Popular Media
Development

Popular Media, Democracy and Development in Africa examines the role that popular media could play to encourage political debate, provide information for development, or critique the very definitions of 'democracy' and 'development'. Drawing on diverse case studies from various regions of the African continent, the chapters employ a range of theoretical and methodological approaches to ask critical questions about the potential of popular media to contribute to democratic culture, provide sites of resistance, or, conversely, act as agents for the spread of Americanized entertainment culture to the detriment of local traditions. A wide variety of media formats and platforms are discussed, ranging from radio and television to the Internet, mobile phones, street posters, film and music.

Grounded in empirical work by experienced scholars who are acknowledged experts in their fields, this contemporary and topical book provides an insight into some of the challenges faced throughout the African continent, such as HIV and AIDS, poverty and inequality, and political participation. Examples are grounded in a critical engagement with theory, moving beyond descriptive studies and therefore contributing to the intellectual project of internationalizing media studies.

Popular Media, Democracy and Development in Africa provides students and scholars with a critical perspective on issues relating to popular media, democracy and citizenship outside the global North. As part of the Routledge series *Internationalizing Media Studies*, the book responds to the important challenge of broadening perspectives on media studies by bringing together a range of expert analyses of media in the African continent that will be of interest to students and scholars of media in Africa and further afield.

Herman Wasserman is Professor of Journalism and Media/Cultural Studies at Rhodes University, Grahamstown, South Africa and Honorary Senior Lecturer in Journalism Studies at the University of Sheffield. He is a Fullbright alumnus and editor of the journal *Ecquid Novi: African Journalism Studies*. Recent publications include *Tabloid Journalism in South Africa: True Story!* (2010) and *Media Ethics Beyond Borders* (co-edited, 2010).

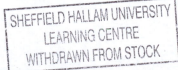

Internationalizing Media Studies
Series Editor: Daya Kishan Thussu
University of Westminster

Internationalizing Media Studies
Edited by Daya Kishan Thussu

Popular Media, Democracy and Development in Africa
Edited by Herman Wasserman

Popular Media, Democracy and Development in Africa

Edited by Herman Wasserman

Routledge
Taylor & Francis Group

LONDON AND NEW YORK

First edition published 2011
by Routledge
2 Park Square, Milton Park, Abingdon, Oxon OX14 4RN

Simultaneously published in the USA and Canada
by Routledge
270 Madison Avenue, New York, NY 10016

Routledge is an imprint of the Taylor & Francis Group, an informa business

© 2011 Herman Wasserman, editorial selection and material;
individual chapters, the contributors

Typeset in Bembo by Wearset Ltd, Boldon, Tyne and Wear
Printed and bound in Great Britain by CPI Antony Rowe,
Chippenham, Wiltshire

British Library Cataloguing in Publication Data
A catalogue record for this book is available from the British
Library

Library of Congress Cataloging in Publication Data
Popular media, democracy and development in Africa/edited by
Herman Wasserman. – 1st ed.
p. cm. – (Internationalizing media studies)
Includes bibliographical references and index.
1. Mass media–Political aspects–Africa. 2. Democratization–
Africa. I. Wasserman, Herman.
P95.82.A4P67 2011
302.23096–dc22

2010011259

ISBN13: 978-0-415-57793-9 (hbk)
ISBN13: 978-0-415-57794-6 (pbk)
ISBN13: 978-0-203-84326-0 (ebk)

Contents

PART II
Popular media, politics and power: engaging with democracy and development

PART III
Audiences, agency and media in everyday life

PART IV
Identity and community between the local and the global

Contributors

Abdalla Uba Adamu is Professor of Curriculum Studies, and Media and Cultural Studies in Bayero University, Kano, Nigeria. His main research focus is on transnational media flows and their impact on the transformation of Muslim Hausa popular culture especially in literature, film, music and performing arts. He is the creator of the Foundation for Hausa Peforming Arts (Kano, Nigeria) whose main focus is archiving the traditional performing arts heritage of the Muslim Hausa. His most recent book is *Transglobal Media Flows and African Popular Culture: Revolution and Reaction in Hausa Popular Culture* (Kano: VEP, 2007), based on the Mary Kingsley Zochonis Lecture he delivered for the African Studies Association of the UK at SOAS, London, in September 2006. His other recent publications include chapters in *Media and Idenity in Africa* (ed. Kimani Njogu and John Middleton, 2009), *Global Soundtracks: Worlds of Film Music* (ed. Mark Slobin, 2008) and *Beyond the Language Issue – The Production, Mediation and Reception of Creative Writing in African Languages* (ed. Anja Oed, 2008). He is also a filmmaker for his own production company, Visually Ethnographic Productions, whose most recent film is *Equestrian Elegance: The Hawan Sallah Pageantry of Kano Emirate* (2009), which records the Sallah durbar pageantry of Kano.

Victor Ayedun-Aluma is a senior lecturer in mass communication at the University of Lagos, Nigeria. He holds a PhD in Communication from the University of Ibadan, Nigeria and is an alumnus of the International Institute for Journalism, Germany. His research and publications are in the areas of political and development communication as well as broadcast and new media technologies and processes. In 2008, he edited a volume on investigative journalism commissioned by the Wole Soyinka Centre for Investigative Journalism. He has served as research consultant on communication and development programmes of the United Nations Children's Fund, the International Labour Organisation, the News Agency of Nigeria, the Nigerian Television Authority and the Human Development Initiatives, receiving the latter's Certificate of Appreciation in 2007. He is a published poet and an art-music enthusiast.

Tanja Bosch is a senior lecturer in the Centre for Film and Media Studies at the University of Cape Town, South Africa. She completed her MA in International Affairs while a Fulbright Scholar at Ohio University, where she also graduated with a PhD in Mass Communication. Her dissertation, which was awarded the Broadcast Educational Association (BEA) Outstanding Dissertation Award 2003, was an ethnographic study of community radio and identity in South Africa. Tanja teaches radio journalism, new media, health communication and media theory and research. Her areas of research and publication include talk radio and democracy, community radio and youth use of mobile media, particularly mobile phones and Facebook.

Inge Brinkman has been attached to the African Studies Centre, Leiden, the Netherlands, since 2008 while she carries out research into communication technologies and social relations in Angola. She is engaged in a case study on the legacy of war and new ICT in southeast Angola and in studying the historical relations between literacy/orality, elite-formation and communication technologies in northern Angola. These case studies form part of a larger programme, entitled 'Mobile Africa Revisited', aimed at studying the relations between mobility, communication technologies and social relations in various case studies in Chad, Mali, Senegal, Cameroon, Angola and South Africa. Within this programme, Inge has a coordinating and supervising role. Her former research includes a study on mobile telephony in Sudan, writing a history of a Dutch development organization and a PhD project on morality and identity in Kenyan literature, concluded in 1996.

Monica B. Chibita is a senior lecturer in the Department of Mass Communication, Makerere University and a senior researcher under the Makerere-Sida research collaboration. She is a member of the Editorial Board of *Communicatio*, the Advisory Board of the *Westminster Papers in Communication and Culture* (*WPCC*) and Associate Editor with the *Journal of African Media Studies* (*JAMS*). She has presented papers and published on media history, media policy, the media and participation and indigenous language broadcasting. She has also been involved in various aspects of curriculum development and review over the last decade.

Mirjam de Bruijn is a senior researcher at the African Studies Center in Leiden, the Netherlands, where she is part of the research management team. In June 2007 she was nominated Professor of African Studies (Contemporary History and Anthropology of West and Central Africa) at Leiden University. She has conducted research in various countries in West and Central Africa (from 1986 to the present): Cameroon, Mali and Chad. The main themes are: nomadic societies, inequality and social relations, (contemporary) slavery, children and youth, cultures of poverty, mobility, war and climate change, and communication technology. She completed (interdisciplinary) projects on climate change, migration, conflict and poverty, and did project evaluations. She is coordinator of the partnership programme between ASC and CODESRIA (CDP) and partner in a research programme on mobility and resources that was granted by the Volkswagen Foundation in 2008. She was awarded a research grant for a five-year research programme on marginality, communication and mobility in Africa that started in 2008. Recent publications include M.E. de Bruijn, F. Nyamnjoh and I. Brinkman (eds), *Mobile Phones: the New Talking Drums of Everyday Africa* (Bamenda, Cameroon: Langaa Publishers, 2009) and M.E. de Bruijn and R.A. van Dijk, 'Questioning Social Security in the Study of Religion in Africa: The Ambiguous Meaning of the Gift in African Pentecostalism and Islam', in C. Leutloff-Grandits, A. Peleikis and T. Thelen (eds) *Social Security in Religious Networks: Anthropological Perspectives on New Risks and Ambivalences* (New York/Oxford: Berghahn Books, 2009, pp. 105–27).

Marie-Soleil Frère is an associate researcher at Belgium's National Fund for Scientific Research and also professor of journalism, specializing in the African media, at the University of Brussels. Her recent publications include *Presse et democratie en Afrique francophone* and *The Media and Conflicts in Central Africa*.

Audrey Gadzekpo is a senior lecturer and Head of the School of Communication Studies, University of Ghana. Her research interests are in the area of media, gender, development, politics and governance. In 2005 she was Visiting Scholar at the Programme of African Studies, Northwestern University, USA, where she taught a course on Gender, Communication and Women's Rights in Africa. She has more than 25 years' practical experience as a journalist, working variously as a reporter, editor, contributor, columnist, talk show host, socio-political commentator and magazine publisher/editor. Her publications include: *When the Watchman Slips: Media Accountability and Democratic Reforms in Ghana*; *Selected Writings of a Pioneer West African Feminist: Mabel Dove* and *What is Fit to Print: The Language of the Press in Ghana*.

Sean Jacobs is an assistant professor of international affairs at The New School in Manhattan. He is a native of Cape Town, South Africa. Adam Esrig provided research assistance for his chapter in this volume.

Siri Lamoureaux is a linguist and anthropologist who graduated from the African Studies Centre/University of Leiden in the Netherlands. Her interests in language, society and new media recently brought her to Sudan where she looked at the social and linguistic features of text messaging in Khartoum. The thesis resulting from this research, entitled *Message in a Mobile: Mixed Messages, Tales of Missing and Mobile Communities at the University of Khartoum* (ASC/Langaa Publishers), will soon be published. She is now involved in the Mobile Africa Revisited research programme at the African Studies Centre and planning for a PhD focusing on language and ICTs in the Sudan.

P. Eric Louw, now based in the School of Journalism and Communication, University of Queensland, Brisbane, Australia, previously taught at the University of Natal, University of South Africa and Rand Afrikaans University.

He has also run a non-government organization engaged in development work and been a journalist on the *Pretoria News*. His primary area of research is political communication. Professor Louw's books are: *The Rise, Fall and Consequences of Apartheid* (Praeger); *Roots of the Pax Americana* (Manchester University Press); *The Media and Political Process* (Sage); *The Media and Cultural Production* (Sage) and *South African Media Policy* (Anthropos). Louw also co-edited *The South African Alternative Press* (Anthropos).

Winston Mano is a senior lecturer and course leader at the University of Westminster, in London. He has been a member of the Communication and Media Research Institute (CAMRI) since 2000 and obtained his doctoral degree in 2004. He teaches undergraduate and postgraduate courses in media and communication. Mano has published articles and chapters in books on African media topics. He also edited (in 2005) *The Media and Zimbabwe*, a Special Issue of *Westminster Papers in Communication and Culture*. He is the founding editor of the *Journal of African Media Studies* published by Intellect and is on the board of many journals. In 2009, he helped establish the University of Westminster's Africa Media Centre. He can be contacted at: University of Westminster, Harrow Campus, HA1 3TP, Harrow, UK. E-mail: manow@wmin.ac.uk.

Daniela Merolla lectures on African Literatures and Media at the Institute for Cultural Disciplines, Leiden University, the Netherlands. On African websites she published 'Digital Imagination and the "Landscapes of Group Identities": Berber Diaspora and the Flourishing of Theatre, Videos, and Amazigh-Net', *The Journal of North African Studies* Winter 2005: 122–31; 'Migrant Websites, WebArt, and Digital Imagination', in D. Merolla and S. Ponzanesi (eds) *Migrant Cartographies, New Cultural and Literary Spaces in Post-colonial Europe* (Lexington Books, 2006, pp. 217–28); 'Le théâtre et la production médiatique berbère entre le Maroc et l'Europe', *Études Littéraires Africaines* 21: 44–7. Her most recent publications are E. Bekers, S. Helff and D. Merolla (eds) *Transcultural Modernities: Narrating Africa in Europe* (Amsterdam: Rodopi, 2009); D. Merolla and M. Schipper (eds) *Creation Myths and the Visual Arts: An Ongoing Dialogue between Word and Image*, Special Issue of *Religion and the Arts* 13 (2009) and 'Dangerous Love in Mythical Narratives and Formula Tales', *Religion* 39(3): 283–8.

Okoth Fred Mudhai is a senior lecturer in Journalism and Global Media/Communication and Course Director, Specialist Journalism Postgra duate Programme in the Media and Communication Department, Coventry University, UK. He is co-editor of *African Media and the Digital Public Sphere* (Palgrave Macmillan, 2009). He was part of IT and Civil Society Network of the IT and International Cooperation Programme, US Social Science Research Council (2003–5). His PhD (the Nottingham Trent University, UK) and MA (Leeds University, UK) theses focused on Information and Communication Technology (ICT) access-usage in Africa. He has won a number of media awards for journalistic stories, two on ICT at global level. He has previously worked as a journalist with The Standard Media Group (Nairobi) and contributed to various print and broadcast outlets based in Kenya, South Africa, the UK and the USA.

Sonja Narunsky-Laden is a senior lecturer in the School of Communication, University of Johannesburg. Her doctoral research interests addressed the emergence of a black middle class in South Africa, as represented in and mediated by magazines published for black South African readers. Her current research interests include magazine research as a yardstick of social change, processes of self- and social-identity within contexts of socio-cultural change, questions of 'cultural economy', market devices and the cultural embeddedness of money, and how patterns of consumer culture and lifestyle reorganize the broader socio-cultural entities in which they operate. She co-edited with Leon de Kock and Louise Bethlehem the award-winning special issue of *Poetics Today* entitled *South Africa in the Global Imaginary*, published in book form by Unisa Press (2004).

Francis B. Nyamnjoh has taught Sociology, Anthropology and Communication Studies at universities in Cameroon, Botswana and South Africa, and served as Head of Publications with the Council for the Development of Social Science Research in Africa (CODESRIA), Dakar, Senegal. He is currently Professor of Social Anthropology at the University of Cape Town in South Africa.

Levi Obijiofor is a senior lecturer in Journalism at the School of Journalism and Communication, The University of Queensland, Brisbane, Australia. His research interests are: the impact of new technologies on journalistic practices; international news reporting across cultures; and media representations of ethnic minorities. He has published widely across a range of peer-reviewed journalism and communication journals. He was at various times Sub-Editor, Production Editor and Night Editor of *The Guardian* newspapers in Lagos, Nigeria. Between March 1995 and May 1996, he worked in the Division of Studies and Programming (BPE/BP) at the Paris headquarters of UNESCO where he edited the bulletin *FUTURESCO* and also coordinated the future-oriented studies programme. He holds a PhD and a Master's degree in Communication from the Queensland University of Technology (QUT), Brisbane, Australia. He also holds a Bachelor's degree (First Class Honours) and a Master's degree in Mass Communication from the University of Lagos, Nigeria.

George Ogola is a senior lecturer at the School of Journalism, Media and Communication, University of Central Lancashire. He holds an MA in Journalism and Media Studies and a PhD from the University of the Witwatersrand, South Africa. His research interests include journalism studies, popular media in Africa, popular culture, political communication and media cultures in 'transitional' societies in the global South.

H. Leslie Steeves is Professor and Associate Dean for Graduate Affairs and Research in the School of Journalism and Communication, University of Oregon. Much of Steeves' research centres on two areas and their intersection: communication in developing countries, particularly in sub-Saharan Africa, and gender and media. She has published many articles in these areas, as well as two books: *Gender Violence and the Press: The St. Kizito Story* (Athens, Ohio: Ohio University Monographs in International Studies, 1997) and *Communication for Development in the Third World: Theory and Practice for Empowerment, 2nd Edition* (co-authored with Srinivas Melkote, New Delhi: Sage, 2001). Her present work additionally examines media entertainment and tourism representations of Africa. She has had two Fulbright grants for teaching and research in Kenya and Ghana, and she directs an annual study-abroad programme in Ghana.

Herman Wasserman is Professor of Journalism and Media/Cultural Studies at Rhodes University, Grahamstown, South Africa and Honorary Senior Lecturer in Journalism Studies at the University of Sheffield, UK. He is editor of *Ecquid Novi: African Journalism Studies* and serves on the editorial board of several other journals including the *Journal of African Media Studies*, *Journal of Global Mass Communication*, *Journal of Mass Media Ethics* and *Communicatio*. He is a Fulbright alumnus (Indiana University) and a former visiting Resource Person at the Council for the Development of Social Science Research in Africa in Dakar, Senegal. He has published widely on media in Southern Africa. His most recent book, *Tabloid Journalism in South Africa*, is published by Indiana University Press.

Wendy Willems is Lecturer in Media Studies in the School of Literature and Language Studies at the University of Witwatersrand in Johannesburg, South Africa. She completed her PhD entitled *Imagining the Power of the Media: Global News, Nationalism and Popular Culture in the Context of the 'Zimbabwe Crisis' (2000–2007)* in the Centre for Media and Film Studies, School of Oriental and African Studies, University of London in 2009. Her research interests revolve around popular culture, new media and informal politics in Africa and Zimbabwe in particular. She is Associate Editor of the *Journal of African Media Studies* and Book Review Editor of *Ecquid Novi – African Journalism Studies*.

Acknowledgements

I would like to use the opportunity to thank each of the authors for their valuable contributions, delivered under extreme time pressure. I am very grateful for their inspiring visions of African media, their expert knowledge of the continent and the vigour with which they conducted their investigations into this fascinating and complex field. My thanks also goes to Daya Thussu for his invitation to join this project. It is an honour to be associated with his invaluable efforts to broaden the field of international media studies.

Herman Wasserman, March 2010

Permissions

Chapter 1 draws on a previously published interview article in *Journalism Studies*:

Introduction

Taking it to the streets

Herman Wasserman

In December 2008, shortly after the historic election of Barack Obama to the presidency of the United States, I encountered a street vendor selling cheap copies of DVDs on the pavement in Yaoundé, Cameroon. Wearing a T-shirt proclaiming 'Barack Obama for President 2008', he was inviting patrons coming from the bakery across the street to browse his selection of titles. These included not only biographical films presenting Obama as a son of Africa, but also some that offered critical perspectives on his predecessor, George W. Bush, by exposing the 'relationship between Bush and Osama Bin Laden', for instance, recounting conspiracy theories about the 9/11 attacks, or including Bush in a documentary about famous dictators. The proximity of this exchange on the pavement (in close proximity to the bakery selling fine pastries and ice cream across the bustling street) struck me as a vivid illustration of the multiple histories, alternative visions of modernity and the layered identity positions occupied in everyday Africa. It also suggested how global popular culture gets sampled, re-made locally and re-circulated in order to attain political significance, even if the counter-hegemonic impact of such popular engagement with the political sphere remains debatable. The pavement discussions ensuing from the selling of DVDs about Barack Obama and George W. Bush, shaped to relate to Cameroonians' daily lived experience, would resemble not so much the elitist public sphere envisaged by Habermas as the vibrant, convivial *radio trottoir* (Ellis 1989; Nyamnjoh 2005) where current affairs are discussed in informal networks. The overlaps and interfaces of popular media, politics and everyday lived experiences in Africa are at the centre of this book.

The example of Obama's representation in African popular media (see also the cover illustration of this book, where residents of Kibera slum in Nairobi follow the inauguration of Obama on television with expectation and jubilation) furthermore reminds us that African media cannot be studied in isolation from global political events nor could local engagement with global media events be understood as passive consumption. An essentialist view of African media as locked in a binary opposition to those in the Global North could be just as reductive as one which views African media audiences as the passive dupes of American cultural imperialism or an approach to African media which neglects the differences between African countries, regions or internal contestations in African nation-states. Insights from international scholars like Straubhaar (2007), Kraidy (2005) and Thussu (2006, 2009) have refocused attention on the ways in which global media are shaped by global flows, contraflows and hybrid transculturation. As Nixon (1994: 3) has shown in his study of the ties between South African culture and the United States, these global allegiances are also marked by slippages and barriers, so that connections between African culture and global culture remain partial and intermittent. The visibility of these local–global connections in the realm of the popular should not be mistaken as evidence for equality between the partners involved in cultural exchanges. Critics (see for example Sparks 2007) of globalization theory have pointed to the stubborn persistence of global inequalities in media ownership, production and consumption. These continued imbalances between media-rich and media-poor, both globally and within nations themselves, raise critical questions about the much-heralded demise of the nation-state brought on in part by the globalization of mass media, and underline the continued relevance of critical political-economic approaches to the study of media in Africa. When studying popular media in Africa, one cannot avoid the continued global asymmetries of economic and political power, and one is led to ask how popular media can contribute to the very real, urgent and tangible issues which confront the continent.

Given these persisting inequalities in the global media arena, one is compelled to not only celebrate the vibrancy of popular media in Africa in terms of their creative articulations of everyday life, but to examine the relationship between these forms of popular expression and the political and economic spheres on the continent as these relate to global geopolitics and the hegemony of neoliberalism. The popular in Africa, as Barber (1997: 3) notes with reference to Bourdieu, is a site 'inscribed with the history of political and cultural struggles'. Neither the dismissal à la the Frankfurt School of the popular as material for brainwashing, nor the uncritical acceptance that 'what is popular is by definition good' (Barber 1997: 3) can be the only response to the vibrant array of popular media on the continent today.

For instance, while critics have denounced tabloid newspapers in Africa as cheap sensationalism that depoliticizes citizens, others have pointed to the way these newspapers articulate the experience of the poor and the marginalized who seldom take centre stage in the mainstream press. Tabloid papers such as the *Red Pepper* in Uganda, and the *Daily Voice, Son* and *Daily Sun* in South Africa have enjoyed tremendous popularity in the past decade. The *Daily Sun* is now the biggest daily newspaper in South Africa, with a readership of around five million among the poor and working-class black population (see Wasserman 2010). These tabloids have been lambasted for their sensational content, homophobia and xenophobia, accused of diverting readers' attention from important news with stories about sex and gossip, and providing entertainment instead of information. While these accusations are not without truth, these tabloid newspapers may also be read as part of political discourses in African countries where access to the mainstream media or participation in political debate remains the preserve of the elite. One of the arguments for the positive potential of tabloids is that they provide readers who feel excluded from dominant discourses and social processes with the pleasure of seeing the establishment's norms subverted, undermined or satirized. This is the point of view of John Fiske, for whom the existence of tabloids should be read as an index of the 'extent of dissatisfaction in a society, particularly among those who feel powerless to change their situation' (1989: 117). The distance experienced between 'democracy' and 'development' (Pillay 2008) often expresses itself as apathy, ridicule or mocking. West and Fair (1993: 104), referring to development theatre in Tanzania, invoke Bakhtin's work (e.g. Bakhtin 1968) on the carnival to suggest that 'laughter, frivolity, and the carnivalesque open up an "unofficial" discursive space from which the "official" world may be ridiculed and resistance sustained'. As Bosch points out in Chapter 5 in this volume, tabloids, like other forms of popular media, may therefore not be dismissed outright as having no political relevance or public value.

Tabloid newspapers in Africa are an example of how complex issues are raised by the introduction of global popular formats into the local media landscape in Africa. This engagement between the global and the local is not a one-way street, however. Africans display agency in the way they engage with global popular media formats in the international arena. The popularity of global television formats among African viewers, for instance, does not preclude viewers from challenging representations of themselves, constructing counter-discourses to the dominant ones presented in global television, or negotiating the meanings presented to them. Nor are these engagements limited to a geographically bounded African context, but also take place among Africans in the diaspora, as Mano and Willems (2008) have shown in their analysis of online debates among diasporic Zimbabweans in response to the appearance of a Zimbabwean nurse, Makosi Musambasi, on the British *Big Brother* reality television show. Their example is interesting not only for its illustration of how diasporic audiences can make use of entertainment media formats to challenge xenophobic and racist representations of Africans (in this case the antagonism against Musambasi stoked up in the British tabloid press), but also for how local (gendered) politics became articulated through global genres and platforms. This appropriation and abrogation of global media paradigms by Africans, with political aims of subverting racist discourses (even as racism became replaced by gender stereotyping), illustrates that the relation between the global and the local in popular media, and the various relations of power entwined in that relationship, are too complex and contradictory to be described by crude media imperialism paradigms. The examples of creative appropriation of popular media by Africans can easily seduce the optimistic observer into celebrating their potential as vehicles to escape the tenacious communicative imbalances between the Global North and South. Nowhere is the emancipatory promise that popular media hold for Africans more clearly seen than in the field of information and communication technologies (ICTs). New media in African have often been seen as an instigator for social change and 'moves toward democratization' (Mudhai *et al.* 2009: x) or unproblematically embraced as tools for 'leapfrogging' stages of development (Mudhai *et al.* 2009: 1). Mobile phones, the 'new talking drums of Africa' (De Bruijn *et al.* 2009) are becoming increasingly central to the way Africans interact with the online public sphere. With their vast penetration in Africa, mobile phones are challenging endogenous and exogenous hegemony (Eskine 2010) and can amplify other ICTs to form 'new solidarities to challenge undemocratic forces, ideologies and practices that stand in the way of social progress' (Nyamnjoh, in Wasserman 2009).

Yet the initial optimism surrounding new media in Africa has been tempered by more realistic and nuanced assessments of their potential as well as limitations. For critical scholars of new media, the creative appropriation of new media technologies has to be considered against 'old questions about access, inequality, power, and the quality of information' (Mudhai *et al.* 2009: 1).

The nuanced stance required for the study of new media technologies on the continent is also advisable for popular media in Africa more broadly. Instead of merely celebrating the existence and vibrancy of popular media in Africa, this book explicitly wants to critically examine how these media relate to discourses of African democracy and development. The danger exists that studies of popular media phenomena might only be celebrating the insignificant without scrutinizing them for ways in which they may feed meaningfully into a process of substantial political engagement. Whether through surveys and interviews, theoretical interventions or political economic critiques, the chapters in this book investigate how audiences/consumers/users use popular media, under which conditions they are doing so and whether such usage may empower them as citizens to participate in political processes or challenge established centres of power.

At the same time, the meaning of the very concepts of 'democracy' and 'development' cannot be taken for granted, nor can the relationship between them be seen as without contradictions and tensions. These concepts are interrogated in the book, both in theoretical interventions and in context-based case studies.

The examples shared in the chapters in this book are not only aimed at proving or disproving the potential of popular media to disseminate information necessary for social change – in the 'entertainment for development' tradition – nor are they singularly concerned with ways in which popular media can provide spaces for democratic deliberation and the performance of citizenship. While these perspectives are included, and are important, the book as a whole attempts to illustrate how discourses about 'popular media', 'development' and 'democracy' intersect. Discourses about 'development' and 'democracy' are not always innocent, but may also serve to hide other agendas. H. Leslie Steeves' chapter in this volume (Chapter 10), discussing the reception of the reality television show *The Amazing Race*, provides a convincing illustration of how popular genres on global entertainment media platforms may entrench neoliberal hegemony even as they engage in the seemingly benevolent rhetoric of 'democracy' and 'development'. Yet popular media may also make visible the loss of legitimacy of African democracies, satirize the powerful and create alternative modernities, as several other chapters show. The field of popular media is indeed multifaceted, consisting of different dimensions and contradictions.

Although the relation between popular media, public communication and political life is often underestimated, popular media are deeply implicated in the 'struggle for access to knowledge' (Conboy 2002: 2). The fact that popular culture, and popular media as one of its manifestations, may be seen as linked to lucrative global economic concerns, has given rise to debates around the extent to which these media are vehicles for hegemony or may be appropriated and adapted by audiences with sufficient agency to use such popular forms in their own interests (cf. Conboy 2002: 15). Although the broad field of cultural studies has established the legitimacy of the popular as an area of scholarly inquiry, this enthusiasm has led to cultural studies often being accused of naïvely celebrating the political potential of the popular, with not enough attention being paid to the continuing limitations on popular discourses imposed by the state and capital. On the other hand, a reluctance can often still be noted in the field of mass communication and journalism studies to take popular culture seriously, with the moral panics around tabloid newspapers – widely seen both in Western and African democracies as a constituting a 'crisis for democracy' (Sparks 2000: 11; cf. Wasserman 2010).

The political implications of media use have also been central to scholarship on media in Africa, yet arguably such research has hitherto mostly focused on formal, mainstream media. Media in Africa are widely regarded as having the potential to contribute to the exercise of civic rights and responsibilities, the communication of political information, the (re)construction of cultural identity and the achievement of developmental goals. Informed by the Habermasian notion of the public sphere as a space for rational deliberation, elite print media, public broadcasting or community media have been foregrounded as tools for development and deepening of liberal democracy. While a significant body of literature on African popular culture exists, this work has not always directly engaged with the implications of popular media for contested terms such as democracy and development.

The dominant frames for investigations into the relation between media, democracy and development in Africa have been those derived from political economy and democratization theory, often incorporating discussions of policy and regulation, press freedom and normative issues (see for instance Bourgault 1995; Eribo and Jong-Ebot 1997; Horwitz 2001; Hyden et al. 2002; Tomaselli and Dunn 2001) – focusing on the role of (often state-owned or controlled) radio and television and mainstream newspapers, with little attention to more informal, popular forms of communication. While it has been argued that popular culture has been 'assigned a marginal position in scholarship on the arts in sub-Saharan Africa' (Barber 1997: 1), this neglect seems to be especially striking in the field of African journalism and media studies. The reason for the different perspectives on popular culture might have to do with the dominant normative frameworks for media on the continent, which sees the African media's role as predominantly concerned with deepening democracy and furthering socio-economic development (although what form these contributions should take has been the subject of much debate). While in the broader field of African studies, incorporating African cultural studies, popular culture has been seen in terms of the opportunities it offers for anti-hegemonic resistance (albeit by often naïvely exaggerating the extent of individual agency, as Wendy Willems points out in Chapter 3 in this volume), the emphasis in African journalism and media studies has fallen on the contribution formal media could (and, normatively, should) make to democracy and development on the continent. This book attempts to cross what often seems like a disciplinary divide between studies of popular culture in Africa on the one hand and the role of media in democracy and development on the other. It wants to explore the overlaps and interstices between mainstream, formal media and popular mediated communication; between cultural discourses and those of democracy and development; and between various disciplinary and methodological approaches to the study of popular culture, media, democracy and development. The contributions collected in this volume display an array of perspectives on popular media and its relation to African politics, society and culture. Some of these chapters employ critical theory to denounce the impact of popular media as tools of global cultural imperialism, while others follow ethnographic approaches to celebrate the ways in which Africans have appropriated and adopted popular media to fashion new identities and provide cultural contraflow; some chapters argue normatively for the regulation of popular media while others rejoice in the opportunities popular media offer for the subversion of authoritarian control; some unpack the political economy of these media forms against the specificities of African contexts while others take a more global view to discuss the position of African popular media in the age of globalization and the advent of new media technologies. While some chapters discuss popular media primarily in terms of its implications for democratic politics, others emphasize its relation to developmental issues or the overlap between discourses of development and democracy.

It was the clear intention not to impose a particular vision of popular media or prescribe a specific theoretical or methodological approach to authors, but instead invite contributors to provide different perspectives on these issues. Contributors were encouraged to approach popular media in Africa from a comparative perspective, preferably including more than one African country in their purview or to view African popular media against the background of international debates or transnational trends. The objective of this comparative approach was to avoid a set of nation-based case studies but instead provide local, specific responses to more general themes and questions. The choice against following one particular theoretical or methodological approach was made to demonstrate the contested nature of popular culture and its manifestations in media on the continent. A simplistic celebration of its potential or a critique of its limitations would fail to capture the many different dimensions of popular media as social, cultural, economic and political phenomena.

This book not only wants to refocus attention on the interface between popular media, democracy and development, but also wants to do so very specifically from the perspective of Africa. The book responds to Thussu's call (2009: 1) in the introductory volume of the Routledge series *Internationalizing Media Studies*, of which this book also forms part, for a broadening of the discourse on globalization of media and communication beyond Northern perspectives on the phenomenon. This broadening needs to take place both in terms of critical considerations of media globalization as this process plays out in various parts of the world, as well as in the field of media scholarship itself. This book aims to contribute to both these aspects: several chapters in this book deal with globalization as this process is reflected through popular media in Africa. Some of them critique the way in which globalization remains a highly uneven process, with corporate-owned, profit-driven popular media a manifestation of the global reach of neoliberal hegemony. On such a critical view, media globalization can exacerbate the symbolic and material marginalization of Africa. Others highlight the hybrid identities, contraflows and creative appropriations of media in African popular culture which may lead to moments of resistance or reversal of the dominant global flows.

As a contribution to what may be called the project of de-Westernizing media studies (Park and Curran 2000; Wasserman and De Beer 2009), one of the book's objectives is to engage with media studies on a theoretical level from the perspective of African experience. A focus on 'African media' immediately raises the problem of homogenizing and/or essentializing a whole continent with 54 countries, a host of languages and cultures and diverse histories. Yet as Mano (2009: 277) points out, these countries have in common the experience of domination and resistance. This shared experience of colonial subjection, struggles for independence and continued geopolitical and economic marginalization in the era of globalization, suggests that a transnational study of popular media on the continent would approach such media in relation to the lived experience of their audiences, as social phenomena, and within relations of power, both internal and global. Such an attention to power relations should have as its basic assumption the location of Africa on an 'unequally positioned global traffic of knowledge' (Shome 2009: 696). The very attempt to 'internationalize' media studies should therefore raise the question *for whom* media studies needs to be internationalized (Shome 2009: 701). If the internationalization of media studies through projects such as this book serves to entrench the primacy – both in temporal terms, as being 'first' on a trajectory of progress, and hierarchically first, as occupying the highest rung – of media studies theories in the Global North, the project would have the opposite effect as was its intention. The vantage point, the point of departure into the 'international' or 'global' (Shome 2009: 700) cannot remain the existing frameworks of the North, but should be rooted in the experiences of those in the South for whom the routes into media and cultural studies have always been negotiated between local and global frameworks and experiences (Shome 2009: 701).

Although some of these experiences may be shared among countries in Africa and the South more generally, homogenization of entire regions just based on their difference from the North should be avoided. An approach that links together popular media in ostensibly very diverse African countries on the basis of the continued resonance of history in the political, social and economic conditions shaping the production and consumption of media on the continent, would go beyond the presentation of a set of individual nation-based case studies. Furthermore, such an historical-social approach would avoid representing African media as either an exotic Other to the Global North, an interesting curiosity that need not be taken seriously in theoretical debates, or disciplined into following the same trajectory of development, modernization and progress as media in developed, media-saturated and established democratic societies. The former would exclude African media forms and practices from ongoing theory-building in global journalism and media studies scholarship; the latter may restrict African media to enter academic debates only when it is framed in terms of 'media development' or 'media democratization' that seek to fashion African media in the North's image. When instead the current 'globalized' mediated lived experience of Africans is viewed through the long lens of history, earlier unequal symbolic and economic exchanges and relations of power may be recalled to understand the rejection by some African scholars of the 'universalizing pretensions of Western theorizing and evidence' (Mano 2009: 277). The embrace of indigenous forms of communication, even though they may sometimes verge towards essentialism and dichotomous thinking (see Tomaselli 2003), may be understood against this background as manifestations of the 'disillusionment and resentment of Western domination in intellectual, political and economic terms' (Mano 2009: 277). As Francis Nyamnjoh points out in Chapter 1 in this volume, closer attention to the role of media in African lived experience should remind us that no theorization takes place in a void. Media theory as developed in the Global North habitually masks its own situatedness, often laying claim to universal pronouncements with very little cognizance of media developments elsewhere. This book aims to encourage a sustained and open engagement between media theories developed in the Global North and theoretical perspectives emerging from encounters with African popular media. The contributions also raise questions about the very notions of 'democracy' and 'development' in media theory – notions which are still all too often programmatically superimposed from an Northern analytical perspective on African media without due cognizance of the rich textures and complex contradictions characteristic of media in everyday life in African societies. It is hoped that the perspectives offered in this book, coming as they are from a wide range of experiences and contexts on the continent, would again emphasize the extent to which dominant media theories in the Global North about the relation between media, democracy and society are in themselves also localized and contextual, even if they tend to become axiomatic despite their own parochialism. The point is however not to create a dichotomy between media theory in the Global North and South – that way essentialism and theoretical absolutism lie. Attention to the varied and complex ways in which media are produced, consumed and re-mediated (to use a term from De Bruijn *et al.*'s study of how diasporic African identities are constructed online in Chapter 15) cannot afford shallow or binary thinking.

The contributions in this volume have been organized so as to speak to major themes in the study of popular media, democracy and development in the African context.

Part I deals with theoretical debates around popular media as they apply to the African context. The book's central notions of democracy and development, as well as the very definition of popular media, are interrogated first against the broad backdrop of the position popular media in Africa play in relation to global cultural economies (Chapters 1 and 2). The key contention in these two chapters takes place around the power struggle between the local and the global. At stake is the relative ability of African producers and consumers to either resist Northern hegemony by creatively appropriating and adapting popular media, or whether popular media facilitates the spread of Northern cultural content in a way that further subjects and marginalizes African cultures and subjectivities. For P. Eric Louw in Chapter 2 popular media in Africa are less a site of resistance than a tool with which to enlist the services of comprador classes, a form of 'soft power' with which to extend the influence of the 'Pax Americana'. From this perspective, discourses of 'democratization' and 'development' may bring about social and cultural change in African societies that undermines local traditions.

In Chapter 1, Nyamnjoh also points to the marginalization of Africa, in the area of popular media practices as well as in the academic study thereof, but remains optimistic that there would always be 'room for initiative or agency at an individual or group level to challenge domination, exploitation and the globalization of indifference to cultural diversity'. This important question about the extent to which popular media in Africa may be seen as a site for resistance or domination is illuminated further from the perspective of specific African settings, such as Zimbabwe (Chapter 3), Ghana and Nigeria (Chapter 4) and South Africa (Chapter 5). In Chapter 3 Willems discusses the implications of convergence culture in Zimbabwe for the theoretical understanding of how popular media in Africa is related to more formal media platforms, critiques the ways in which audience agency has been variously celebrated or ignored in different scholarly traditions, and argues for a more productive dialogue between the fields of journalism and mass communication and African cultural studies. In Chapter 4 Ayedun-Aluma argues for a reconceptualization of community media as popular media where competing interpretations of democracy and development may be offered to those found in mainstream, elite media. For Ayedun-Aluma, the preferred meaning of democracy and development constructed on a community level would be one which endorses a principal role for non-elites in the attainment of democratic and developmental goals. But he critiques existing community media practices in Ghana and Nigeria as falling short of this people-centred ideal. In Chapter 5, Tanja Bosch also seeks to broaden theoretical constructs of the popular by revisiting Habermas' concept of the 'public sphere'. While Habermas' ideas have been subject to much critique for their perceived social exclusions and emphasis on formal deliberation and consensus (rather than discord or conflict) Bosch uses the example of commercial talk radio in South Africa to envisage a reconceptualization of the public sphere in Africa that would occupy a middle ground between the informal *radio trottoir* (a concept which features in several chapters in this book) and the more elitist, formal platforms for political communication.

Part II deals with the question of popular media's relation to power. A central concern in these chapters is the extent to which popular media can challenge, resist or subvert dominant power structures in African society – be these authoritarian governments, global cultural imperialism, the contestations between cultural formations within one society or nation-state, or commercial pressures on the media itself. The chapters in this section eschew a naïve celebration of resistance offered by popular culture, instead offering a nuanced assessment of the potential and the limitations of popular media in African contexts. These assessments often have as a starting point the inability of mainstream media to offer a platform for the articulation of controversial or popular political views, as a result of either severe political pressure or state control, because of an ideological proclivity towards economically powerful audiences, or because of socio-economic impediments like low literacy rates which restrict access to mainstream news media like newspapers.

Several examples, ranging from Fela Kuti's Nigeria to Oliver Mtukudzi's Zimbabwe, by way of Cameroon, Kenya, Congo and South Africa, are offered by Winston Mano in Chapter 6 to argue that the definition of African journalism should be broadened to include popular music. Mano argues that in African countries where public communication is constrained, popular music can perform the journalistic functions of informing and mobilizing citizens on issues related to democratic politics as well as matters pertaining to socio-economic developments such as health. The lack of access to mainstream media, which leads to the emergence of alternative, popular forms of expression, is also the subject of Audrey Gadzekpo's discussion of street news posters in Ghana in Chapter 7. These visual media have provided illiterate Ghanaians with the means to engage in the discussion of news events ranging from community (what in contemporary journalism parlance in the North may have been called 'hyperlocal') news such as accidents and funerals, and national news about celebrities and sports, to global news events like the election of Barack Obama as US president. These posters are a good example not only of the alternative modes of news delivery in Africa, but also of how that news gets appropriated and recirculated in overlapping circuits of communication: images for these posters are sometimes literally taken out of mainstream publications or news websites, or co-exist with those provided by photographers (who again in the current journalistic nomenclature may be called 'citizen journalists'), the photographs get annotated in a popular linguistic register, and the meanings thus created are recirculated orally in the informal networks of *radio trottoir*. Gadzekpo's study is a vivid illustration of the way in which audiences create meaning in everyday African contexts, creatively appropriating and adopting the channels available to them.

The resistance offered by popular media to state censorship and control, this time in the Kenyan context, is the topic of Chapter 8 by George Ogola. While the chapter considers the ways in which popular culture in Kenya have provided the vocabulary as well as the site for the mediation of contemporary social and political experiences, it also offers a sober assessment of the transformative effects of popular media. The chapter views the resistance offered by these media in Fabian's terms as 'moments of freedom' rather as the romantic ideal of total liberation. Yet, as Ogola concludes, the point of these instances of popular challenges to state power is not so much their efficacy in achieving political or social change, but the fact that they point to the porousness of mainstream media and the inability of political power to completely foreclose on popular expression.

Challenges to state power in South Africa also form the focus of Sean Jacobs' discussion of filmic representations of post-apartheid social movements in South Africa in Chapter 9. A range of new social movements have emerged after the advent of democracy in South Africa to challenge the limits of the democratic transition. Although formal apartheid was abolished in 1994, the black majority in the country still experience continued social and economic marginalization, with deepening inequality between rich and poor. The two social movements Jacobs focuses on – Abahlali baseMjondolo and the Treatment Action Campaign – respectively campaign for the rights of shackdwellers and for equal access to antiretroviral drugs for people living with HIV/AIDS. While these movements have demonstrated skilful use of media to further their cause, they have also increasingly made use of opportunities to collaborate with filmmakers to highlight their cause to audiences beyond their immediate support base. Jacobs discusses the politics of representation in this cinematic mediation of the activities of the two movements. Issues of control, the negotiation of meaning and the creation of cultural capital are brought into focus as Jacobs differentiates between the different relations these two social movements have with mainstream media.

Central to an understanding of popular media has been their claims to represent the voice of 'the people'. Even if these rhetorical claims may be exposed as a 'vernacular ventriloquism' (Conboy 2006: 14) on the part of commercial media aimed at maximizing profits, the link between media and commerce does not necessarily negate the possibility of popular media to 'articulate the lifeworld of the majority of ordinary men and women excluded from the mainstream of political power' (Conboy 2002: 2).

The popular representation of daily life might at first glance not seem political in the same way as political communication in mainstream media, and often leads to accusations of popular media creating diversions from more 'serious' news, 'dumbing down' or depoliticizing audiences. A closer, contextual reading of popular media however often brings to light a different kind of political engagement, one which could be termed the 'politics of the everyday' (Wasserman

2010), and which breaks down boundaries between the 'knowledge class' and 'ordinary people' (Hermes 2006: 28).

These questions are dealt with in Part III of this book, where the dynamics of audiences, the possibility of agency and the role of popular media in everyday life in an African context are explored. The section is introduced by a critical analysis of an episode of the US-produced (but internationally popular) television show *The Amazing Race* set in Burkina Faso. H. Leslie Steeves' trenchant investigation into the relative agency of Burkinabé in influencing the representation on this show, the experiences of local participants and observers of the production, and their perspectives on what the production's costs and benefits might be to them draws on ethnographic research within the theoretical framework of postcolonial criticism. Her analysis brings to light a host of misrepresentations and exoticizing embellishments, a power differential between the Northern participants and producers and subaltern local subjects and collaborators, fitting into an overall paradigm of neoliberalism and cultural commodification. The political economy of popular media representations of developing countries presented in this analysis is hardly cause for celebration. As a reminder of the exploitative potential of the encounter between global popular media and the inhabitants of African locales, Steeves' chapter serves as a cautionary prologue to the rest of the chapters in this volume where the agency of popular media audiences are cast in a more positive light.

In Chapter 11 on popular magazines in South Africa, Sonja Narunsky-Laden argues that the commercial logic of these publications does not necessarily preclude them from functioning as agents of social and cultural change in an African postcolonial setting. From this perspective, these publications promote a sense of 'cultural citizenship'. She provides a nuanced reading of these magazines in order to conclude that despite their commercial orientation as print commodities, these publications may be seen as enabling participation in 'procedures of socio-cultural change, democratization, and cultural citizenship'.

As in the case of commercial magazines in South Africa, popular television shows in the Democratic Republic of the Congo might at first glance seem an unlikely space for discourses of democratic citizenship to emerge. But as Marie-Soleil Frère argues in Chapter 12 on popular television programmes and audiences in Kinshasa, these programmes have gained the trust of audiences in the Congolese capital for whom these sensational, dramatic television shows provide a more accurate portrayal of their daily reality than the public broadcaster or commercial stations. Although Frère stresses that the excesses and ethical breaches of these television shows should not be condoned, she concludes that it would be much more important to attempt to understand what the popularity of these programmes says about the failures of mainstream media to win the trust of audiences and to express the concerns of those marginalized members of the polity for whom politics have become remote from their daily lived experience. Frère points out that the correct response would not be to condemn these popular media forms on the basis of existing normative standards moulded on elite media practices, but instead examine the reasons for their popularity and on that basis revisit the existing normative and professional frameworks.

The normative assumption that popular media are hierarchically inferior to 'serious' news media in terms of their ability to facilitate democratic participation is also interrogated by Levi Obijiofor in Chapter 13. In his chapter, Obijiofor focuses on an audience that have been referred to – at least in the media-saturated contexts of the Global North – as 'digital natives' (Prensky 2001), i.e. the young generation of media users who were born when new media technologies such as mobile phones, the Internet, etc. were already commonplace and thus have grown up with these technologies. Obijiofor examines the use of new media among students at universities in Nigeria and Ghana to evaluate claims that new media tend to be used more for diversion and entertainment than for public deliberation and civic engagement. He finds that students' engagement in social networking sites like Facebook is not dichotomous to more 'serious' uses of new media, but can facilitate the creation of networks within which democratic participation may take place. The political economy of access is however never far from any analysis of new media in Africa, and Obijiofor also points to the limitations imposed on such participation by infrastructural and socio-economic impediments.

In the final section of the book, Part IV, questions of identity take centre stage – again in relation to contestations between local and global, national and transnational signifying frameworks. In Chapter 14 on transnational flows and local identities in Nigerian film, Abdalla Uba Adamu explores the reworkings of a Hollywood film, *Dead Poets Society*, in two countries in the Global South, India and Nigeria. Adamu illustrates through a critical reading of these adaptations how popular media provide a platform for the renegotiation of racial, gender and national identities. Linking the impact of local political developments in Nigeria on the film industry to global cultural flows, understood through the theoretical framework of hybridity, Adamu demonstrates that postcolonial hybridity should be understood not as a superficial intertextual mixing devoid of power struggles. Instead, the appropriation and reworking of cultural content derived from the Global North, by means of 'small media technologies', can be seen as an attempt by African media producers and consumers to control their own self-image and reclaim the right to cultural self-representation.

The (re)construction of cultural identity is also the subject of Chapter 15 by Inge Brinkman *et al*. In their contribution, the authors examine and compare four case studies of websites related to various regions in Africa in which ethnic or regional identities are considered of political importance. These websites contain debates about Moroccan Berber, 'Kongo' 'Nuba' and anglophone West-Cameroonian identities, informed by experiences of marginality and mobility. The study brings to light the replication of social and class hierarchies from the 'offline' world in the 'online' sphere, with production of and participation in these websites mostly restricted to male elites. The nuanced and critical analysis provided in this wide-ranging study makes a strong case against overly celebratory and optimistic views of the Internet as an open and democratic space for deliberation and identity construction. Factors such as residence, computer access and class still circumscribe the limits of online debate of this nature.

Okoth Fred Mudhai gives a more optimistic assessment of the potential of new media technologies to contribute to democratic participation in Chapter 16 on the converged new media environment in several African settings. Mudhai examines the interface between new media technologies and the older, and in Africa most pervasive, medium of radio. He situates his discussion against the background of the 'third wave of democratization' sweeping Africa since the 1990s, which has led to the liberalization of media in many African countries. The licensing of private radio stations has rekindled what Mudhai calls a 'radio culture', which has now been boosted by social networking applications via the Internet and mobile phones. This new networked environment is characterized by an unprecedented level of audience feedback and participation, which Mudhai sees as giving shape to alternative discourses of development and democracy outside the established mass media channels. Mudhai's discussion links to the other chapters in this part through his examination of ethnic-based radio, which could either be seen as exacerbating ethnic exclusivity and conflict in African countries such as Kenya and Rwanda, or could lead to the hybridization of identities and holding an emancipator promise in the way they facilitate open and free identity debates.

The issue of cultural diversity is also the topic of the final chapter in this part and in the volume, in which Monica Chibita examines the function of popular media as an arbiter of cultural recognition. Situating her discussion in the framework of critical political economy, and supported by illustrations from Kenya, Nigeria and Uganda, Chibita argues for the need for media regulation of the popular media sphere. Such regulation is especially necessary, the chapter concludes, in the African context characterized by major social and economic inequalities and a weak production sector. From Chibita's perspective, ensuring cultural diversity in African media is crucial in an era where media globalization tends to lead to concentration and marginalization of local cultures.

Taken together, the chapters summarized above present a picture of popular media in Africa which attests to its vibrancy as well as its many contradictions and complexities. The arguments and cases presented here show how popular media in Africa serve as sites for multiplicitous constructions of citizenship, identity and democratic participation, but also as terrains of conflict, where notions of nationhood and citizenship are contested against the background of accelerated globalization, the colonial legacy of imposed ethnicities, political transformations and economic struggles.

References

Bakhtin, M. (1968). *Rabelais and His World*, trans. Helene Iswolsky. Cambridge, MA: MIT Press.

Barber, K. (1997). 'Views of the Field', in Barber, K. (ed.) *Readings in African Popular Culture*. Bloomington: Indiana University Press, pp. 1–12.

Bourgault, L. (1995). *Mass Media in Sub-Saharan Africa*. Bloomington: Indiana University Press.

Conboy, M. (2002). *The Press and Popular Culture*. London: Sage.

——. (2006). *Tabloid Britain. Constructing a Community through Language*. London: Routledge.

De Bruijn, M., Nyamnjoh, F. and Brinkman, I. (eds) (2009). *Mobile Phones: The New Talking Drums of Africa*. Leiden: African Studies Centre, and Douala: Langaa.

Ellis, S. (1989). 'Tuning in to Pavement Radio', *African Affairs*, 88(352): 321–30.

Eribo, F. and Jong-Ebot, W. (eds) (1997). *Press Freedom and Communication in Africa*. Trenton: Africa World Press.

Eskine, S. (ed.) (2010). *SMS Uprising: Mobile Activism in Africa*. Oxford: Fahamu Books.

Fiske, J. (1989). *Understanding Popular Culture*. Boston: Unwyn Hyman.

Hermes, J. (2006). 'Hidden Debates: Rethinking the Relationship between Popular Culture and the Public Sphere', *Javnost The Public*, 13(4): 27–44.

Horwitz, R.B. (2001). *Communication and Democratic Reform in South Africa*. Cambridge: Cambridge University Press.

Hyden, G., Leslie, M. and Ogundimu, F.F. (2003). *Media and Democracy in Africa*. Uppsala: Nordiska Afrikainstitutet.

Kraidy, M.M. (2005). *Hybridity, or the Cultural Logic of Globalization*. Philadelphia: Temple University Press.

Mano, W. (2009). 'Re-conceptualizing Media Studies in Africa', in Thussu, D.K. (ed.) *Internationalizing Media Studies*. London: Routledge, pp. 277–93.

Mano, W. and Willems, W. (2008). 'Emerging Communities, Emerging Media: The Case of a Zimbabwean Nurse in the British *Big Brother* Show', *Critical Arts*, 22(1): 101–28.

Mudhai, F., Tettey, W.J. and Banda, F. (eds) (2009). *African Media and the Digital Public Sphere*. New York: Palgrave Macmillan.

Nixon, R. (1994). *Homelands, Harlem and Hollywood*. London: Routledge.

Nyamnjoh, F.B. (2005). *Africa's Media, Democracy and the Politics of Belonging*. London: Zed Books.

Park, M.-J. and Curran, J. (2000). *De-Westernizing Media Studies*. London: Routledge.

Pillay, S. (2008). 'The ANC as Government. Contesting Leadership Between Democracy and Development', *Perspectives*, newsletter of the Heinrich Boell Foundation, No. 12.

Prensky, M. (2001). 'Digital Natives, Digital Immigrants', *On the Horizon*, 9(5): 1–6.

Shome, R. (2009). 'Post-colonial Reflections on the "Internationalization" of Cultural Studies', *Cultural Studies*, 23(5): 694–719.

Sparks, C. (2000). 'Introduction: The Panic over Tabloid News', in Sparks, C. and Tulloch, J. (eds) *Tabloid Tales: Global Debates over Media Standards*. Lanham: Rowman & Littlefield, pp. 1–40.

——. (2007). *Globalization, Development and the Mass Media*. London: Sage.

Straubhaar, J.D. (2007). *World Television*. London: Sage.

Thussu, D.K. (ed.) (2006). *Media on the Move: Global Flow and Contraflow*. London: Routledge.

——. (ed.) (2009). *Internationalizing Media Studies*. Oxford: Routledge.

Tomaselli, K.G. (2003). ' "Our Culture" vs "Foreign Culture": An Essay on Ontological and Professional Issues in African Journalism', *International Communication Gazette*, 65(6): 427–41.

Tomaselli, K. and Dunn, H. (eds) (2001). *Media, Democracy and Renewal in Southern Africa*. Colorado Springs: International Academic Publishers.

Wasserman, H. (2009). 'Extending the Theoretical Cloth to Make Room for African Experience: An Interview with Francis Nyamnjoh', *Journalism Studies*, 10(2): 281–93.

——. (2010). *Tabloid Journalism in South Africa: True Story!* Bloomington: Indiana University Press.

Wasserman, H. and De Beer, A.S. (2009). 'Towards De-Westernising Journalism Studies: The Case of Africa', in Hanitzsch, T. and Wahl-Jorgensen, K. (eds) *Handbook of Journalism Studies*. Mahwah: Lawrence Erlbaum, pp. 428–38.

West, H.G. and Fair, J.E. (1993). 'Development Communication and Popular Resistance in Africa: An Examination of the Struggle over Tradition and Modernity through Media', *African Studies Review*, 36(1): 91–114.

Part I

The popular media sphere
Theoretical interventions

Chapter 1

De-Westernizing media theory to make room for African experience[1]

Francis B. Nyamnjoh

Theorizing the local and the global in Africa

How should one think about popular media in the African context? Should we attempt to understand and analyse the increasing proliferation of tabloids, reality television shows, pop music, websites and mobile communications through the analytical frameworks constructed by scholars in the Global North, or does Africa pose unique research questions? Is there a danger of either essentializing Africa by treating her as 'different', or by ignoring her specificity by approaching her media via Western theoretical constructs?

The scholar wishing to understand the interface between popular media, development and democracy in contemporary African societies is faced with a complex double bind. Elsewhere (Nyamnjoh 2005: 2–3) I have argued that African worldviews and cultural values are doubly excluded from global media discourses, first by the ideology of hierarchies and boundedness of cultures, and second by cultural industries more interested in profits than the promotion of creative diversity and cultural plurality. Little attention is accorded to how Africans negotiate and navigate the various identity margins and cultural influences in their lives, in ways that are not easily reducible to simple options or straightforward choices. The consequence of rigid dichotomies or stubborn prescriptiveness based on externally induced expectations of social transformation is an idea of democracy hardly informed by popular articulations of personhood and agency in Africa, and media whose professional values and content are not in tune with the expectations of those they purport to serve.

The predicament of media practitioners in such a situation, as well as those wishing to understand African media practice through media theory, is obvious: to be of real service to liberal democracy and its expectations of modernity, they must ignore alternative ideas of personhood and agency in the cultural communities within which such practices take place and of which such practitioners and, often, scholars form part. Attending to the interests of particular cultural groups as strategically essential entities risks contradicting the principles of liberal democracy and its emphasis on civic citizenship and the autonomous individual, which media practitioners in African societies are being held accountable to.

Torn between such competing and conflicting understandings of democracy, the media find it increasingly difficult to marry rhetoric with practice, and for strategic instrumentalist reasons may opt for a Jekyll and Hyde personality that is, at the end of the day, of service neither to democracy nor to development (Nyamnjoh 2005).

Yet despite this critique of the dominant liberal democratic normative paradigm, one should avoid the trap of an idealization of Africa or the romantic essentialism of 'African values' that many proponents of Afrocentric thought are prone to (Kasoma 1996; Pecora *et al.* 2008). A flexible theoretical position is needed, one which takes into account the multiple, overlapping spaces and flows in the era of globalization yet refuses to gloss over global power imbalances and material inequalities (Ferguson 2006). For instance, while the potential contribution of information and communication technologies (ICTs) to development in Africa has widely been lauded by cyber-optimists, such euphoria should be mitigated (see Nyamnjoh 1999) by a sober assessment of the political economy of access to new media technologies, and by the reality of the social shaping of these technologies by Africans who harness these technologies to simultaneously reproduce and contest existing social structures in ways that technological determinism masks more than elucidates (Mbarika 2003; Nyamnjoh 2005; de Bruijn *et al.* 2009). In this light one should hold out hope for the creative ways in which recent developments in media technologies can give rise to participatory movements like 'citizen' journalism which could open new opportunities for democratic citizenship and flexible mobility (Bahree 2008; Panos 2008; Dibussi 2009). Africa's creativity simply cannot allow for simple dichotomies or distinctions between old and new technologies, since its peoples are daily modernizing the indigenous and indigenizing the modern with novel outcomes.

No theorization takes place in a void. Meaningful theorization about media has to be contextualized, and African scholars should critically situate their scholarship in relation to theories from Europe and North America. The test of the theoretical pudding being in the practical eating, no scholar should enter the marketplace of ideas without fully being aware where they're coming from, and the extent to which the theories on display in the shop windows of ideas, make sense. When you buy a dress you don't buy it to hang in a wardrobe, you buy it to wear it, so you try on different dresses to see which one fits your bulk. If you're a bulky person and you go and buy a Barbie-like dress just because it's fashionable to be a Barbie, you won't have the opportunity of wearing that dress. The dress would not be relevant to your reality, because your reality is simply too large for the Barbie-like dress, no matter how appealing that dress might appear. It is not a question of finding a dress somewhere that fits you. It is a question of finding a dress which has room for expansion, a dress you could extend to accommodate the fullness of your being. There should be room on the sides of existing theories for African scholarship to extend the cloth (Nyamnjoh 2004a).

If critical-cultural theory as it has historically emerged from European media and cultural studies, finds reason to be critical of American scholarship because it is too narrowly focused, either because of a focus on American society or an American understanding of what society should be like, then it is normal that an African who buys into Western theoretical articulations would say that as much as it makes sense when you narrow it down to comparing European and American societies, these theories don't quite make that much sense when you compare Western societies taken together with non-Western societies like those in Africa. So if African scholars find inspiration from critical thinking, they still need to open up this dress and beat it and stretch it, because of the African colonial experience and because of the African postcolonial situation of living in the shadows of global forces, and then come up with something that is not radically different as such but has different nuances in tune with the African experience (Ferguson 2006; Zeleza 2006).

Providing for African creativity

An African proverb says: 'Until the lions produce their own historian, the story of the hunt will glorify only the hunter' (Achebe 2000: 73). The wisdom of this proverb is brought home not only through an analysis of writings on Africa, but also and perhaps more sensationally through the images of Africa captured in the cinematic gaze of the supposedly superior others. As the bottom rungs of the ladder of race and place, Africa has through the centuries provided especially Euro-American cultural entrepreneurs with a rich catalogue of stereotypes, prejudices and other negations on which to capitalize. If this is true of publishing, cinema and television have, since the twentieth century, offered more efficient vehicles for effective traffic in such misrepresentations (Walker and Rasamimanana 1993; Barlet 2000; Gugler 2003; Harding 2003).

In their study of educational films on Africa in American schools, Walker and Rasamimanana (1993) discovered not only the prominence of Tarzan films in the repertoire of 'America's most consistent cinematic denigration of Africans', but also a tendency in Hollywood films to persist in presenting Africa as a continent of negations inhabited by stupid, bloodthirsty savages who are incapable of teaching anyone anything of value, but who must learn all from others to make progress. Hardly ever is there mention of the Africans who 'fought determinedly against European aggression and influence to preserve their indigenous and sovereign ways'. Nor do the films recognize that many contemporary, well-educated, and cosmopolitan Africans have chosen to maintain their indigenous values and behaviours, or that many others have eclectically adapted or 'Africanized' some elements of Western culture while deliberately and consciously rejecting others as inferior to their own.

If stereotypes and prejudices are this evident in educational films, the situation is worse with commercial films. An effect of feeding school children and adults alike with a consistent menu of misrepresentations about Africa and the African diaspora is the reproduction of hierarchies that exclude and render invisible

African humanity and creativity (Walker and Rasamimanana 1993: 7–16). We could add to this study examples of Hollywood movies (*Blood Diamond, Lords of War*, etc.) that articulate African predicaments in ways that fail to do justice to the nuances and complexities of the realities they seek to capture.

Since colonial times, Africans have been confined largely to consuming (even if creatively) pervasive 'mythic Hollywood screen imagery' (Ambler 2001), and to feeding the Africa misrepresentation industry (Barlet 2000; Harding 2003). In a context like this, where Africans find themselves peripheral to global trends and subjected to the high-handedness and repression of their own governments, it is easy to slip into meta-narratives that celebrate victimhood. While there is genuine reason to be pessimistic and cynical, there is often, on closer observation, also reason to be hopeful. However repressive a government may be and however profound the spiral of silence induced by standardized and routinized global cultural menus, few people are completely mystified or wholly duped. There is always room for initiative or agency at an individual or group level to challenge domination, exploitation and the globalization of indifference to cultural diversity. Histories of struggle in Africa are full of examples in this connection. In cinema, just as in publishing, Africans have found myriad creative ways of participating as active agents in national life and global cultural processes, and of re-imagining their continent, its struggles, victories, challenges and aspirations (Gugler 2003).

As Eddie Ugbomah, a renowned Nigerian filmmaker, observes, in Africa 'There are many trained filmmakers who can make films better than Hollywood directors, but they do not have Hollywood money' (Ukadike and Ugbomah 1994: 157). They are making do with their widow's mite, seeking to fill the cinematic vacuum on the positive contributions of African cultures. In the face of global cinematographic indifference and caricature of their realities, the African lions have sought – despite financial, political and other hurdles – to enrich or contest the accounts of the Euro-American cinematic hunters through films of their own (Medjigbodo 1980; Ukadike and Ugbomah 1994; Barlet 2000; Gugler 2003; Harding 2003: 79–83; Ngugi 2003).

In response to many of these dilemmas, the vibrant Nigerian video-movie industry, with its highly localized locations, settings, dress and narratives, has responded with direct-to-video marketing, cutting out theatre-going, which is perceived as not being central to African cultural patterns and practices. The assumption is that given the tendency for Africans to view movies in their own homes, movies need not necessarily be distributed mainly for cinemas, where they would have to compete with Hollywood blockbusters. Through direct-to-video sales, the Nigerian movie industry is making a name for itself locally and internationally, notably amongst Nigerians and Africans in the diaspora (Adejunmobi 2002: 77–95; Ambler 2002: 119–20; Harding 2003: 81–3; see also Chapter 14 in this volume).

Though sometimes overly dramatic, sensational and stereotypical in their portrayal, especially of the occult and ritualized practices drawn largely from ethnic

Igbo, Yoruba and Hausa cultures (Okwori 2003), the Nigerian video-movie industry covers themes and uses language in creative ways relevant to and popular with its African audiences (Adejunmobi 2002). Throughout Africa and thanks to flexible mobility, cities are full of shops owned mainly by the Nigerian Igbo business community selling Nigerian-made and pirated films from Hollywood, Bollywood and Nigeria's very own popular Nollywood, at affordable prices. The fact of the films being a mixture of English, pidgin English and indigenous Nigerian languages does not seem to detract from their popularity across Africa. Commercial and public television stations throughout Africa feed heavily on Nollywood videos (through popular digital channels like Africa Magic), while from Maputo to Dakar through Harare, Nairobi, Accra and Freetown pirated latest Hollywood films proliferate at US$5 and less. Indeed, 'video dens and theatres have become ubiquitous features on African landscapes', offering new forms of leisure to urban and rural Africa alike, ranging from establishments where funds are informally collected in exchange for film shows, to more formal movie theatres, through obscure backrooms and home viewing (Ambler 2002: 119).

Pirating may be a breach of copyright but it is also an indication of the desire to belong by those who are denied first-hand consumption of the cultural products in question. Using very basic equipment and releasing its products directly on video cassettes and CDs, Nigerian filmmakers have captured a large market among Africans at home and in the diaspora, offering films more culturally relevant than even the most sympathetic Hollywood product (Adejunmobi 2002). It is estimated that the Nigerian movie industry, which produces thousands of video films every year, yields about $45 million in revenues each year (Ambler 2002: 119–20). To Nigeria, one could add South Africa, Ghana and Burkina Faso – countries where the cinematic industry is considerable in its production, ranging from films to serials, and consumed both locally and abroad. This creativity in African cinema does more than re-imagine Africa and the challenges of being African. It also tells the story of how Africans are actively modernizing their indigeneities and indigenizing their modernities, often in ways not always obvious to those obsessed with cultural hierarchies.

So when you apply Western theory to African experience, you have to modify it. When we don't speak in terms of levels, and we don't bring condescension to bear unduly, but stick to the science, and provide room for dialogue and cross-fertilization, such an approach really opens up new ways of seeing Western societies, just as it does for the African context. There is a lot of room for enriching theory if we don't allow science to serve ideology as is often the case. If we are modest enough to know that science is not the monopoly of any given individual or group, and that conferencing and interaction between scholars globally – much more possible today in a context of flexible mobility – is imperative, media scholarship would be all the richer for that.

The problem is that African scholars are trapped in local and global hierarchies that inform how they relate to the rest of the world – whether those hierarchies are based on race, geography, gender, generation or whatever – they are all part and parcel of these hierarchies, and they bring them into the workplaces and into their scholarship.

Lessons in creative appropriation from the margins

Good theories, sophisticated theories, lasting theories have got to be able to serve as navigators of various identity margins, various margins of reality, being able to capture reality in its wholeness and nuanced complexities. A good theory should not be like an undertaker who stubbornly imposes Lilliputian coffins on gargantuan realities. Listening to dynamic social reality and the creativity diversity of our world is the business of good theory building.

So where are the areas, the points of focus, where a Western study of the interface between popular media, democracy and development can benefit from being more open and having more dialogue with African scholars and African experiences? What is the contribution that African scholars can make to such a study? By simply asking how do people on the margins – margins of every society – come by information? How do they communicate with one another and with others over and above those margins? How do they relate? When you start asking those questions you will find out that instead of the focus and the exchange being centred on mainstream media, you will see that these people bring on board a buffet of communication possibilities that at different levels might involve the mainstream media, soap operas, alternative media, as well as just straightforward word of mouth and symbolic communication. Ordinary people at the margins of focus of technology use a combination of possibilities to relate and to exchange in ways that can be quite instructive about theory building. They use a combination of different factors in ways that mean that media theories of communication which only focus on possibilities as if people were autonomous and atomized individuals, miss the point about the creative domestication of individual agency by the groups and communities to which various individual actors belong. It is people on the margins, in economic difficulties, that bring the complex and comprehensive nature of communication home to us. It's not a question of dichotomies, of either/or. Often we talk about the haves and the have-nots, in a way that does not quite capture the situation. Instead we should try as much as possible to allow the given situation or context that we are researching to tell its story, rather than saying 'this is the storyline'.

The different types of communication that are typical to African settings can also be seen as a metaphor for the different forms of communication within Western societies. It has nothing to do with geography or race. It has to do with marginality, regardless of where that marginality happens to be, or who happens to inhabit it. Only in Africa's case it happens to be a potent concoction of racial, spatial, economic and cultural marginality. Marginality can take different forms, and Africa's experience in that regard can be very useful in theory building, especially if we don't get carried away with the superiority complex that a feeling or perception of relative comfort tends to engender.

That marginality itself impacts on scholarly production, on the ability for these very alternative perspectives to enter the Western theoretical dialogue. That is a problem, because the person who has the power to define has that power not only to define the self, but also to define others. That means that Western scholarship tends to determine who is going to be included and who excluded, and that does not always have to do with the quality of scholarship being produced. A journal that is based in the UK, run by somebody who has assumptions about the world and North/South divisions, might take positions about which papers will be published. Those decisions have very little to do with science, but more with the politics of scholarly production. It therefore becomes very difficult for African ideas, African scholarship, African research to filter through. But fortunately we are living in the twenty-first century, where you have alternative ways of surviving even while you are being excluded. There are possibilities through new technologies of dissemination – just by putting something on a listserv or online, even if you have limited bandwidth, means that you increase the chances of excluded scholarship, of excluded theoretical contributions, thereby preventing them from dying simply because they haven't been published in a mainstream channel.

The likelihood exists that knowledge produced in the South might not always make its way to publication or public debate for various reasons – economic, political or otherwise – but also thanks to recent developments in technologies, even if they cannot quite make it, the chance of them being accessed by those who really want to know, who really want to relate, are greater than before.

I have argued before (Nyamnjoh 2004b) that African scholars have to focus their attention so much on entering and impacting on the Western theoretical discourse that they lose sight of the imperative of speaking to people closer to home. But I think it is something that is easily corrected. However generous these new technologies might be to the margins, and however accommodating of the margins the metropolis might be, only the elite can filter through. So it creates the imperative of other, alternative centres within Africa, like the Council for the Development of Social Science Research in Africa (CODESRIA) or the Organization for Social Science Research in Eastern and Southern Africa (OSSREA), to promote such scholarly exchanges. But there is also the danger of locking yourself up in your alternatives, and creating a new form of fundamentalism that excludes everything that differs from you and then you become just as bad as those you are critical of. We must create room to reach out while at the same time encouraging exchanges within the continent. It's in some ways the same as the classic debate – how well do you provide for gender in scholarship? Do you do it by creating room for gender in the mainstream, or by creating a forum for gender in its own right without creating a ghetto? Both these options should be pursued at the same time.

Being African is not a birthmark

The African context and experience should contribute towards theory building. The African condition is not a birthmark, it is not exclusive to Africa. At this point in history Africa has those conditions that make such a view possible, but it can also outgrow that reality. The precepts of journalism, for instance, that apply currently in Africa are largely at variance with dominant ideas of personhood and agency (and by extension society, culture and democracy) shared by communities across the continent, as it assumes that there is a 'one-best-way' of being and doing to which Africans must aspire and be converted in the name of modernity and civilization. This divorce is at the heart of some of the professional and ethical dilemmas that haunt journalism in and on Africa, a journalism whose tendency is to debase and caricature African humanity, creativity and realities. It is a constraint that renders African journalism a journalism of bandwagonism, where mimicry is the order of the day, as the emphasis is less on thinking than on doing, less on leading than on being led. In relation to popular media, although commendable progress is being made by the local cultural industry on the continent to be relevant (take film and music production for example), the tendency remains (especially in broadcasting and publishing), to rely overly on imported content, and to resort to mimicry of Western programmes instead of creative production of local content (Pecora *et al.* 2008).

Introducing 'African studies' programmes is not always the answer to the challenge of directing more theoretical attention to African media. You run the risk of making it stand apart, as something 'out there', something to be studied by those who are interested in those margins. The main business, of studying the disciplines and universal concerns, takes place elsewhere. But if African studies programmes are structured in such a way that their discussions are not incestuous, just maintaining mediocrity amongst themselves, people just interacting among themselves like a religious sect, then they can be very useful.

The relationship between the study of African media and global media theory is best captured by the notion of flexibility – flexible mobility, flexible belonging, flexible citizenship. That's the only way to challenge these things, by questioning the tendency to essentialize even when it's important to draw attention to some things that have been overlooked or some specific experiences that stand apart.

There is also the danger that theories from the North are used to underpin normative assumptions of what media in Africa *should* look like. This is why African media often does poorly on global indices of press freedom, for instance, because freedom is measured in a particular way. Normative theories are good in that there is already a social consensus about values we share and about the social order that we need. But when normative theories take upon themselves an export component, it can become very dangerous, because you are glossing over power relations and unequal encounters and unequal exchanges. You are providing for norms without knowing where they are coming from. If we think about North–South divisions, and we believe in geopolitics and that factors such as gender, class, race and age can impact on the social values at play, then we should be much more careful in negotiating and arriving at the ethics and values that we think we can afford to impose on African media. Norms require far more negotiation, especially when you are talking between societies.

How well popular media, especially those formats taken over from elsewhere in the world, is relevant to Africa and Africans depends on what value such media gives African humanity and creativity. If a media practice is such that it privileges a hierarchy of humanity and human creativity, and if such media believes that African humanity and creativity are at the abyss of that hierarchy, such media are bound to be prescriptive, condescending, contrived, caricatured and hardly in tune with the quest by Africans for equality of humanity and for recognition and representation.

And if African media practitioners were to, wittingly or unwittingly, buy into that hierarchy, they would in effect be working against the interests of the very African communities they claim to serve. But if one convinces one's self that one is at the abyss, that one is a veritable heart of darkness, one doesn't need much convincing to buy into prescriptions on how to fish one's self out of the abyss or the heart of darkness, especially if such prescriptions are by those one has been schooled to recognize and represent as superior.

Recognizing indigenous African forms should not be mistaken for throwing the baby of adaptability out with the bathwater. African popular musicians for example have evolved and continue to develop musical idioms that capture ongoing processes by Africans at modernizing their cultures and traditionalizing their modernities. Indeed, the mechanisms developed by Africans in response to the above scenarios are complex, fascinating and informed by ideas of personhood and agency that simply refuse to be confined to the logic of dichotomies, essentialism, the market and profitability, as the rich personal account of one of Africa's leading contemporary musicians, Manu Dibango, demonstrates (Dibango 1994). As an African musician who has lived the best part of his professional life in Paris and whose music has been enriched by various encounters, Manu Dibango describes himself as 'Négropolitain', 'a man between two cultures, two environments', whose music cannot simply be reduced to either, without losing part of his creative self (Dibango 1994: 88–130). It appears that no one is too cosmopolitan to be local as well. We only have to note the creative ways Africans have harnessed the mobile phone to interlink town and home village, to know how disinterested in a culture of winner-takes-all Africans are.

Equally, to recognize the cosmopolitan nature of Africans and their identities does not necessarily imply to argue in favour of cultural homogenization implicit in the rhetoric of globalization. Although globalization is homogenizing consumer tastes, the same globalization, through the unequal relations it generates, provides consumers (big and small) with the means to create individual and social identities, which are variant and diverse in a way that speaks less of a synthesis of cultures. Not even in the United States, where much has been achieved in the area of the 'McDonaldization of Society' (Ritzer 2000), is that synthesis possible.

It is more a type of unity in diversity, where the fact of Africans belonging to the same popular media consumer club (wanting computer games, television programmes, books, animated cartoons, films and music, and longing for the same blogs, YouTube feeds, online networking possibilities) does not guarantee cultural synchronization.

The way forward

The way forward for theory-building around popular media, development and democracy in Africa is in recognizing the creative ways in which Africans merge their traditions with exogenous influences to create realities that are not reducible to either but enriched by both. The implication of this argument is that how we understand the role of African media depends on what democratic model we draw from. Under liberal democracy, where the individual is perceived and treated as an autonomous agent, and where primary solidarities and cultural identities are discouraged in favour of a national citizenship and culture, journalism is expected to be disinterested, objective, balanced and fair in gathering, processing and disseminating news and information. Media are supposed to inform, educate and entertain. The assumption is that since all individuals have equal rights as citizens, there can be no justification for bias among journalists. But under popular notions of democracy where emphasis is on interdependence and competing cultural solidarities are a reality, the media are under constant internal and external pressure to promote the interests of the various groups competing for recognition and representation.

The tensions and pressures are even greater in situations where states and governments purport to pursue liberal democracy in principle, while in reality they continue to be high-handed and repressive to their populations. When this happens, journalists and other mainstream media practitioners are at risk of employing double-standards as well, by claiming one thing and doing the opposite, or by straddling various identity margins, without always being honest about it, especially if their very survival depends on it. In these contexts where mainstream media are failing or are hampered, alternative forms of popular media, ranging from websites, street posters and pop songs to mobile phones and clandestine radio, can often step into the breach to provide a platform for democratic debate and channels for competing discourses of development may emerge. To democratize means to question basic monolithic assumptions, conventional wisdom about democracy, development, journalism, government, power myths and accepted personality cults, and to suggest and work for the demystification of the state, custom and society.

To democratize African media is to provide the missing cultural link to current efforts, links informed by respect for African humanity and creativity, and by popular ideas of personhood and domesticated agency. It is to negotiate conviviality between competing ideas of how best to provide for the humanity and dignity of all and sundry. It is above all to observe and draw from the predica-

ments of ordinary Africans forced by culture, history and material realities to live
their lives as 'subjects' rather than as 'citizens', even as liberal democratic rhetoric
claims otherwise. The mere call for an exploration of alternatives in African
media is bound to be perceived as a threat and a challenge.

One development in African media that one could be very enthusiastic about
is what is termed 'citizen journalism'. Mainstream media in Africa can often be
detached from what is really going on in the lives of ordinary people and how
they make news, how they gather news and how they communicate. It is because
African mainstream media practitioners, by sticking to Western canons, often miss
the point of African value added in terms of how people communicate and how
they share communication with one another. And Africa has a much richer landscape in this regard that can inform journalism. Before citizen journalism came to
the West, you had citizen journalism all over Africa. So, how did the excluded
succeed in making news about their experiences and sharing this news among
themselves? Today, with ICTs, this seems like something new, but if we look at
Africa, people have been using ways like *radio trottoir* to obtain information, share
it and create possibilities where normal channels were beyond their reach. So
citizen journalism is something that helps me to revisit an old problem, that of
understanding popular forms of communication and how they blend in with conventional media for the benefit of society.

Citizen journalism and user-generated content is currently high on the
research agenda of media studies in the North. The question, however, is to what
extent that debate is relevant for Africa, given problems of infrastructure and
access. Journalism, to be relevant to social consolidation and renewal in Africa,
must embrace professional and social responsibilities in tune with the collective
aspirations of Africans. This is true of popular media as well, which, as is evident
from the popularity of Nollywood films across the continent, are highly regarded
even when very poorly produced, once they reflect the cultural realities and lived
experiences of their target audience. To be African in matters of journalism or
popular media implies to privilege contextual relevance over professional recognition. In a context where economic and political constraints have often hindered
the fulfilment of this expectation, the advent and increasing adoption in Africa of
information and communication technologies (ICTs) offer fascinating new
possibilities. While journalists are usually open to new technologies in their work,
their practice of journalism has not always capitalized upon the creative ways in
which the public they target for and with information adopt, adapt and use the
very same technologies. The future for democracy and the relevance of journalism therein would have much to learn from the creative ways in which Africans
are currently relating to innovations in ICTs. The same popular creativity that
has been largely ignored by conventional journalism in the past is remarkable
today all over Africa and amongst Africans in the diaspora. The body of literature
informed by empirical research is considerable to suggest that individuals and the
cultural communities they represent often refuse to celebrate victimhood. They
seek to harness, within the limits of the structural constraints facing them,

whatever possibilities are available to contest and seek inclusion. Hence the need to highlight the importance of blending conventional and citizen journalism through the myriad possibilities offered by ICTs to harness both democracy and its nemesis. The current context of globalization facilitated by the ICTs offers exciting new prospects not only for citizens and journalists to compete and complement one another, but also an opportunity for new solidarities to challenge undemocratic forces, ideologies and practices that stand in the way of social progress.

The lessons for African media scholarship of such creative appropriation processes underway are obvious. Comprehending the overall development, usage and application of ICTs within African social spaces would take the fusion of keen observation and complex analysis to capture structural, gendered, class, generational, racial and spatial dimensions of the phenomenon. A dialectical interrogation of the processes involved promises a more accurate grasp of the linkages than would impressionistic, linear and prescriptive narratives of technological determinism. If theories of African media could pay closer attention to the creative usages of ICTs by ordinary Africans, African media practitioners could begin to think less of professional media, including journalism, in the conventional sense, and more of seeking ways to blend the information and communication cultures of the general public with their conventional canon and practices, to give birth to a conventional-cum-citizen journalism that is of greater relevance to Africa and its predicaments.

Note

1 This chapter is based on an article in *Journalism Studies*, used here with permission: Wasserman, H. (2009) 'Extending the Theoretical Cloth to Make Room for African Experience: An Interview with Francis Nyamnjoh', *Journalism Studies*, 10(2): 281–93.

References

Achebe, C. (2000) *Home and Exile*, New York: Anchor Books.

Adejunmobi, M. (2002) 'English and the Audience of an African Popular Culture: The Case of Nigerian Video Film', *Cultural Critique*, 50: 74–103.

Ambler, C. (2001) 'Popular Films and Colonial Audiences: The Movies in Northern Rhodesia', *The American Historial Review*, 106(1): 81–105.

—— (2002) 'Mass Media and Leisure in Africa', *The International Journal of African Historical Studies*, 35(1): 119–36.

Bahree, M. (2008) 'Creative Disruption: Citizen Voices', *Forbes Magazine*, 12 August. Available online: www.forbes.com/free_forbes/2008/1208/083.html (accessed 11 November 2009).

Barlet, O. (2000) *African Cinemas: Decolonizing the Gaze*, London: Zed Books.

De Bruijn, M., Nyamnjoh, F.B. and Brinkman, I. (2009) *Mobile Phones: The New Talking Drums of Everyday Africa*, Bamenda: Langaa RPCIG and African Studies Centre, Leiden.

Dibango, M. (in collaboration with Danielle Rouard) (1994) *Three Kilos of Coffee: An Autobiography*, Chicago: University of Chicago Press.

Dibussi, T. (2009) *Scribbles from the Den: Essays on Politics and Collective Memory in Cameroon*, Bamenda: Langaa RPCIG.

Ferguson, J. (2006) *Global Shadows: Africa in the Neoliberal Order*, Durham, NC: Duke University Press.

Gugler, J. (2003) *African Film: Re-Imagining a Continent*, Bloomington: Indiana University Press.

Harding, F. (2003) 'Africa and the Moving Image: Television, Film and Video', *Journal of African Cultural Studies*, 16(1): 69–84.

Kasoma, F.P. (1996) 'The Foundations of African Ethics (Afriethics) and the Professional Practice of Journalism: The Case for Society-centred Media Morality', *Africa Media Review*, 10(3): 93–116.

Mbarika, V.W.A. (2003) 'The State of Teledensity Diffusion in Least Developed Countries: A Review of the Literature', Idea Group Inc.

Medjigbodo, N. (1980) 'Afrique Cinématographiée, Afrique Cinématographique', *Canadian Journal of African Studies*, 13(3): 371–87.

Ngugi, N. (2003) 'Presenting and (Mis)representing History in Fiction Film: Sembene's "Camp de Thiaroye" and Attenborough's "Cry Freedom"', *Journal of African Cultural Studies*, 16(1): 57–68.

Nyamnjoh, F.B. (1999) 'African and the Information Superhighway: The Need for Mitigated Euphoria', *Ecquid Novi: African Journalism Studies*, 41(3): 69–91.

—— (2004a) 'Africa in 2015: Interrogating Barbie Democracy, Seeking Alternatives', *Democracy & Development – Journal of West African Affairs*, 4(2): 107–12.

—— (2004b) 'From Publish or Perish to Publish and Perish: What "Africa's 100 Best Books" Tell Us About Publishing Africa', *Journal of Asian and African Studies*, 39(5): 331–55.

—— (2005) *Africa's Media: Democracy and the Politics of Belonging*, London: Zed Books.

Okwori, J.Z. (2003) 'A Dramatized Society: Representing Rituals of Human Sacrifice as Efficacious Action in Nigerian Home-Video Movies', *Journal of African Cultural Studies*, 16(1): 7–23.

Panos Institute for West Africa (2008) *Usages innovants des TIC en Afrique: La Presse au Coeur de l'analyse*, Dakar: Institut Panos Afrique de l'Ouest.

Pecora, N., Osei-Hwere, E. and Carlsson, U. (eds) (2008) *Yearbook 2008: African Media, African Children*, NORDICOM Goteborg University: The UNESCO International Clearinghouse on Children, Youth and Media.

Ritzer, G. (2000) *The McDonaldization of Society*, London: Pine Forge Press.

Ukadike, N.F. and Ugbomah, E. (1994) 'Toward an African Cinema', *Transition*, 63: 150–63.

Walker, S.S. and Rasamimanana, J. (1993) 'Tarzan in the Classroom: How "Educational" Films Mythologize Africa and Miseducate Americans', *The Journal of Negro Education*, 62(1): 3–23.

Zeleza, P.T. (ed.) (2006) *The Study of Africa: Disciplinary and Interdisciplinary Encounters*, Dakar: CODESRIA.

Chapter 2

Revisiting cultural imperialism

P. Eric Louw

Is the notion of cultural imperialism helpful when applied to Africa? Certainly the concept has long been popular in Africa. But has 'cultural imperialism' been overtaken by notions like cultural hybridization; by the growth of popular culture and popular media; and by the idea that active audiences and/or active local cultural producers now 'resist' external 'imperial' culture by producing their own local culture?

For some the emergence of new media and local popular media renders the idea of cultural imperialism redundant because such local media apparently generate a communicative 'antidote' to global media and to any externally-imposed 'imperial' communication flowing through the global media. This raises a related question – is popular media an effective site of 'resistance' to cultural imperialism or is it simply a platform that facilitates the process of Americanization and semi-Americanization (hybridization) by passing on a 'reworked' version of the global media's content?

This chapter revisits cultural imperialism with a view to opening debate about whether development, democratization and popular media should be viewed as necessarily 'anti-imperial'. This question is raised in the context of the assumption built into this chapter that America currently operates a global informal empire. The resultant Pax Americana is seen to have a vested interest in promoting global trade, socio-economic development (Westernization) and the building of liberal-democratic states across the globe (Louw 2010). Within this context those promoting the discourses of 'development', 'democracy' and 'good governance' effectively promote American cultural modernization within a second wave of globalization. (Globalization's first wave was driven by the British Empire). By promoting the discourse of 'development' they become agents of modernization, Westernization, economic growth and hence the expansion of (Pax Americana) trading opportunities. One of the consequences of this 'development' and 'democratization' is that people in places like Africa are experiencing a form of cultural change that encodes significant Americanization and semi-Americanization (cultural hybridization). Africa's popular media naturally provide a platform for the circulation of these Americanized and semi-Americanized cultural forms. So, effectively, certain forms of popular media can also become 'helpful' to the operation of an informal empire.

Informal empire, compradorism and cultural imperialism

Cultural imperialism is, as Tomlinson (1991) has noted, a poorly defined concept: 'There are hardly any precise definitions of "cultural imperialism". It seems to mean that the process of imperialist control is aided and abetted by imposing supportive forms of culture' (Barker, in Tomlinson 1991: 3). Tomlinson (1991: 19–28) suggests the notion of cultural imperialism appears to draw upon four strands of thinking:

- It involves the imposition of cultural domination, such that weak societies/states have the culture of strong societies/states imposed upon them.
- It is enmeshed with 'media imperialism', i.e. an Anglo-American built media system has become globally dominant, and serves as a conduit for the export of Anglo-American culture to the far reaches of the globe.
- This Anglo-American culture is deemed to be a 'foreign' culture that is effectively invading the 'cultural spaces' of other sovereign nations.
- The processes of imperialism are seen as driven by global capitalism. Hence the notion of cultural imperialism became enmeshed with a critique (often Marxist-aligned) of global capitalism and capitalist-driven modernization.[1]

This chapter will propose some realignments to the notion of cultural imperialism.

In particular, the notion of an 'invasion' of foreign culture, and of cultural domination being 'imposed' by 'outsiders' needs to be modified.[2] Essentially, the idea of cultural imperialism involving the imposition of outside culture on a bunch of (Third World) 'dupes' is not helpful.

Instead, this chapter suggests that because the Pax Americana functions as an informal empire it generates a particular kind of 'cultural imperialism'. The building of the Pax Americana as an informal empire began after the Second World War, and within this informal empire, comprador-partners (drawn from middle classes across the globe) actively import American culture. It is not imposed upon them. These comprador-partners (who are not 'dupes') service the Pax Americana by being embedded within a global alliance of (First and Third World) middle classes. These Third and First World middle classes work together to facilitate the flow of American culture to Africa, Asia, Europe and Australasia. Within the Third World, comprador-partners act as middle-class Jacobin social engineers promoting 'development', social change, modernization, nation building, etc. These compradors work to bring about social and cultural change in their societies that undermines traditional cultures by Westernizing and semi-Westernizing the Third World's traditional people.

So understanding contemporary 'cultural imperialism' requires some examination of the role of compradors and of 'development' within the Pax Americana.

A key feature of this informal empire is that independent states are enmeshed as clients into an American global trading network. Consequently, the Pax

Americana annexes no territory for incorporation into America; neither are territories organized as (formal) overseas possessions of America. Instead, America invests great energy into building middle-class comprador-partners in independent states. In Africa this has involved using development programmes to build a Westernized middle class; and then using these African middle classes as partners in running still more development programmes.

The point is, to function well, the Pax Americana as a (comprador-based) informal trading empire needs independent states run by people 'sympathetic' to tying their countries into the American trading network. Since the best comprador-partners are middle-class people, it is not surprising to find that since the Second World War much energy has been invested in encouraging the growth of middle-class elites across the Third World, with a framework called 'nation building'. From this, in the 1950s and 1960s, grew a development industry operating from North America and Western Europe. In the first instance, this industry was geared to preparing Europe's empires for independence by 'developing' urban middle classes with the necessary political, economic and administrative skills to lead each imperial possession to independence. Consequently, 'development' effectively meant 'liberalization' – i.e. an attempt to promote liberal-democracy and capitalism in these new Third World states. Because this was essentially an exercise in Westernization, the provision of Western education to Asians and Africans became a central feature of this development process.

The problem faced by an informal empire (like the Pax Americana) is that when its trade-promotion agendas are impeded by 'underdeveloped states' (i.e. states with poor infrastructures, poor governance and populations without the cultural capital required to run Western economies and be good trading partners), it needs to employ 'indirect' methods to try and rectify the situation. Such 'indirect' methods deliberately eschew drastic actions like annexation (used by formal empires), but they still involve intervention. And the preferred intervention of the Pax Americana has been to deploy specialists in Third World development – i.e. people working in the 'development industry' (often linked to the West's 'foreign aid industry' visible across Africa and Asia). This development industry has come to be inspired by a form of Jacobin thinking – i.e. a belief in middle-class driven social engineering (of either a liberal or socialist variety). It is social engineering that intervenes in other people's lives to change them. Presumably those doing the intervening believe that what they are doing is good – i.e. bringing about socio-economic change. In many ways this makes the development industry a form of contemporary 'missionary' activity within which (Western) 'believers' work to 'improve' non-Western societies.[3] But today's missionaries do not promote Christianity. Instead, the contemporary development agenda is driven by a secular (liberal) vision of social engineering that grew up in the context of building a Pax Americana after 1945. This agenda has been closely associated with a strong belief in 'education' as a key mechanism to roll out the skills (and attitudes) needed for 'progress'. But, in addition, the Pax Americana has also recognized the importance of media networks as 'soft power'[4] agents, geared to promoting the diffusion of an

American zeitgeist, and those values, lifestyles and consumption patterns that complement 'development' – i.e. the Westernization (or semi-Westernization) required to underpin the expansion of global trade. This Pax Americana development agenda was well encapsulated by President Clinton when he announced 'we have it within our means ... to lift billions and billions of the people around the world into the global middle class'. As Bacevich notes, the barely disguised subtext in this statement was one that most Americans would find reassuring, namely, globalization means that 'they' would become more like 'us' (Bacevich 2002: 40–1). However, the process of making Africans more like Americans has involved undermining traditional African culture and its associated traditional (tribal) authority structures. Effectively, the Pax Americana has unleashed a process of creative destruction across Africa, associated with the rapid diffusion of both Western culture (especially American culture) and the English language. Significantly, it is an alliance of (local) African compradors and (overseas) Western development agents who drive this process of creative destruction.

So the key to understanding the nature of contemporary 'cultural imperialism' is to recognize the role middle-class partner-allies play in running their states in accordance with the needs of the American trading empire. Central to running such an informal (trading) empire is thus clientship and/or compradorship, with America using 'soft power' (Nye 2004) to build comprador compliance. In addition, the Pax Americana has constructed a complex system of multilateral regulations that constitutes the global governance structure for this informal trading empire. The whole edifice rests upon America having more military power at its disposal than any other nation in history. This makes the potential of American military violence an omnipresent reality across the entire globe.

Exercising global hegemony through running an informal empire is a complex business. Hence, Washington deploys all manner of 'global governance' tools, including financial and trade regulations; negotiations and diplomacy; military coercion; financial coercion (sanctions); dollar diplomacy; and cultural influence. But within this spectrum of tools, one of the defining characteristics of the Pax Americana is that 'soft' (cultural) power plays a core role in building and maintaining American global hegemony. The Pax Americana has made 'culture' an important hegemonic tool, and Americans have become extraordinarily adept at using 'soft' power. Having created a culture industry that delivers global 'influence' (and even makes a profit from doing so), Americans have accumulated high levels of expertise in this 'cultural' area.

Global media: the Pax Americana's soft power asset

The key soft power asset of America is its dominance over a significant part of the global media industry including film and television production, news agencies, book publishing and the Internet. This is important because media plays a major role in organizing culture.

Tunstall (1994: 18) has suggested that the world's media operate at three levels:

1   at the international level an American-led cartel dominates;
2   at the national level one finds media that are hybridized (i.e. hybrids of local national cultures and American culture); and
3   at the local level one finds ethnic media.

Tunstall (2008: 11) subsequently modified this model by suggesting that the world's ten most populous countries (China, India, Bangladesh, Pakistan, Indonesia, Japan, Brazil, Mexico, Nigeria and Russia) had become media self-sufficient. However, if one examines Tunstall's modified ('the media were American') model, one finds it is not as modified as it first appears because the evidence in the book does not overturn the reality of powerful Americanization pressures within the global media system. As Olson (1999: vii) has noted, 'American media are everywhere'. Effectively, 'Hollywood has conquered the world' (Olson 1999: vii), with American products especially dominant in the world's film and television sectors (Herman and McChesney 1997: 41). US images are quite literally a globalized phenomenon. Global news flows are also dominated by Anglo-American media with three of the four big print-based news agencies being Anglo-American; and both the major television news agencies being Anglo-American (Herman and McChesney 1997: 49). These shape the presentation of news around the globe (Herman and McChesney 1997: 49). And the most recent reconfiguration of the media system, namely the Internet, is also largely American-driven with American companies like Microsoft and Google at the heart of this system.

Not only is Tunstall's (1994) observation that the 'media are American' still essentially true, but because the global media system is 'an American, or Anglo-American, built box' (Tunstall 1994: 63) there seems to be little prospect of escaping Anglo-American media dominance, given there seems no prospect of anyone else building another 'box'. The much vaunted example of Al-Jazeera as an 'alternative' box ignores the fact that Al-Jazeera was built by staff retrenched by the BBC, which is why Al-Jazeera media practices are discernibly Anglo-American. What is more, the growth of the Internet as the most recent media platform has only served to enhance this dominance of Anglo-American media messages and Anglo-American cultural content. This dominance is illustrated by the fact global media networks are dominated by ten or so media conglomerates, most of which are based in America (Sparks 2007: 172–4; Herman and McChesney 1997: 104). Similarly, the top seven World Wide Web providers are America-based. Equally important, since the end of the Cold War, the American commercialized and liberalized model of media (and Internet) organization has increasingly been cloned across the globe (Herman and McChesney 1997: 137). In Africa, this cloning process was strongly promoted by American diplomats and the American aid industry. This cloning process, coupled with the growing global impact of American advertising (Herman and McChesney 1997: 58), has generated a growing homogenization of the world's culture industries. Consequently, even though Hollywood, for example, has become less American-owned (Herman and McChesney 1997: 40), this does not alter the fact that the 'box' remains essentially American in terms of its key practices and discourses. This is well illustrated by Africa's multi-channel television service, Multichoice DStv. Multichoice Africa, which is beamed from South Africa, targets sub-Saharan Africa's middle classes. The Multichoice Africa 'box' may not be Anglo-American owned, but it is operated by (South African middle class) people trained to use Anglo-American practices; and the content of the Multichoice Africa service is overwhelmingly filled with 'Hollywood' genre films and television. So Multichoice ensures that even if the bulk of Africa's masses do not have access to 70 television channels and 40 audio channels of Anglo-American programming, the middle-class comprador elites of sub-Saharan Africa do. So even those compradors living in one of the smallest and most provincial of Africa's capital cities can now have access to the same television available to those in the heartland cities of the Pax Americana.

What is clear is that the global media now have a distinctively 'American' feel, and the Anglo-American global media 'box' helps create the frame within which the world is seen. Although this does not mean the Anglo-American global media is able to force the rest of the world to accept its worldview, it grants America many possibilities for agenda-setting, and for presenting America and American values in a positive light.

Lying at the heart of the Anglo-American built 'box' is a huge media and culture industry built by the Americans during the twentieth century. This multi-faceted culture industry – whose two main production hubs are located in Los Angeles and New York – is often collapsed into the rubric 'Hollywood'. This industry's influence is now global, because 'American media are everywhere' (Olson 1999: vii). US-made images and their accompanying soundtracks (carried by film, television, videos, DVDs and the Internet) now reach every corner of the globe. Clearly these images and sounds are not value-neutral. They expose the world to American products, how to use these products, and the lifestyles accompanying the use of such products. Hence, they overtly and subliminally diffuse models of behaviour, dress codes, eating habits and values. And they do so within a format that is highly entertaining and pleasurable. In this way, an American zeitgeist is diffused – a way of seeing the world that naturalizes consumerism, materialism, secularism, individualism and middle-classness, which are all values conveniently helpful for promoting global trade and hence for underpinning the Pax Americana (as an 'informal' global trading empire).

Because exposure to American media is more pleasant, and appears more 'innocent' than exposure to an imperial official, there may be greater openness/willingness to absorb such media-delivered culture. This would explain the 'Americanization' of so many people across the globe since 1945. In the case of Africa, much of the initial Americanized media content was actually diffused by the British. During the 1950s, the British (under pressure from America) began implementing 'development' programmes that included media infrastructures. This coincided with the rapid spread of American media content to Britain itself. Not surprisingly, this American content then found its way from Britain into Britain's African colonies, while after independence, these British-built media infrastructures continued to serve as conduits for the dissemination of US content. It was young Africans (particularly those in the cities) who were, of course, especially susceptible to being influenced by American music, fashion and popular culture. The importance of this diffusion of American popular culture should not be underestimated, because this greatly enhances America's abilities to win friends, allies and comprador-partners – which effectively translates into 'soft power'.

America has developed a phenomenal capability to project 'attractiveness'. This translates into the ability to get others to 'buy into' its values, which makes it easier for America to sell its policies as legitimate (Nye 2004: x). Hence, America can lead by example, and so can often get its way without having to use threats and violence. Effectively, soft power grows out of an ability to attract, co-opt and set agendas (Nye 2004: 8), all three of which are tied to two of America's key strengths, namely, its ability to project positive images into the world (through the culture industry) and having a strong economy, which provides the resources for largess, leverage and influence (or sanctions).

Building soft power

America's soft power has emerged from building a pool of overseas goodwill. Essentially America has proved to be adept at constructing a sense of 'affinity' and 'comfort' with American culture and ideas. There are a number of ways this happens.

First, constant exposure to images of America and Americans creates a sense of 'familiarity', and identification with American celebrities can generate a sense of 'bonding' with America. Since America is by far the world's number one exporter of films and television programmes its capacity to globally project positive images is phenomenal (Nye 2004: 33). And since 'pictures often convey values more powerfully than words' Hollywood has a huge capacity to 'Americanize', modernize and 'de-traditionalize' people across the world (Nye 2004: 33). Further, American popular culture portrays Americans as open, mobile, individualistic, anti-establishment, pluralistic, voluntaristic, populist and free (Nye 2004: 47). These are all values with great appeal to middle-class people across the world – the very people America seeks as comprador-partners. Amongst those places where America has been relatively successful in building African middle-class partners are Kenya, Botswana, South Africa, Zambia, Uganda, Ghana and Senegal.

Second, America has for decades run a foreign visitors' programme on an industrial scale. Foreigners identified as movers and shakers, and potential future

leaders are brought to America on 'familiarization tours' geared to building positive feelings and networking comprador-linkages.

Third, millions of foreign students study at American universities. This is
encouraged because it is understood university graduates are more likely to end
up in leadership positions back home, and American education promotes American middle-class values.

Fourth, foreign scholars are encouraged (and financially assisted) to spend time
in America, which helps diffuse American values throughout the world's middle-
class communities.

Fifth, America is the world's leading importer of migrants. Significantly,
America deliberately encourages immigration from every country in the world.
This means people from all over the world 'recognize' Americans who 'look' like
them. The way in which this can translate into goodwill is best illustrated by how
Obama's brown complexion became a major diplomatic asset in Africa and the
Middle East.

Sixth, as an immigrant nation, America has borrowed freely from the
traditions of waves of migrants, with such borrowings having almost come to
define 'American-ness'. Thus pizza, burritos, frankfurters and bagels now seem
American. This is significant because once 'American culture' is viewed as being
mongrel, hybridized and globalized, the idea of becoming 'Americanized' starts
to shift. Hence, instead of 'Americanization' being negatively viewed as an 'imperialist' imposition, it can now be positively interpreted as joining 'globalized
culture', and even become fashionable for some. Hence one sees American
culture being adopted even by Third World groups who believe themselves to be
rebellious and opposed to the Pax Americana; and popular culture and popular
media in places like Africa become infused with American and semi-American
cultural forms.

In addition, America is the largest seller of music to the world (Nye 2004: 34),
publishes more books than any other country (Nye 2004: 34), hosts more websites than any other country, and Americans are the most prolific publishers of
academic journal articles in the world (Nye 2004: 34). All of this translates into
soft (cultural) power. Although much of this soft power derives from non-
government sources – e.g. Hollywood film studios or the music industry – some
soft power is consciously organized by the government in the shape of government information, public relations, public diplomacy and military psychological-
operations (Nye 2004: 107–13). Importantly, America's culture industry has
proved to be extraordinarily successful at generating products and ideas that
appeal to middle-class audiences around the world. And since it is this middle-
class sub-culture that American policy-makers are the most interested in (as
comprador-clients), American media messages have, on the whole, proved to be
key soft power assets.

Cultural imperialism by invitation

Because Americans run an informal empire the Pax Americana exercises its global hegemony in indirect ways. The same holds true for the way American cultural influence is diffused.

In order to understand the way the Pax Americana's cultural machinery works to produce a form of cultural imperialism, it is necessary to begin by examining the global economic system America created after 1945. This trading and financial system was designed to service the needs of American liberal-capitalism. Technically, no independent country can be forced to join this system. But there are benefits to joining and penalties for refusing to cooperate with this American-designed trading system. Coercion comes in many forms and the Pax Americana has shown a willingness (and skill) to deploy the mechanisms of the global financial and trading system as a weapon. Alternatively, America dispenses financial inducements to those who collaborate. This may not be the sort of power associated with a formal empire, but it is power and it is imperial. Clearly, not every independent state has generated the same sort of ruling elite, however, the Pax Americana (through its global regulatory system and system of inducements) has been remarkably successful in producing middle-class comprador-partners in a wide variety of independent states across the world. Of course, things go wrong for the Pax Americana, and this informal empire has often found that its comprador-partners are either incompetent or unwilling to run their societies in ways deemed appropriate by Washington. When this happens the Pax Americana intervenes in various ways. At one extreme, such governments are removed (e.g. Saddam Hussein in Iraq, the Taliban in Afghanistan and Charles Taylor in Liberia). Peacekeeping forces are also deployed to establish appropriate governance, law and order, and service delivery (e.g. Bosnia, Congo, Côte d'Ivoire, Liberia, Sudan, Chad and Central African Republic). But sometimes interventions are less extreme, and simply involve pressure to establish 'good governance' and 'development' to bring about good governance. Much foreign aid to Africa is now conditional upon such good governance clauses. The end goal of such good development aid is the building of states conforming to America's democratic-capitalist model of good governance – i.e. functional states that can operate as good trading partners for America's informal trading empire. Post-apartheid South Africa would be an example of such a state.

As noted, the Pax Americana resembles, in many ways, a huge global alliance of middle-class people who share similar lifestyles. Many comprador-partners were drawn from the middle classes, while others learned to become middle class. Whatever path they took to get there, middle class-ness is a common characteristic of those occupying the governance structures of the Pax Americana across all continents, including Africa.

These comprador-partners tend to regularly expose themselves to products of the American culture industry. Many of these compradors aspire to adopting American lifestyles (given the status that power confers upon imperial cultures).

But whether they 'aspire' to it or not, members of the Pax Americana comprador-alliance imbibe heavily of American culture – consuming American television, films and Internet products and enjoying the benefits of America's consumption-based culture. Effectively, a 'cloning process' can be observed in which the comprador classes absorb America's middle-class materialist values. American media (film, television and the Internet) are the 'cultural reservoirs' from which they consume these values. What often emerges from this is hybrid-ized culture – i.e. many comprador-classes effectively build new cultures by com-bining American cultural material with their indigenous cultural materials. Consequently, 'Americanization' does not look the same everywhere. However, some American cultural influence is discernable in all states, from which is emerg-ing a globalized cultural 'convergence' or 'synchronization' (Hamelink 1983).

Comprador-partners reconfigure their economies to suit the Pax Americana's needs because it is in their interests to do so. These configurations impact on how people function and live within these states. The cultural shifts produced by the Pax Americana are most visible where modernization is occurring in Third World contexts. These cultural shifts are not imposed by America. Instead, they are the result of comprador-allies implementing socio-economic policies that more effectively mesh their states into the Pax Americana. So cultural change is brought about in a two-step process: Washington influences its compradors; these compradors then create altered socio-economic and cultural conditions that stim-ulate cultural shifts associated with economic modernization. Such modernization has generally served to undermine Africa's traditional (tribal) cultures and indi-genous languages. Media and education are often important mechanisms for inducing such socio-cultural changes. The result is a form of two-step cultural imperialism in which local (middle-class Westernized) compradors become the primary agents driving change.

As a result, 'supportive forms of culture' associated with new values and habits are being imported to assist with Pax Americana imperial control and economic development. However, the cultural changes associated with the Pax Americana should not be seen as planned 'invasions' of foreign culture that undermine the 'cultural sovereignty' of these states. Rather, these changes are brought about by one section of the indigenous population (the comprador-partners) who, as agents of the Pax Americana, actually 'invite' the empire in. Their own consumption and adoption of American values is voluntary. Consequently, 'Americanization' and cultural hybridization is not something one can simplistically 'blame' on Americans – rather, it is Americanization (and/or semi-Americanization) by invi-tation. On the other hand, the cultural devastation being wrought on traditional cultures across the world is not happening by invitation. Rather, this devastation is being driven by an alliance of local-compradors and Western 'development' agents from the metropolitan core. In this regard, 'nation building' (so beloved by America and its comprador-partners) is a significant driver of cultural imperial-ism. These nation-building projects involve local compradors trying to invent new 'national cultures'. By importing American culture they unleash cultural hybridization, while their countries' traditional cultures are modernized out of existence. Consequently, the cultural imperialism of the Pax Americana is a mixture of invitation and imposition, depending on which sub-culture one belongs to.

The majority of those doing the 'developing' and 'nation building' do not see themselves as engaged in 'cultural imperialism' or in promoting Americanization. In part this is because the discourses of 'development', 'nation building', 'democracy' ('democratization') and 'good governance' have been skilfully packaged and sold to the world in ways that belie their value to the governance of America's informal empire. In this regard it is interesting to note that it is non-governmental organizations (NGOs) (who do not generally see themselves as agents of 'America' or 'Western imperialism') who are now often at the forefront of promoting discourses ('development', 'democracy' and 'good governance') that effectively promote American cultural modernization. By promoting the discourse of 'development' they become agents of modernization, Westernization, economic growth and hence the expansion of trading opportunities. By promoting the discourses of 'democracy' and 'good governance' they become agents for spreading the kind of governance preferred by Washington (which just happens to be governance helpful for promoting precisely the kind of globalized capitalist-based trade network being run from America). And one of the consequences of this 'development' and 'democratization' is that people in places like Africa are experiencing a form of cultural change that encodes significant Americanization and semi-Americanization (cultural hybridization). And Africa's popular media circulate these Americanized and semi-Americanized cultural forms.

What is Americanization?

Americanization is the outcome of propagating American ideas, customs, social patterns, language, industry and capital around the world (Ritzer and Ryan 2004: 47). Defining exactly the 'content' of Americanization is difficult for two reasons. First, America does not itself have a single, uniform or static monoculture. Second, there are multiple responses to American culture around the world, so different cultural contexts are impacted differently. Hence, Americanization is a complex process rather than a clear-cut phenomenon. Nonetheless, it is possible to describe the broad outlines of the cultural residues left by the Americanization process.

Perhaps the place to start is inside America because the process of Americanization also occurs inside America itself. A key feature of America is that it is a nation of immigrants. This means 'being American' is, in many ways, the outcome of being inducted into a new culture – of being born 'anew' in ways that Americans see as being better than the 'old cultures' being 'replaced'. Essentially, American culture has a northwest European, specifically Anglo, core. America's Hispanic, African-American and native-American sub-cultures are dominated by a mainstream white (Anglo) culture (Campbell *et al.* 2004: 16). However, since the 1960s there has been a growing tendency to de-emphasize (and even try and 'hide') America's Anglo roots by trying to promote instead the idea of cultural hybridity (Olson 1999: 166). This is tied to the notion that America is building an 'international culture' by specifically drawing migrants from every country in the world (Campbell *et al.* 2004: 19). This idea has been codified into the ideology of multiculturalism, which promotes the idea of America as a culturally hybridized, 'post-ethnic nation' (Campbell *et al.* 2004: 19). America's post-ethnic nation ideology reached new heights with the election of President Barack Obama. This ideology serves the needs of the Pax Americana by creating a new set of myths about American society and its relationship to the world. Obama exemplifies how this ideology works because despite having an African father, Obama is culturally indistinguishable from a white middle-class American. But because he looks different, Obama can be used to sell the post-ethnic nation 'brand' and so make the Pax Americana look less 'imperialist' to non-Americans, especially Africans. The idea of a post-ethnic nation serves two purposes. First, it offers an apparent 'cure' to America's guilt over slavery. Second, it makes American imperialism look more benign and disguises the 'ethnic continuity' between the Pax Britannica and Pax Americana's globalization projects. If the ideology is to be believed, both the American nation and American imperialism are being de-racialized, 'multiculturalized' and 'post-nationalized' such that a new (utopian) post-conflict world is being built. This provides the Pax Americana with a new missionary impulse – a new 'civilizing mission' geared to universalizing the American dream. In this dream the world is run by a multiracial network of middle-class comprador-partners scattered around the globe who all share America's 'post-national' and 'democratic capitalist' vision of how societies ought to be run. It is the perfect ideology for running an informal empire like the Pax Americana.

However, the notions of post-ethnic nation, multiculturalism and cultural hybridization make the Pax American's version of globalization far more culturally destructive than the Pax Britannica's because these notions trivialize (and relativize) the differences between cultures. America's post-ethnic nation vision encodes the idea that history and culture 'do not matter', or even worse are 'bad' (because cultural differences and cultural boundaries 'cause' conflict). Effectively, this post-ethnic nation idea decontextualizes people by devaluing the complex relationships between history, cultural difference and place. In its stead Americans are building a culture of 'uniformity and placelessness' of shopping malls (that look much the same), and synthetic landscapes and pseudo places (e.g. 'Disneyfication' and 'museumization') (Campbell *et al.* 2004: 17). Filling the world with shopping malls may be an efficient way to promote consumption, global trading and a mobile workforce, but it erodes both the sense of living in a distinctive place and of 'belonging' to a culture rooted temporally and geographically. In place of 'rootedness' comes an homogenizing culture built on second-hand media images geared to generating conspicuous consumption in the 'here and now'– a culture that de-historicizes by inducing a 'forgetfulness' or even 'contempt' for cultural heritage and 'difference'.

Americanization also alters people's lifestyles and perceptions by promoting consumerism. Across the world American visual media (films, television and advertising) actively promote (American-style) consumer-driven lifestyles, and the products supporting such a lifestyle (from fashion and mobile phones to processed foods and modes of recreation). But this Americanization not only diffuses consumerist values, it also alters the actual ways in which people consume. Hence, in the latest waves of Americanization, consumption is associated with glitzy shopping malls, franchises, fast food, superstores, theme parks and casino-hotels (Campbell *et al.* 2004: 47–8). The effects of this are the homogenization of the consumption experience such that the products being consumed, and the experience of purchasing them, are now remarkably similar in Atlanta, Johannesburg, Singapore or Munich. The result has been to reconfigure our cities, architecture and socio-cultural landscapes, and alter the way people now interact with each other and with their material world. These changes, broadly labelled MacDonaldization (Ritzer 1998), change business practices and how ordinary people consume and behave in everyday life (Campbell *et al.* 2004: 18). Of course, the extent of this cultural change varies from place to place, such that Europe is more Americanized than Africa, and Japan is more Americanized than China. But even within a continent like Africa, which is generally seen as a 'development laggard', there are still hotspots of cultural change – i.e. nodes of Americanization and semi-Americanization (hybridization). Amongst these would be Nairobi, Lagos, Accra, Douala, Harare and all of South Africa's cities. These social change hotspots effectively serve as America's trading and cultural 'gateways' into Africa. In these cities we find the processes of Americanization and cultural hybridization well advanced.

Will there be resistance and contestation to the penetration of America's informal empire into Africa? And might some of this contestation be cultural in nature and be generated by local popular media? Empires usually generate such resistance and contestation, and the Pax Americana is unlikely to escape such contestation. However, the Pax Americana is an informal empire which gives it an advantage over the formal empires it replaced, namely it is an opaque empire. It is not that the Pax Americana is invisible, but it is hard to see, and the processes of penetration (especially cultural penetration) are backed by powerful players – including Africa's Westernized (comprador) ruling elites, the NGOs and a huge development industry, plus a whole network of trading interests. The reality is that the Pax Americana, its trade networks, its military reach, plus its media and cultural forms dominate the globe. And so, although one might expect to see some local cultural producers contesting Americanization, one can also expect to see many local producers and media in places like Africa become either agents for diffusing or mimicking Americanized culture, or for the production of hybridized (semi-American) culture. The reality is, no one on the planet can escape the influence of America's informal empire and the cultural imperialism that follows in the wake of the (hard and soft) power this empire can project. For these reasons, cultural imperialism is far from being a dated concept (albeit that the concept would benefit from being stripped of some of its 1960s and 1970s political agendas).

Notes

1 Although the notion of cultural imperialism was enmeshed with a Marxist political agenda (of replacing capitalism with socialism) during the 1960s and 1970s, there is no reason why the concept of 'cultural imperialism' has to encode such a political agenda. It is not necessary for this concept to encode a *critique* of capitalism. The concept can simply be used to describe a post-1945 Pax Americana-driven process of socio-cultural change that has been unfolding across the globe (i.e. the second wave of globalization).
2 This vision of an 'imposition' by 'outsiders' is tied to the idea that imperialism is necessarily bad. This author makes no such assumption – there is no assumption encoded into this chapter that either formal or informal empires are necessarily bad.
3 The 'Western believers' can, of course, be Third World people who have been Westernized.
4 Nye (2004) defines 'soft power' as cultural power. It is the exercise of hegemony through 'ideas' and 'influence'. Soft power involves shaping others' perceptions, and so, as Nye notes, soft power resources are generally slower, more diffuse and more cumbersome to wield than hard power resources. At the heart of America's soft power lies its culture industry – an industry that projects images of America into the world; images that others find 'attractive'.

References

Bacevich, A.J. (2002) *American Empire. The Realities and Consequences of US Diplomacy.* Cambridge, MA: Harvard University Press.

Campbell, N., Davies, J. and McKay, G. (eds) (2004) *Issues in Americanisation of Culture.* Edinburgh: Edinburgh University Press.

Hamelink, C. (1983) *Cultural Autonomy in Global Communication.* New York: Longman.

Herman, E.S. and McChesney, R.W. (1997) *The Global Media.* London: Cassell.

Louw, P.E. (2010) *Roots of the Pax Americana. Decolonization, Development, Democratization and Trade.* Manchester: Manchester University Press.

Nye, J.S. (2004) *Soft Power.* New York: Public Affairs.

Olson, S.R. (1999) *Hollywood Planet.* Mahwah: Lawrence Erlbaum Associates.

Ritzer, G. (1998) *The McDonaldization Thesis.* London: Sage.

Ritzer, G. and Ryan, M. (2004) 'Americanisation, McDonaldisation and Globalisation', in Campbell, N., Davies, J. and McKay, G. (eds) *Issues in Americanisation of Culture.* Edinburgh: Edinburgh University Press, pp. 41–60.

Sparks, C. (2007) *Globalization, Development and the Mass Media.* London: Sage.

Tomlinson, J. (1991) *Cultural Imperialism.* London: Continuum.

Tunstall, J. (1994) *The Media are American.* London: Constable.

——. (2008) *The Media were American.* New York: Oxford University Press.

Chapter 3

At the crossroads of the formal and popular

Convergence culture and new publics in Zimbabwe

Wendy Willems

The study of formal and popular media in Africa is associated with two separate bodies of knowledge which insufficiently engage with each other. In the field of media and communication, formal media in Africa are often studied in order to assess the extent to which these contribute to democracy, hold the state to account and inform voters about their options in elections. In the field of African studies, on the other hand, popular media such as music, video and comics have sometimes been naïvely celebrated as forms of resistance against those in power. This chapter argues that there is a need for more engagement between the two fields in order to investigate the way in which formal and popular media become entangled in a dialogue with each other, hereby constituting what Jenkins (2006) has referred to as 'convergence culture'. A focus on the entanglement of formal and popular media provides an insight into the way in which ordinary people engage with political elites through the state and its media outlets. The dominant liberal-democratic model of media–state relations considers formal media such as state-owned broadcasting media or the private press as the main vehicles through which the state and citizens communicate with each other and as means through which democracy is promoted and state accountability is enhanced. However, in reality, these formal media are often shaped and accessed only by an elite minority. While conventional analyses of media in Africa adopt a definition of media as elite consensus, this chapter advocates for a more radical definition of democracy as dissensus. This enables us to take into account alternative, popular forms of media through which citizens in Africa either receive information on political affairs or contest political elites. An analytical focus on 'convergence culture' highlights the multiple, conflictual and dialogical ways in which the state and citizens communicate with each other. The chapter uses the case study of Zimbabwe in order to interrogate the intersection of different forms of media – informal, formal, old, new, state-owned, privately owned.

Formal media and the elite public sphere

In the field of political communication, formal media such as television, radio and the press have been conceptualized as crucial in communication between the state and citizens. In the late 1950s and 1960s, media were considered to play an important role in the creation of harmonious nation-states, particularly in developing countries that had just obtained independence and whose borders were imposed as artificial boundaries during colonial rule (Lerner 1958; Pye 1963; Schramm 1964; Lerner and Schramm 1967). Media could aid in the process of building a loyal citizenry and in bringing about economic and political development. The key role of media in national development justified government control of media and saw the establishment of state monopolies in the press and broadcasting in many developing countries. In the context of the Cold War, the First World did not consider the libertarian model of media–state relations to be desirable for developing countries as it could increase their vulnerability to the dangers of communism. State ownership of media was crucial in order to guide the process towards the development of fully fledged nation-states.

However, perceptions on the normative role of media changed fundamentally after the end of the Cold War in the late 1990s and early 2000s when a consensus emerged that liberal democracy was the best recipe for development in Africa (Abrahamsen 2000). Key principles of a liberal democracy included frequent conduct of free and fair elections; the existence of multiple political parties; and respect for basic human rights such as freedom of speech, freedom of the press and freedom of association. In a liberal democracy, media fulfil an important role in strengthening the democratic process and holding government to account over its performance. Mass media – and particularly the press – are expected to act as watchdogs guarding against possible abuses of power by governments. They must act as a 'fourth estate'. Press freedom is seen as a vital guarantee to enable the media to play this role. The state is expected to create an open environment in which different media can flourish and compete by abolishing its monopoly on broadcasting and the press in order to allow a range of private media to monitor state performance. Private media are then attributed with the potential to advance democratic values (DfID 2001; World Bank 2002; BBC World Service Trust 2006).

With the gradual replacement of African one-party states with multi-party administrations in the late 1980s and early 1990s, many studies began to focus on the role of media in this transition process. Academic research on media and communication in Africa increasingly adopted the liberal-democratic model of media–state relations as the normative ideal in Africa. For example, Ogbondah sees the ideal role of the press in Africa as being free to 'investigate and report the misconduct, corruption, illicit spoils, embezzlement, bribery, inefficiency and lack of accountability that have characterised post-independence African governments' (1997: 291).

Based on this ideal role specified for the media, scholars[1] have then often assessed the extent to which media–state relations in Africa have met the key principles of the liberal-democratic model. Academic discourse on media, governance and democracy in Africa has been closely tied in with the perspectives of donor and civil society organizations like the Freedom Forum and Reporters

Without Borders (RSF) that offer normative assessments of media–state relations worldwide against the benchmarks of the liberal model such as RSF's Press Freedom Index.[2]

The liberal-democratic model of media–state relations considers media as an important arena for public debate, or 'public sphere' in the words of Jürgen Habermas (1989). Habermas considers the public sphere as a space for rational debate that, according to him, would ultimately give rise to a consensus on public affairs. Media scholars have used Habermas' theory on democracy to conceptualize media as a public sphere (Garnham 1986; Dahlgren 1993, 1995). Media then constitute a discursive space, a space in which issues of public concern are deliberated. Media are considered as important in carrying information that enables citizens to make informed political choices (Bignell 2000: 155). Audiences are seen as citizens engaged in public dialogue in and through the media. A major task of media is to provide information in order to enable citizens to participate meaningfully in political life, e.g. to provide fair and 'objective' coverage on all major candidates in elections which allows citizens to make a well-informed choice.

Critics have pointed out that Habermas' focus on rational-critical debate is based on an elitist conception of liberal democracy. For example, Negt and Kluge (1972) have argued that the Habermasian public sphere was essentially a bourgeois space and not easily accessible. Nancy Fraser (1992) particularly highlights the way in which women were excluded from the liberal public sphere, while Todd Gitlin (1998) has problematized Habermas' idea of a unitary public sphere and notes a trend towards a segmented public sphere split into what he calls 'public sphericules'.

Habermas' liberal concept of democracy can be contrasted with a more radical conceptualization of democracy as dissensus and conflict (Laclau and Mouffe 1985; Mouffe 2000). Laclau and Mouffe (1985: xv) have argued that:

> the problem with 'actually existing' liberal democracies is not with their constitutive values crystallized in the principles of liberty and equality for all, but with the system of power which redefines and limits the operation of those values. This is why our project of 'radical and plural democracy' was conceived as a new stage in the deepening of the 'democratic revolution', as the extension of the democratic struggles for equality and liberty to a wider range of social relations.

More recently, Laclau and Mouffe's concept of radical democracy has been used by media scholars to assess the democratizing potential of new media such as the Internet (Dahlberg and Siapera 2007). Drawing upon Gramsci's work on popular culture and hegemony, other scholars have looked at the role of popular forms of media in constituting a public sphere. In the African context, popular culture and media have been essential means through which ordinary people have sought to engage, debate and contest the state.

Popular culture and the celebration of agency

While scholars focusing on the role of media in the process of democratization in Africa have concentrated on the part that formal media such as radio, television and the press played, the field of African studies has seen a growing body of research on informal media and popular culture. In the Anglo-Saxon canon of media and cultural studies, popular culture generally refers to the space in which mass-produced products such as soap operas, magazines and clothes are *consumed*. However, in African studies the term has mostly been used to refer to the *production* of popular arts or artisanal forms of cultural expression. Popular culture, then, is not the result of an interaction between a product and a consumer but is often defined as a tangible product which can be passed on from one person to another such as music, songs, theatre, clothes and more recently video (Fabian 1978, 1990, 1996, 1998; Vail and White 1978, 1983; Coplan 1985; Barber 1987, 1997; Gunner 1994; James 1999; Haynes 2000; Nuttall and Michael 2000; Adamu *et al.* 2004; Nyairo and Ogude 2005). Furthermore, while cultural studies primarily looks at popular culture in relation to the culture industries and economic elites, African studies has mostly examined popular culture in its relation to the state and political elites.

An advantage of conceptualizing African publics as sites of popular culture is that it avoids the elitist connotations attached to Habermas' concept of the public sphere. Popular culture is frequently defined in terms of its oppositionality to power, as is apparent from Stuart Hall's (1981: 238) definition: 'The people versus the power-bloc: this, rather than "class-against-class", is the central line of contradiction around which the terrain of culture is polarised. Popular culture, especially, is organised around this contradiction: the popular forces versus the power-bloc.' Hall derives his definition from Antonio Gramsci who considers popular culture as the arena where hegemony is continuously contested. As opposed to Habermas' emphasis on consensus, work on popular culture generally stresses dissensus and conflict. Through the production of forms of popular culture, ordinary Africans are able to debate issues and bring up matters of concern; this in stark contrast to the elite public sphere described by those scholars inspired by Habermas' work. Karen Barber has argued that the most important attribute of popular culture in Africa is its power to communicate, because 'for the majority of Africans, the arts are the only channel of public communication at their disposal' (1987: 2). And as Barber (1987: 3) points out, this is especially so in a climate where the ruling elite dominate public space:

> In Africa ordinary people tend to be invisible and inaudible. In most African states, numerically tiny elites not only consume a vastly disproportionate share of the national wealth, they also take up all the light. Newspapers, radio and television offer a magnified image of the class that controls them. Not only does the ruling elite make the news, it is the news – as endless verbatim reports of politicians' speeches, accounts of elite weddings and birthday parties, and the pages and pages of expensive obituaries testify.

Hence, the importance of songs, jokes and drama as crucial channels of communication for people who are not being granted access to official, formal media outlets. Similarly, James and Kaarsholm (2000: 193–4) have argued that in countries

> where colonial and more recent histories have left legacies of stark inequality and violent intolerance, the building of a democratic culture has often necessitated more informal means of expression. Sometimes this is because what is understood to be institutionalized as 'politics' has become the scene of such alienation, self-seeking and irrelevance that a real articulation of needs and values appears possible only within cultural realms which do not, at first sight, appear to be really political. Sometimes it is because the sphere of politics seems remote and inaccessible.

In many African countries, formal media continue to be associated with the state, and for this reason they enjoy minimal legitimacy among citizenries. In countries where media are not owned or controlled by the state but in private hands, they often target the wealthiest segment of the population in order to generate sufficient revenue from advertising.[3] Hence, in these circumstances, informal means of expression through, for example, popular forms of art are crucial channels through which ordinary people gain information about the formal realm of politics and also through which they express their views about the state.

A central problem, however, with studies on popular culture in Africa is that these have often ended up naïvely celebrating agency, hereby neglecting the question of power.[4] Some critical scholars have begun to articulate their unease about the way in which the agency of the African subject has increasingly been 'celebrated'.[5] For example, Achille Mbembe has expressed his concern about what he calls 'the rediscovery of the subaltern subject and the stress of his/her inventiveness' which has 'taken the form of an endless invocation of the notions of "hegemony", "moral economy", "agency" and "resistance"' (2001: 5). Similarly, Jonathan Haynes argues that while initially Africans were predominantly seen as passive victims, in recent years 'the problem is perhaps the opposite: that the study of the African popular arts will be assimilated into the version of postcolonialism that looks for no more than a playful, textual subversiveness' (2000: 16–17). As Lila Abu-Lughod has pointed out in more general terms, care should be taken not to read 'all forms of resistance as signs of the ineffectiveness of systems of power and of the resilience and creativity of the human spirit in its refusal to be dominated' (1990: 41). As she argues, '[b]y reading resistance in this way, we collapse distinctions between forms of resistance and foreclose certain questions about the workings of power' (Abu-Lughod 1990: 42). By focusing on the agency, creativity and subversiveness of Africans, scholars have downplayed the constraints imposed by the state or capital on the emancipatory potential of popular culture as well as the role of the state or capital in the production and co-optation of popular culture.

Towards an analysis of convergence cultures in Africa

If we define media in a broader manner so as to encompass both formal and informal channels of communication, we can thus identify two quite separate fields of scholarship. On the one hand, there is work on political communication, which tends to focus on elite media and often adopts a political economy approach in which either the state or the market control and shape media and communication. Audience members are generally absent from these analyses. On the other hand, there is the body of work in African studies, which celebrates the production of popular culture by Africans in response to those in power (Fabian 1978, 1990, 1996, 1998; Barber 1987, 1997). While the first field assesses the role and normative value of media in enabling a liberal democracy, the second field generally does not get tempted to engage in normative debates on democracy and citizenship.

A more productive dialogue between the two fields could be fruitful in order to remedy the weaknesses and oversights of both fields. What has been lacking in previous scholarship is a more detailed analysis of the different ways in which both formal media and forms of popular culture are implicated in mediating the relation between the state and citizens. A focus beyond formal media such as television, radio and the press – traditionally the focus of scholars examining media and democracy in the field of political communication – is even more crucial in Africa where media density is generally relatively low. Many Africans, particularly those resident in rural areas, might not have regular access to formal mass media but instead rely upon more informal means of communication to obtain information about or to comment upon the affairs of the state.

Increasingly, new media also fulfil an important role in this respect, albeit often only accessible to urban elites. For example, immediately after the death of Zambian President Levy Mwanawasa in August 2008, the national broadcaster, the Zambia National Broadcasting Corporation (ZNBC) screened condolence messages sent by Zambians via SMS. During the eruptions of violence following the December 2007 elections in Kenya, government issued a media blackout on live radio and television broadcasts for a number of days. According to government, the emotions demonstrated during live broadcasts would 'incite further violence'. In response, Kenya's blogosphere and mobile phones filled an important gap in information through their continued reports and their dissemination of the latest news on the post-election violence (Mäkinen and Wangu Kuira 2008). For example, the website Ushahidi ('testimony' or 'witness' in Swahili, www. ushahidi.com) played a crucial role in collecting eyewitness reports on violence sent in by email and SMS. Similarly, in February 2009, the Elders' Council of the ruling South West Africa People's Organization (SWAPO) in Namibia criticized state-sponsored newspaper *The Namibian* for publishing SMS messages which 'insulted the entire Namibian nation' and argued that SMS messages should instead promote 'peace, harmony and mutual understanding between individuals in society' (Maletsky 2009).

In order to explore the dialogue between different forms of media and communication, Henry Jenkins' concept of 'convergence culture' proves useful. Jenkins defines convergence culture as the space 'where old and new media collide, where grassroots and corporate media intersect, where the power of the media producer and the power of the media consumer interact in unpredictable ways' (2006: 2). Convergence culture refers to the space in which these different forms of media – informal, formal, old, new, global, local, state-owned, privately owned – meet, intersect, shape, reinforce or resist each other, and the new publics that they constitute in the process. Whereas convergence is often understood as a technological process where multiple media functions are brought together in one device, Jenkins focuses on the cultural aspects of convergence, on the way in which media consumers are actively participating in circulating, subverting and creating media content through new media such as the Internet. According to Jenkins, '[c]onvergence involves both a change in the way media is produced and a change in the way media is consumed' (2006: 16). He primarily discusses the situation in the United States where despite a growing concentration of ownership in the hands of a few media corporates, spaces remain for consumers to shape, appropriate and recirculate these media.

While in Jenkins' US context, the corporate market is crucial in shaping the American media environment, in many African countries, the state continues to have an essential role in shaping the media. Convergence then should be primarily understood as the dialogue between state-owned media and small, informal media technologies used by ordinary people. As this chapter explores, within the constraints imposed by the state, many opportunities remain for ordinary people to use, adopt or contest media content through both old and new media technologies. African studies scholars such as Spitulnik (2002) have highlighted how in many African countries, media consumers have recirculated state media discourse in very inventive ways such as by adopting slogans from radio and television, by creating parodic phrases and by renaming acronyms. While old media – i.e. oral culture, rumours and jokes – have always played a crucial role in enabling participatory media cultures in Africa, new media are also increasingly being used to comment upon state media discourse. It is at the intersection of the old, older and the new that convergence culture is created.

Convergence culture and new publics in Zimbabwe

Because of the economic and political turbulence in the early 2000s in Zimbabwe, mass media emerged as a particularly sensitive issue for government elites who considered radio, television and the press as crucial weapons in their hold onto power. For Zimbabweans, on the other hand, the unpredictable nature of the crisis made it even more crucial to be able to access adequate information about events. However, this was increasingly more difficult for both economic and political reasons. Due to the enormous inflation, the real incomes of Zimbabweans were drastically reduced, hereby limiting their ability to purchase newspapers, buy radio batteries, access satellite television or browse the Internet. Zimbabweans' access to a wide range of media sources and diversity of viewpoints was further impeded by the tight government control on radio and television and government's refusal to liberalize the broadcasting sector.

According to a survey undertaken by the Zimbabwe Advertising Research Foundation (ZARF) in 2001, Radio 2 (now known as Radio Zimbabwe), which broadcasts in local languages such as chiShona and siNdebele, was the most accessible and frequently listened to medium in Zimbabwe (ZARF 2001; see also Table 3.1). In the urban areas, ZTV1 had the widest audience. Whereas less than 10 per cent of all Zimbabweans had access to private newspapers, 57 per cent listened to ZBC Radio 2 at least once a week (70 per cent in high-density urban areas and 52 per cent in rural areas) and 43 per cent watched ZBC television at least once a week (80 per cent in high-density urban areas and 22 per cent in rural areas).[6] Out

Table 3.1 **Proportion of Zimbabwean population (as a percentage) who read a daily or weekly publication in the last six months, listened to a radio station in the last seven days or watched a television station in the last seven days**

	High-density urban	Rural	Total
Daily newspapers			
The Daily News	58	26	38
The Herald	44	30	35
None	19	57	43
Weekly newspapers			
The Sunday Mail	45	20	30
Kwayedza	16	15	15
The Financial Gazette	13	5	9
The Zimbabwe Independent	5	2	4
The Standard	5	1	3
The Zimbabwe Mirror	3	1	2
None	27	62	49
Radio channels			
Radio 1	7	2	4
Radio 2	70	52	57
Radio 3	46	12	25
Radio 4	7	3	4
BBC World Service	0	0	0
None	8	43	31
Television channels			
ZBC TV1	80	22	43
Joy TV	30	3	13
SABC 1/2/3	2	0	1
Multichoice/DStv	1	–	1
None	17	77	55

Source: ZARF (2001).

of all newspapers, *The Daily News*, *The Herald* and *The Sunday Mail* enjoyed the largest readership, particularly so in the urban areas. Private weekly newspapers such as *The Financial Gazette*, *The Zimbabwe Independent* and *The Standard* were accessible only to a minority of readers in urban and rural areas.

Because of their limited readership, predominantly in the urban areas, and their business-oriented nature, government cautiously tolerated the existence of private weekly newspapers such as *The Zimbabwe Independent*, *The Standard* and *The Financial Gazette* although it regularly threatened these papers with closure. While the government introduced new legislation such as the Access to Information and Protection of Privacy Act (AIPPA), which was introduced in 2002 and resulted in a government-controlled licensing system of print media houses and journalists, most private weekly newspapers – except for the popular *The Daily News* which was shut down in September 2003 – continued to be able to publish their critical news stories on the crisis and government's complicity in it, albeit they had to be careful about charges that could be laid by the government in response to their reporting. Some articles on the new pieces of legislation that were introduced by government in the early 2000s were formulated in an extremely vague manner that made it relatively easy for government to charge newspapers. However, within the constraints, both local reporters and foreign correspondents were to a certain extent still able to continue their critical coverage of the crisis. Foreign correspondents, for example, found ways to circumvent the compulsory accreditation with the government-appointed Media and Information Commission (MIC) that they were required to register with in order to be able to report from Zimbabwe. Instead, they often simply entered Zimbabwe as tourists and continued to file their stories 'undercover'.

Hence, in this situation, the media that were relatively more accessible to Zimbabweans comprised mainly television (particularly for urban Zimbabweans) and radio (for all Zimbabweans). Because of the monopoly that government held on broadcasting, this meant that most Zimbabweans became largely dependent on the national broadcaster ZBC. Because radio and television had a much wider reach and therefore posed a bigger threat to government, it introduced a range of measures such as the Broadcasting Services Act (BSA) in order to ensure that no private players could enter the broadcasting sector.[7] Self-censorship practices at the national broadcaster Zimbabwe Broadcasting Corporation (ZBC) and the introduction of local content regulations resulted in the mediation of a narrow national imaginary on radio and television. The introduction of local content quota did not only lead to the removal of critical foreign news bulletins but also resulted in the virtual banning of radio airplay of locally produced songs that were critical of government.

In addition to these measures, which sought to restrict critical content on radio and television, the government took a number of affirmative measures to mediate official versions of the 'nation'. Nationalist television talk shows, a revival of 1970s *Chimurenga*[8] songs on radio and television and the launch of a series of televised 'music galas' all sought to communicate a particular national imaginary which was by no means an inclusive definition of the 'nation' but should rather be seen as the mediation of a 'party-nation' which was aimed at legitimizing continued reign of the ruling party, Zimbabwe African National Union-Patriotic Front (ZANU-PF) (Ndlovu-Gatsheni and Willems 2009; Willems 2009). The revival of *Chimurenga* music and state attempts to co-opt popular musicians such as Oliver Mtukudzi into its project are crucial in order to gain a full understanding of the different forms of communication that mediated the relation between state and citizens in Zimbabwe. While Mtukudzi had strictly distanced himself from party politics in the past, he agreed to play at an event in March 2005 to celebrate Joyce Mujuru's appointment as Vice-President. Subsequent to the event, the ruling party ZANU-PF used one of Mtukudzi's songs in a campaign advert. The response of fans to the event was one of disappointment. The popular website 'NewZimbabwe' published some of the emails it had received from fans who felt 'betrayed' by Mtukudzi and pledged to auction off Mtukudzi's records and CDs in their possession.[9] In an attempt to appease his fans, Mtukudzi issued a statement in which he denied being a ZANU-PF supporter.[10] This example demonstrates the attempts the Zimbabwe government has made to appropriate popular culture for its own political ends. Hence, popular culture cannot simply be regarded as a free space where ordinary people can exert their agency but instead should be considered as an arena which is constantly eyed by those in power, resulting in constraints and limitations on agency.

In a context in which Zimbabweans had restricted access to alternative views of the crisis due to the high costs and lack of availability of print media and alternative broadcasters, they began to express themselves through a range of popular and informal media. New technologies such as the Internet and mobile phones played an important role in enabling the spread of dissenting voices. A rising number of websites began to challenge official views of the crisis, often set up by exiled Zimbabwean journalists in the growing 'diaspora'. As a result of the spiralling economic and political crisis, many Zimbabweans decided to leave the country in search of greener pastures in the United Kingdom, the United States and South Africa. New websites such as *NewZimbabwe*, *ZWNews*, *ZimDaily* and *ZimOnline* carried their own news stories and opinion articles on the crisis, or brought existing news stories about Zimbabwe from different news sources together on one webpage. However, these websites were mostly available to the growing number of diasporic Zimbabweans and for economic reasons were only accessible to a minority of Zimbabweans within Zimbabwe. According to 2007 statistics, out of a total population of 13.1 million Zimbabweans[11], 1.35 million people reported to use the Internet but only 99,500 Zimbabweans subscribed to an Internet provider and just 15,200 of these subscribed to broadband Internet. The high costs of the Internet and the rapid increases in costs of living further negatively impacted on Internet access within Zimbabwe.

Within these constraints, jokes and rumours then emerged as important popular forms of commentary on the economic and political crisis as well as on the attempts of the state to restrict the public arena. In the African context, these informal media have often been referred to as 'radio trottoir' ('pavement radio' in English) which Stephen Ellis has defined as 'the popular and unofficial discussion of current affairs in Africa' (1989: 321).[12] Against the background of the growing economic and social crisis and the attempts of the state to monopolize the public sphere and to clamp down on dissent, the practice of joking became increasingly prevalent in Zimbabwe. In the numerous queues for fuel, cooking oil and sugar, which rapidly appeared and have grown in length since 2000, Zimbabweans actively debated the state of politics in the country, irrespective of their fears in openly discussing these issues in public. Jokes were not only transmitted orally in queues, public transport, beer halls and hair salons but also increasingly began to be shared through private newspapers,[13] mobile phones, email newsgroups and websites such as Nyambo ('joke' in chiShona). Mobile phones, in particular, were important because these media were relatively accessible to Zimbabweans as compared to television, Internet and newspapers. As Table 3.2 demonstrates, mobile phones are the most accessible medium in Zimbabwe after radio.[14]

The mobile phone did not only connect rural and urban Zimbabweans but also linked those resident within Zimbabwe to those based in the diaspora. The practice of joking in itself and the distribution of jokes via SMS and email defied government's attempts to monopolize the public sphere and its efforts to dominate the public sphere. Irrespective of government's lack of respect for freedom of expression, Zimbabweans ridiculed their president or rubbished the national broadcaster ZBC through jokes. The growing disillusionment with the national monopoly broadcaster is well-captured in the following joke which narrates a visit by a diasporic Zimbabwean to an electronics shop in the United Kingdom:

> In UK last year I was shopping things to take home kuZimbabwe when I came into this shop selling Tvs. The shop attendant was showing me this latest TV which listens to spoken commands. He commanded 'CNN', and we flipped into CNN then again to 'BBC' and we had it on the screen at once. I asked how much it was and he told me 300.00 pounds in which I replied, 'Nonsense (I was shocked by the price)', but then to my amazement there was Judesi Makwanya on ZBC News Harare.[15]

This joke represents ZBC's television content as 'rubbish' and also comments on the growing Zimbabwean diaspora in the United Kingdom. While the joke does

Table 3.2 Comparative availability of different media to every 1,000 Zimbabweans

Radio receiver owners (1997)[16]	102
Mobile phone owners (2007)[17]	92
Television receiver owners (1997)[18]	33
Buyers of daily newspapers (1996)[19]	19
Internet subscribers (2007)[20]	7.5

not explicitly describe BBC and CNN in positive terms, it posits ZBC in opposition to BBC and CNN and hereby mirrors the distinction often invoked by the Zimbabwean government. While government considered ZBC as a patriotic channel, BBC and CNN were seen as tools used by foreign governments to promote regime change in Zimbabwe. Through jokes, Zimbabweans did not only criticize the discourse of state media but the practice of joking in itself should be seen as a comment on the very absence of tolerance and freedom of expression in Zimbabwe as well as on the disarticulation of ordinary people in state media.

Conclusion

This chapter has highlighted how an analysis of convergence culture – defined as the intersection between different forms of media, informal, formal, old, new, global, local, state-owned, privately owned – can provide us with better insights on the multiple and divergent ways in which the relationship between the state and citizens is mediated. This concept is also useful in bringing together two bodies of literature which have not been in sufficient dialogue: on the one hand, studies on media, governance and democracy in political communication and work on popular culture in African studies on the other hand. While the first field has ignored the crucial role of popular culture in political communication, the second body of literature has insufficiently theorized the contribution of popular culture to democratic engagement and has also often neglected the constraints imposed by the state on popular culture. The Zimbabwean case study used in this chapter has demonstrated the attempts of the state or political parties to co-opt or incorporate popular culture in order to win support from citizens. Ordinary Zimbabweans, on the other hand, have been creative in appropriating, recirculating and subverting state media discourse through popular cultural forms such as jokes. While Jenkins (2006) introduces the concept of convergence culture to describe recent changes in the American media environment, the term is very suitable in the African context in order to grasp the multidimensional aspects of political communication between the state and citizens. A mere focus on formal media misses out the other, popular ways in which both the state and citizens seek to engage each other.

Notes

1 See, for example, Ansah 1988; Zaffiro 1988, 1989, 2000, 2002; Faringer 1991; Karikari 1992; Martin 1992; Lardner 1993; Kasoma 1995, 1997; Eribo and Jong-Ebot 1997; Ogbondah 1997; Ogundimu 1997; Berger 1998, 2002; Pitts 2000; Tettey 2001; Jacobs 2002; Hyden *et al.* 2003; Ojo 2003; Nyamnjoh 2005.

2 For more information see: www.rsf.org/en-classement1003-2009.html (last accessed 8 December 2009).

3 Perhaps an exception to this is the 'tabloid revolution' in South Africa where privately owned tabloid newspapers have become increasingly popular among a relatively poorer segment of the population (see Wasserman 2010).

4 While many studies celebrate agency, Johannes Fabian has been more careful to emphasize that popular culture in Africa can only emerge during what he calls 'moments of freedom', which are moments when dissent and resistance are possible. As he argues,

> popular culture emerging under colonial domination *demanded freedom* in more than one sense: politically, it asked for freedom for the people; theoretically, it *required* freedom among those who created and lived it [...]. That freedom must exist for cultural creation to take place.
>
> (Fabian 1998: 18)

5 See also other recent work in African studies which has often emphasized the agency and creativity of Africans. Scholars have, for example, highlighted the way in which global culture is creatively appropriated by Africans (Van Binsbergen and Van Dijk 2004), have sought to move away from notions of Africans as victims and shifted attention to their ability to negotiate the ecological, economic and political constraints which they face (Chabal *et al.* 2007), have emphasized the creativity of African urban-dwellers in their survival strategies (Konings and Foeken 2006) and have explored the notion of local vitality in Africa (Probst and Spittler 2004).

6 Zimbabwe Advertising Research Foundation (2001).

7 While the government of Zimbabwe introduced a range of measures to ensure ZBC could maintain a monopoly on broadcasting, a number of radio stations based overseas such as SW Radio Africa and the broadcasting arm of the US government, the VOA, managed to broadcast their programmes to Zimbabweans via the shortwave. It is unclear what number of listeners these stations attracted.

8 The chiShona word *Chimurenga* refers to a traditional warrior and legendary hero in the 1890s, Sororenzou Murenga, who was renowned for his fighting skills. The word is normally used to refer to the early Shona and Ndebele uprisings of 1893 and 1896 against white settler rule (*First Chimurenga*) and to the liberation struggle against the Rhodesian Front regime in the 1960s and 1970s (*Second Chimurenga*). In the course of the major land occupations which commenced in February 2002, the government came to refer to these invasions and to the fast-track land reform programme as the *Third Chimurenga*.

9 'Outrage as Tuku backs Mugabe', *NewZimbabwe*, March 2005, www.newzimbabwe.com/pages/tuku15.12411.html (last accessed 15 March 2008).

10 'Mtukudzi, Oliver: "I am not a Zanu PF supporter"', 25 March 2005, available from *NewZimbabwe* website, www.newzimbabwe.com/pages/tuku20.12423.html (last accessed 15 March 2008).

11 For population statistics, see Human Development Report of the United Nations Development Programme (UNDP), http://hdrstats.undp.org/countries/data_sheets/cty_ds_ZWE.html (last accessed 9 January 2009). For Internet statistics, see International Telecommunication Union (ITU), www.itu.int/ITU-D/icteye/Reports.aspx# (last accessed 6 January 2009).

12 The term *radio trottoir* was invented by inhabitants of Brazzaville and Kinshasa in Congo but there are equivalent terms in other parts of Africa such as 'Radio Mall' in Botswana, 'Radio Kankan' in Guinea, 'Radio Treichville' in Cote d'Ivoire, 'Radio Potato' in South Africa, 'Radio Boca Boca' in Lusophone Africa and 'le téléphone arabe' in North Africa (Ellis and Ter Haar 2004: 28; Nyamnjoh 2005: 210). Similar terminology can also be found elsewhere in the world such as in Armenia where the term 'Radio Yerevan' referred to the practice of joking during the Soviet period.

13 Several private newspapers carried special sections with jokes such as 'A lighter world' in *The Standard*, the daily joke on the Arts & Culture page in *The Daily News*, the satirical column 'Cabinet Files' in *The Financial Gazette*, which is a mock weekly letter

to the 'Dear Comrades', written by the President. Most newspapers, including the Zimpapers' titles, also carried political cartoons and comic strips.

14 Recent data on television and radio ownership as well as purchases of daily newspapers are unavailable. It is, however, unlikely that these figures have radically changed in the past ten years. This table represents those who 'own' a certain medium. The number of users is of course likely to be higher given the common practice in Zimbabwe of sharing newspapers, watching television and listening to radio in groups, and using the Internet at the workplace, at a friend's house or in an Internet café.

15 Message posted to ZvaJokes (http://groups.yahoo.com/group/ZvaJokes) on 14 February 2002 by Tapiwa Mlangeni.

16 See UNESCO (1999).

17 See International Telecommunication Union (2008a).

18 See UNESCO (1999).

19 See UNESCO (1999).

20 See International Telecommunication Union (2008b).

References

Abrahamsen, R. (2000) *Disciplining Democracy: Development Discourse and Good Governance in Africa*, London: Zed Books.

Abu-Lughod, L. (1990) 'The romance of resistance', *American Ethnologist*, 17(1): 41–55.

Adamu, A.U., Adamu, Y.M. and Jibril, U.F. (2004) *Hausa Home Videos: Technology, Economy and Society*, Kano: Centre for Hausa Cultural Studies in conjunction with Adamu Joji Publishers.

Ansah, P.A.V. (1988) 'In search of a role for the African media in the democratic process', *Africa Media Review*, 2(2): 1–16.

Barber, K. (1987) 'Popular arts in Africa', *African Studies Review*, 30(3): 1–78.

Barber, K. (1997) *Readings in African Popular Culture*, Oxford: James Currey.

BBC World Service Trust (2006) *African Media Development Initiative. A Summary Research Report*, London: BBC World Service Trust.

Berger, G. (1998) 'Media and democracy in Southern Africa', *Review of African Political Economy*, 25(78): 599–610.

Berger, G. (2002) 'Theorizing the media–democracy relationship in Southern Africa', *Gazette: International Journal for Communication Studies*, 64(1): 21–45.

Bignell, J. (2000) *Postmodern Media Culture*, Edinburgh: Edinburgh University Press.

Binsbergen, van W.M.J. and Dijk, R. van (2004) *Situating Globality: African Agency in the Appropriation of Global Culture*, Leiden: Brill.

Chabal, P., Engel, U. and Haan, L. de (2007) *African Alternatives*, Leiden: Brill.

Coplan, D. (1985) *In Township Tonight! South Africa's Black City Music and Theatre*, London: Longman.

Dahlberg, L. and Siapera, E. (2007) *Radical Democracy and the Internet: Interrogating Theory and Practice*, Basingstoke: Palgrave Macmillan.

Dahlgren, P. (1995) *Television and the Public Sphere: Citizenship, Democracy, and the Media*, London: Sage Publications.

Dahlgren, P. and Sparks, C. (1993) *Communication and Citizenship: Journalism and the Public Sphere*, London: Routledge.

Department for International Development (DfID) (2001) *The Media in Governance: a Guide to Assistance. Developing Free and Effective Media to Serve the Interests of the Poor*, London: DfID.

Ellis, S. (1989) 'Tuning in to pavement radio', *African Affairs*, 88(352): 321–30.

Ellis, S. and Ter Haar, G. (2004) *Worlds of Power: Religious Thought and Political Practice in Africa*, London: Hurst and Company.

Eribo, F. and Jong-Ebot, W. (1997) *Press Freedom and Communication in Africa*, Trenton: Africa World Press.

Fabian, J. (1978) 'Popular culture in Africa: findings and conjectures', *Africa*, 48(4): 315–34.

Fabian, J. (1990) *Power and Performance: Ethnographic Explorations through Proverbial Wisdom and Theatre in Shaba, Zaire*, Madison: University of Wisconsin Press.

Fabian, J. (1996) *Remembering the Present: Painting and Popular History in Zaire*, Berkeley: University of California Press.

Fabian, J. (1998) *Moments of Freedom: Anthropology and Popular Culture*, Charlottesville: University Press of Virginia.

Faringer, G.L. (1991) *Press Freedom in Africa*, Westport: Praeger.

Fraser, N. (1992) 'Rethinking the public sphere: a contribution to the critique of actually existing democracy', in C. Calhoun (ed.) *Habermas and the Public Sphere*, Cambridge, MA: MIT Press.

Garnham, N. (1986) 'The media and the public sphere', in P. Golding, G. Murdock and P. Schlesinger (eds) *Communicating Politics: Mass Communications and the Political Process*, New York: Holmes & Meier.

Gitlin, T. (1998) 'Public spheres or public sphericules?', in T. Liebes and J. Curran (eds) *Media, Ritual and Identity*, London: Routledge, pp. 175–202.

Gunner, L. (1994) *Politics and Performance: Theatre, Poetry and Song in Southern Africa*, Johannesburg: Witwatersrand University Press.

Habermas, J. (1989) *The Structural Transformation of the Public Sphere: an Inquiry into a Category of Bourgeois Society*, London: Polity Press.

Hall, S. (1981) 'Notes on deconstructing the "popular"', in R. Samuel (ed.) *People's History and Socialist Theory*, London: Routledge and Kegan Paul, pp. 227–40.

Haynes, J. (2000) *Nigerian Video Films*, Athens, OH: Ohio University Press.

Hyden, G., Leslie, M. and Ogundimu, F.F. (2003) *Media and Democracy in Africa*, Uppsala: Nordiska Afrikainstitutet.

International Telecommunication Union (ITU) (2008a) *Mobile Cellular Subscribers per 100 People*, available at: www.itu.int/ITU-D/icteye/Reports.aspx# (last accessed 6 January 2009).

International Telecommunication Union (ITU) (2008b) *Internet Indicators: Subscriptions and Users*, available at: www.itu.int/ITU-D/icteye/Reports.aspx# (last accessed 6 January 2009).

Jacobs, S. (2002) 'How good is the South African media for democracy?', *African and Asian Studies*, 1(4): 279–302.

James, D. (1999) *Songs of the Women Migrants: Performance and Identity in South Africa*, Edinburgh: Edinburgh University Press.

James, D. and Kaarsholm, P. (2000) 'Popular culture and democracy in some Southern contexts: an introduction', *Journal of Southern African Studies*, 26(2): 189–208.

Jenkins, H. (2006) *Convergence Culture: Where Old and New Media Collide*, New York: New York University Press.

Karikari, K. (1992) 'Africa: the press and democracy', *Race and Class*, 34(3): 55–66.

Kasoma, F. (1995) 'The role of the independent media in Africa's change to democracy', *Media, Culture and Society*, 17(4): 537–55.

Kasoma, F. (1997) 'The independent press and politics in Africa', *Gazette: International Journal for Communication Studies*, 59(4–5): 295–310.

Konings, P. and Foeken, D. (2006) *Crisis and Creativity: Exploring the Wealth of the African Neighbourhood*, Leiden: Brill.

Laclau, E. and Mouffe, C. (1985) *Hegemony and Socialist Strategy: Towards a Radical Democratic Politics*, London: Verso.

Lardner, T. (1993) 'Democratization and forces in the African media', *Journal of International Affairs*, 47(1): 89–93.

Lerner, D. and Pevsner, L.W. (1958) *The Passing of Traditional Society: Modernizing the Middle East*, New York: Free Press.

Lerner, D. and Schramm, W. (1967) *Communication and Change in the Developing Countries*, Honolulu: Hawaii University Press.

Mäkinen, M. and Wangu Kuira, M. (2008) 'Social media and post-election crisis in Kenya', *The International Journal of Press/Politics*, 13: 328–35.

Maletsky, C. (2009) 'Elders spew fire over SMSes', *The Namibian*, 2 February. Available at: www.namibian.com.na/news/full-story/archive/2009/february/article/elders-spew-fire-over-smses/ (last accessed 9 February 2009).

Martin, R. (1992) 'Building independent mass media in Africa', *Journal of Modern African Studies*, 30(2): 331–40.

Mbembe, A. (2001) *On the Postcolony*, Berkeley: University of California Press.

Mouffe, C. (2000) *The Democratic Paradox*, New York: Verso.

Ndlovu-Gatsheni, S.J. and Willems, W. (2009) 'Making sense of cultural nationalism and the politics of commemoration under the *Third Chimurenga* in Zimbabwe', *Journal of Southern African Studies*, 34(4): 945–65.

Negt, O. and Kluge, A. (1993) [1972] *Public Sphere and Experience: Toward an Analysis of the Bourgeois and Proletarian Public Sphere*, Minneapolis: University of Minnesota Press.

Nuttall, S. and Michael, C.-A. (eds) (2000) *Senses of Culture: South African Culture Studies*, Oxford: Oxford University Press.

Nyairo, J. and Ogude, J. (2005) 'Popular music, popular politics: unbwogable and the idioms of freedom in Kenyan popular music', *African Affairs*, 104(415): 225–49.

Nyamnjoh, F.B. (2005) *Africa's Media, Democracy and the Politics of Belonging*, London: Zed Books.

Ogbondah, C.W. (1997) 'Communication and democratization in Africa', *Gazette: International Journal for Communication Studies*, 59(4): 271–94.

Ogundimu, F.F. (1997) 'Mass media and democratization in sub-Saharan Africa', *African Rural and Urban Studies*, 4(1): 7–18.

Ojo, E.O. (2003) 'The mass media and the challenges of sustainable democratic values in Nigeria: possibilities and limitations', *Media, Culture and Society*, 25(6): 821–40.

Pitts, G. (2000) 'Democracy and press freedom in Zambia: attitudes of members of parliament toward media and media regulation', *Communication Law and Policy*, 5(2): 269–94.

Probst, P. and Spittler, G. (2004) *Between Resistance and Expansion: Explorations of Local Vitality in Africa*, Munster: Lit Verlag.

Pye, L.W. (1963) *Communications and Political Development*, Princeton: Princeton University Press.

Schramm, W.L. (1964) *Mass Media and National Development: the Role of Information in the Developing Countries*, Stanford: Stanford University Press.

Spitulnik, D. (2002) 'Alternative small media and communicative spaces', in G. Hyden,

M. Leslie and F.F. Ogundimu (eds) *Media and Democracy in Africa*, Uppsala: Nordic Africa Institute, pp. 177–205.

Tettey, W.J. (2001) 'The media and democratization in Africa: contributions, constraints and concerns of the private press', *Media, Culture and Society*, 23(1): 5–31.

UNESCO (1999) *UNESCO Statistical Yearbook 1999 – Culture and Communication Statistics*, available at: www.uis.unesco.org/TEMPLATE/html/CultAndCom/Table_IV_14_Africa.html (last accessed 30 January 2009).

Vail, L. and White, L. (1978) 'Plantation protest: the history of a Mozambican song', *Journal of Southern African Studies*, 5(1): 1–25.

Vail, L. and White, L. (1983) 'Forms of resistance: songs and perceptions of power in colonial Mozambique', *American Historical Review*, 88: 883–919.

Wasserman, H. (2010) *Tabloid Journalism in South Africa: True Story!*, Bloomington: Indiana University Press.

Willems, W. (2009) *Imagining the Power of the Media: Global News, Nationalism and Popular Culture in the Context of the Zimbabwe Crisis (2000–2007)*, unpublished PhD thesis, London: School of Oriental and African Studies, University of London.

World Bank (2002) *The Right to Tell: the Role of the Mass Media in Economic Development*, Washington, DC: World Bank.

Zaffiro, J. (1988) 'Regional pressure and the erosion of media freedom in an African democracy: the case of Botswana', *Journal of Communication*, 38: 108–20.

Zaffiro, J. (1989) 'The press and political opposition in an African democracy: the case of Botswana', *Journal of Commonwealth and Comparative Politics*, 27(1): 51–73.

Zaffiro, J. (2000) 'Broadcasting reform and democratization in Botswana', *Africa Today*, 47(1): 87–102.

Zaffiro, J. (2002) *Media and Democracy in Zimbabwe, 1931–2002*, Colorado Springs: International Academic Publishers.

Zimbabwe Advertising Research Foundation (ZARF) (2001) *Zimbabwe All Media Products Survey (ZAMPS)*, Harare: Zimbabwe Advertising Research Foundation.

Chapter 4

Theorizing popular community media for democracy and development

Victor Ayedun-Aluma

Introduction

The media structure of anglophone West Africa is commonly viewed as comprising three components: traditional or indigenous media; modern 'mass' media; and post-modern 'new' media (Ansu-Kyeremeh 1998; Wilson 1998). And in the ambit of modern mass media, three tiers are identified: government and public media; private and commercial media; and community media. The concept and practice of community media within this environment raises fundamental problems about its potential utility as agents of democracy and development. This chapter explores these problems. It critiques current conceptualizations of community media in light of their primary rationales as facilitators of democracy and development, suggests the reconceptualization of community media as a form of popular media (defining it as 'popular community media'), and analyses the community radio process in Ghana and Nigeria in terms of this definition of popular community media.

Conceptualizing the popular community media

Opubor (2000: 16) asserts that community media are 'techniques and technologies for responding to community communication needs'. He further asserts that community media are created by a community as part of its communication system. Wanyeki (2000) regards community media as technologies through which marginalized groups are enabled to participate in issues of development, politics and cultural preservation. She describes community media as those 'produced, managed and owned by, for and about the community they serve' (Wanyeki 2000: 30); thus, distinguishing between community media and community-oriented media. The former are owned, managed and operated by members of the community they serve, while the latter are owned by independent corporations which have a community development orientation and development agencies which encourage community participation in media.

For Karikari (2000: 47), community media 'present an alternative discourse from the communication agenda set by the dominant socio-political or even cultural order'; thus, community media are identified by their pursuit of a social and political agenda different from the mainstream. In Karikari's definition, community media are those media which 'are devoted to the social, political and cultural interests and aspirations of identifiable groups resident in particular geographical areas within a country or within its provinces and/or sharing common specific social economic cultural or political experiences and interests'. He further notes that community media must be distinguished from rural media, and that failure to do so results in the misdefinition reflected in the discourse of authors like Kasoma (2002).

Departing sharply from the foregoing conceptualizations, Berger (1996) stipulates the possession and exercise of a 'liberatory' ethic as the fundamental attribute of community media. He acknowledges the importance of qualities such as community ownership, control and participation, non-profit orientation and development-centred activities, but gives primacy to the pursuit of what he calls 'a progressive agenda' in the context of the promotion of democracy. This is an agenda informed by and working out the 'liberatory' ethic. Such an ethic, which he argues should be the defining property of community media, involves 'a sense of advancing the rights of [a community] against those forces that would deny them'. It entails acting 'as an agent with a relative autonomy, centred around the participating activists, that intervene in community power relations (and media consumption patterns)'. In this liberatory view of community media, 'a community media agenda should ... start from the point of view of liberation from dominant power structures, and where communication is a tool in a larger social praxis' (Berger 1996).

Some critical remarks are in order at this juncture. Opubor's conceptualization emphasizes the need for community media to be the creation of the communities they serve. He criticizes what he calls 'exogenous definitions of communities and the imposition of narrow based solutions to the cultural communication and survival problems which communities face' (Opubor 2000: 13). This perspective underlines the importance of the social and cultural origins of the media technologies being defined as community media. It would appear that different problems arise from differences in the origins of media. Where media are exogenous creations, problems of incapacitation of the host community, maladaptation of the media, and possibly rejection of the media by the community might arise. But where media are endogenous creations, it might be expected that these problems will not arise due to the processes of the social shaping of these media.

The issue of the social and cultural origins of media is echoed in Wanyeki's (2000) conceptualization when she stresses community participation as fundamental to the idea of community media. The point is how deep is community participation to be? Can it go beyond the usual questions of involvement in content production and operations management? Can participation include creation and choice of media technologies by the community? It is conceivable that were such depths of participation to take place community media might move out of the modern mass media category into the traditional or indigenous media category; or it might straddle both categories.

Karikari's view basically sees community media as a form of alternative media, pursuing dissenting political agendas. This squares somewhat with Berger's conceptualization. However, Karikari stretches the requirement of community ownership to cover the individual entrepreneur, group, association or institution as long as they are 'non-sectarian, non-partisan and open'. Thus, he falls into self-contradiction on at least two points. First, a medium that exists to promote alternative discourses and orders may not really be described as non-partisan. Second, it is difficult to see how a medium owned by an 'individual entrepreneur' may continually uphold the community media ideal of reflecting a plurality of voices.

The foregoing discussion points out the following aspects of the mainstream conceptualization of community media. Community media are owned by the communities they serve. They involve participation by these communities. They are not motivated by commercial gain, but by the promotion of the communal good. The issues that remain problematic, however, include: in what way might a structurally complex formation as a community be said to own a medium of communication? To what extent might the social and cultural origins of media affect their ownership and utilization by a community? In what ways might the communal good be defined?

The idea that community media should exist to promote the communal good is a prominent one in the mainstream conceptualization of community media; and the communal good is usually defined in terms of the actualization of democracy and development (Berger 1996; AMARC 1998; Wanyeki 2000; Alumuku 2007). The question is what views of democracy and development are community media as presently defined likely to promote? This question is addressed by first problematizing the concepts of democracy and development, and thereafter underlining how the mainstream conceptualization of community media privileges some views of democracy and development.

Essentially, democracy is a political system or style of governance which vests power in the people, operationalized as the majority of the people. It encourages the building of consensus or coalitions as a mechanism for mediating the differences among the people, thus facilitating the exercise of people power; and fosters the expression of the will or perspective of the different subgroups among the people, thus permitting the airing of the view of minority groups (Tourraine 1991). In this understanding are embedded the concepts of a community, the people and the culture of the people.

A community may be seen as a group of persons who have important attributes in common, are conscious of this commonality, and interact at varying levels of intensity in order to pursue an agenda that is valuable to them. The bases of commonality may be the geographic location, the interests (AMARC 1998), a common heritage (Moemeka 1998), or the presence of 'social linkages and flows of resources' (Wellman and Leighton 1988). The people and the culture of the people, on the other hand, may be read as more of a construct of the elites than of the people themselves. Boëthius (1995), for instance, shows how the concept

of popular culture is a product of the transforming influence of the modernization processes that European society underwent between the medieval and the
late modern times. Boëthius argues that the idea of the people's culture became
separated from the culture of the aristocracy and the bourgeoisie as European
societies underwent processes that re-valued and, indeed, devalued important features of folk European culture and sought to remould these pristine ways of life
in a fashion sanctioned by the ideals of the European religious and commercial
elites. McQuail (1987), Cawelti (1999) and Garofalo (1999) also draw attention
to the fact that apart from the distinction between high and low culture, with
popular culture being seen as low in relation to the culture of the elite, there is a
range of phenomena to which the culture of the people might apply. This ranges
from the folk culture in which there is little or no social distance between the
producers and consumers of culture through mass culture in which there is a
significant social distance between the producers and consumers of culture. Here
the producers are industrial organizations whose action is geared towards transforming elements of people's culture into commodities with high market
exchange values.

The concepts of community, the people and popular culture provide further
refinement of the notions of democracy discussed so far. Community underlines
the factors of commonness as well as differences in the democratic process.
Democracy is built on the perception of a commonality of values and interests,
but it is also driven by differences and the handling – whether by reconciliation
or domination – of the differences. The concept of 'the people', as shown by
Boëthius, indicates the presence of power differences in the community, while
the culture of the people constitutes a site in which such differences are handled
through mediation or domination. Thus, through the frames of these concepts,
we understand how the meanings of democracy may vary.

Development is the other communal good that community media is usually
said to promote. It may be defined as the attainment of growth and transformation in the economic and political systems of countries (McMichael 2000). Such
developmental change may be driven either by endogenous forces and models or
by exogenous ones. Additionally, development may be seen as the attainment of
an improved physical and mental quality of life among target human populations.
The difference in emphases of these definitions underlines variation in the meanings of development. Thus, the primary focus of development may be seen as
economic and political systems or as people's quality of life, even as no claim is
made that the two foci are mutually exclusive.

Which meanings of democracy and development might the existing concepts
of community media currently be promoting? And how might community media
be reconceptualized in order to facilitate its utility as a promoter of preferred
understandings of democracy and development? Existing concepts of community
media are apparently driven by a desire to affirm communities – seen as marginalized – through communication institutions and practices. As a result, the community media idea is constructed to emphasize the properties of community

ownership, community participation – origination and/or utilization, non-commercial motivation, and alternative – even liberationist – political agendas. The problems arising from the construction of each of these properties have been alluded to earlier in this chapter. What should be highlighted at this point is the possibility that specific constructions of these properties of the community media concept are likely to privilege some meanings of democracy and development over others. For example, the view of community media as the pursuit of a liberationist agenda is likely to privilege a meaning of democracy as a process of mediating or negotiating power differences between social classes; and a meaning of development as a process of attaining systemic political and economic transformation in which the people, rather than indigenous or exogenous elites, are in the driving seat. Further, an understanding of community media which emphasizes community ownership and participation is likely to promote a view of democracy as a process of reconciling differences and building consensus in order to strengthen commonality of perception and action. It is also likely to privilege a meaning of development which centres more on the attainment of social transformation than on the class identities of the drivers of such transformation.

The argument of this chapter is that the conceptualization of community media privileges specific meanings of democracy and development through intervening constructions such as community, the people and popular culture. This situation is possible because community, the people and popular culture might be regarded as constructions embedded in the ideas of community media and of democracy and development. To the extent that this is the case, the key to promoting preferred meanings of democracy and development through the reconceptualization of community media should be found in these embedded constructions. Assuming then that a preferred meaning of democracy and development is one that endorses a principal role for the non–elite classes, an appropriate conceptualization of community media should enhance its people component. Such enhancement should be found in constructions of community, the people and popular culture.

A concept of community media which foregrounds the people factor may be labelled the popular community media. How might popular community media be conceptualized? It should represent the use of communication for community self-affirmation in ways that take cognizance of national and global contexts. It should promote community origination, adaptation and utilization of media technologies as a tool and product of the everyday life of the people. It should encourage structures of media ownership that accommodates diversity, benefiting majorities and valuing minorities, within the community. At a fundamental level, the popular community media should be motivated by the desire to promote the common good and should, therefore, seek to advance group and individual rights. The popular community media idea should, in the West African context, also be cognizant of the complexity of the people-concept. Ake's (1981) analysis suggests at least three types of popular realities that have resulted from the political-economic forces set off by colonialism and postcolonialism in Africa.

Thus, one type of popular reality might be labelled the 'disarticulated oasis' – a largely urban formation oriented to lifestyles at comparable social levels in the mother cities of Europe and the United States. Another type would be one created through situations of interaction between indigenous cultures, a sort of intercultural borderland. And a third type would be uni-cultural, 'folk' and largely rural. Each of these popular realities would shape the specific manifestations of popular community media.

Actualizing the popular community media: examples from Ghana and Nigeria

To what extent might the community radio processes in Ghana and Nigeria be said to exemplify the popular community media concept? Ghana's first community radio station, Radio Ada, began regular broadcasts in February 1998. By December 1999, the number of community radio stations had grown to seven, thus inspiring the establishment of the Ghana Community Radio Network to serve as an operations support organization for the stations. Out of these seven stations, however, only three had their own broadcast frequencies (Whaite 2005). The stations that did not have their own frequencies instituted temporary arrangements that enabled them to transmit their programmes. For example, a regional station of the state-funded Ghana Broadcasting Corporation provided a two-hour daily slot to enable a community station to broadcast its programmes. As of 2007, Alumuku (2007: 169) identified 13 operational community radio stations in Ghana.

There appears to be some confusion about the inauguration date of community radio broadcasting in Nigeria. According to one view (shared by Bello (2006: 104) and Ojo (2005: 21)), the honour of being Nigeria's first community radio should go to the University of Lagos' Radio Unilag 103.1 FM, which began operations in 2004. Other 'community' radio stations would then include 11 campus radio stations since licensed by the Nigerian Federal Government (Dunu 2009: 153). The basis for this view is provided by the revised Nigerian Broadcasting Code, which categorizes campus broadcasting as a form of community broadcasting, defining the university campus as an academic community (Ojo 2006: 38). A contrary view, however, maintains that Nigeria is yet to have its first community radio station since the existing campus stations operate essentially as training laboratories for students under the supervision of senior faculty; thus, large sections of the university community, particularly non-academic staff, are excluded from participation in the station's operations and decision-making (Dunu 2009: 163–4).

In Ghana, the impetus for institutionalizing community radio was provided by civil society groups, chief among which was the Ghana Community Broadcasting Services founded by Alex and Wilna Quarmyne. The peculiar moment of history in which community radio emerged is poignantly captured in this statement from Radio Ada's training manual:

The deregulation of broadcasting in Ghana was in response to pressure from libertarian press interests rather than from organised community radio activists, of which there were none in the country at the time. Community radio in Ghana, therefore, did not start from a grassroots movement. Neither did it come with any concessions. In fact, the deregulation of broadcasting was so indeterminate that community radio has had to define itself.

(Quarmyne 2001: iii)

Another example is Radio Progress, Wa, which was established by Mass Media for Development, an organization promoted by the Catholic Diocese of Wa (Alumuku 2007: 196). The feature worth noting is that the primary drivers of community radio in Ghana were a coalition of indigenous and exogenous elites rather than people at the grassroots. This feature is evidenced also in Nigeria where civil society groups have engaged in advocacy and capacity building for community radio since November 2003. Institutional platforms such as the Initiative on Building Community Radio in Nigeria and later the Community Radio Coalition have been developed and used to advance the cause of community radio. According to Akingbulu and Menkiti (2008: 9), the Initiative on Building Community Radio in Nigeria was started by 'two international organisations, the Panos Institute West Africa (PIWA) and the World Association of Community Radio Broadcasters (AMARC), in partnership with the Institute for Media and Society (IMS-Nigeria)'. The target audiences have been government officials, executives of the national broadcast regulatory agency, media scholars, journalists and social activists. The purpose has been to build consensus among the elite classes on pressure points defined around the establishment of appropriate legal and policy frameworks, the development of requisite human and technical capacities, and the trialling of actual community broadcast station projects. Training workshops and seminars have also been held in virtually all the regional centres in Nigeria in an effort to clarify and crystallize a mainstream perception of community radio and to increase awareness and interest in it as well. A notable achievement has been the development of a model training curriculum to be used for prospective community radio workers.

The response of government officials to the push for community radio has tended to be tardy or lukewarm in both countries. On the constraint posed by the relative indifference of government and the competitive action of the commercial broadcasters, a station executive at Ghana's Radio Ada said:

The policies are too liberal and the regulatory mechanism in the broadcasting industry is not effective. Therefore many of the radio stations, particularly the commercialized ones, operate to thwart the efforts of the few radio stations which attempt to be principled. For example it is the policy of the Radio Ada not to broadcast any claim by any individual or group that he/they has/have cure for AIDS. Yet there are other radio stations in the country which are making huge monies by constantly advertising and promoting certain questionable medicines which they claim can cure AIDS. This, of course negates any effort at campaigning against irresponsible sexual habits that may result in the spread of the disease.

(Anon 2005: 9–10)

And, in reviewing the challenges on the road to institutionalizing community radio in Nigeria, Akingbulu and Menkiti asserted that:

> Government machinery has been slow. The final documents from the three policy processes which were initiated in 2004 and 2006 have not been released to the public. Inconsistency is also evident. Government said in mid-2006 that it wanted a policy in place before licensing community radio stations. But while it has not released the community radio policy, it approved licences for stations in educational institutions. The understanding with stakeholders was for grassroots community radio, but no approval has yet been given for any in this category.
>
> (Akingbulu and Menkiti 2008: 10–11)

It was earlier noted that the Nigerian regulatory agency lumped academic broadcasting through campus radio with community broadcasting. The implication of this conceptual confusion also needs to be underlined. As currently formulated in the Nigeria Broadcasting Code (2002: 28), campus broadcasting as a form of community broadcasting does not require that the campus radio station be owned and managed by members of the university community or their elected representatives. It also does not require the station to represent the interests of the community aside from promoting learning. In these circumstances, it can only be concluded that the envisaged campus radios are likely to function as instruments of the university administration rather than of the university communities.

The emerging community radio process in Nigeria is clearly being defined by the action and inaction of the elite classes, which for now are directed at other elite groups. This reflects the Ghanaian experience at a similar stage. Why in the case of Nigeria is this so? It may be that the civil society group which functions as the arrowhead lacks the capacity to mobilize the common people or it may be that the international financial support institutions which empower the civil society group lack the means and the plan to directly take on the non-elite classes. Whichever the case, the dominant strategy of intra-elite action which is shaping the community radio process in Nigeria may be expected to fundamentally mark the operation and impact of the community radio stations when they take off as 'grassroots community radio'. Thus, what emerges may be more of an elite-oriented community media than popular community media.

To what extent then might the Ghanaian community radio story be said to exemplify popular community media? The people factor is played out in terms of making contributions to the funding of the station's operations, volunteering time and labour, as well as providing an active listenership. Ale relates the comments from the station manager of Radio Ada, Kofi Larweh, that

> Radio Ada's workforce … comes from the market women, fashion designers, drivers, shoe makers, watch repairers and others. During important village functions, recorded tapes are brought into the station for use. Sometimes we use them like that, sometimes we edit them if necessary.
>
> (Ale 2008: 36)

Also, local languages and development-support programming are used as strategies for increasing community participation in station operations. For example, Radio Ada broadcasts in the Dangme language, the indigenous language of its locality in the Greater Accra region; and Radio Peace based in Winneba employs several local languages, including Fanti and Ewutu, thus the majority of the people who are not speakers of the English language are encouraged to become involved as audiences of the broadcasts. The focus of programming at these and other community radio stations in Ghana include religious exhortation, health and sanitation, commerce and small business, civic education, political awareness and gender issues. Describing some modalities of 'popular' participation in Radio Peace, for example, Alumuku observes that

> Members of the community also participate through phone-in programmes, although not many members of the audience in the community have telephones. The radio also receives many letters from their audience. Opinion leaders who represent groups within the community participate in programmes and are able to express the opinion of groups which otherwise would have remained unheard.
>
> (Alumuku 2007: 189)

This observation underlines the constraints imposed on the efficacy of community media when they are not driven by the people. The example of Radio Peace, Winneba, indicates that generally inaccessible communication technologies such as telephones are likely to be used, while more accessible ones such as traditional festivals are likely to be devalued; literacy, a skill not widely possessed at the grassroots, is likely to be required for participation, while the more widespread orality is minimized; and 'opinion leaders', that is, elite members of minority groups, are likely to become the oracles 'representing' the views of their groups. The result of these features is that existing inequalities and inequities in power and wellbeing in the community are not likely to be radically addressed and revised through the agency of community radio. The complex realities of the people as suggested by Ake (1981) are unlikely to be meaningfully engaged. And community media becomes a site for popular reaction to elite constructions rather than avenues for grassroots self-affirmation.

Conclusion

In the West African space, community media has been promoted as a tool for the attainment of democracy and development. Its current conceptualization, however, raises problems regarding its potential for actualizing democracy and development since it fails to foreground the agency of the people as the fundamental drivers of community media. A reconceptualization is needed if the potential of community media as tools of democracy and development is to be realized. Such a reconceptualization is advanced in this chapter. It is argued that the conceptualization of community media as a form of popular media, highlighting the fundamental role of the people, is better placed to facilitate the achievement of democracy and development in West Africa. It is suggested that this concept be referred to as popular community media, and its essential properties be identified as: a community self-affirmation agenda that is cognizant of national and global realities; community origination, adaptation and utilization of media technologies; structures of media ownership that accommodate social complexity; and protection and advancement of group and individual rights.

The community radio processes in Ghana and Nigeria were evaluated in light of this characterization of popular community media. It was found that current practice in the two countries fell short of the popular community media idea, particularly in the areas of community origination and adaptation of media technologies, structures of media ownership sensitive to social complexity, and concurrent advancement of group and individual rights. To the extent that current practice of community radio fails to represent popular community media, it is unlikely to fully release popular imaginations and energies in the service of democracy and development. This failure is corroborated by Bathily's (2006: 59) analysis using a different set of criteria derived from the African Charter on Broadcasting in which he asserts that 'community radio as it exists now on the ground, in most African countries, is on the WRONG TRACK'. It is therefore recommended that the community radio process in Ghana and Nigeria be reformed along the lines indicated by the popular community media concept in order to better realize its potential for democracy and development.

References

Ake, C. (1981) *A political economy of Africa*, Essex: Longman.

Akingbulu, A. and Menkiti, M. (2008) 'Building community radio in Nigeria: how far?', in A. Akingbulu (ed.) *Rooting for community radio in Nigeria*, pp. 9–11, Lagos: Institute for Media and Society.

Ale, A. (2008) 'How community radio aids development', in A. Akingbulu (ed.) *Rooting for community radio in Nigeria*, pp. 35–7, Lagos: Institute for Media and Society.

Alumuku, P.T. (2007) *Community radio for development*, Nairobi: Paulines Publications.

AMARC Africa and Panos Southern Africa (1998) *What is community radio? A resource guide*, Johannesburg: AMARC Africa.

Anon. (2005) Radio Ada, interim document for 'Community television – A scooping study'. Online, available at: www.tv4d.org/Ghana_Field_Study_Radio_Ada.pdf (last accessed 28 October 2009).

Ansu-Kyeremeh, K. (1998) 'Indigenous communication in the age of the Internet', in K. Ansu-Kyeremeh (ed.) *Perspectives on indigenous communication in Africa, volume II, dynamics and future directions*, pp. 245–54, Legon: School of Communication Studies, University of Ghana.

Bathily, A. (2006) 'General reflections on community radio concepts and models in Africa', in A. Akingbulu (ed.) *Building community radio in Nigeria: issues and challenges*, pp. 53–61, Lagos: Institute for Media and Society.

Bello, A.W. (2006) 'Radio in an academic community: the case of Unilag FM', in A. Akingbulu (ed.) *Building community radio in Nigeria: issues and challenges*, pp. 101–5, Lagos: Institute for Media and Society.

Berger, G. (1996) 'What is community media?', paper delivered at Community Voices Conference, Media Institute of Southern Africa, Mangochi, Malawi, 6–11 October. Online, available at: http://guyberger.ru.ac.za/fulltext/commmediamisa.rtf (last accessed 24 October 2009).

Boëthius, U. (1995) 'The history of high and low culture', in F. Fornäs and G. Bolin (eds) *Youth culture in late modernity*, pp. 12–38, London: Sage.

Cawelti, J.G. (1999) 'Popular culture/multiculturalism', in J. Hanson and D.J. Maxcy (eds) *Sources: notable selections in mass media*, pp. 176–84, Guilford: Dushkin/McGraw-Hill.

Dunu, I.V. (2009) 'An appraisal of audience involvement in university campus radio operations in south-east Nigeria', *Journal of Communication and Media Research* 1(1): 153–65.

Garofalo, R. (1999) 'Definitions, themes, and issues', in J. Hanson and D.J. Maxcy (eds) *Sources: notable selections in mass media*, pp. 277–86, Guilford: Dushkin/McGraw-Hill.

Karikari, K. (2000) 'The development of community media in English-speaking West Africa', in S.T.K. Boafo (ed.) *Promoting community media in Africa*, pp. 43–60, Paris: UNESCO.

Kasoma, F.P. (2002) *Community radio: its management and organisation in Zambia*, Lusaka: Zambia Independent Media Association.

McMichael, P. (2000) *Development and social change, a global perspective*, 2nd edn, Thousand Oaks: Pine Forge Press.

McQuail, D. (1987) *Mass communication theory, an introduction*, London: Sage.

Miller, T. and McHoul, A. (1998) *Popular culture and everyday life*, London: Sage.

Moemeka, A.A. (1998) 'Communalism as a fundamental dimension of culture', *Journal of Communication*, 48(4): 118–41.

National Broadcasting Commission (2002) *Nigeria Broadcasting Code*, Abuja: National Broadcasting Commission.

Ojo, E. (2005) *Survey on design of model community radio for Nigeria*, Lagos: Institute for Media and Society.

Ojo, E. (2006) 'Legal framework for community radio in Nigeria', in A. Akingbulu (ed.) *Building community radio in Nigeria: issues and challenges*, pp. 37–44, Lagos: Institute for Media and Society.

Opubor, A.E. (2000) 'If community media is the answer, what is the question?', in S.T.K. Boafo (ed.) *Promoting community media in Africa*, pp. 11–24, Paris: UNESCO.

Quarmyne, W.W. (2001) *Radio Ada, building participation into training for community radio*, Accra: Ghana Community Broadcasting Services.

Tourraine, A. (1991) 'What does democracy mean today?', *International Social Science Journal*, 43(2): 259–68.

Wanyeki, L.M. (2000) 'The development of community media in East and Southern Africa', in S.T.K. Boafo (ed.) *Promoting community media in Africa*, pp. 25–42, Paris: UNESCO.

Wellman, B. and Leighton, B. (1988) 'Networks, neighbourhoods and communities', in L. Tepperman and J. Curtis (eds) *Readings in sociology, an introduction*, pp. 644–55, Toronto: McGraw-Hill Ryerson.

Whaites, N. (2005) 'Tuning in: an inventory of rural FM radio in Ghana', unpublished MSc thesis, the University of Guelph, Canada.

Wilson, D. (1998) 'Towards effective communication policies and strategies for Africa', in K. Ansu-Kyeremeh (ed.) *Perspectives on indigenous communication in Africa, volume II, dynamics and future directions*, pp. 233–43, Legon: School of Communication Studies, University of Ghana.

Chapter 5

Talk radio, democracy and citizenship in (South) Africa

Tanja Bosch

Introduction

Discussion and debate has always been considered integral to democracy. Talk has been seen as constitutive of publics, with talk among citizens seen as fundamental to their participation (Dahlgren 2002). This talk, or discursive interaction among diverse individuals and groups, is what leads to the creation of a public. Media scholars have examined the role of independent mass media systems in Africa and argued that the primary role of the media in these societies is to inform citizens about public policy so that they become a more informed electorate (e.g. Sandbrook 1996). In this way, it is generally agreed that the mass media can promote democratization by making citizens more aware of their roles in a democracy (see for example Hyden and Okigbo 2002).

Talk radio is particularly important in African democracies, which often struggle to escape the legacy of repressive regimes in which censorship, state victimization or imprisonment is most often the direct result of individuals publicly critiquing the state. In South Africa, and other African societies, open debate is often discouraged for a number of political and cultural reasons. With this in mind, this chapter argues that talk radio in Africa has the potential to make positive contributions towards democracy, channelling public opinion and offering a space for political discussion and debate. Radio broadcasting is usually considered the most prevalent medium in Africa, mostly because of high penetration compared to television and print; and because radio does not require literacy, can be broadcast in multiple languages and can reach large geographical areas.

This chapter reflects on talk radio broadly, but draws largely on the practices of commercial talk radio in South Africa, arguing that it illuminates debates about the nature of the public sphere, despite its interpellation of citizens as consumers. The term talk radio is thus used in this chapter to refer primarily to commercial talk radio, although there is also reference to radio practices elsewhere on the continent, and to community or local radio.

The chapter argues that public discursive arenas such as radio become important sites where social identities can be 'constructed, deconstructed and reconstructed' (Fraser 1990). Using the theoretical frameworks of Habermas' public sphere, Nancy Fraser's counterpublics, and Bourdieu's field theory and constructs of capital, this chapter argues that commercial talk radio becomes the unlikely site where public opinion is formed as individuals use the airwaves to participate in critical discussion and debate, and in doing so, organize themselves as a public. To some extent, commercial radio might be considered a form of 'popular media' as it attempts to draw larger audiences to satisfy a largely commercial imperative, with a fair amount of 'frivolous' or entertainment directed talk. But despite these limitations, the audience engages in more structured discussion and debate on socio-political issues, even when not prompted to do so. Drawing on Fraser's (1990) conceptualization of a 'public', this chapter uses the term as it emphasizes discursive interaction directed by a plurality of perspectives; whereas 'community' suggests a degree of homogeneity.

Background: talk radio

Talk radio is generally defined as a format characterized by conversation that is initiated by a programme host and usually involves listeners who telephone to participate in the discussion about topics such as politics, sports or current events (Rubin and Step 2000).

Talk radio has increasingly played a role in political discussion and debate in the United States, and a growing body of literature further explores the phenomenon of this so-called 'dial in democracy' (Bolce 1996). In particular, Bolce (1996) refers to the 1994 elections in the United States as the first talk-radio election, with listeners forming a significant category of voters. Much of the scholarship on talk radio has shown that the development of a 'talk radio democracy' has changed the way in which people obtain political information, and that as a result, regular talk radio listeners are also more politically active (Capella Turow and Jameson 1996).

While there is a growing consensus that talk radio provides a forum for public deliberation, some scholars also regard talk shows as a form of infotainment that is incongruous with serious political journalism (Lee 2002).

In Africa, the notion of pavement radio (Ellis 1989) has often been raised to illustrate how public opinion can be shaped by citizens' direct engagement with a mediatized public sphere. Pavement radio, a direct translation from the more commonly used French term *radio trottoir* refers to informal communication networks on the continent where the distinction between listener and broadcaster becomes somewhat blurred, and story selection is dependent on the popularity of stories, which are often located in folklore and mythology (Bourgault 1995). Nyamnjoh (2005) has shown how pavement radio and other similar informal information sources are used by poorer citizens frustrated with the mainstream state and private media in Cameroon. This is very similar to the emergence of tabloids, where a radical departure from the mainstream press has resulted in a different kind of journalism. Some have critiqued these tabloids as being purely sensationalist entertainment (e.g. Berger 2005; Froneman 2006), while others have explored tabloids as a contribution towards giving a voice to ordinary people and contributing towards a democratic public sphere so that the elite do not dominate mediated debate (Wasserman 2008). In many ways, talk radio in Africa begins to negotiate a middle line between these two extremes, i.e. politically significant infotainment and a populist 'pavement' radio. While talk radio is populist and participatory, it begins to emerge as a kind of citizen and civic journalism. Within this context, there emerges a justification for the conflicts with dominant Western journalistic norms of accuracy, truth and independent verification of facts.

In Africa, the power of talk radio has been effectively demonstrated by *Radio des Milles Collines* (Radio of a Thousand Hills) in Rwanda, often referred to as hate radio (Kellow and Steeves 1998). This government-controlled radio station played a key role in inciting the 1994 Rwandan genocide, using an ethnic framework to report a political struggle and broadcasting repeated calls to violence. However, there are also numerous counter-examples of how radio has been used for social change and peacebuilding. The *Talking Drum Studio* in Sierre Leone, for example, hosted by former senior combatants who were once bitter enemies, discussed methods of reconciliation and uniting the deeply fragmented society with their listeners.

Similarly, in Ghana, talk radio has become the means for citizens to discuss sensitive or controversial political and social issues without fear of government intimidation, in the absence of other spaces to do so. Radio programmes have given citizens the opportunity to engage in formal and informal debate in a range of local languages, as the 'easiest, quickest and relatively inexpensive means to bring issues to the court of public opinion' (Boateng 2003: 19). Boateng (2003) has demonstrated how private media participation has led to the use of Akan forms of representation to facilitate communication, through the articulation of national issues among an ethnically diverse population of Accra. In Mali too, talk radio has increased political knowledge, with radio use significantly associated with higher levels of democratic orientations (Nisbet 2009).

In South Africa, as elsewhere on the continent, media liberalization in the 1990s paved the way for a proliferation of new community and commercial radio stations. Radio 702 was established in Johannesburg in 1980 and intended as a youth music station, but was repositioned as a talk radio station in 1986. The station's inability to compete with existing music station Radio 5, and the political context at the time of heavy state censorship of media content, made this an ideal historical moment for the emergence of the station, which became the only independent source of broadcast news (De Beer 1998). In 1997, 702's sister station, 567MW Cape Talk, was conceptualized, and programming is frequently simulcast on both stations. Owned by the South African media conglomerate Primedia, these stations are the only commercial format talk radio stations in South Africa. The Afrikaans talk radio station, Punt Geselsradio, was also formed in 1997, around the same time as 567MW, but its licence was revoked about five years later as a result of the station's failure to apply for amendments to its license conditions (Bizcommunity 2002) as well as financial difficulty (*Independent Online* 2001).

Talk radio and the public sphere

Discussions on talk radio are most often approached through the theoretical frame of the public sphere as conceptualized by Jürgen Habermas (1989). For Habermas, the *Öffentlichkeit* or public sphere comprised the press, institutions of political discussion (e.g. parliament, literary salons etc.) and other public spaces where political discussion occurred.

Key criteria for the formation of the Habermasian public sphere are universal access, autonomy and the quality of the contributions or a rational-critical debate. In other words, the public sphere is not formed merely by the expression of sequential public opinions by private individuals, but rather the engagement of a rational-critical debate, which leads to the formation of consensus and group public opinion. It is at this juncture that talk radio in Africa departs most radically from its counterparts in North America, or the same format on television, where the talk format has been most commonly associated with controversial so-called 'shock jock' radio.

In new democracies like South Africa, radio emerges as one form of public 'space' which embraces the principles of the Habermasian public sphere, primarily encouraging open discussion of general socio-political issues in a process in which discursive argumentation is employed to identify issues of common concern. While the station is driven by its commercial imperative, the callers set the agenda with their on-air interactions. Callers participate via calling in to the station, or by sending text messages to the station, which are then read out on air. The latter function has broadened participation, with landline access no longer a prerequisite for participation in on-air discussions, particularly as South Africa currently has almost 100 per cent mobile phone penetration (*Mail and Guardian* 2009).

Schudson (1978) has argued that mediated communication is more relevant to democracy than face-to-face interpersonal communication; though others (see for example Kim 2009) have shown how non-purposive communication can be central to formation of opinions on political matters. In some ways, talk radio is a middle ground as it brings personal opinions into a public space by providing an accessible alternative to interpersonal interaction, especially for listeners who may find face-to-face interaction less rewarding (Armstrong and Rubin 1989). While mediated, there is the simulation of a personal conversation with other listeners or between caller and host. Talk radio has been shown to serve various needs, including seeking political information, interpreting reality or merely serving the purpose of companionship (Hofsetter and Gianos 1997). Commercial talk radio features programme hosts who initiate conversation on a range of serious and trivial topics, and one might argue that the type of discussions that occur on talk radio are frequently of a personal nature, thus paving the way for more serious political discussions.

The author has previously argued how talk radio may serve the purpose of confession (Bosch 2008). This argument arises from the notion that traditional African cultures usually do not sanction the public display or discussion of private problems. On commercial talk radio in South Africa, serious political talk shows exist side-by-side with more frivolous non-purposive talk. Listeners frequently call in to discuss issues of public concern, but then continue their argumentation by drawing on personal subjectivities. The second more explicit way in which this occurs is when listeners expressly move private issues into the public domain, to seek advice on health or financial matters, as part of shows designed for this purpose (e.g. on sexual health or behavioural health). Here one sees listeners seeking affirmation of self-identity via their discursive engagement with the 'experts' in studio, the hosts, and with the silent empathetic audience via a complex process of authentication. Rather than reaffirm a social hierarchy via the notion of 'expert' opinions versus public knowledge, this is subverted with the active participation of the host, who also usually plays the role of 'expert', asking questions and probing the callers.

While African discussions of politics in private spaces are common, many countries suffer the legacy of repressive and authoritarian political cultures in which speaking out on a controversial political matter could result in state victimization. While political dissent was also muffled under an apartheid regime, there has been increased citizen participation in the public and political sphere since the first democratic elections in 1994.

On South Africa's commercial talk stations, e.g. Radio 702 in Johannesburg and 567MW in Cape Town, callers engage with programme hosts and with each other on a range of socio-political issues. Talk is often listener-directed with a so-called 'open line', which means that callers direct the conversation and raise their own topics of interest. Issues raised are often socio-political in nature – ranging from the performance of local government structures, to questions such as the purchase of toy guns for children as Christmas presents. Other themes have included the education system and matric results and teaching, affirmative action in sports, environmental policy, the 2010 football World Cup and other similar topics. Talk radio, in this instance, moves beyond the traditional reporting of the mainstream press, by allowing citizens to engage with each other on a range of, often controversial, issues.

One example of this is the deliberation on race that followed the reporting on Brandon Huntley, a South African citizen granted refugee status in Canada on the grounds of his assertions that he would be persecuted if he returned home because he was white. Huntley was granted asylum in September 2009 because he did not believe that the South African government could protect him from criminal persecution on the grounds of his race (*News24* 2009). The coverage of the story on talk radio prompted broad discussion on the topic, as well as related topics of race, racial discrimination and crime. Most importantly though, callers placed race firmly on the agenda, and felt no need for politically correct views in the ensuing debate.

In these discussions, racial identifiers were used, but more often there were also discussions in which racial meaning was conveyed implicitly. The discussions on crime in particular were often framed in an 'us versus them' oppositional tone. The rhetoric of these deliberations on race may not have conformed to the Habermasian ideal speech situation of rational-critical debate, as the argumentation did not reveal any particular consensus. However, these ongoing discussions present a rare opportunity for a racially diverse listening public to engage on an issue of national salience in a neutral 'space'. The conversation moved substantially from mere expression of private opinion – i.e. for or against Huntley's argument – to a broader public opinion that Huntley's case was unjustified, regardless of individual callers' private opinions on the links between race and crime. This was interesting as race is usually avoided in public debate as a result of sociocultural norms or a desire to be politically correct.

Talk radio and democracy

Talk radio contributes to a discursive or deliberative democracy, in which public participation and citizen deliberation is considered more important than voting alone. Given its commercial imperative, commercial radio seems an unlikely space for such deliberation, and in a developing context one might imagine community radio to serve a more powerful role as spaces for parallel discursive arenas where members of subordinated social groups invent and circulate counterdiscourses (Fraser 1990). Hundreds of community radio stations are active throughout the continent, with a proliferation of stations emerging in postapartheid South Africa after media liberalization. The discussions on community radio are mostly of a frivolous nature with many call-ins linked to music requests and other entertainment shows; and in cases of more serious discussions, listener comments are often one-way, limited to the hyper-local, and of a homogenous nature. It is perhaps the broader and more diverse audience of commercial talk radio that generates public and collective discussions of nationally salient issues. Talk radio, Coleman argues, 'in a deeply divided society, of segregated communities and hostile publics largely devoid of a shared identity of nationhood, is of more than usual significance' (1998: 10). In the South African context where communities are still geographically, socially and often also politically divided, over a decade after the end of apartheid, talk radio has the potential to play a key unifying role. By giving members of these various 'imagined communities' around the country an equal opportunity to engage in public argumentation, this talk-radio audience might 'imagine' themselves as a public.

In the South African context talk radio becomes the main authoritative site for mediated discussions. Press conferences centred on fairly major political events are frequently held at the studios of Talk Radio 702 in Johannesburg. Here we see the newsmakers coming to the journalists, instead of vice versa, as is usually the case for press conferences. One example was the press conference delivered by former ANC chairperson, Mosiuoa Lekota, in the run up to the formation of the breakaway political party, Congress of the People (COPE) live on the Redi Direko show on 8 October 2008. At this press conference Lekota made the announcement of his intention to start a new political party to oppose the African National Congress (ANC).

During the 1999 national elections several live debates were held between representatives of political parties, allowing listeners to address them directly. Similarly, politicians frequently appear on the station's talk shows to answer questions live from callers and to engage with the audience directly. In this way, the radio station becomes an intermediary between the public and policy-makers, and a space where citizens can directly speak to policy-makers and politicians, and receive instant feedback. Further examples of this are regular shows on 567MW where the mayor and the Premier are hosted on call-in shows where they engage directly with the public.

This has been developed even further, with the policy-makers directly approaching the radio station to interact with listeners. For example, when callers raise issues of policing, Western Cape police commissioner Zwandile Petros regularly calls the station and answers listeners' questions or concerns on the air. The station hosts an event that asks listeners to nominate someone who needs assistance. The '567 Cape Talk birthday wish' provides financial assistance to various people who are nominated by others as being needy.

Interestingly, again these issues seldom seem to make it onto the agenda of discussions on community radio stations, and policy-makers do not appear as regularly. One possible explanation might be that the listening public of commercial talk radio raise issues so frequently that politicians have to be available to answer them, so that their appearance is as a result of increased demand; but also that the role of commercial talk radio, despite its commercial imperative, has expanded to allow an authentic space where the public can hold policy-makers accountable, with talk radio playing a kind of 'watchdog' role as an authentic 'fourth estate'.

Challenges to the public sphere hypothesis

Habermas has been widely criticized, most notably for his idealization of the bourgeois public sphere by presenting it as a forum of rational debate and discussion while in fact participation was limited. In particular, women and working-class people (and poor blacks in a South African context) were excluded (see for example Fraser 1990; Kellner 2000). While the concept of the public sphere is still widely used, the theoretical terrain has since shifted away from the notion of one democratic public sphere, to a theorization of a multiplicity of public spheres, which sometimes concur, sometimes overlap, but also sometimes come into conflict with one another.

With commercial talk radio we see a 'refeudalization' of the public sphere, similar to the nineteenth-century trend Habermas identified in which private interests assumed direct political functions when powerful corporations started controlling and manipulating the media and the state. Habermas argued that this 'refeudalization' resulted in a breakdown of the boundaries between the public and private sphere, with citizens becoming consumers and dedicating themselves to passive consumption and private concerns rather than issues of the common good (Kellner 2000). While occupying the journalistic field, commercial talk radio is simultaneously positioned within the economic field, continually caught between the competing imperatives of press freedom and journalistic practice and the laws of the market, with this tension becoming quasi-permanent as the symbolic power of talk radio increases (Benson and Neveu 2005). However, through the analysis of broadcasts on commercial talk radio one can argue that it provides a site for the production and circulation of discourses, and becomes a 'theatre for debating and deliberating rather than for buying and selling' (Fraser 1990: 57).

Broadcasts sometimes highlight what Bourdieu (1986) would refer to as markers of 'distinction'. Broadcasts are exclusively in English, presupposing the requisite amount of linguistic capital as a precondition to participation and 'thereby making discursive assimilation a condition for participation in public debate' (Fraser 1990: 69). In the post-structuralist/constructivist view, language is integrally related to power and as such becomes the instrument of particular social interests that construct discourses, conventions and practices, while embedding language and communication in hegemony.

Judging by the advertisements placed on the station, there is the assumption that listeners have a fairly high degree of economic capital; the key, as Bourdieu (1986) argues, to access other forms of capital such as social capital. The high number of general knowledge related competitions on the station create the notion of a hyper-intelligent listening public, in possession of the requisite amounts of cultural capital (i.e. formal education) to participate. Moreover, callers frequently express admiration for the talk-show hosts' skills or abilities, even during serious talk shows. Fiske (1992) argues that this type of fandom provides social prestige and self-esteem, which is associated with cultural capital. Through admiration of a host who is in possession of the desired level of cultural capital, perhaps reflected through their linguistic capital or intellectual abilities, the listener assumes a degree of homogeneity with the host, even if it is at a spatial distance.

While Bourdieu uses economics and class as the major dimensions of social capital, gender and race could be added as further axes of discrimination. While women are not excluded or prevented from participating, they seldom call in to the station to join political deliberation and discussions, though they do participate on the lighter entertainment shows. Similarly, contributions from callers are not always racially diverse, and so the listenership may be diverse, but the callers are not. With some exceptions, they appear to be primarily middle class, and possibly quite similar to talk-radio listeners in the United States who have been found to be 'better educated, more affluent, slightly older, and more involved in the political process than others' (Wilcox 1995: 3). The Cape Talk audience is certainly in possession of a certain degree of economic, social and cultural capital;

and the elitist competitions discussed earlier form one way of self-differentiation of the talk-radio listener, who is purposely positioned as being more intelligent and therefore more capable of meaningful discussion than the average citizen. If cultural capital is manifest through fashion and lifestyle, this is constantly reinforced when presenters talk about subjects ranging from the mundane, like wearing denim tops with denim jeans as an inexcusable faux pas, or the more socially responsible notion of being environmentally aware on a daily 'Green Tip' segment (both on the Redi Direko show).

While Bourdieu uses economics and class as the major dimensions of social capital, in the South African context race could be added as another axis of discrimination. In fact, callers sometimes express a certain degree of rudimentary biological determinism, the most notable example being when popular presenter Mike Wills left the station in 2006 to make way for black breakfast host Aden Thomas. Informal discussions (summarized in a listener blog[1]) reflect a perception of Cape Talk as a 'white' station, together with concerns that black presenters are used merely to fill quotas, but do not intellectually measure up to their white counterparts. In many ways the introduction of Aden Thomas was most likely a deliberate strategy to increase the diversity of the listenership (personal communication, Aden Thomas, April 2007), but this kind of ethnocentrism or racism is sometimes reflected in on-air discussions on language and pronunciation. 'It's wonderful how you people [presumably black South Africans] learn the [English] language so beautifully and thoroughly' (paraphrased comment from a caller to the Redi Direko show, 4 July 2008). Bourdieu (1986) identifies this as linguistic capital, the acquisition of which is a clear prerequisite for membership of the talk-radio community. In South Africa, modes of pronunciation or accent are markers of race, class and social mobility. If, as Bourdieu (1991) argues, linguistic exchanges are also relations of symbolic power in which power relations are actualized, the Cape Talk broadcasts may involve a certain level of inevitable intimidation, which is exerted on those who are predisposed by virtue of their habitus to feel it; or those who are aware of the implications of status and power within the symbolic exchange, perhaps one reason that the callers to the station are largely homogenous in terms of class and race.

Hage (in Dolby 2000) has gone so far as to theorize whiteness itself as a form of cultural capital, or a 'shifting set of cultural practices' (Dolby 2000: 49), with the nation as a circular field with whiteness at the centre and others at the periphery. If years of racialized privilege and access to education and other forms of cultural capital during apartheid created the power and status of this embodied cultural capital, then certainly Hage's analysis is relevant in our consideration of Cape Talk radio. One might argue that white citizens (especially males) have been groomed for participation in the public sphere; and even from a simplistic political economy perspective which argues that race has made way for class as the new marker of division, the majority of wealthy citizens are white. As Bourdieu (1986) argues, economic capital is at the root of all other forms of capital, even if only in making affordable the time required for the acquisition of other forms of capital.

To extend the argument even further, if Cape Talk values cultural capital in the form of a certain level of intellectual ability usually acquired through years of schooling, then the racial composition of its listenership is not surprising. What is surprising, however, is the limited interaction of the number of black South Africans who do have access to this economic and cultural capital, at least on the air. One possibility has already been outlined above, and another might be that black listeners do tune in, but simply do not call in to the station, perhaps because they have other outlets for discussion or complaints, and do not need to use radio for confession. Regardless of class, it is possible that traditional African cultures do not sanction the public display or discussion of private problems. While African discussions of politics are common, these tend to take place in private spaces, with many cultures suffering the earlier mentioned legacy of a political culture under which speaking out on a political matter could result in victimization by the state.

Another possibility is that the symbolic power wielded by current callers (via their linguistic capital) acts as an explicit strategy of domination, meaning that black listeners don't call in as frequently simply because they do not feel part of the imagined community of the radio station. This may represent a problematic in that race and culture are obviously not synonymous, but the limited participation of middle-class black callers is an interesting issue to be flagged for further research.

It is also important to realize that the talk-radio audience is probably not uniform, and the Cape Talk listener is probably a complex composite more reflective of the diversity of the city. Clearly the notion of a singular, monolithic audience is outdated (Livingstone and Lunt 1994), as it is revealed to be a 'self-deceiving ideological assumption made in the interest of potting discrete publics through the blender of national unity' (Coleman 1998: 8). Either way, a clear racial distinction emerges, the significance of which is yet to be explored. The introduction of black presenters is a clear station strategy to increase the diversity of the listeners (or perhaps just the callers), perhaps spurred by what seems to be a fairly constant trend, at least within the period of this analysis – shows hosted by black presenters such as Redi Direko or Eric Miyeni seem to elicit more calls from black listeners. But if the public sphere is, as Habermas argued, an imagined community where everyone has the ability for equal participation, then Cape Talk satisfies at least the first criterion, even if not everyone participates.

Another broad theme that emerges in consideration of the talk-radio audience is fan culture, which might be more usually associated with television stars or the commercial radio disc jockey. Cape Talk listeners often pay personal compliments to programme hosts, many of these often reflecting on their personal appearances, particularly if they also appear at public events or in other media, e.g. Redi Direko also appears on the satellite channel e.tv's 24-hour news.

Despite the possible and partial exclusion of marginal groups, commercial talk radio in South Africa appears to be promoting an unspoken national project, and an attempt to create a nationalistically democratic public sphere. This is further evidenced by how it constantly blurs the boundaries between mass medium and civil society. Listeners often call in to the station with complaints about service delivery, e.g. street lights not being repaired quickly enough in certain areas, open manholes on public roads, traffic disturbances not dealt with quickly enough, etc., and the station then follows up and reports directly back to the audience. In many instances, listeners do not call service providers (e.g. the police or the city council) directly with their grievances, but instead call the radio station hosts who mediate on their behalf. This demonstrates the symbolic power of commercial talk radio, defined by Thompson as 'the capacity to intervene in the course of events, to influence the actions of others and indeed to create events, by means of the production and transmission of symbolic forms' (1995: 17).

Conclusions

In some ways one might consider talk on radio as forming part of everyday conversation. However, this chapter has argued that the mediated nature of conversations and debates on the radio move it towards a special mode of interaction. In particular, the move beyond the mere expression of personal opinions towards a collective deliberation of salient issues of public concern reveals commercial talk radio as a democratic public sphere. The symbolic power of talk radio becomes apparent as various degrees of economic and social capital are required for participation, and talk radio sometimes becomes the vehicle for the transmission of the discourse that produces social hegemony.

But talk radio becomes an institutionalized arena of discursive public interaction. It is one of few national and neutral spaces where controversial issues can be discussed even if consensus is not always reached. This may result in what Fraser refers to as a 'weak public', 'publics whose deliberative practice consists exclusively in opinion-formation and does not also encompass decision-making' (1990: 75).

But it is a public nonetheless that arises out of the on-air deliberations of the radio station. Diverse individuals come together for rare moments of interaction as we see how 'public spheres are not only arenas for the formation of discursive opinion; in addition, they are arenas for the formation and enactment of social identities' (Fraser 1990: 68). Thus while commercial talk radio is largely a form of popular media, it has great potential to play a strong role in promoting democracy and development through the creation of a democratic and mediated public sphere.

Note

1 www.timokeller.net/2006/06/30/mike-wills-leaves-cape-talk-567/.

References

Armstrong, C. and Rubin, A. (1989) 'Talk radio as interpersonal communication', *Journal of Communication* 39(2): 84–94.

Benson, R. and Neveu, E. (eds) (2005) *Bourdieu and the journalistic field*. Cambridge: Polity Press.

Berger, G. (2005) Remarks at Mondi Shanduka Newspaper Journalism Awards. Sandton, Johannesburg. Online, available at: http://journ.ru.ac.za/staff/guy/fulltext/mondi05.doc (last accessed 15 October 2009).

Bizcommunity (2002) 'Punt geselsradio licenses revoke'. Online, available at: www.biz-community.com/Article/196/59/813.html (last accessed 16 November 2009).

Boateng, K. (2003) 'Radio in Accra: a confluence of national and traditional representations', paper presented at the annual meeting of the International Communication Association, Marriott Hotel, San Diego, 27 May 2003. Online, available at: www.allacademic.com/meta/p112119_index.html (last accessed 15 October 2009).

Bolce, L. *et al.* (1996) 'Dial in democracy: talk radio and the 1994 election', *Political Science Quarterly* 111(3): 457–81.

Bosch, T. (2008) 'Radio as confession: religious community radio in South Africa', *Journal of Theology in Southern Africa* 131: 84–99.

Bourdieu, P. (1986) 'The forms of capital', in J.E. Richardson (ed.) *Handbook of theory of research for the sociology of education*, translated by Richard Nice. New York: Greenwood Press, pp. 241–58.

Bourdieu, P. (1991) *Language and symbolic power*. Cambridge: Polity Press.

Bourgault, L. (1995) *Mass media in sub-Saharan Africa*. Bloomington: Indiana University Press.

Capella, J., Turow, J. and Jamieson, K. (1996) 'Call-in political talk radio: background, content, audiences and portrayal in mainstream media', a report published by the Annenberg Policy Centre, University of Pennsylvania. Online, available at: www.annenbergpublicpolicycenter.org/Downloads/Political_Communication/Political_Talk_Radio/1996_03_political_talk_radio_rpt.PDF (last accessed 15 October 2009).

Coleman, S. (1998) 'BBC Radio Ulster's talkback phone-in: public feedback in a divided public space', *The Public* 5(2): 7–19.

Dahlgren, P. (1995) *Television and the public sphere: citizenship, democracy and the media*. London: Sage.

Dahlgren, P. (2002) 'In search of the talkative public: media, deliberative democracy and civic culture', *The Public* 9(3): 5–26.

De Beer, A. (1998) *Mass media towards the millennium: the South African handbook of mass communication*. Pretoria: J.L. van Schaik Publishers.

Dolby, N. (2000) 'Race, national, state: multiculturalism in Australia', *Arena Magazine* 45: 48–51.

Ellis, S. (1989) 'Tuning in to pavement radio', *African Affairs* 88(352): 321–30.

Fiske, J. (1992) 'The cultural economy of fandom', in Lisa Lewis (ed.) *The adoring audience: fan culture and popular media*. London: Routledge, pp. 30–49.

Fraser, N. (1990) 'Rethinking the public sphere: a contribution to the critique of actually existing democracy', *Social Text* 25(26): 56–80.

Froneman, J. (2006) 'In search of the Daily Sun's recipe for success', *Communitas* 11.

Habermas, J. (1989) *The structural transformation of the public sphere*, translated by Thomas Burger and Frederick Lawrence. Cambridge, MA: MIT Press.

Hofstetter, C. and Gianos, C. (1997) 'Political talk radio: actions speak louder than words', *Journal of Broadcasting and Electronic Media* 41(4): 501–15.

Hyden, G. and Okigbo, C. (2002) 'The media and the two waves of democracy', in Goran Hyden, Michael Leslie and Folu F. Ogundimu (eds) *Media and democracy in Africa*. New Brunswick and London: Transaction Publishers, pp. 29–53.

Independent Online (2001) 'Punt hopes to keep on talking'. Online, available at: www.iol.co.za/index.php?set_id=1&click_id=13&art_id=qw979068423949U153 (last accessed 16 November 2009).

Kellner, D. (2000) 'Habermas, the public sphere and democracy: a critical intervention'. Online, available at: www.gseis.ucla.edu/faculty/kellner/papers/habermas.htm (last accessed 15 October 2009).

Kellow, C. and Steeves, H. (1998) 'The role of radio in the Rwandan genocide', *Journal of Communication* 48(3): 107–28.

Kim, J. (2009) 'The significance of non-purposive dialogue for democracy in the age of interpersonal media', paper presented at the annual meeting of the International Communication Association, New York. Online, available at: www.allacademic.com/meta/p14110_index.html (last accessed 15 October 2009).

Lee, F. (2002) 'Radio phone-in talk shows as politically significant infotainment in Hong Kong', *The Harvard International Journal of Press/Politics* 7(4): 57–79.

Livingstone, S. and Lunt, P. (1994) *Talk on television: audience participation and public debate*. London: Routledge.

Mail and Guardian (2009) 'Africa calling: cellphone usage sees record rise', *Mail and Guardian* online, 23 October 2009. Online, available at: www.mg.co.za/article/2009-10-23-africa-calling-cellphone-usage-sees-record-rise (last accessed 10 November 2009).

News 24 (2009) 'Refugee decision "shocking"', News24.com. Online, available at: www.news24.com/Content/SouthAfrica/News/1059/71b1696cef6542c4a6f1278e126ad02e/02-09-2009-08-02/Refugee_decision_shocking (last accessed 10 November 2009).

Nisbet, E. (2009) 'Mass media use and democratic consolidation: the case of Mali', paper presented at the annual meeting of the International Communication Association, Sheraton New York, New York City. Online, available at: www.allacademic.com/meta/p14252_index.html (last accessed 15 October 2009).

Nyamnjoh, F. (2005) *Africa's media: democracy and the politics of belonging*. London and New York: Zed Books.

Rubin, A.M. and Step, M.M. (2000) 'Impact of motivation, attraction, and parasocial interaction on talk radio listening', *Journal of Broadcasting & Electronic Media* 44: 635–54.

Sandbrook, R. (1996) 'Transitions without consolidation: democratization in six African cases', *Third World Quarterly* 17(1): 69–87.

Schudson, M. (1978) 'The ideal of conversation in the study of mass media', *Communication Research* 5(3): 320–9.

Wasserman, H. (2008) 'Attack of the killer newspapers! The "tabloid revolution" and the future of newspapers in South Africa', *Journalism Studies* 9(5): 786–97.

Wilcox, T. (1995) 'Squawk talk: call-in talk shows and American culture'. Online, available at: web.mit.edu/comm-forum/forums/squawktalk.html (last accessed 17 August 2009).

Part II

Popular media, politics and power

Engaging with democracy and development

Chapter 6

Popular music as journalism in Africa

Issues and contexts

Winston Mano

Introduction

Popular musicians in Africa do not just entertain their listeners. They also provide 'news' through music (Mano 2007). African musicians inform and mobilize citizens on topical issues, including health, economic and political hot topics that are usually neglected or insufficiently covered in many fledgling democracies in modern Africa. The launch of '8 Goals for Africa' on 8 June 2010, three days before the start of the World Cup tournament in South Africa, for example, show how the continent's musicians help raise awareness in the fight against hunger and poverty in Africa. The song, copyrighted to the United Nations, was meant to popularize the Millennium Development Goals (MDGs) and was distributed free of charge and made available for download at www.8goalsforafrica.org.

African musicians' journalistic role, as will also be shown by the discussion below on the life and work of Fela Anikulapo-Kuti, the late popular Nigerian musician (Olaniyan 2004), is especially noticeable in times of crises, and where the political space is narrowing. Popular music's meanings benefit from the fact that much of Africa has cultures with strong pre-capitalist peasant 'residues' that still have a strong belief in the *word* (orality), which they rightly associate with the power to change reality (Gecau 1995; Vambe 2001).

Musical texts authored in upheavals and crises are invested with meanings that offer an important avenue to mediate key political topics that their public yearn for but cannot find in the mainstream media. The existence of this news-through-music element is crucial, because across Africa some mainstream journalists have suffered intimidation, arrest and have even been killed by undemocratic forces. The poor working conditions make African journalists vulnerable and less expressive. The journalist wanting to keep his job survives by self-censorship, which is unhealthy for most of the continent's young democracies. Politically sensitive topics are left out and people's democratic choices, and public dialogue in general, become narrow and unconstructive. At such times, musicians sometimes fill in this void by subtly communicating matters of the day, providing information and news that helps keep alive the hopes of African citizens. Music with political characteristics can produce messages that foreground matters of the day in ways similar to journalism. The popularity of this music among African publics is unsurprising because it is authored within a context shared by musician and listener. Apart from entertainment, musicians on the continent have been able to effectively articulate political and non-political matters in ways that reflect and affect the concerns, fears, losses and aspirations of many Africans. Both in colonial and postcolonial Africa, there are plenty of examples of musicians who have been vocal on everyday issues. This chapter reviews issues and contexts where African popular musicians have managed to take to the streets social justice issues relevant to democracy and development.

Popular music as journalism

Music plays an important role in most societies. Musicians on the continent are often at the centre of social, economic and political struggles (see, for instance, Mano 2007; Lwanda 2009; Schumann 2009). Both traditional and contemporary musicians 'are continually expected to use their privileged access to a platform to engage in socio-political issues – even to reveal wrong doing if necessary' (Allen 2004: 1). To understand the role of music and other media on the continent, it is important to understand the relationship between mass communication media, interpersonal media and 'small media'. Modern African music has to a large extent built on traditional musical practices and formats, which were based on themes and styles familiar to their audiences. This is the reason why others question 'the assumption that the media are always experienced as exogenous to Africa – whether as imperialist aggression or as opportunities to enter new imaginative realms'   (Barber 2009: 4). African music draws its strength from live homegrown popular traditions in Africa, which have now been popularized and enhanced by new technologies. The existing popular music genres in modern Africa are constitutive of evolving local and foreign influences, especially waltzes, foxtrots, ragtimes, Charlestons and cha-cha-cha that galvanized local musicians and were catalysts in the generation of new popular musical genres – highlife, juju, Congolese jazz, marabi – now in use across the continent (Barber 2009). These have been brought in to produce 'music that has social and political features, among many other things' (Thorsen 2004: 11).

Popular music arises in response to adverse conditions within societies. It is a way of questioning and challenging that which does not make political sense to the people. It is one of the options available to the oppressed to question and fight oppressive power-holders who ignore popular will. Popular music 'asks questions and creates conditions' for change in society (Fabian 1978: 19). Popular music is alternative communication (Atton 2002) that helps galvanize forces at the margins to recognize and do something about their unfavourable conditions of life. 'Popular' has a dual reference here: first it points to how the music is consumed by many in large numbers, hence the popularity of the artists in society; second, and more crucially, how it engages with concerns that matter for those below. It speaks against the 'power blocs' on behalf of those without political power (Sparks 1992: 24). Writing about the role of popular music in Kenyan society, Kimani Gecau (1995: 558–9) observes that in situations of inequality and domination:

> audiences composed of ordinary people 'read' and interrogate messages. They scrutinise the message and 'contextualise' it by analysing, accepting, modifying or rejecting according to what experience, infused with handed down acquired knowledge, has taught them. This continuously critical interrogation of what comes through the official 'national' and international media establishes a tension between the dominant 'top-down' vertical communication and the tendency among the subordinate groups toward the 'horizontalisation' of the flow of information and opinion.

Similarly, Fiske suggests that this opposition derives from the way in which public communication (news) has traditionally been produced and dominated by a 'power-bloc', whereas popularity is the product of the 'people' (Fiske 1992: 46). Popular culture arises, therefore, from below, and differs from and challenges that which the power-bloc wishes the generality of the people to have (Mano 2007).

In Africa, popular music serves as journalism especially in situations where public communication is constrained. It expresses majority will when all other avenues seem to be closed. It is journalism in the way it sets the agenda or what to talk about among the people and in the way the music texts meet with and generate new forms of knowledge among members of the audience. This awareness not only induces 'sceptical laughter' but it opens up to 'pleasures of disbelief, the pleasures of not being taken in' (Fiske 1992: 49). Popular culture makes the oppressed more aware of their circumstances and that is precisely the reason why those with power campaign to have it banned. Although music texts are polysemic, it is important to note that the sense listeners make of popular music depends at least in part in what musicians have actually 'written in the first place' (Sparks 1992: 37).

Popular music plays a journalistic role by communicating messages and meanings, often of a political nature, that are not fully represented in the mainstream mass media. Popular music texts, just like journalism texts, project multifaceted versions of realities that are meaningful to their audiences. The main ways of achieving this are through ridicule, or what Gecau (1995: 558) calls a language of 'fables and innuendo'. Such language is familiar to ordinary people in the streets because the musicians live with them, often in deprived conditions (Mano 2007). As with other popular cultural forms, such as street theatre, street radio and cartoons, popular music is talked about in the streets, homes, in the mass media, online and in other ordinary contexts outside the elite spaces. Popular songs are what they play in the crowded salons, barber shops, people's markets, shopping centres, farming areas, rural shopping centres, informal industries and in crowded people-carriers that daily ferry the poor in Durban, Johannesburg, Lusaka,

Nairobi, Accra, Lagos and Kampala, to mention but a few cities. This does not mean that music meanings are obvious. Nor does it mean that music meanings are the preserve of the musicians. However, 'of importance specifically to songs (and this may be more or less true of other forms of communication) is that the source may be less important than whether the songs are (or not) to the people's way of thinking and feeling' (Gecau 1995: 559). Meanings in both journalism and popular music are socially structured, articulated and circulated in cultural settings (Dahlgren 1992: 5). Popular culture, including popular music, is the way that the 'lower classes employ and deploy symbolic forms to define their changing relations with each other and with centres of power; to negotiate or contest, consciously or unconsciously, dominant meanings and to create alternative "meanings"' (Gecau 1995: 560). Music is a key part of African popular culture.

It is worth remembering that 'A record is ... not a piece of pure art; it is the result of countless choices and compromises, using criteria that mix the aesthetic, the political and the economic' (Street 1986: 6). However, 'what distinguishes a popular song within the context of a nation and its culture is neither its artistic aspect nor its historical origin, but the way in which it conceives the world and life, in contrast to official society' (Gramsci 1985: 195). Like popular journalism, popular music is complicated both in its production and consumption. The record is a result of many factors and not necessarily what the popular musicians wish. This is the reason why what musicians claim to be the focus of their music is often contradicted by what the listeners say about it. Musicians cannot control or tell their listeners how to listen to their music.

As will be seen from the examples provided below, popular music periodically extends the political public sphere and it is also the case that popular topics and discussions in the public sphere are covered by popular music. For example, at the height of the Zimbabwe Crisis from 2000–4, *The Daily News*, which was the only 'independent' daily newspaper in Zimbabwe, devoted 'five pages everyday to the arts, music being the main subject' (Sibanda 2004: 8). This was because popular music was at that time communicating issues in ways similar to journalism and filling the information void caused by censorship.

African popular music as journalism: cases and contexts

Popular African musicians have acted as barometers during times of political crisis. When life is good, it is known that African musicians sing the praises of those in power, but when life is not so good for ordinary people, the very same musicians voice people's concerns to the establishment. This is not just a contemporary development because music has been 'one of the key ways in which political crises — from colonialism and the demands for independence, to political assassinations, to ethnic cleansing and so on — have been documented' (Nyairo and Ogude 2005: 237). The continent is full of examples where musicians have bravely and explicitly challenged power-holders when they neglect the people.

By far the most prominent example is how popular music played a key role in the struggle to end apartheid in South Africa. Michael Drewett (2003) discusses how many musicians, prior to the 1994 South African democratic elections, opposed racial discrimination through their music and support of the anti-apartheid political cause. The South African apartheid government attempted to minimize the impact of musicians by preventing controversial music from being heard and by repressing the musicians themselves. However, 'no matter what their message was, censored musicians developed strategies to reach as wide an audience as possible. In doing so, they articulated and transformed culture, opening spaces in which particular forms of artistic expression emerged' (Drewett 2003: 153). It is this agency in African music and musicians that I take to be the 'journalistic' function of popular music. Music increases communicative options where the public sphere is constrained.

In majority-ruled South Africa, popular music is also playing an important role in society. For example, popular music was part of the 2006 succession battle by members of the ruling elite. Jacob Zuma had been removed from the vice presidency by Thabo Mbeki after being charged with corruption and rape. However, for most ordinary South Africans, this move was politically motivated and strategically meant to undermine Zuma's chance of assuming the presidency after Mbeki's tenure. There were also fears that the incumbent wanted to change the constitution and stand for an extra term, which was illegal under the South African constitution. There were also complaints that judges and the mainstream media were biased and were being influenced by the incumbent. Many ordinary South Africans, including the vocal Congress of Trade Unions of South Africa (COSATU) took to the streets in support of Zuma. Websites were set up in support of Zuma and also a march to the Durban offices of the South African Broadcasting Corporation (SABC), the national broadcaster. Eventually, the group Ingane Zoma produced 'Msholozi', a popular pro-Zuma song. The sales of the record soared to 50,000 in weeks (BBC 2006). The SABC's response was to exclude the title track from the airwaves, arguing that it would incite the public and undermine the principles of public service broadcasting (BBC 2006). The main message in the song was to call for Zuma to be made the next leader of South Africa and for all charges against him to be dropped. The SABC excluded (not banned) it from their playlist but, owing to South Africa's diverse media, other radio stations played it. A spokesperson of Ingane denied that the song was political: 'Our song is not political, we just write about what is happening and what people think' (BBC 2006). The song was sold to pro-Zuma crowds who gathered outside the courts. The song captured the public mood in favour of a candidate who was being ostracized by the system. All charges against Zuma were later dropped and in 2008 'popular will' saw him elected as a successor to Mbeki, both as head of the South African government and of the ruling African National Congress (ANC). Here it is clear that Ingane, the three Zulu women behind the song, interacted with the audience and, following Gecau (1995: 559), one can say they based their 'perception and practice on a collective memory, values, beliefs and identity rooted in past history and experiences'. In this case, it was what they knew about Zuma and his ANC history as background to understanding the reasons Zuma was now being 'unfairly treated' by the establishment. The song became a mobilizer in a situation where there were organized and non-organized groups on the ground, able to read and share the meanings of the popular song. To a large extent the song was a public communicative text, which helped challenge officialdom.

Kenyan popular music has similarly provided news and information to ordinary people, particularly at times of political crisis. This dates back to the pre-colonial era but was more noticeable during the Mau Mau uprisings against the British and more recently in the challenge that led to the downfall of the undemocratic rule of Arap Moi. Opposition to Moi included musical mockery of his unbecoming authority and borrowed power. Gecau argues that 'collective memory and ways of perceiving changing social life and relations of power have primarily, but not solely, been developed and communicated through popular song, which has remained an important means of expression and representation since the pre-colonial past' (1995: 560). Song and dance forms in Kenya have come from Asia, Europe, America and from within Africa itself and were later used to communicate anti-colonial sentiments in local languages. An example of the musicians discussed by Gecau is Daudi Kabaka, who by the late 1960s was singing about 'ways of the city', covering the meaning of urbanization in social relations which made him produce music that depicted Nairobi as a 'place of hardship and harsh ways of survival for the poor, who are waylaid by crooks at every turn' (Gecau 1995: 571). The music was not all about negatives, however. In the 1960s, when the postcolonial government was new, it was celebrated by the musicians for being led by black people. The celebration of changes to social life and identity was reflected in music that focused on love, beauty and femininity. The Kenyan context shows that popular music, and popular culture on the whole, is not only produced by the subordinate groups but also borrows from the dominant culture through adaptation and incorporation.

In Nigeria, Fela Anikulapo-Kuti (born in 1938 – died on 2 August 1997) remains a leading example of a 'political musician' whose music articulated sentiments from those at the bottom of his society. Fela's popular music style developed over time. As in the Kenyan context discussed above, popular music in Nigeria benefited from local and international styles and forms. Fela was not always the people's musician but his style evolved from experience. During the Biafran War in 1967–70, Fela even produced 'Viva Nigeria' which was supportive of the government's call to 'keep Nigeria one' and to achieve national unity in the face of a secessionist war. Back then, Fela was reportedly desperate for recognition and, therefore, financial assistance from the Nigerian government (Olaniyani 2004: 27). Fela later regretted having produced the song, claiming that he was actually on the side of Biafra: 'Anyway, at that time ... I wasn't politically minded at all ... What did I know?' (Fela cited in Olaniyan 2004: 29). His role as a political musician started in the United States, after meeting Sandra

Isidore and other activists, and reading books on black political consciousness. On his return to his native Nigeria in March 1970, Fela had a difficult start and it was not until 1971 that he met real success with the hit 'jeun Ko Ku', about gluttony, which sold 200,000 copies within six weeks of its release. From 1970 to 1975 Fela sang about the quotidian urban experiences of the lower- and under-classes. In 'Je' Nwi Temi' ('Don't Gag Me'), released in 1973, he expressed his determination to fight for social justice. His first anti–state composition was 'Alagbon' – about lack of human rights and his determination to speak out, which was released in 1974. Another hit, 'Upside Down', was a political afrobeat recorded with Sandra Isidore, his American activist friend. Fela sang against corruption and misrule. Olaniyan also describes how Fela, at his Africa Shrine, his base, often launched 'running commentaries on local and global headlines as they affected Nigerians in particular and withering satires against public institutions or officials whose actions or policies he considered untoward' (2004: 51). This is a very clear example of popular music as advocacy journalism or news through music. Fela was using his music to politically educate the poor about their rights. This practice drew the anger of the establishment so much that he was constantly attacked by government-uniformed forces and on one such occasion:

> a half-literate officer of the Nigerian army and lorry-loads of fully armed soldiers swooped down on the venue of a performance by Fela, their AK–47s fully drawn. Amid the commotion by the startled audience, the officer bellowed out to his soldiers, 'Arrest the music!' At first unsure what next to do, the soldiers were later to oblige by carting away Fela's instruments to stop him from performing.
>
> (Olaniyan 2004: 1)

In his three decades as a people's musician Fela met with many violent visitations from the army and police. Another example is from 18 February 1977, which resulted in the invasion and ransacking of his residence by nearly 1,000 soldiers:

> Residents – including Fela – and guests were brutally beaten and bayoneted and some, including Fela's ailing mother, received serious injuries. The government ordered a commission of enquiry into the cruelty by its agents and it unsurprisingly concluded that 'unknown soldiers' had committed the acts.
>
> (Olaniyan 2004: 1)

Fela responded by producing an album called *Unknown Soldier*. Fela's afrobeat music articulated the concerns of the subordinate classes who were neglected under Nigerian dictatorships. He championed their cause and was not afraid to speak up.

In Cameroon, popular music has also been a formidable weapon against injustices committed by those in power. Nyamnjoh and Fokwang (2005) analysed the political role of popular music in Cameroon and discovered that the most popular songs criticized the economic crisis, denounced social injustices and the slow pace of development, and condemned the government's inaction and complicity in the face of corruption. For example, popular music criticized the president's inaction in the face of schools without teachers, hospitals without drugs, and harvests not fetching money. Musicians, through their music, urged the state to stop the rot.

In 2008, Cameroonian musicians Lapiro de Mbanga and Joe La Conscience were arrested for criticizing constitutional amendments which allowed the incumbent, President Paul Biya, an unlimited term of office and immunity when he left power (Freemuse 2009). They were accused of inciting demonstrations against the amendments, even though all the other rioters had been officially pardoned. Mbanga and La Conscience were arrested on 9 April and 20 March 2008, soon after the deadly riots. In his 'Constipated Constitution', Mbanga, whose real name is Pierre Roger Lambo Sandjo – warns President Paul Biya about the dangers the constitutional amendments could create. Mbanga, both a popular musician and a member of the opposition party, the Social Democratic Front (SDF), explicitly sings about corruption in the Cameroonian government. The government used the riots as an opportunity to charge him. He was accused of instigating the violent demonstrations by the youths in the Mbanga area during the February 2008 demonstrations. La Conscience was similarly jailed for organizing resistance against the constitutional amendments. The Cameroon authorities arrested him for a sit-in at the US embassy in Yaoundé. In both cases, these musicians are prominent examples of how popular music journalists sing about, and even organize the masses against, oppression in society. The Constitutional Amendment Bill was adopted on 10 April 2008. It allows an unlimited number of presidential mandates and guarantees the president immunity for any acts committed by him during his time in office. At the time of writing, Mbanga had just lost his appeal, which meant that he was likely to serve the full three-year jail term (Freemuse 2009).

During Zimbabwe's first and second wars of liberation, *Chimurenga* music or rebel music emerged as a formidable force for mobilizing and documenting the people's struggles against colonial domination. Popular music was part of the struggles for social justice. However, Zimbabwean music in the twenty-first century only came into being after the country's majority independence in 1980. Scannell observes that popular Zimbabwean music only came into being, and was promoted on the radio, in the newly established political and social circumstances after the achievement of democratic rule. 'Thus, the moment of independence, which gave birth to the African nation-state of Zimbabwe, freed up already-existing musical life and practices so that they achieved public recognition and legitimacy as "Zimbabwean music"' (Scannell 2001: 21). However, for Fred Zindi (1997), Zimbabwean music is a blend of local, regional and international music forms that has evolved into a unique popular music: 'Most of Zimbabwe's music expresses the social life and hardships experienced by the people. It talks about the Liberation War, the social conditions of ordinary people, poverty and injustices in society. At times it talks about romance' (Zindi 1997: 5).

This is not unlike what we found in the Nigerian and Kenyan contexts, where many influences have shaped what can be described as national music. Zimbabwean popular music is integral to Zimbabwean everyday life and history. The performance and consumption of popular music in Zimbabwe not only predates colonialism but also is linked to Zimbabwean historical and cultural processes (Kwaramba 1997; Pongweni 1982; Vambe 2004; Zindi 1985).

Popular music as journalism is evident in the meanings and consumption of popular music in the country. Popular music in Zimbabwe sells relatively well, for example Aleck Macheso's *Zvakanaka Zvakadaro* selling more than 100,000 copies in barely a week after its release in 2001. This is a huge achievement in a country where the sale of 5,000 units is considered a hit.[1] Previously Macheso's *Simbaradzo* sold 118,000 copies within two months of its release (*The Daily News*, 19 December 2001). The reason why popular music sells easily in Zimbabwe is because it addresses issues that are rarely included in the mainstream media. For instance, Andy Brown and his group The Storm, produced a song entitled 'A Nation of Thieves' that was 'excluded' on state media playlists. Brown was quoted as saying: 'They [ruling party politicians] have been stealing all the money, so as a result the whole infrastructure is beginning to fall apart' (interviewed by Farai Sevenzo, BBC website 2005). Lovemore Majaivana, the late Bulawayo-based musician, has similarly attacked the government in Harare for discriminating against the Ndebele people in Matabeleland. Using ridicule, innuendo and sarcasm, Majaivana's music carried sentiments of disbelief and anger at the high levels of corruption by elites in Harare, Mashonaland. Albert Nyathi, the dub poet from Bulawayo, has similarly sung against political repression in Zimbabwe and Africa as a whole. He has sung about the vices of apartheid, including the killing of the South African activist Chris Hani. His music asks questions and makes the listener think about answers that help improve their awareness of their conditions.

The late Simon Chimbetu, of Zimbabwean *Sungura*[2] music fame, was a good example of the popular as meaning not the elites but ordinary people. He was a veteran of Zimbabwe's liberation war who sang about ordinary everyday issues that have resonance for the poor working class and unemployed Zimbabweans. Chimbetu's top selling songs were about ordinary everyday issues like death, love, relationships and the economic struggles of ordinary Zimbabweans. One of his songs famously appealed for a stay in the price of basic commodities, especially bread and maize. Most of Chimbetu's music chronicles the everyday problems of people in Zimbabwe. In the post-2000 crisis many groups used music to communicate political messages but also issues ranging from love, romance, politics, religion, corruption, unemployment, disease and AIDS to moral decadence (such as prostitution). The inclusion of such popular causes increases the popularity of the music. To illustrate my point I will focus on three of the top selling and most controversial artists in the post-independence era.

As will be discussed below, Leonard Zhakata and Oliver Mtukudzi are leading Zimbabwean musicians who have described themselves as 'fighters', 'journalists' and generally as people who 'fight' on behalf of the voiceless. They are all popular with rural and urban music listeners, especially those from the underclasses. Some of the music they have produced has been excluded from the airwaves by the national broadcaster because it is deemed too critical of the government of Robert Mugabe.

Leonard Zhakata also describes his work in ways similar to journalism and sees his music as a 'recording of events as they occur' (Zhakata 2005). Zhakata's music focuses on social realities. By having music that records 'events as they occur' in Zimbabwe, Zhakata serves as a journalist and his music is a form of journalism. It is a sharp satire on the social, economic and political aspects of Zimbabwean everyday life. From love to politics, Zhakata provides popular lyrics with which many Zimbabweans seem to identify. Most of his albums have sold over 100,000 copies. His 1994 debut album, *Maruva Enyika* (Flowers of the World), sold 120,000 copies. In 1996, he released *Nzombe Huru* (The Bull), which sold 130,000 copies. *Vagoni Vebasa* (The Professional Workers) in 1997, *Ndingaitesei* (What Can I Do) in 1998, *Pakuyambuka* (On Crossing) in 1999, and in 2000, an album called *Original Rhythms of Africa*, all sold over 100,000 units. In 2002 he released the top selling *Mubikira* (The Silent Victim) (Mano 2007).

In the early 1990s, at the height of Zimbabwe's acute economic problems resulting from the government's bad implementation of the World Bank and International Monetary Fund (IMF)'s Economic Structural Adjustment Programme of 1991, Zhakata led other musicians in communicating the economic plight faced by ordinary people. His hit song, 'Mugove' ('Pay') subtly pointed out that workers' incomes had been eroded by inflation and could barely sustain them (Vambe 2000: 9). More importantly the song, sung in a local language, Shona, focused attention on the workers, and on their view of social realities: 'Vakuruwe indepeiwo kamuka kekuti ndiyambira vaye vakawana mukana we kukwira pamusoro … zvichema zveavo vari pasi' ['elders give me an opportunity to warn and remind those who chanced their way to the top … about the grievances from those below']. The songs carried the lament of workers who were 'being worn out' by the rich and powerful. If the singer were the one in power they would share the rewards of independence with all. Needless to say it has remained an all-time hit in Zimbabwe because of persistent economic problems.

Another of Zhakata's controversial albums, called *Hodho* (Shotgun), produced in 2003, was initially excluded from the playlists of the national broadcaster. Following an outcry, a ZBC official explained that the album would continue to be played by ZBC, adding that: 'We will promote everything that seeks to build the nation, but the national broadcaster will not give room to music that seeks to denigrate and undermine our national identity and aspirations' (*The Daily News*, 26 June 2003). The album was reportedly doing well in sales and the charts. The Zimbabwe Music Corporation, who manage Zhakata's music, claimed that *Hodho* was their 'top selling album at the moment' (*The Daily News*, 26 June 2003). The

Zimbabwean government was not happy with Zhakata's music. It came as no surprise when, in early 2004, Zhakata was quizzed for more than 30 minutes by Harare police over the appearance of his song, 'Ngoma Yenharo' ('Sounds of Resistanc') on an album compiled by a shadowy pressure group called Zvakwana (Enough) (Mano 2007).

The singer has lamented the fact that his music is now forced underground because of the openly political interpretations of his texts. The official media denounces him as a 'spent force' and restricts airplay of his music. Although independent media have tried to give him fair coverage, the banning of *The Daily News* in 2003 meant that even this was now limited. Zhakata's position is that:

> I would continue to record music in the format I have been [using] all along. I will not change my style. I will not tone down my lyrics and will continue to sing about issues affecting the people of Zimbabwe.
>
> (Zhakata 2005: 12)

Zhakata approaches music as journalism to 'cover' the problems of ordinary Zimbabweans as 'they occur' in society.

Oliver Mtukudzi has actually described himself as a 'journalist'. Mtukudzi clearly stated that his 'lyrics have always been drawn from people and their day-to-day issues and not just their difficulties but also their humour, happiness, irony' (Oliver Mtukudzi, interviewed by Michael 2003). Mtukudzi clearly states what I believe is the journalistic function of his music in troubled Zimbabwe. With over 47 music albums to his name, Mtukudzi ranks among the most known Zimbabwean musicians. His career started in the colonial era, in the late 1970s, when he was part of the resistance to minority white rule in Rhodesia, with liberation war rallying cry songs such as 'Ndipeiwo Zano' ('Please Advise Me') released in 1978. By far the most controversial track by Mtukudzi is 'Wasakara' ('Accept That You are Worn Out'), from his 2001 album *Bvuma* (Tolerance). 'Wasakara' urges old people to retire:

Wasakara (You are Worn Out)
Bvuma
Bvuma bvuma iwe
Bvuma bvuma chete
Bvuma wasakara,
Bvuma wawinyana
Kuchembera, Chiiko kuchembera...
[Accept
Just accept it
You must accept it
Accept you are now worn out
Accept you are now wrinkled
What does getting old mean to you?]

The song criticizes those who do not accept the fact that they are old and need to retire from certain 'jobs'. To most Zimbabweans this was an indirect reference to the country's then 81-year-old president, Robert Mugabe, who had been the country's ruler since 1980. In 2000, Mugabe had disappointed other presidential hopefuls by refusing to step down. The succession debate was virtually absent in government, in the ruling party meetings and in the official news media. Mtukudzi's song, through metaphor and innuendo, successfully focused people's attention on the issue. In their discussion of popular music and politics in Cameroon, Nyamnjoh and Fokwang (2005: 263) similarly discovered that for musicians 'any criticism had to be very subtle and deep in metaphor to avoid the risk of repression for the artist concerned'. Mtukudzi sang against violence when there was widespread violence, particularly against farm workers, urban workers, white farmers and opposition party supporters. Needless to say he was obviously inspired by conditions in Zimbabwean society. As observed by Farai Sevenzo (BBC website 2005) conditions that prompted people to write songs during the time of the independence war in the 1960s and 1970s were almost identical to the conditions that people were finding themselves in, especially from 1999 to 2005.

Concluding reflections

This chapter has discussed the rise of the trajectory of music as journalism in Africa. The examples discussed clearly show that popular music provided much needed 'news' when it mattered most in the history of African societies. The musicians skilfully bring together social experiences as they experience a changing life. The African popular singer as a journalist has a big responsibility:

> The singer is assumed to be a part of the 'community' who is, just as the nationalist leader, privileged by his audience to act as a 'teacher' and to *mediate* local, national, regional and global experiences and interpretations. This sense of responsibility imposes a need for an appropriate idiom and discourse, thus the songs are not simply the arbitrary individualistic expressions of the singer, nor are they the unmediated reflections of an external reality. The singer at once wants to 'name' and 'defamiliarise' the known and common while at the same time transmitting what is considered new and informative.
>
> (Gecau 1995: 573)

The singer, without much education, asks questions and invites the listeners to help answer them. In this process it is important to think of this role played by popular musicians as a form of journalism.

The performance and consumption of popular music can also be seen as involving the contestation of power in African society, defined as 'that which enables a social actor to influence asymmetrically the decisions of other social actor(s) in ways that favour the empowered actor's will, interests, and values' (Castells 2009: 10). Research needs to focus not only on the flow of power in the practices and texts but also on the actions of the audiences who consume popular music. Studies can also be done on the responses that they receive. The Zimbabwean government, for instance, has actually produced its own popular music in order to counter-communicate on issues about land, imperialism and national unity. All this clearly shows that the trajectory of popular music as journalism has many issues and angles that need to be further examined.

Notes

1 Zimbabwe has a population of 11.6 million people and a relatively small music market. Sales are affected by the prevalence of piracy.
2 *Sungura* refers to a genre of local popular music, with Shona lyrics accompanied by a distinctive Zimbabwean dance.

References

Allen, L. (2004) 'Music and Politics in Africa', *Social Dynamics* 30(2): 1–15.

Atton, C. (2002) *Alternative Media*. London: Sage.

Barber, K. (2009) 'Orality, the Media and New Popular Cultures in Africa', in Kimani Njogu and John Middleton (eds) *Media and Identity in Africa*. Edinburgh: Edinburgh University Press for the International African Institute.

BBC (2006) 'Soaring Sales of ProZuma Song'. Online, available at: http://news.bbc.co.uk/1/hi/world/africa/4720532.stm (last accessed 10 August 2009).

Castells, M. (2009) *Communication Power*. Oxford and New York: Oxford University Press.

Dahlgren, P. (1992) *Journalism and Popular Culture*. London, Newbury Park and New Delhi: Sage Publications.

Drewett, M. (2003) 'Music in the Struggle to End Apartheid', in Martin Cloonan and R. Garofalo (eds) *Policing Pop*. Philadelphia: Temple University Press, pp. 153–65.

Fabian, J. (1978) 'Popular Culture in Africa', *Africa* 48(4): 18–28.

Fiske, J. (1992) 'Popularity and the Politics of Information', in P. Dahlgren (ed.) *Journalism and Popular Culture*. London, Newbury Park and New Delhi: Sage Publications.

Freemuse (2009) 'Cameroon: Imprisoned for Singing "Constipated Constitution"', 24 April 2008. Online, available at: www.freemuse.org/sw26753.asp (last accessed 2 December 2009).

Gecau, K. (1995) 'Popular Song and Social Change in Kenya', *Media, Culture & Society* 17: 557–75.

Gramsci, A. (1985) *Selections from Cultural Writings*. London: Lawrence and Wishart.

Kwaramba, D.A. (1997) *Popular Music and Society*. IMK-Report No. 24, University of Oslo.

Lwanda, J. (2009) 'Music Advocacy, the Media and the Malawi Political Public Sphere', *Journal of African Media Studies* 1(1): 135–54.

Mano, W. (2007) 'Popular Music as Journalism in Zimbabwe', *Journalism Studies* 8(1): 61–78.

Mbiriyamveka, J. (2002) 'My Job isn't about Politics', *The Herald*, 21 September 2002.

Michael, T.M. (2003) 'Song of Zimbabwe: Interview with Oliver Mtukudzi', 4 April 2003. Online, available at: www.worldpress.org (last accessed 3 November 2005).

Nyairo, J. and Ogude, J. (2005) 'Popular Music, Popular Politics: Unbwogable and the Idioms of Freedom in Kenyan Popular Music', *African Affairs* 104(415): 225–49.

Nyamnjoh, F.B. and Fokwang, J. (2005) 'Entertaining Repression: Music and Politics in Postcolonial Cameroon', *African Affairs* 104(415): 251–74.

Olaniyan, T. (2004) *Arrest the Music! Fela and His Rebel Art and Politics*. Bloomington: Indiana University Press.

Pongweni, A. (1982) *Songs that won the Liberation War*. Harare: College Press.

Scannell, P. (2001) 'Music, Radio and the Record Business in Zimbabwe Today', *Popular Music* 20(1): 13–27.

Schumann, Anne (2009) 'Popular Music and Political Change in Cote d'Ivoire: the Divergent Dynamics of Zouglou and Reggae', *Journal of African Media Studies* 1(1): 117–33.

Sevenzo, F. (2005) 'Zimbabwe Turbulent Times', BBC Rhythms of the Continent. Online, available at: www.bbc.co.uk/worldservice/africa/features/rhythms/Zimbabwe. shtml (last accessed 3 November 2005).

Sibanda, M. (2004) 'Complete Control: Music and Propaganda in Zimbabwe', Freedom of Music Expression, 23 September 2004. Online, available at: www.freemuse.org/sw7086.asp.

Sparks, C. (1992) 'Popular Journalism: Theories and Practice', in P. Dahlgren (ed.) *Journalism and Popular Culture*. London, Newbury Park and New Delhi: Sage Publications.

Street, J. (1986) *Rebel Rock: The Politics of Popular Music*. Oxford and New York: Basil Blackwell.

Thorsen, S.M. (2004) *Sounds of Change: Social and Political Features of Music in Africa*. Sida Studies No. 12.

Vambe, M.T. (2000) 'Popular Songs and Social Realities in Post-Independence Zimbabwe', *African Studies Review* 43(2): 73–86.

Vambe, M.T. (ed.) (2001) *Orality and Cultural Identities in Zimbabwe*. Gweru: Mambo Press.

Vambe, M.T. (2004) 'Thomas Mapfumo's "Toi Toi" in Context: Popular Music as Narrative Discourse', *African Identities* 2(1): 89–112.

Zhakata, L. (2005) 'Personal Experience', *Six Articles on Music Censorship in Zimbabwe*, paper prepared in connection with a seminar on Music and Censorship in Zimbabwe held on 28 April 2005 at Mannenberg Jazz Club, Harare. Online, available at: www. freemuse.org/sw11081.asp (last accessed 1 November 2005).

Zindi, F. (1985) *Roots Rocking in Zimbabwe*. Gweru: Mambo Press.

Zindi, F. (1997) *Music YeZimbabwe*. Harare: Fred Zindi and Morgan Chirumiko.

Chapter 7

Street news

The role of posters in democratic participation in Ghana

Audrey Gadzekpo

Introduction

In the last two decades there has been substantial scholarship generated on the contributory role of the African media in facilitating (and in some cases undermining) democracy within the context of a growing culture of media pluralism and freedom on the continent (Karikari 1994; Bourgault 1995; Chalk 1999; Hyden 2003; Nyamjoh 2005; Gadzekpo 2008). Much of this scholarly enquiry has been limited to traditional mass media (print, radio, television) and, increasingly, new media platforms (the Internet, social media, blogging, mobile telephony, etc.). And while research in the area of popular culture has produced a corpus of material on music, oral and popular literature that illuminates the diverse ways in which Africans assert their speech rights (Barber 1997; Fabian 1997; Mbembe 1997; Newell 2001; Ogude and Nyairo 2007), not enough attention has been paid to visual media forms such as posters.

Two publications from South Africa – *Images of Defiance: South African Resistance Posters of the 1980s* by the South African History Archive (1991) and *African Posters: A Catalogue of the Poster Collection in Basler Afrika* by Miescher and Henrichsen (2004) – demonstrate that despite the dearth of research on the subject, a rich harvest of posters has been produced on the continent. The range of posters contained in both books reflects the diverse roles posters play in African society – from political education and mobilization during undemocratic rule, to galvanizing people during elections and raising awareness on health and education issues. The salience of posters in Africa is illustrated also in Fourie's (2008) study on political campaign posters in South African elections. Fourie (2008) argues that beyond image building such posters set the agenda for political party campaigns and in so doing contribute to the formation of democratic value.

Compared to Western countries, posters have had a short trajectory in Africa. The earliest poster in the collection of about 900 posters contained in the Miescher and Henrichsen catalogue is a Namibian election poster from the 1930s. According to Deirdre Donnelly (2005) the peak of poster production in Africa was in the 1970s and 1980s when solidarity movements were encouraged to produce posters to educate and mobilize people in response to apartheid-era violence.

Although posters are not new to Ghana, re-democratization in 1993 and media liberalization resulting from stronger constitutional provisions on media freedoms, have encouraged a distinct genre of street posters that are fast becoming an integral part of the market-based news media system. Sold alongside newspapers on the streets and at vendor booths, these posters are distinguishable as a popular idiom for expressing titillating newsworthy events rather than for achieving propagandist, political, educational, informational or publicity goals.

This genre of poster, perhaps best described as a street news poster, has provided an avenue for illiterate and semi-literate people to actively engage in the public sphere by widening the range of modes through which 'news' is delivered. The street news poster, therefore, can be perceived as a growing part of the 'complex of distinctive expressions of life experiences' (Fabian 1997: 18), which provides opportunities for ordinary people to participate in national conversations at a transformative moment in the history of Ghana. This role is especially important in a developing nation context where low literacy rates place strictures on people's ability to read and understand newspapers.

Research on Ghanaian posters is still in its rudimentary stages and there are gaps in the knowledge on their history, variety and function. It is not the ambition of this chapter to address all of these gaps. Rather, the aim is to begin an exploration into poster production in Ghana by scrutinizing a particular genre of poster that has recently emerged and which coincides with Ghana's successful transition to democracy. Specifically, therefore, this chapter focuses on the original and creative processes behind the production, distribution and consumption of street news posters in Ghana and interrogates how they serve as alternate vehicles for orienting public awareness on topical issues in Ghana's growing democratic culture.

As research on popular culture has shown, alternative modes of communication can be a powerful means of bypassing official or hegemonic sources of information and in engaging the marginalized segments of society (Mbembe 1997). Indeed, Donnelly (2005) observes that Nelson Mandela, in the foreword to the original edition of *Images of Defiance: South African Resistance Posters of the 1980s*, remarked on the influence of posters in raising political consciousness among some of the young prisoners he met while in prison.

Poster culture in Ghana

In an attempt to understand the sites of agency underpinning the fast-growing market of street news posters semi-structured interviews with vendors and customers were conducted in July 2008. Since the aim was mainly exploratory, a total of 12 street vendors and 15 customers found selling and buying posters on the street were interviewed, as well as two sales attendants who worked at a poster storage warehouse we visited. Most were willing to share information but did not want to be identified, and most spoke in the local dialect of Twi.

It is difficult to come across literature specific to posters in Ghana, thus impossible to pinpoint precisely when posters first made their appearance in the country. However, it is fair to observe that public education and health posters, as well as posters advertising commercial goods and services similar to those chronicled by Miescher and Henrichsen (2004), have been in existence for some time. A typical example of a commercial service poster commonly found in Ghana is one that features new fashions or hairstyles. They are often displayed in dressmaker shops or in hair salons and provide models of dress or hair style from which customers can choose. Also, political party campaign posters, for example those produced by the Convention People's Party (CPP), have been around since the advent of multi-party politics in the 1950s. The street news poster, which is the subject of this chapter, on the other hand, is a more recent phenomenon and thus of greater interest.

These news-purveying posters started appearing on the streets in the 1990s when, as part of Ghana's re-democratization effort, licensing restrictions on print media were lifted and a proliferation of newspapers – tabloid, quality and entertainment – emerged. A typical street poster comprises a collage of six to eight related visual images selected from news events that are already in the public domain. These might include local news like accidents or funerals, or international news events. The images on the posters are usually photographic images culled from newspapers and Internet news sites, although sometimes images come in the form of cartoons. Increasingly, original pictures from paid photographers or agents who follow up on 'breaking news events' (e.g. accident sites, or funerals of celebrities) are being used in place of, or to augment, those that appear in the news. Most posters come with calendars underneath the images as an added attraction.

The narrative of the street poster is driven by images complemented by short headlines, captions, bullets of information, one-liners and speech balloons in simple, sometimes pidgin English ('so wicked', 'so far so good', *'wetin you go fit do for Ghana'*,[1] 'seeing is believing', etc.). In Ghana, pidgin English is the linguistic register most associated with people who, because of poor education or illiteracy, have difficulty speaking standard English. The frequent use of that register in poster texts suggests they are targeted not at an elite class of consumers but as a subordinate social group.

Classification of street posters

Barthes' often-quoted observation that 'what is noted is by definition notable' (Allan 2000: 62) applies to how the rules of newsworthiness, which guide news selection by professional journalists, are also (albeit informally) applied to street posters. Poster salience is of course variable and dependent on the impact and timeliness of the news items. As one vendor explained, 'it is what people are already talking about and what people want to see and read'. Thus posters of President John Evans Atta Mills as the winner of the Ghanaian elections of December 2008 hit the streets immediately after these closely run elections were declared in his favour. And with almost equal alacrity, posters depicting a victorious Barack

Obama and his family were available the day after he was pronounced winner of the US presidential elections (see Figure 7.1).

The selection process is guided by other news values as well – prominence, conflict, novelty, bizarre/oddity, relevance, simplification, personalization, cultural specificity, negativity, etc.

Street news posters can be grouped into five heuristic classifications:

- celebrity posters
- event-driven posters
- political posters
- bizarre and sensational posters
- instructional and educational posters.

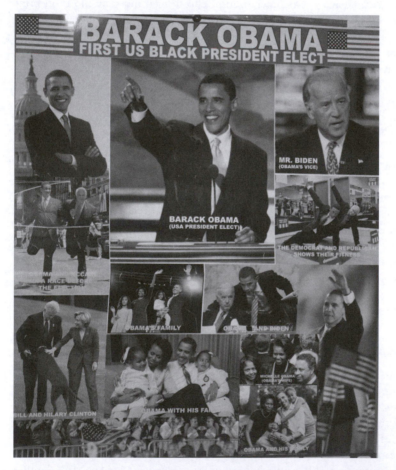

Figure 7.1 Images associated with Barack Obama's victory in the 2008 US presidential elections, including representations of vice-presidential candidate Joe Biden and Obama's family.

Celebrity posters: prominence is an important news value and as such celebrities – entertainers, sports figures, flamboyant religious leaders – attract the attention of poster-makers. Popular entertainers are often the subject of posters not when they create something new, but when they are involved in tragedy. Thus, pictures of the sites of car wrecks of local celebrities or their funerals are a popular subject of posters. As elsewhere, international and local musical stars, especially hip hop and rap artists, are favourite subjects as well. Also, an expanding pentecostalite public culture (Meyer 2004), coupled with the growing influence of mega charismatic churches, has produced celebrity church leaders who are featured on posters. Their celebrity status as televangelists, radio preachers and religious pundits, gives them visibility beyond their churches, and thus their lifestyles provide titillating news for newspaper tabloids and street gossip. Posters of religious celebrities usually depict images of flamboyant pastors juxtaposed with pictures of their spectacular church buildings and large congregations.

Another very popular type of celebrity poster is that of sporting heroes. The Cup of African Nations (CAN) football tournament, which was hosted in Ghana in 2008, for example, provided the impetus for a slew of posters featuring the lifestyles of players of the national football team, the Black Stars, who were in the public limelight during that period (see Figure 7.2).

There were posters featuring football stars and their mothers, or their luxury homes and cars, or with their children or girlfriends. One poster provided a collage of images of the popular Black Stars player, Junior Agogo, including a photograph of his mother and one he took with his famous uncle, the perennially newsworthy Jerry John Rawlings, Ghana's former president. More recently, posters featuring scenes from the historic win of the country's under-20 football team, the Black Satellites, in the FIFA U-20 World Cup Championship, were hot-sellers on the street (see Figure 7.3).

Aside from valorizing sports celebrities, sporting events produce another kind of poster, usually about the winning teams of major local matches. Posters generated on the premier league club, Asante Kotoko, the winners of the 2008 One Touch League Cup, are examples. One such poster features pictures of the players, the cup they had won, and scenes from some of their matches. Sometimes the sporting events poster goes international by highlighting football clubs such as Manchester United, Chelsea and Liverpool, who have a strong local support base. These posters are timed to coincide with international league matches, which are keenly followed by Ghanaian fans.

Event-driven posters: these posters provide a window on the outside world as well as on local happenings. Street news posters have captured particularly salient international news events such as 9/11 terrorist acts in New York, associated images of Osama Bin Laden, the capture of Saddam Hussein following the invasion of Iraq (see Figure 7.4), the 29 March 2006 eclipse of the sun and the US presidential race between John McCain and Barack Obama.

Political posters: these posters, which touch on the political public sphere and political issues, are not political party campaign posters. They are big sellers and generate a lot of interest, especially during election periods. In addition to portraying the actual outcomes of the elections, they capture a range of scenes from the processes leading up to the actual polls, for example the presidential primaries of major political parties, the choosing of running mates, and huge political rallies. Some political posters provide background and history to national politics. There are posters of candidates and their wives, and posters of former presidents with captions indicating their tenure of office. During the 2008 elections there were posters depicting the excesses of the 1979 military coup d'états which first brought Rawlings to power. Although he was not a candidate in those elections, as the founder of the ruling National Democratic Congress (NDC) government which was vying for power, Rawlings was considered central to the political campaign.

Political posters sometimes come in the form of satire, functioning much like cartoons in newspapers and magazines by providing a configuration of striking,

Figure 7.2 Representations of the lifestyles of Ghana's international football stars.

humourous images that poke fun at political personalities or events. After Ghana's 2008 elections, which produced a change in administration, posters depicted images satirizing the losing incumbent party – the New Patriotic Party (NPP). One such poster was made up of eight different frames of images, including an image representing the two final presidential candidates as boxers in a boxing ring accompanied by speech balloons. The losing candidate – the NPP's Nana Addo Dankwa Akuffo-Addo – was depicted as saying, 'I am finish [*sic*]', while the smiling winning candidate – Atta Mills of the (NDC) – was shown repeating the same words but in the local Ga dialect, 'Agbena'. Another frame showed members of the NDC, including the president, vice-president and ex-president Rawlings pushing an elephant, the NPP symbol, into a bush.[2]

Figure 7.3 The 2009 Under–20 World Cup winners, the Black Satellites, captured in various celebratory shots.

Bizarre or sensational posters: events that defy our sense of normalcy satisfy the news criterion of the bizarre or sensational. Just as this news value is a staple of tabloid journalism, news of bizarre or sensational happenings are a favourite poster subject. Posters in this genre are generated out of news stories of gruesome or ritualistic murders, acts of cannibalism, occult practices, the activities of fake pastors, graphic pictures of persons engaged in unnatural sexual practices, etc. An example is a poster on Dr Ram Beckley, an occultist and a medical practitioner, who was accused of kidnapping a teenage girl for ritual purposes in April 2002. Beckley's photograph was juxtaposed with several images of human skulls and bones, and an image of a uniformed school girl. Speech balloons had Beckley, nicknamed in the poster as Ghana Bin Laden, proclaiming, 'You are lucky'.

Instructional or educational posters: this type of poster is often produced to coincide with public education campaigns that are of particular salience to ordinary people. Posters featuring new ministers after a change in administration or a cabinet reshuffle fall into this category. Another example is the posters that were produced when the local currency (the cedi) was re-denominated in 2007 as part of measures taken to address currency depreciation. Following the exercise 10,000 old cedis were converted to one Ghana cedi.

The political economy of posters

Street news posters have sprouted a parallel market alongside mainstream newspapers and are part of the distribution chain of printed material sold at news vendor booths and on the streets of urban centres in Ghana. The locus of production is Accra, Ghana's capital city, but they are distributed and sold to vendors in other big cities such as Kumasi, Takoradi and Koforidua. The production of street posters is controlled by a small group of businessmen who own printing presses and who supplement printing orders with poster production. There are about four main producers of posters in Accra, but two – Justdan Press and Krobia Services – are the market leaders. The nerve centre of distribution is a warehouse in the heart of Accra, which stores thousands of posters cutting across all the different classifications described above.

Poster making and selling is a lucrative business for those involved in the chain of this cultural production – producers, distributors and vendors. They yield 100 per cent profit for vendors who buy them from distributors at 50 Ghana pesewas (less than 50 US cents) and sell them for one Ghana cedi (less than a US dollar). However, the poster cycle is short. Typically, an edition of a news poster does not last beyond a month within which period a vendor can sell an average of 2,000 posters. Understandably, the peak period of sales occurs soon after 'the news' hits the street. Vendors usually sell between 50 and 100 posters a day initially, before slowing down to between ten and 15 towards the end of the news poster cycle.

Street posters cater largely to under-educated readers but are not exclusionary of the educated. Vendors report that bank workers and secretaries, for example, are among their regular clientele. Still, as one vendor explained, many people cannot read and understand a newspaper but they can make a lot of meaning from looking at the pictures. This alternate form of news production can therefore be perceived as a response to the material conditions of many ordinary Ghanaians who do not possess enough literacy or money to efficiently engage with mainstream newspapers. The adult literacy rate in Ghana is only 65 per cent (United Nations Development Programme [UNDP] Human Development Report 2009) yet newspapers are predominantly in English. Also newspapers cost on average one Ghana cedi each, the same price of a poster, which can be read wherever they are displayed rather than individually purchased.

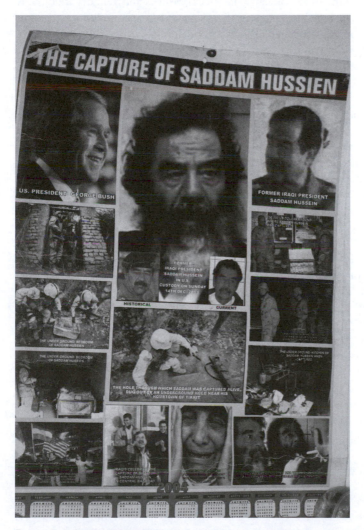

Figure 7.4 Saddam Hussein's capture and associated images, including a smiling George Bush.

Another advantage of the poster lies in the fact that the gate-keeping process that determines what is fit to print is less hierarchical than in traditional media and involves complex interactions at the level of poster production and consumption. Socially-relevant posters require an eye for news events already in the public domain and an ear to the ground for conversation topics among potential audiences. This is because the decision on what makes the final cut from the plethora of news stories available to poster-makers is often predicated on feedback from vendors, agents and customers. It is they who constantly suggest to the producers what news subjects they would like to see amplified in posters. Thus, although poster story ideas come from conventional media, readers and vendors are directly implicated in their material production; their suggestions and feedback determining new editions or the continued production of already existing posters. Vendors play an especially powerful role as the arbiters of the field of discourse contained in posters, because to a large extent it is their views as middlemen that guide the production process and the ultimate product.

Poster appeal cuts across gender and age, but vendors have observed that consumption is gendered: young women buy more posters than men because, as posited by a vendor, 'women are inquisitive'; they want sensational news and like to buy posters just to generate discussion at home or amongst their friends. Still, according to some vendors, men buy posters also and generally prefer sports and politically-related ones, while young adult males tend to patronize posters of musicians because they like to emulate their way of dressing.

Included in the diverse indeterminate poster clientele are also visitors from the rural areas that are underserved by newspapers and who take street news posters back as evidence of news from the big cities. Ghanaians living abroad and non-Ghanaian West Africans also make up the poster clientele, the latter group preferring mostly fashion and global news-related posters to take back to countries such as Nigeria, Togo and Benin. Street posters make novel souvenirs for friends and family living abroad. At one news vendor's we came across a woman who bought a variety of news posters to send to her daughter in the United States because she wanted her to 'keep abreast of what was happening at home'.

Like other mass media, street posters satisfy a range of other cognitive, diversionary and social utility needs in those who patronize them. In terms of cognition they are used for reference, didactic and informational purposes. Readers can derive a sense of what is happening around them from street posters as well as important information that helps them function. A reader explained she buys posters of celebrities in order 'to know them better'. Some readers claim posters help to generate conversation and deepen discourse on salient issues, thus owners of drinking bars, beauty salons and barber shops are regular customers for posters.

The referential role of posters is best exemplified by those that were produced around the time when the Ghanaian currency was re-denominated in 2007. Poster-makers targeted re-denomination posters at traders, particularly market women, who needed help converting the old currency into the new. The posters matched visual images of the old currency with the corresponding value of the new currency making it much easier for people to convert between old and new currencies.

Fiske (1998: 513) has observed that popular culture that works in the interests of 'the subordinate is often a provoker of fantasy'. This assertion finds support in the gratification some poster readers claim to get from posters depicting the luxurious lifestyles of sporting heroes such Chelsea midfielder Michael Essien and Black Star captain Stephen Appiah. Such posters do not only encourage fantasy, they are motivational and aspirational. A vendor explained that sometimes coaches buy the posters of sporting heroes to demonstrate to young aspiring footballers what they might also become if they perform well.

Making meaning

The complementarity between the street news poster and the mainstream media from which it draws its material would suggest that it is part of a larger hegemonic process of production that privileges dominant ideology. After all, the posters draw on the agenda set by mainstream news media. But, the street poster reflects an unstable ideology. The act of selectivity involved in determining what images make up a poster suggests that it is also capable of setting its own agenda that may or may not coincide with that of the media from which it emanates.

The street poster is essentially a cultural commodity through which meanings, pleasure and social identities are constantly being provoked and circulated (Fiske 1998). The consumption and production processes of posters reflect two main forms of social power as defined by Fiske (1998) in relation to cultural commodities: the power to construct meanings, pleasures and social identities, on the one hand; and the power to construct a socio-economic system, on the other. The first indicates semiotic power, which is exercised through representation, the second involves social power.

On the semiotic level there is little guarantee that the encoding of a story in mainstream media would be symmetrical to the encoding of the same narrative in visual form because the process of encoding and decoding news posters occurs at multiple levels. The first level involves mainstream media encoding an event in a newspaper or on an Internet site. At the second level, poster-makers decode that event, select visual representations from it and then encode it in the new form of a poster. The final stage in the process occurs when a poster reader decodes the poster and makes meaning from it. This stage provides opportunity for meaning making that could be within a hegemonic framework, or a negotiated or even oppositional framework.

The ability to provide alternatives to the hegemonic tendencies of traditional news media was conveyed through one of the hottest selling street posters in 2008. The poster was of the popular comedian Kofi Adu, aka Agya Koo, who was given a national award – the Order of the Volta – during a controversial national awards ceremony. Though he commands mass appeal, Agya Koo's award was derided by mainstream media as an example of the 'dumbing down' of prestigious national honours. The reason may have been based on social class: Agya Koo performs in the local dialect Twi, is a semi-educated concert party[3] comedian and an actor in Ghanaian movies. For the media establishment he is not the quintessential national award winner. For producers of street posters, however, Agya Koo is a 'living legend', as the title of one poster proclaimed, and consequently he was the only one of the 240 awardees who was immortalized in a poster (see example in Figure 7.5).

Like all posters street news posters provide visual communication in public spaces that allows them to participate in everyday experiences (Miescher and Henrichsen 2004). As visual forms they can 'transform otherwise complex and opaque social events and situations into quick and easily readable depictions that facilitate comprehension of the nature of social issues and events' (Abraham 2009: 119). And as Abraham contends of other visual forms such as cartoons, posters 'present society with visually palpable and hyper-ritualized depictions' that can 'reveal the essence and meaning of social events' (Abraham 2009). The visual and textual content of some street news posters exemplify the tendency towards hyper-ritualized depictions that, unlike factual news, embellish significantly in order to convey meaning beyond what the original news item may have intended. In this sense the poster can be read as a provider of infotainment rather than objective news events.

Importantly, street news posters are an ideal tool for framing social meanings and for reconstructing news and social issues. Framing is a particularly useful concept in our understandings of how the street poster creates meaning because it offers a way to describe the power of the poster as a communicative text. Analysing the news frames that provide meaning to the images in the poster can help illuminate the influence these visual texts are meant to have on readers because essentially framing involves selection and salience (Entman 2003). As Allan (2000: 64) contends, frames 'help to render an "infinity of noticeable details" into practicable repertoires' and in so doing 'facilitate the ordering of the world in conjunction with hierarchical rules of inclusion and exclusion'. Similar to the task of professional journalists, poster producers carefully select a news event, exclude or include elements that advance their message, frame the issues with the selected images for the poster and in so doing orient readers' understanding of the issue.

A degree of manipulation of photographic images takes place in the process of framing. This is especially evident with the cartoonized images that form part of the composition of posters. Many of these images are not sketches or drawings; they are essentially an amalgamation of spliced photographs of faces of newsmakers superimposed on other human forms engaged in actions that support the narrative of the poster. An Obama victory poster, for example, shows the US president crossing the finishing line in a physical race with his political opponent McCain. Clearly headshots of Obama and McCain had been superimposed on the image of two men racing each other. In a similar vein a popular street poster predicated on a bizarre news story of a man charged for bestiality showed the man in the act with a goat even though there is little evidence to show he had actually been photographed in flagrante delicto.

Poster-makers claim to discourage manipulated images and insist that 'the pictures we print are real'. But clearly, most poster news is both constructed and reconstructed. Because of their indexical nature it is easy to consider photographs

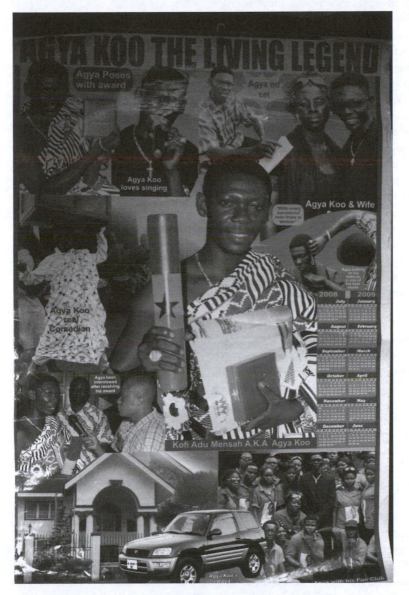

Figure 7.5 Popular comedian Agyaa Koo won the Ghanaian national award – the Order of the Volta – in 2008.

as 'real' or factual representations; a phenomenon aptly described by Barthes (2003: 296) as 'the myth of photographic naturalness'. Far from capturing what is, however, a poster rendition of news constructs a codified definition of what should count as the reality rather than a true reflection of reality. The images that make up the collage of photographs selected for a poster are thus re-presentations rather than representative of a social reality.

A degree of objectivity is often expected of news but posters make little attempt at objectivity. Often there is a highly ideological procedure embedded in the selection of the iconic news frames that constitute the poster. The poster depicting the excesses of the 1979 coup d'état, for example, reinforces the anti-coup, pro-democracy attitudes of a majority of Ghanaians that have been confirmed in opinion surveys (see, for example, Afrobarometer surveys on Ghana, Afrobarometer 2008). Also, the sub-texts of many political posters reflect a partisan slant directed at appealing to particular political interests and factions. A poster 're-presenting' the NPP presidential primary race, for example, has one of the front runners riding in a luxury car with his nickname – Alan Cash – on the number plate, while his contenders are riding in a *trotro*[4] with the inscription – 'poverty no be economics'. The preferred reading of such a poster is likely an endorsement for 'Alan Cash' and a denigration of the other candidates.

Posters also reinforce ongoing discourses occurring in society as well as providing social commentary. For example, the rhetoric of God-inspired peaceful elections that characterized the language of opinion leaders and phone-ins during national elections in 2004 is captured in a political poster that depicted angels praying for peaceful elections. Similarly, the framing of a 2004 election-inspired street poster featuring a boxing scene in which Kufuor knocks out Mills, while Rawlings lurks in the background, harkens back to discussions on the overbearing influence of Rawlings in NDC politics, which was a recurring theme in public conversations at the time.

Abraham (2009) argues that even though some scholars consider visual modes of communication deficient in performing analytical communication, they can rise above the purely descriptive level of communication fostered by iconic signs to allow for the kind of abstract analytical communication made possible by the symbolic. This analytic capacity enables them to offer deep social commentary about issues and not just a 'simple passing glance at society' (Abraham 2009: 155). Nowhere is the analytical function of posters more evident than in the satirical political posters. Like cartoons in a newspaper, this genre of posters functions as persuasive communication and appears deliberately constructed to mould or influence public opinion as well as to elicit 'a passing chuckle' (Abraham 2009).

A poster titled 'Who Bears the Flag' exemplifies this (see Figure 7.6). The poster can be read as social commentary on the NPP presidential primaries in which there were as many as 17 contenders. The crowded sense of the race is communicated by the cramming of more than 20 images into the poster. Most posters are composed of six to eight images. The poster successfully captures the drama of the event through cartoon-like manipulations of photographic images of

Figure 7.6 Headshots of contenders in the ruling New Patriotic Party's race for presidential candidate. Sitting President John Kufuor is portrayed as a headmaster with a whip in hand in two frames and as a traditional king in another frame.

the contenders. Thus, juxtaposed with headshots of the candidates are also cartoon images of them packed in a classroom listening to a lecture by their leader, President Kufuor. In the dominant frame, Kufuor, dressed like a colonial-era headmaster with cane in hand, appears to be directing the candidates, who are portrayed as marching schoolboys, at a parade. Another frame shows most of the candidates crammed in an old *trotro* emblazoned with a party banner. Driving a new Peugeot saloon car with the number plate 'Alan Cash' is a candidate widely rumoured to have been the favourite of the president. Reinforcing that street rumour is a scene showing the president in royal Asante regalia (the king maker). The poster is liberally sprinkled with one-liners ('Who will be the next successor?'), captions ('*We de go learn how to chop president*') and speech balloons from some of the candidates ('Haha ha, *money dey talk*').

On a purely denotative level the sensory impressions obtained from the different photographs of the contenders represented in that poster communicate efficiently the subject matter – the NPP presidential primaries. But the deliberately framed reconstructed photographic and cartoon images, combined with the linguistic text, go beyond the descriptive to provide a more interpretive, hyper-ritualized dimension where the knowledge on which the signs depend is heavily cultural and contextual.

Conclusions

This chapter has attempted to demonstrate how a new genre of posters that has emerged in Ghana is serving as an alternative medium for the reconstruction of news and an avenue for integrating subordinate groups into mainstream news-making. Described in this chapter as street news posters, this visual form of communication has significant implications for Ghanaian democracy because it provides a mode through which social and political messages can reach ordinary people in a form that excites and informs them.

Street news posters amplify ongoing discourses already in the public sphere and, in the case of those on politics especially, allow subordinate groups of people to become part of national conversations on governance in language that they can understand. They may have been culled from mainstream newspapers, but ultimately poster images are directed at serving the interest of the majority population of poorly literate Ghanaians who form the core of readership, rather than the educated elite towards whom newspapers are primarily targeted.

The visual simplistic mode in which poster messages are delivered may cause us to overlook them entirely or dismiss them as shallow forms of infotainment, but the range and regularity of posters predicated on issues of national salience suggests they play a role in how citizens are being engaged in the democratic process.

As has been shown, street news posters constitute novel ways in which information and news can be delivered, especially to those with limited ability to read and comprehend the contents of opinion-forming media such as newspapers. Their capacity to provide social commentary and satire as exemplified by some of the political posters is another demonstration of their ability to raise consciousness on salient issues and to assert speech rights by poking fun at 'the important' in society.

There are many dimensions to the street poster that are still under investigation, especially how readers decode and act on poster messages. This is only an exploratory study on an emerging genre of an old communicative form. And even though we are not yet certain about their impact, the ability of street news posters to orient social issues and to engage in social criticism positions them as items of democratic expression worthy of further attention and research.

Notes

1 Pidgin English for 'what can you do for Ghana'.
2 The notion of driving the elephant into the bush was often expressed by opponents of the New Patriotic Party (NPP) during the campaign and after elections when the party lost power.
3 Concert parties are a popular form of comic variety show targeted at ordinary Ghanaians rather than the elite.
4 A *trotro* is a cheap means of transportation for the masses, usually a minivan.

References

Abraham, L. (2009) 'Effectiveness of Cartoons as a Uniquely Visual Medium for Orienting Social Issues', *Journalism, Communication Monographs*, 11(2).
Afrobarometer (2008) 'Survey Results by Country: Ghana'. Online, available at: www.afrobarometer.org/ghana.htm (retrieved 3 January 2010).
Allan, S. (2000) *News Culture*, Buckingham and Philadelphia: Open University Press.
Aulich, J. and Sylvestrová, M. (1999) *Political Posters in Central and Eastern Europe, 1945–95: Signs of the Times*, Manchester: Manchester University Press.
Barber, K. (1997) 'Popular Reactions to the Petro-Naira', in Barber, K. (ed.), *Readings in African Popular Culture*, London: James Currey, and Bloomington: Indiana University Press, pp. 91–8.
Barthes, R. (2003) 'Rhetoric of the Image', in McQuail, D. (ed.), *McQuail's Reader in Mass Communication Theory*, London: Sage, pp. 289–97.
Bourgault, L.M. (1995) *Mass Media in Sub-Saharan Africa*, Bloomington: Indiana University Press.
Chalk, F. (1999) 'Hate Radio in Rwanda', in Adelman, H. and Suhrke, A. (eds), *The Path to Genocide: The Rwandan Crisis from Uganda to Zaire*, New York: Transaction, pp. 93–109.
Donnelly, D. (2005) 'African Posters', *Critical Arts*, 19(1 and 2): 187.
Entman, R. (2003) 'Framing: Towards Clarification of a Fractured Paradigm', in McQuail, D. (ed.), *McQuail's Reader in Mass Communication Theory*, London: Sage, pp. 390–7.
Fabian, J. (1997) 'Popular Culture in Africa: Findings & Conjectures', in Barber, K. (ed.), *Readings in African Popular Culture*, London: James Currey, and Bloomington: Indiana University Press, pp. 18–28.
Fiske, J. (1998) 'The Popular Economy', in Storey, J. (ed.), *Cultural Theory and Popular Culture: A Reader*, London and New York: Pearson Prentice Hall, pp. 504–21.

Fourie, L. (2008) 'South African Election Posters: Reflecting the Maturing of a Democracy?', *Communication*, 34(2): 222–37.

Gadzekpo, A. (2008) 'Guardians of Democracy: The Media', in Agyemang-Duah, B. (ed.), *Ghana: Governance in the Fourth Republic*, Accra: Ghana Center for Democratic Development, pp. 195–214.

Hyden, G. (ed.) (2003) *Media and Democracy in Africa*, Uppsala: NordiskaAfrikainstitutet.

Karikari, K. (ed.) (1994) *Independent Broadcasting in Ghana. Implications and Challenges*, Accra: Ghana Universities Press.

Mbembe, A. (1997) 'The "Thing" & its Doubles in Cameroonian Cartoons', in Barber, K. (ed.), *Readings in African Popular Culture*, London: James Currey, and Bloomington: Indiana University Press, pp. 151–63.

Meyer, B. (2004) '"Praise the Lord": Popular Cinema and Pentecostalite Style in Ghana's New Public Sphere', *American Ethnologist*, 31(1): 92–110.

Miescher, G. and Henrichsen, D. (2004) *African Posters: A Catalogue of the Poster Collection in Basler Afrika*, Switzerland: Basler Afrika Bibliographien.

Newell, S. (2001) *Readings in African Popular Fiction*, Oxford, London and Indiana: James Currey, International African Institute and Indiana University Press.

Nyamnjoh, F. (2005) *Africa's Media, Democracy and the Politics of Belonging*, London: Zed Books.

Ogude, J. and Nyairo, J. (eds) (2007) *Urban Legends, Colonial Myths: Popular Culture and Literature in East Africa*, Trenton: Africa World Press.

South African History Archive (1991) *Images of Defiance: South African Resistance Posters of the 1980s*, Johannesburg: STE Publishers.

United Nations Development Programme (UNDP) (2009) Human Development Report. Online, available at: http://hdr.undp.org/en/reports/global/hdr2009/ (retrieved 4 January 2010).

Chapter 8

'If you rattle a snake, be prepared to be bitten'[1]

Popular culture, politics and the Kenyan news media

George Ogola

Introduction

In March 2006, the Standard Media Group's (SMG) head office in Nairobi was raided by masked gunmen who shut down the Group's Kenya Television Network (KTN) studios, confiscated several computers from the newsroom, disabled printers and destroyed copies of the following day's newspapers. The government had previously expressed indignation at the Group's criticism of the Mwai Kibaki administration. A year earlier, with six bodyguards in tow, Kenya's first lady stormed the Nation Media Group's (NMG) newsroom just before midnight, assaulted a cameraman while bitterly complaining about the manner in which the Group's flagship title, the *Daily Nation*, had been covering her family. She was particularly riled by the newspaper's coverage of her disagreements with Abdoulaye Makhtar Diop, then outgoing Country Director of the Word Bank, who was her neighbour in an upmarket Nairobi suburb. When asked to explain the raid on the SMG, the Internal Security Minister defiantly warned critics thus: 'If you rattle a snake, be prepared to be bitten.'

Despite the re-introduction of political pluralism in Kenya in 1991 and a significant expansion of the democratic space, the political landscape remains unpredictable, often with very direct implications for media freedom. Indeed, not until January 2009 when the controversial Communications Amendment Act[2] was passed, did Kenya have a media law. The Kenyan constitution guarantees the freedom of the press but only by way of inference (KHRC 1997: 36). Section 79 (1) of the constitution expresses this freedom thus:

> Except with own consent, no person shall be hindered in the enjoyment of his freedom of expression, that is to say, freedom to hold opinions without interference, freedom to receive ideas and information without interference (whether the communication be to the public generally or to any person or class of persons) and freedom from interference with his correspondence.

But this freedom remains subject to other 'rights' and can be revoked in the 'interests of defence, public safety, public order, public morality or public health' which are contained under the Penal Code. These are vague constructs which can only be determined by the state and the courts. Laws such as The Law of Contempt, Incitement to Disobedience, Preservation of Public Security Act, The Law of Defamation, The Books and Newspapers Act, The Public Order Act and The Official Secrets Act, and others on libel and defamation have all been used by the state and politicians to frustrate the press. The Penal Code gives the government inordinate powers which it often uses to control the news media. This control has historically been exercised in two ways; through direct intimidation and or litigation. Several news organizations have previously been forced to shut down having been slapped with hefty fines after losing libel cases. In one such ruling, *The People*, a highly abrasive oppositional newspaper known in the late 1990s for its incisive investigative reporting, nearly collapsed when Nicholas Biwott, then a powerful Kanu politician, was awarded KSh 20 million in damages after a story adversely mentioning him was published by the newspaper.

Precisely because of this unpredictable environment, Kenyan journalists, alongside cultural and literary writers, have routinely created new ways to circumvent censorship and possible confrontation with the state. This chapter seeks to discuss the ways in which journalists and other cultural producers have kept the Kenyan news media porous. Broadly, the chapter explores the way popular culture interfaces with politics within Kenya's mainstream news media. The chapter focuses on a newspaper serial and stylized comedy programmes to interrogate this interface. The chapter first examines how popular culture provides the idioms but also the site within which contemporary social and political experiences are mediated. It then proceeds to historically situate the stylization of the Kenyan news media to accommodate appropriated forms of popular cultural productions such as popular fiction and comedy, which allow for the creation of both sites and 'moments of freedom' (Fabian 1998) and, within them, new political subjectivities. The chapter seeks to demonstrate how popular cultural forms and popular media articulate various forms of social and political consciousness and thus encourage participatory democracy.

Popular culture and the 'dramaturgy of power'

As an entry point to this discussion, this chapter finds significant John Street's thesis about the relationship between politics and popular culture, particularly his argument that this relationship is not just about popular culture 'reflecting' or 'causing' political thoughts. Street contends that popular culture does not make people think and act in particular ways. Yet this is not to suggest popular culture has no political agency. Street merely cautions that posing the debate in a manner that 'looks for cause and effect' may not be useful, arguing that popular culture 'neither manipulates nor mirrors us ... [w]e are not compelled to imitate it, any more than it has to imitate us. Instead, we live through and with it' (1997: 4).

A number of scholars of popular culture typically characterize the relationship between politics and popular culture in terms of 'cause and effect'. Achille Mbembe's ambivalence towards certain forms of popular culture such as the use of laughter as a means of ridiculing power being necessarily fatalistic is a case in point (1992a). This chapter does not discuss what popular culture 'causes'. Instead, it teases out how the political, more appropriately how the 'dramaturgy of power', is enacted in sites of popular cultural production. The chapter argues that the public face of power in Kenya is 'a performance', 'a drama', in essence, a 'dramaturgy of power'. This 'performance' is perhaps best captured by Mbembe's description of the postcolony as a 'simulacrum', which he defines as 'a regime of unreality' (1992a: 8). Within this performance, this chapter is particularly interested in how certain forms of cultural production, to paraphrase Street, shed their pleasures and become – through the uses to which they are put and through judgments made of them – forms of political practice (1997: 12). James Scott reminds us that popular culture makes public 'hidden transcripts', in which are written 'the anger and reciprocal aggression denied by the presence of domination' (1990: 19). Scott notes that the 'hidden transcripts' can be found in rumour, gossip, folktales, songs, rituals, codes and euphemism – a good part of the folk culture of subordinate groups (Scott 1990). Reflecting on the same argument, Street argues that such a culture 'becomes part of a political struggle to establish a particular view of the world, one which challenges the conventions of the dominant common sense' (1997: 12). But it is to be noted that the 'hidden transcripts' are not just statements of suppressed emotions; they are a kind of action. Indeed, as Scott reminds us, it is important to think of the 'hidden transcripts' as a 'condition of practical resistance rather than a substitute for it' (1990: 191). This chapter, however, concedes that not all popular culture can be treated as forms of political resistance. Although interested in oppositional practices within popular cultural forms as they are enacted in the news media, the chapter acknowledges this site as comprising multiple contradictory voices simultaneously occupied by both ruler and ruled.

Since independence, Kenya has had a turbulent political history, now the subject of a rich corpus of literature (see Atieno-Odhiambo 1987, 2002, 2004; Cheeseman and Branch 2008; Haugerud 1995; Throup and Hornsby 1998). This history reveals a predominantly anxious relationship between news media and the successive administrations.

At independence, the news media was co-opted into supporting Jomo Kenyatta's 'nation-building project', one invented by the government as unequivocal although part of the administration's regime-building strategy. Kenyatta argued that as a newly independent state, Kenya had various competing interests – ethnic, religious, political, racial – which, unless checked, would impede the country's development. By using state institutions and other instruments within the public and private sphere such as the media, Kenyatta ensured that opposition to his rule was delegitimized on the grounds that this was inconsistent with the needs of the young nation. Yet what Kenyatta created was a 'coercive political superstructure' (Hyden 2006) sustained through force but also through a regime of invented mythologies that constituted a very specific 'ideology of order' (Atieno-Odhiambo 1987). The media became a part of Kenyatta's political project, circulating and popularizing state mythologies under the guise of promoting national development.

When Daniel Moi ascended to power in a constitutional succession in 1978 following Kenyatta's death, political repression continued, but so did the regime-building process. In consolidating his power, Moi made Kenya a one-party state by law and then systematically cracked down on the opposition especially after an attempted coup to topple him in 1982. The 1980s were therefore a highly repressive epoch in Kenya's history. Meanwhile, the government attempted to monopolize various public sites for popular expression, particularly the news media. The ruling party Kanu bought Hillary Ng'weno's *Nairobi Times* and renamed it *Kenya Times* to act as its mouthpiece. Kanu functionaries also took control of the *East African Standard*, the second largest newspaper, while Moi also managed to exercise influence through his business relations with the owners of the two main newspaper groups, His Highness the Aga Khan and Lonrho Africa's Roland 'Tiny' Rowland.[3]

The government also clamped down on the alternative media. Indeed, between 1988 and 1990, more than 20 publications were proscribed including *Beyond Magazine, Financial Review, Nairobi Law Monthly* and *Development Agenda* (Mbeke and Mshindi 2008).[4] Yet even as the crackdown on the opposition continued, there was a thriving oppositional counter-culture that found space within the mainstream news media. It is instructive to note that the Kenyan newspapers comprised several sub-genres, which provided opportunities for creative exploitation. From 1983 through 2003, for example, Wahome Mutahi published a hugely popular fiction column at different times in the *Sunday Nation* and the *Sunday Standard*. 'Whispers' was one of a number of fictionalized reality columns that kept the Kenyan mainstream newspapers porous.[5] This column was subversive and mainstream, its oppositional politics veiled in humour and satire. Although it started off as a didactic column relying on mundane stock mannerisms, the column gradually became a public space where Kenya's postcolonial existence, in its many guises, was constantly interrogated. In many ways, the column defined the 'Kenya(n) becoming', exploring his hopes and fears, his existential dilemmas as he grappled with the vagaries of African modernity and the ruthlessness of the postcolonial political order.[6] In Mutahi's work, laughter was employed in the Bakhtinian sense, it allowed authority as well as the common-place to be 'drawn into a zone of crude contact ... fingered familiarly, turned upside down, inside out and peered at from above and below ... dismembered' (Bakhtin 1981: 23). But above all else, Mutahi highlighted the realm of the 'popular' as being capable of engaging with the complex contradictions and ambiguities of postcolonial Kenya.

Mapping politics through fiction

'Whispers' was set in a fictional universe. Mutahi created a fictional family modelled partly on his own family. He explicitly intended his column to be read as a form of political intervention. His decision to use the domestic space as a narrative space was strategic on several grounds. First, the domestic space was a familiar cultural template acceptable across Kenya's multiple cultures. Second, this space appeared politically innocuous. A political event narrated as a family feud would not easily rile authority.

The writer thus collapsed the domestic space with the public space so that what was discussed within the family was read against the backdrop of national issues. Anne McClintock provides a good discussion of the allegorical potential of the family by arguing that nations are 'symbolically figured as domestic genealogies' (1995: 357) and that the 'nation' is frequently figured through the iconography of familial and domestic spaces. The family in 'Whispers' was thus used allegorically to mean the 'nation'. And thus in the 'Whispers' household was the head of the family, the eponymous character Whispers, a self-indulgent, self-deprecating, chauvinistic man who seemed to struggle with the challenging city life in Nairobi. He was the butt of many jokes but also the main protagonist in the column. Whispers, also referred to as 'Son of the Soil', was narrated as one of the millions of rural migrants in Nairobi who now call the city home. But he was not 'weaned' of his village upbringing just yet. Using the allegorical form of a journey, we see this character move back and forth between the village and the city both physically and psychologically, what Mbugua wa Mungai has called the 'the cultural and spatial crossings of the postcolonial Kenyan subject' (2004: 4). Through his journeys we experience his traumas and predicaments as he attempts to make sense of his two worlds, the village and its cultures and the city with its own. The author's use of the personal voice, of Whispers as the narrator, was particularly telling of his role as a collective voice in the column. Even without the use of the collective pronoun 'we', one still gets a sense of plurality in the narrator's first-person voice.

'Whispers' was not a celebratory narrative, it was a lamentation of 'things falling apart', a narrative of dislocation. The main character was portrayed as a victim of this dislocation and, upon him, the effects of social and political changes played out. Whispers' family also comprised Whispers' wife Thatcher, an iron-willed woman who always kept Whispers in check. Named after the former British prime minister who was a particularly visible figure in the Kenyan popular press and known for her aggressive political style, Thatcher became a symbol of the 'new' woman in Kenya. Her fictional character in the column undermined patriarchy and was used to subvert the negative inscriptions on the female gender in Kenya. Yet Thatcher was also in part an allegory of the 'nation' rebelling against state domination. The couple had two children, Whispers Junior and the Investment, deployed as tropes through which to read various youth experiences rather than merely acting as literary types. While it is impossible to conduct an inventory of all the thematic issues that 'Whispers' explored, the stories that featured in the column in the 1990s are broadly reflective of its defining traits.

Politically, perhaps the column's most significant engagement with the political process was in 1992. This year remains especially important in the reading of Kenya's transitional politics in the early 1990s. It was in 1992 that Kenya held its first multi-party elections following the re-introduction of political pluralism. 'Whispers' captured how an oppositional cultural and political aesthetic flourished even amid the various constraints on not only the 'expressible' but also the 'thinkable'. Among the most salient issues that emerged from the column are narratives that dramatize the tyranny of the state, political betrayal, the political culture of accumulation, tribalism, etc. It was a catalogue of all that has gone wrong with post-independence Kenya. As one of the templates for discussing Kenya as a failing state, Mutahi focused on the 'politics' of political pluralism. The following sample articles are illustrative of the discussions: 'SOS, Madd *defect: the greener the grass the better*' (*Sunday Standard*, 5 January 1992); 'SoS *multi-party* mouth pays off' (undated); 'Trouble over Kislopes', 'Scared mouth goes on *strike*' (*Sunday Standard*, 29 March 1992); '*Ethnic clashes* in Whis' neighbourhood' (*Sunday Standard*, 26 April 1992); 'SOS thinking of *defecting* from the shilling economy' (*Sunday Standard*, 28 June 1992); 'Whispers offers *hire services*' (*Sunday Standard*, 2 August 1992); '*Total man's House* divided: *Agip House* raring to go to war' (*Sunday Standard*, 13 September 1992); 'Ambushed by mean *warriors*' (*Sunday Standard*, 4 October 1992); '*Operation Whispers Out*' (*Sunday Standard*, 15 November 1992); '*Secret Weapon* exposed' (*Sunday Standard*, 22 November 1992); 'The *Mheshimiwa* culture and *eating*' (*Sunday Standard*, 6 December 1992); 'Meet the *rigging* master: when it's hard to play fair game' (*Sunday Standard*, 20 December 1992) (emphasis mine).

These titles quite literally hint at discourses revolving around political pluralism in Kenya in the 1990s. They paint images of violence, betrayal, corruption and poverty in the country. In 'SOS, Madd defect: the greener the grass the better', Mutahi narrates as well as comments on political defections and the formation of political alliances which were particularly in vogue in the country in the early 1990s. The defections and political alliances are narrated as demonstrative of the political betrayal of the public by the country's leaders. The alliances are narrated as mutual dealings between the political classes. Between 1992 and 1995, 'Whispers' especially examines the centrality of class in Kenya's transitional politics as it became evident that class-based political dealings had replaced genuine political reform. This period witnessed numerous discussions on the legitimacy of political coalitions in the country, often pejoratively called the 'politics of co-operation', a term coined following the decision by two political parties, the ruling party Kanu and the National Development Party (NDP) to 'co-operate'. The column narrates this 'co-operation' as an alliance of convenience among the elite. Such coalitions in Kenya have been what Throup calls 'ephemeral accommodations', often short-lived because they lack a firm ideological base (1997: 37). Mutahi interprets the coalitions as a political strategy by the ruling political class to safeguard the status quo. Other stories that enact this problem include: 'Thatcher's unity pact flops: *co-operation* with Son of the Soil comes unstuck' (*Sunday Nation*, 24 October 1993); 'Tricky task of retrieving "*defecting*" husbands' (*Sunday Nation*, 29 August 1993); 'Trouble for out-dated elder. SOS finds the going tough as *sheng*' rocks delicate *negotiations*' (*Sunday Nation*, 30 October 1994); 'Thatcher, SOS, breaks links: *co-operation* resumes as rhino horn brings the promise of a bright future to the family' (undated) (emphasis mine). The emphasized words *co-operation, defecting, negotiations* were words popularly used by the mainstream press, hence familiar to readers. When used in the column, they come inscribed with particular histories and quite often with negative political connotations. Mutahi exposed these terms as euphemisms used to hide more specific class interests. Scott reminds us that such euphemisms on the 'public transcript' mask the many nasty facts of domination, giving it a harmless or sanitized face (1990: 53). In the stories, Mutahi revises and recasts these euphemisms/words within the family space to critique the political class. Alliances are thus struck between man and wife at the expense of their children, or between daughter and mother at the expense of the father. The stories are narrated as normal domestic feuds but they mirror betrayal at the national level. Being able to muster an ethnic constituency (the Luo), Raila Odinga, then leader of the NDP in the 1990s, was an important player in the schemes by Kanu to maintain its grip on power. Similarly, for the NDP, 'co-operation' with Kanu would provide it with access to power and state resources. Mutahi thus echoes John Lonsdale's argument that politicians see the state itself as a resource and that 'ready access to state institutions is literally what makes classes dominant' (Lonsdale 1981: 162). The column thus exposes these political alliances as acts of political betrayal of the public.

'Whispers' also took stock of the various political (pseudo)ideologies, myths and political metaphors that are constantly employed in the 'dramaturgy of power' in Kenya, using these to discuss questions on power and the perceived majesty of that power. Scott has noted that 'rulers who aspire to hegemony in the Gramscian sense of that term must make an ideological case that they rule, to some degree, on behalf of their subjects' (1990: 18). He explains that although this claim, in turn, 'is always tendentious', it is 'seldom completely without resonance among subordinates' (Scott 1990). Providing a similar argument are Schatzberg (1988) and Diouf (1996) who note that in 'Middle Africa', state-sanctioned ideological myths and imagery are crucial in the performance of power. In Kenya, especially in the first and second republics, these were continuously used as important instruments in the performance of power. Although variously consumed, they were employed by actors both within and outside the state to define social and political relationships. Among the most persistent in this range of constructions was the (il)legitimacy of paternal systems of authority, drawn directly from the family and the various 'ideologies of development' such as Jomo Kenyatta's 'Harambee motto' (pulling together) and Moi's famous political slogan of 'Peace, Love and Unity'.

At independence, Kenyatta emphasized the validity of the metaphor of a united family with the father as head. Kenyatta was referred to as Baba wa Taifa (Father of the Nation).[7] Like Kenyatta, Moi too became Baba wa Taifa and, when discussed in 'Whispers', is parodied as such. Moi had a dominant presence in the serial. The political narratives mainly revolved, although not exclusively, around him. As 'Father of the Nation', Moi had to assume the title Mzee, a title which is as honorary as it is functional. In Kiswahili, Mzee literally means 'the old wise man' and is used to show respect to old men. But this title is also significant in structuring relationships in Kenya. Moi, a fairly youthful politician in 1978 when he came to power, became Mzee, in effect fabricating and legitimizing his 'wisdom' despite his youthful age. As Baba wa Taifa, Mzee Moi was able to rule over 'his children'. The title Mzee culturally generates a hierarchy and legitimizes domination.[8]

Below are a few examples of how Mutahi appropriates these titles in his fiction to critique authority. In an evocative article titled 'The antics of the next "Big man"', Mutahi reproduces the state's symbols but demonstrates how they are ironized by the *plèbe*. Narrating the 'performance' that is orchestrated whenever the president arrives at public functions, the narrator takes the place of the president:

> I have called one Emoite Opotti back from retirement and he is telling the world how wise I am. He is saying: Mtukufu Rais Papa Whis, the very muthoniwa is scheduled to arrive any time now. Hapa kuna vifijo na nderemo [His Eminence President Father Whis ... Here there is great applause] awaiting the arrival of His Excellency Papa Whis. As usual, atakuwa amevalia ile suti yake ya rangi ya udhurungi na ua nyekundu [As usual he will be dressed in his Argyria (blueish-black) coloured suit with red flowers]. His Excellency will be received with thunderous applause by the thousands and thousands of Kenyans who are gathered here. Our beloved president is addressing his first rally after his official visit to the People's Republic of Kyrgystan.
>
> (*Sunday Nation*, 17 February 2002)

While the excerpt above may be read as fictitious, interestingly, apart from the name Whis, the rest of the 'performance' is part of the language of Moi's Presidential Press Service. In fact, the 'ritual' has been reproduced almost verbatim. Yet it becomes obvious that the symbols of the state are being used here to mock power. Part of the article also reads:

> Opotti is saying, Naona msafara wa Mtukufu Rais Papa Whisi approaching [I can see his Eminence President Father Whis' convoy approaching]. Yes, the beloved father of the nation, the Taliban of Talibans, is about to arrive. Parararaparaa! Paraparaa! Mtukufu Papa Whisi ndiye huyo. Ndiye ... [there comes the president ... applause!].

Once again the ritualistic language of the public 'performance' is appropriated. But note the curious allusion to the Taliban. While it adds to the hilarity of the description it simultaneously draws allusions to the murderous Taliban regime.

Dramatizing the ridiculous: *Redykyulass* and *XYZ*

In 2003, having ominously written a piece in which the eponymous character Whispers reflects on his life while on his deathbed, having contracted malaria, Wahome Mutahi passed away following a botched operation to remove a tumour on his neck. However, Mutahi's death did not mark the end of the genre he had helped popularize. 'Whispers' did in fact give rise to a number of spin-offs in both the print and broadcast news media. In the mainstream print media, for example, both *The Standard* and *The Nation* made attempts at 'reincarnating' 'Whispers' with possible surrogates. Benson Riungu, one of the most popular feature writers in Kenya, re-introduced 'Benson's World' in the *Sunday Standard*, although with modest success. Other similar fiction columns were short-lived and failed to generate much interest. Instead, it was the Kenyan television stations that were successful in adopting and then adapting the narrative style developed by Mutahi into widely successful TV programmes.

The most successful of these programmes was *Redykyulass*, a comedy act comprising Walter Mong'are, John Kiarie and Tony Njuguna. The trio formed the group while still students at Kenyatta University. They gained national recognition, however, after winning a popular talent show, the Malibu Star Search held at the Carnivore Restaurant in 1998. The group were signed by Nation Television, who agreed to produce and air their shows. With the heightened agitation for political reform in the country during this time, the Nation Media Group (NMG) had become, almost by default, the de facto media arm of the country's political opposition. *Redykyulass* thus broadly found itself being part of a wider oppositional political infrastructure. The programme became an oppositional space where the excesses of the Moi administration were lampooned. The novelty of *Redykyulass* was, however, the fact that no political story was sacred, no leader beyond the bounds of parody. Although local television comedy was already a popular genre on Kenyan television screens with programmes such as *Vitimbi* and *Vioja Mahakamani* having been around for nearly two decades, these were deliberately depoliticized, not least because both were aired by the state controlled Kenya Broadcasting Corporation (KBC). *Vitimbi* was based on mundane family experiences while *Vioja Mahakamani* was a courtroom comedy structured around the dramatization of common misdemeanours in court.

Politics thus became the mainstay of *Redykyulass*. In part, the name of the act became a figurative reading of the character of Kenya's politics. Not lost to the group was the fact that successive multi-party elections had not radically changed the face of the country's politics. Meanwhile, the unpredictable political landscape did not allow for confrontation of the state through such conventional genres in the news media such as news items, editorials or news features. While the bounds of the expressible had been expanded, news organizations were still unsure of just how far to push the envelope. It is partly for this reason that groups such as the NMG found comedy programmes, especially those featuring political satire, expedient. As Eco argues, through humour 'we can allow ourselves the vicarious pleasure of transgression that offends a rule we have secretly wanted to violate' (1986: 271). *Redykyulass* violated many such rules. Even then, in an interview with Al-Jazeera TV on the programme *People & Power*, the *Redykyulass* cast noted they still had to consult their lawyers before shooting some of the episodes.[9]

Moi's dominance of the political scene made him the 'ogre' of the programme. Monopolizing much of the public news media, his visibility was suffocating. He was on the radio or television, he was on framed pictures hanging in just about every shop, private office or government building. Populating the public space with his image ensured he established a permanent presence in the Kenyan psyche. Yet since humour works through displacement, this omnipresence was subverted in a number of ways. Like 'Whispers', *Redykyulass* dramatized the familiar. Moi became the everyday object of ridicule, the power of his perceived majesty constantly deflated, particularly by those who felt disenfranchised by his regime. What he prohibited became the very targets of popular transgression. This group's pet topics, however, revolved around a broad range of familiar social and political issues, all narrated with ironic humour. Significantly, the subjects of criticism were unambiguous with obvious cues supplied to the audience, mostly through mimicry of familiar speech patterns. But most characters mocked in the show also became tropes used to critique broader issues. Ordinary Kenyans were in fact enjoined as active participants in this discussion. During the interview with Al-Jazeera TV, one of the group's members, John Kiarie, argued that the show partly reflected Kenyan society and not merely specific individuals. He noted that they were keen on pricking the Kenyan political consciousness and wanted Kenyans 'to know that the leaders did not elect themselves'.[10]

The limitation of the genre was exposed, however, with Moi's exit from power. Moi's stylized political leadership provided *Redykyulass* with much of its idioms. The show thus significantly suffered creatively with his departure from power. After a series of poor ratings, *Redykyulass* was dropped by Nation Television. Although it found a new home in KTN with various humorous skits created around the new first family, the show failed to repeat its previous successes. Kibaki nurtured a different style of political leadership and did not 'perform' his power with as much verve as Moi. He was not as visible and, rather than the podium, he preferred news releases and thus was not as susceptible to the kind of gaffes that made Moi so easy to caricature.

The 2008 post-election violence and a new idiom of political consciousness

As noted earlier, multi-party politics in Kenya may have ushered in a new political dispensation but it still failed to re-institutionalize the state. Without claiming to be exhaustive on the pathologies of the post-1992 Kenya state, it is clear that inequitable allocation of resources, the failure to undertake comprehensive constitutional reforms, the monopolization of the political process by the elite, the arbitrary exercise of state power and the informalization of the state, together provided conditions for political instability which ultimately informed the 2007 election crisis (Ogola 2009). The news media found itself at a crossroads. While expected to stand apart from the crisis, it was in fact embedded in the very social and political relations that informed the conflict. Its coverage of the political process leading to and after the elections was so manifestly problematic it has been criticized for partly contributing to the conflagration.[11]

The news media attempted to reclaim the political initiative following the formation of a coalition government in 2008 by the two main parties, PNU and ODM, but which consequently meant the absence of an official political opposition in parliament. Yet because this news media remains inextricably wedded to the state, mainly through the influence of a political class which continues to invest in it, either directly or through proxies, it was once again used as a platform by the political class to re-invent the 'nation-building project' by advocating a new discourse of post–election political consensus.[12] New alternative discursive practices and spaces for their expression were thus forged outside this media even though it still remained important as a platform for their distribution. It is against this background that a number of new comedy acts emerged, the most popular and innovative of which has been *XYZ*, aired on Citizen TV.

XYZ is a satirical puppet show created by Godfrey 'Gado' Mwapembwa, a popular cartoonist with the *Nation* newspaper. The show was inspired by the famous British and French satirical puppet shows, *Spitting Image* and *Les Guignols*. *Spitting Image* was a popular puppet show on the British channel ITV between 1984 and 1996. The show was popular for its spoofs of political leaders, celebrities and the Royal family. The Conservative Party leadership, particularly Margaret Thatcher, was the subject of particularly vicious parody. But with Thatcher's resignation in 1990 the show's popularity also declined, revealing its major limitation of being personality driven. Thatcher's successor John Major failed to inspire the show's creators who even had to 'invent' an affair with one of his ministers, Virginia Bottomley, in an attempt to make him more interesting. This did not however improve the show's poor ratings.

Like *Redykyulass* and *Spitting Image*, *XYZ* targets public leaders.[13] The themes are broadly drawn from circulating social and political stories. Because media freedom still remains subject to the provisions in the Penal Code, which can easily be used to criminalize perceived infractions, the mainstream news media still has to navigate a legal minefield with regard to what can be reported as 'news stories'. Alternative forms of storytelling and techniques such as political satire thus remain ever more important. Through this new idiom, the mystic of power is constantly punctured and a new space for critique established.

XYZ has been brutal in its attack of the coalition government, now the subject of widespread public disillusionment. The subjects of the parodies are wide-ranging but the principle characters have been President Mwai Kibaki and the Prime Minister Raila Odinga, since these two remain arguably the most influential individuals in Kenya's political scene. Having both participated and claimed victory in the disputed 2007 presidential elections, they are used to map Kenya's political weaknesses and absurdities. Also, because the political process is so personalized, the conflation of party and government, party and party leader, leader and ethnic group, makes them figures that represent whole communities, social classes, societal values, aspirations, foibles, etc.

Although only in its second series, the reception of *XYZ* has been broadly positive, albeit not from the government. The show has been criticized by some senior members of the Kibaki administration. The Minister for Public Services, Dalmas Otieno, criticized the group for misrepresenting the president and the prime minister, betraying the anxieties of officialdom and perhaps even confirming that it actually took the show seriously. Otieno has called the show 'weird' and complained that its caricaturing of the president and the prime minister is disrespectful (*Daily Nation*, 14 August 2009). Yet the criticism merely helped underline just how thin the line between fiction and reality is with regard to Kenya's politics.

Conclusion

In 2007, after successfully participating in mobilizing Kenyan youth to vote in that year's general elections, key figures in some of the comedy groups such as John Kiarie of *Redykyulass* decided to vie for parliamentary seats. Others stood for local government seats. Although most of them failed to get elected, the decision to contest for political seats should compel us to reflect on that decision and on the transformative power of popular culture and popular cultural productions. Was it the case that these artists realized the futility of political satire as a means through which to successfully confront the state and contest power? Is it true, as Mbembe argues, that 'although it may demystify the *commandement* or even erode its legitimacy, it does not do violence to the *commandement's* base' and that 'at best, it creates pockets of indiscipline on which the *commandement* may stub its toe, though otherwise it glides unperturbed over them?' (1992a: 10). Re-mythologizing the state's language through political satire may or may not perturb the *commandement* but it is a critique nonetheless. One would also want to contest Mbembe's argument about the masses 'joining in the madness and clothing themselves in cheap imitations of power so as to reproduce its epistemology and the power in its own violent quest for grandeur making vulgarity and wrongdoing its main mode of existence' (Mbembe 1992a). Although the reproduction of the *commandement's* epistemology is key to these forms of narration, one would argue that their recreation is in fact a criticism of the *commandement's* absurdity and the irony of its invented majesty.

To judge the efficacy of these productions, or of popular culture in general, on the basis of their visible transformative power may be to miss the point, for acts of consciousness are not always necessarily tangible or indeed measurable. To reiterate a point made earlier, the question should not be what popular culture affects, rather it is important to acknowledge that when mainstream conventional media spaces are either controlled by the state or subject to a range of legal or political imitations, as has been the case in Kenya, alternative forms of political and social consciousness are forged in spaces where the state cannot exercise control or define the bounds of the expressible. Kenya's news media has therefore played a critical role in sustaining a discourse of political reform and democratic engagement through its appropriation of various popular cultural forms. Yet some of the weaknesses of these forms should also make us reflect on the limits of their transformative power and indeed political agency.

Notes

1 This was a statement by Kenya's Internal Security Minister, John Michuki, defending the government-sanctioned raid on the offices of the Standard Media Group in March 2006.
2 The Kenya Communications Amendment Act, while recognizing the press as an institution, was widely criticized for having provisions which still allow the state, through the Security Minister, to raid and shut down media organizations as well as control programme content. The provisions were however already contained in the Constitution under sections 88–92.

3 The Aga Khan was the principle shareholder at the Nation Group while Lonrho Africa had controlling shares at the Standard Group.
4 The titles of these magazines reflect the repressive character of the period. The titles were meant to read as politically innocuous as possible.
5 Some of these fiction columns included Gakiha Weru's 'Urbanite', and earlier columns such as Hillary Ng'weno's 'My Friend Joe' and Sam Kahiga's 'Kibao'.
6 For a detailed reading on Whispers, see Ogola (2005).
7 For a detailed reading of this metaphor, see Schatzberg (1988).
8 See a detailed discussion of age, gerontocracy and power in Kenya in Ogola (2006).
9 See www.youtube.com/watch?v=Ci6KiFkrf18 (accessed 1 November 2009).
10 See www.youtube.com/watch?v=Ci6KiFkrf18 (accessed 1 November 2009).
11 See Ogola (2009); Wrong (2008); BBC World Service Trust Policy Briefing (2008).
12 A joint editorial titled 'Save our beloved country', published on 3 January 2008 at the height of the post-election violence by leading newspapers and read out by the major TV stations across the country seems to have signalled a shift in the character of the Kenyan media. It marked the beginnings of the negotiation of a post-2007 political consensus, which has since defined much of the local news media's political reporting. But it also appears the news media is simultaneously legitimizing a broader political script; the reinvention of the nation-building project as the political class leans back to the 1960s regime-building political rhetoric of national development.
13 A similar puppet show, ZANEWS, created by cartoonist Jonathan 'Zapiro' Shapiro has courted both praise and controversy in South Africa. It was rejected by the public broadcaster South African Broadcasting Corporation (SABC) and was launched as a web channel (www.zanews.co.za).

References

Atieno-Odhiambo, E.S. (1987) 'Democracy and the ideology of order in Kenya', in Schatzberg, M. (ed.) *The Political Economy of Kenya*. New York: Praeger, pp. 177–201.

——. (2002) 'Hegemonic enterprises and instrumentalities of survival: ethnicity and democracy in Kenya', *African Studies* 61(2): 224–49.

——. (2004) 'Ethnic cleansing and civil society in Kenya 1963–1992', *Journal of Contemporary African Studies* 22(1): 29–42.

Bakhtin, M. (1981) *The Dialogic Imagination: Four Essays*. Ed. Michael Holquist, trans. Caryl Emerson and Michael Holquist. Austin and London: University of Texas Press.

BBC Policy Briefing (2008) 'The Kenyan 2007 elections and their aftermath: the role of the media and communication', *Policy Briefing* (1), London: BBC Service Trust.

Branch, D. and Cheeseman, N. (2008) 'Democratisation, sequencing and state failure in Africa', *African Affairs* 108(430): 1–26.

Diouf, M. (1996) 'Urban youth & Senegalese politics', in Young, T. (ed.) *Readings in African Politics*. Bloomington and Indianapolis: Indiana University Press, p. 41.

Eco, U. (1986) *Travels in Hyperreality*. New York: Harcourt Brace.

Fabian, J. (1998) *Moments of Freedom: Anthropology and Popular Culture*. Charlottesville: University of Virginia Press.

Haugerud, A. (1995) *The Culture of Politics in Modern Kenya*. Cambridge: Cambridge University Press.

Hyden, G. (2006) *African Politics in Comparative Perspective*. Cambridge: Cambridge University Press.

KHRC (1997) *Shackled Messengers: The Media in Multiparty Kenya*. Nairobi: KHRC.

Lonsdale, J. (1981) 'States and social processes in Africa: a historiographical survey', *African Studies Review* 24: 139–225.

McClintock, A. (1995) *Imperial Leather: Race, Gender in the Colonial Contest*. New York: Routledge.

Mbeke, P. and Mshindi, T. (2008) *Kenya Media Sector Analysis Report*. Nairobi: Canadian International Development Agency-Kenya.

Mbembe, A. (1992a) 'Provisional notes on the postcolony', *Africa* 62(1): 3–37.

——. (1992b) 'The banality of power and the aesthetics of vulgarity in the postcolony', *Public Culture* 4(2): 1–30.

Mbugua wa Mungai (2004) 'Wahome Mutahi and Kenyan popular culture', unpublished work.

Ogola, G. (2005) 'Stirring whispers: fictionalising the popular in the Kenyan newspaper', unpublished PhD thesis, University of the Witwatersrand.

——. (2006) 'The idiom of age in a popular Kenyan serial', *Africa* 76(4): 569–89.

——. (2009) 'Media at cross-roads: reflections on the Kenyan news and the coverage of the 2007 political crisis', *Africa Insight* 39(1): 58–71.

Schatzberg, M. (1988) *The Dialectics of Oppression in Zaire*. Bloomington and Indianapolis: Indiana University Press.

——. (2001) *Political Legitimacy in Middle Africa: Father, Family, Food*. Bloomington and Indianapolis: Indiana University Press.

Scott, J. (1990) *Domination and the Arts of Resistance: Hidden Transcripts*. New Haven and London: Yale University Press.

Street, J. (1997) *Politics and Popular Culture*. Cambridge: Polity Press.

Throup, D. (1997) 'The construction and destruction of the Kenyatta state', in Schatzberg, M. (ed.) *The Political Economy of Kenya*. New York: Praeger, pp. 57–64.

Throup, D. and Hornsby, C. (1998) *Multi-Party Politics in Kenya*. Oxford: James Currey; Nairobi: EAEP; Athens, OH: Ohio University Press.

Wrong, M. (2008) 'Don't mention the war', *New Statesman*, 14 February. Available online: www.newstatesman.com/africa/2008/02/wrong-ethnic-kenya-politicians (retrieved 8 January 2010).

Young, T. (ed.) (2003) *Readings in African Politics*. Bloomington and Indianapolis: Indiana University Press.

Online sources

East African Standard online archives. Available online: www.eastandard.net (accessed 1 November 2009).

Nation online archives. Available online: www.nationmedia.com (accessed 1 November 2009).

People & Power – It's Redykulass, Al Jazeera TV. Available online: www.youtube.com/watch?v=Ci6KiFkrf18 (accessed 1 November 2009).

Chapter 9

Post-apartheid South African social movements on film

Sean Jacobs[1]

Introduction

One of the defining characteristics of the post-apartheid polity is the emergence of a range of organizations, outside of legislative politics, that are making direct demands on the state and capital. These movements are collectively known as the 'new social movements'. The main grievances of the new social movements revolve around access to basic needs; that is housing, education, water and electricity and land, among others things, including lack of HIV/AIDS treatment and access to affordable medication. The origins of the new social movements can be traced to the late 1990s. They stem from dissatisfaction with the constraints of liberal democracy and the limited nature of the economic and social transition from apartheid.

The retirement of Nelson Mandela in 1999 and his succession by the younger Thabo Mbeki as South Africa's second democratic president, exposed widespread grievances among poor, black South Africans with the 'new South Africa'. Mandela's conciliatory politics towards whites (who retained the upper hand economically even if political power shifted with the advent of formal democracy) were now openly challenged. The idea of a 'Rainbow Nation', a term coined by Desmond Tutu and championed by Mandela and other ANC leaders as well as the reconciliatory tone of the Truth and Reconciliation Commission could not mask the deepening inequality, degradation and daily humiliation that most black people continued to experience well after apartheid was outlawed. Not surprisingly, in September 2009, the Johannesburg newspaper, *Business Day*, could report that while Brazil and South Africa for a long time vied for the title of 'most unequal' country in the world, Brazil was leaving South Africa behind. While Brazil has decreased its income gap through land reform and social grants, the income gap in South Africa has widened despite its government's goal to halve poverty between 2004 and 2014.

It is in the environment of national inequality and disillusionment that these new social movements link these local, specific, struggles with a critique of both national and global politics. The most active of these movements have been the Anti-Privatisation Forum (APF) and the Soweto Electricity Crisis Committee, both of which agitate for affordable electricity and other municipal services; the Western Cape Anti-Eviction Campaign, which defends poor people evicted from their houses; the Treatment Action Campaign (TAC) which is a national HIV-AIDS pressure group, and Abahlali baseMjondolo, a movement of shack-dwellers based outside Durban on South Africa's northeast coast (Abahlali's name literally translates as 'people living in shacks').

All these organizations have adroitly used mass media, including film (video, documentary film, etc.), and many of them have collaborated with filmmakers and other media activists to promote their struggles. This chapter explores how two of these movements – the Treatment Action Campaign and Abahlali – are represented on film. Do these movements have a say in or control over how they are represented? Who are the protagonists in these films? How are the movements' politics represented? Who appear to be the intended audiences of these films? Finally, what are the impacts of new media technologies on representations of post-apartheid social movements?

Why focus on these two movements? The two movements share a number of characteristics: both movements are explicitly political, linking their specific struggles (healthcare for people living with AIDS or a voice in local government development strategies, respectively) to larger political developments both in South Africa and globally. Both movements are also connected to artists and media workers in South Africa and elsewhere and as a result, on balance, have enjoyed a greater media visibility than any of the other social movements who do not have access to the same cultural capital.

The TAC, however, is a national organization, while Abahlali, despite its affiliation to a national 'Poor People's Alliance' with the landless and housing rights groups, mainly operates locally in informal settlements in and around Durban. While the TAC cultivates relationships with its opponents in government (and pharmaceutical corporations), Abahlali is often depicted as having a more adversarial relationship with local authorities in Durban. This is not entirely the case as Abahlali work very closely with some officials and departments in the Durban Metro Council, have set up safety committees with the police and often work within the law. This includes taking the government to court, as it did when it challenged the constitutionality of a law that would make 'slum clearing' possible for the local authority. Crucially, TAC is a product of the first decade of democracy (the Mandela and Mbeki years), while Abahlali is associated with 'second generation' social movements. Abahlali was formed in 2005, at the start of the second decade of democracy. I would like to suggest that it is particularly this generational factor that is crucial in determining their approach to film. Abahlali came about at a time when new media technologies became more readily available to social movement activists. More significantly, the TAC runs a more professionalized media strategy, while Abahlali's media strategy is less controlled. This will become clear in an analysis of the films.

This chapter connects to the overall themes of the book, namely the connections between popular media (in this case film), democracy and development. At first glance film hardly seems a popular and accessible medium; in its traditional sense South Africa does not have a 'film culture': the country's mainstream cinema houses mainly show Hollywood fare or art house films, while public television, for a brief moment the main outlet for documentary films (see p. 140), has become increasingly subject to management and financial crises. First generation post-apartheid social movements like the TAC were very successful in accessing mainstream filmmakers to tell their stories. In this case, however, the TAC's fate was left to the filmmakers and the vagaries of the film market: at best, they could wish for the films depicting their struggles to be exhibited or screened at film festivals or public television stations outside South Africa. In contrast, Abahlali's bottom-up, informal approach to media, its embrace of the Internet (all films made about Abahlali are posted on their website) and what film observers would describe as the 'DIY feel' of films about it, point to new democratic potential for social movements' relationship to film and cinema.

Some media history

Modern South African social movements have long understood the power of media. However, the state's control of broadcast media – radio (first introduced in 1923) and television (introduced in 1976) – meant that until 1990 (when Nelson Mandela was released from prison) the options for social movements were very limited. What media opportunities existed inside the country were largely limited to print. Whether through publishing its own media, sympathetic mainstream outlets or the 'alternative press' of the 1980s (see Switzer and Adhikari 2000), social movements took advantage of these opportunities.

Though South Africa has a cinema culture that dates back to the silent era, it was only in the early 1950s that the first films with black people as principal cast members appeared (Masilela and Balseiro 2003). These films, however, consisted of musical performances performed on sets that resembled variety shows. In 1959 the American director, Lionel Rogosin, working with local activists, writers and performers, directed the narrative feature, Come Back Africa. The film – which was clandestinely filmed in South Africa – tracked the precarious life of a black migrant worker in Johannesburg, subjected to humiliation, pass laws, police violence, unemployment and poverty. Before it could be shown inside South Africa, however, it was banned (Rogosin 2004). In fact this was the fate of most films, narrative or documentary, which openly exposed the workings of apartheid and the social movements that emerged to challenge its rule. (A similar fate befell the documentary, The Last Graves at Dimbaza, made in 1974 about the 'homelands'.) The censor even felt compelled to ban the sanitized Hollywood biopics of the lives of major anti-apartheid figures Ruth First and Steve Biko (Nixon 1994).

The United Democratic Front (UDF), formed in 1983, and which revived anti-apartheid resistance in the wake of Steve Biko's murder, cultivated journalists and sympathetic filmmakers, both inside and outside South Africa (see Van Kessel 2000). The UDF supported an active underground press and video production. Activist art collectives, such as the Cape Video Education Trust, published poster art, produced videos and documented police brutality or community actions in photos (e.g. the social documentary tradition of groups such as Afrapix).

The transition to democracy introduced a number of new avenues for social movement media. Mainstream media – transformed by ownership and control changes, legal freedom of expression and affirmative action (see Johnson and Jacobs 2004) – began to make their editorial practices more democratic. In addition, the new government deregulated the airwaves. The state broadcaster strove to become a 'public service broadcaster'. In 1993 the state also licensed at least 80 community radio stations. The result was a community radio tier, which came to exist alongside the public and commercial broadcasting tiers. However, community radio stations had their long-term viability compromised by their primary reliance on government and foreign foundation founding, and their lack of a strong advertising base (Bosch 2003).

For a brief period after the transition of democratic rule the state broadcaster, the South African Broadcasting Corporation (SABC), enjoyed what the journalist Allister Sparks (who was briefly head of television at the SABC) described as a 'Prague Spring' (Sparks 2003), before it suffered from interference by the new ruling party, the ANC, and the decline in support for public broadcasting. For a while after 1990, the SABC had a dedicated slot for documentary films on one of its three channels. It has also funded themed documentary films (e.g. *Project Ten*, a series of documentaries that examined the first decade of democracy in 2004).

Though the expected boom in film production did not materialize, documentary film has flourished, creating, for example, opportunities for a crop of young black filmmakers (e.g. Khalo Matabane and Dumisani Phakathi, among others) who emerged to challenge the film industry's majority white composition. Not surprisingly, the new social movements became the subject of several documentary films.

The Treatment Action Campaign

The TAC was founded on 10 December 1998 in Cape Town. It advocates for 'increased access to treatment, care and support services for people living with HIV and campaigns to reduce new HIV infections' (TAC 2009). The TAC's short history has been dominated by its clashes with the government over the latter's refusal to implement a comprehensive AIDS strategy, President Mbeki's denial in the face of an AIDS crisis and pharmaceutical company profiteering from AIDS drugs. (At the time Mbeki, who is not a scientist – he has a graduate degree in economics – denied that there was credible link between HIV and AIDS.)

Since its founding the TAC has cemented its position as the leading AIDS organization, not just in South Africa but also on the continent, if not the world, and achieved a number of victories: President Mbeki publicly ceased to question the link between HIV and AIDS; the government was compelled by the Constitutional Court to make antiretrovirals available to pregnant women and children; the government later announced it would implement a countrywide treatment programme through the public sector. In 2008, the ANC forced Mbeki to resign as South Africa's president. More recently, in December 2009, the new president, Jacob Zuma, announced (during a national address on World AIDS Day) that 'drug therapy for H.I.V.-positive pregnant women and babies would be broadened and start earlier' (Dugger 2009). The TAC has also won a number of victories against multinational drug companies to lower the prices of antiretroviral drugs (TAC 2009).

The TAC also enjoys widespread mainstream appeal. In 2004 Zackie Achmat, the TAC's longtime leader, was a serious contender for the Nobel Peace Prize. Two years later the *New York Times* named the TAC as 'the world's most effective AIDS group' (TAC 2009). Achmat was also included in *Time Magazine*'s '100 Most Influential People' list in 2001 (Karon 2001).

Media coverage of the TAC has generally been positive. TAC officials credit media support as a major factor in the success of the organization's campaigns (Johnson and Jacobs 2004). For example, in 2003 the TAC mounted a civil disobedience campaign and, despite its militant posture during this campaign, to quote the same TAC leader, 'for the most part the media stayed on TAC's side' (cited in Friedman and Mottiar 2006: 22). This was also true of other TAC campaigns, including a highly publicized campaign in which they illegally imported generic AIDS medicine into the country as well as when they shamed government ministers by publicly embarrassing thm.

The Treatment Action Campaign on film

I will discuss representations of the TAC in two films: *It's My Life* (2002) and *State of Denial* (2003).

It's My Life is a documentary feature film that revolves around the decision of Zackie Achmat, the TAC leader, to refuse to take antiretroviral drugs until they are available in the public sector. At the time the film was made in 2002, at least 4.7 million South Africans were infected with the HIV virus (*It's My Life* 2002).

The film is directed by South African Brian Tilley, who had directed a film about the anti-apartheid movement near the end of apartheid. That film, *Fruits of Defiance* (1989), is 'a film about the mass defiance campaign and the release of Nelson Mandela'. It won first prize in the Third World section of the Montreal Television Festival (Steps 2009). The producers are Big World Cinema, a South African company with a strong record of documentary films. The American distributor is Icarus Films, a Brooklyn-based company with a record of socially conscious titles. *It's My Life* won a number of international awards. The film was made for the 'Steps for the Future' project, an international co-production of 40 documentaries and short films that focus on various aspects of the AIDS epidemic in Southern Africa. Funders of Steps for the Future included the Soros Foundation, the Danish and Finnish Film Institutes, the One World Group of Broadcasters and the mobile phone giant, Nokia, which is supporting the training of young filmmakers.

According to the Steps producers the series wanted to avoid 'the usual picture of death and disaster' and instead wanted to focus

> on individual human stories, told in a deeply touching manner that appeal to basic human emotions regardless of the viewer's background. The films promote a better understanding of the many ways that HIV/AIDS is affecting the lives of people in the region ... These stories portray people living with HIV/AIDS as real people who despite their struggles recognize that being HIV positive is not a death sentence and that life is a beautiful thing.
>
> (Steps 2009)

It's My Life was one of two films in the series that focused on the personal life of a social movement activist. The other was *Simon and I*, a 52-minute documentary by lesbian filmmaker, Beverley Ditsie on her relationship with gay activist, Simon Nkoli, who died of AIDS in 1998. (Nkoli's death is credited with galvanizing activists to form the TAC.)

In *It's My Life*, a small film crew followed Achmat around for five months: to the doctor, in his home, on the street campaigning as well as engaging Achmat in discussions about his life, activism and sacrifice, among other topics. We witness Achmat's struggle with his illness as the lack of antiretroviral drugs puts his health at risk. Achmat's close associates try to persuade him to continue his drug treatment. At one point Achmat's doctor tells him: 'Activism is a lot more effective if you stay alive.'

During this time the South African government takes multinational drug companies to court to bring down the price of antiretroviral drugs. The TAC joined the government's case as a friend of the court. Eventually the pharmaceutical industry withdraws its case. Achmat and the TAC celebrate. In a particularly salient moment, Achmat dances by himself in his home to the song 'It's Raining Men'.

Although the government won the case, President Mbeki and his health minister, Manto Tshabalala-Msimang, question the efficacy and safety of antiretroviral drugs, including those that help prevent the passage of HIV from mother to child. The film ends on a pessimistic note as Achmat is forced to continue his and the TAC's fight against the Mbeki government. Achmat continues to struggle with his health, eventually engaging in a debate with the TAC over his decision to boycott anti-viral drugs in solidarity. Towards the end, the film becomes as much about Achmat's battle with his illness as it is about the choices of 'the movement'. The TAC holds a teleconference to report on Achmat's health and to try and change his mind about taking antiretroviral medicines. He sticks to his position.

The technical quality of the film is very high with frequent powerful use of music and editing, cutting from one scenario to another to sway the viewer.

The filmmakers are insiders or 'flies on the wall', following Achmat everywhere. As a result Achmat is the key protagonist. This is primarily a film about him. They have access to his intimate detail, his daily routines, as well as getting him to reveal aspects of his personal history. They are also privy to closed-door meetings of Achmat, the TAC and its allies where sensitive information and strategy is often discussed. Viewers get to see Achmat argue (in a car about what kind of socks he wants to wear), write, travel, speak to crowds at rallies for the TAC's cause, interact with his former partner, his sister and fellow activists, hand out pamphlets, and speak to journalists. Achmat is at once a leader and spokesperson on a large scale – he is portrayed as a crusader against the government and as a martyr for the movement, risking his life in solidarity with the poor – and as a local activist handing out pamphlets in the street. However, the filmmakers were also aware of Achmat's humanity and insecurities. Tilley recalls: 'It was an intense period. Everyone around Zackie was concerned about his health and the last thing they wanted was a film crew hanging about. But we did' (Steps n.d.).

The filmmakers are clear about who the antagonists are: government policy, the pharmaceutical industry, the minister of health at the time (Manto Tshabalala-Msimang who had became a polarizing figure for promoting beetroot, garlic and lemon as a cure for AIDS) and Mbeki himself (in the film, Achmat refers to him as the 'the biggest obstacle' to AIDS policy reform and that 'the leader of our government [Mbeki] is presiding over a holocaust of poor people').[2]

How is the movement identified? Zackie Achmat is very much an embodiment of the movement. We do not get to meet (beyond fleeting screen time) any other members of the TAC or individuals that are active in the TAC. Though other TAC activists enter the fray (most notably, the TAC treasurer Mark Heywood), the focus is on Zackie Achmat: he leads rallies, writes memoranda to Parliament, speaks to crowds, etc. The focus on Achmat is reinforced by the journalists who appear on screen and who are eager to identify Achmat as a hero. One of them even compares Achmat's opposition to the government as 'like David [against] Goliath'.

How is Achmat and the TAC's relationship to the law portrayed? It is not incidental that the film's focus is the TAC's decision to act as 'friend of the court' in the government's case against the pharmaceutical companies. The film shows the TAC (or rather Achmat) as working *within* the law: taking the government to court, and in Achmat's terms supporting the government when it does a good job and opposing it when it doesn't do its work. At the same time, the TAC is also portrayed as engaging in street marches.

Because of its singular focus (Zackie Achmat's decision to not use antiretroviral drugs and viewing the court case from his vantage point), the film contrasts strongly with another film about the TAC, *State of Denial* (see pp. 144–6), which more resembles a conventional television documentary with its talking heads, use of news footage, and which comes across more as an overview about a 'social problem'.

It could be argued that the film's deliberate focus on a biographical/personal struggle obscures a strong advocacy message. At the same time, however, it is also true that the film is as much about Achmat's struggle as it is about 'the movement'. The producers also seem well aware of the maxim that the 'average viewer' is bound to identify more with an individual than a movement. Tilley told an interviewer that despite the individual focus on Achmat: 'The main concern of the film and its character is that South Africa's 4.7 million people living with HIV do not have access to anti-retroviral medicines that could prolong and improve their lives' (Steps n.d.).

State of Denial

State of Denial contrasts the denialism of former President Thabo Mbeki with the everyday experiences of four HIV-positive South Africans. The film, which was shown on public television in the United States, is directed by Elaine Epstein, a New York-based South African director who had a previous career working on AIDS and in public health in South Africa.

According to Epstein, her main objectives as a filmmaker revolved around two main intentions: to produce an 'insider's perspective [of the AIDS pandemic] with South Africans telling their own personal stories'. Second, she wanted to counter Western stereotypes. As she explained it herself:

> I was inspired to make *State of Denial* as I felt that the television programmes I was seeing [in the United States] on AIDS in Africa did not reflect my experience with the epidemic or the people affected by it. I often felt like I was watching a nature programme about the mating habits of some exotic species – always with some white, male, foreign correspondent wandering at a distance through the townships telling viewers how things are, or how he sees them without ever getting up close and giving the people the opportunity to speak for themselves.
>
> (Human Rights Project n.d.)

Despite the title's direct reference to Mbeki's denialism, the film differs from *It's My Life* in that it does not have a singular reference. Instead the film presents the experiences of a cross-section of people living with HIV-AIDS: through their families, or through doctors and health practitioners. However, these stories are linked to wider political factors: whether the legacy of apartheid or Mbeki's decision to 'open the debate' about the causes of AIDS. The filmmaker did not get to interview Mbeki, so inserts news footage of his statement in the South African Parliament that HIV does not cause AIDS. She also includes footage of an interview with Mbeki from a local television news programme where he referred to AIDS testing as 'a paradigm' that he did not want to legitimize.

Mbeki's intransigence is contrasted with those suffering and living with HIV and AIDS. At the beginning of the film we are introduced to Mandla, a HIV-positive family man who has accepted his fate, but is anxious about his wife and children. 'It's up to the government to save us', he tells the filmmaker. Mandla dies shortly thereafter. Mary is an HIV-positive mother of two children: her son Gift and daughter Chipho. The children are able to gain access to some antiretro-viral drugs but the mother cannot. However, by the film's end she eventually does get access to drugs when her health deteriorates. Middle-aged Buyile Montjane is a former nurse who travels to Carletonville, a gold mining town three hours from Johannesburg, where she manages a home-based care pro-gramme for people living with AIDS. Other protagonists include the Zola Support Group, a group of young people infected with HIV in Soweto township in Johannesburg, who speak openly about the discrimination they suffer in their community and families, and Lucky Mazibuko, a HIV-positive columnist for *The Sowetan*, a daily newspaper in Johannesburg. Mazibuko writes a column about his experiences living with AIDS to 'set an example' and eventually joins the TAC.

While most of the protagonists are black, the filmmaker also included a white middle-class couple, Donna and Bowie, who live in the suburbs of Durban. (This was a departure from most representations about AIDS in South Africa – because of the size of the black population, their overwhelmingly working-class position (drugs are expensive) and labour patterns (migrant labour), more black people have been infected with HIV or live with AIDS.) Donna, who is HIV-positive, is pregnant with her second child. Bowie is the father. He was HIV-negative before he met Donna and finds out he is HIV-positive. The couple debate if she should give birth. They can afford drugs (demonstrating racial and economic disparity) and the baby is born HIV-negative.

Though a number of doctors and health practitioners appear in the film, the film focuses on one of these, Dr Daya Moodley, a young research scientist based in Durban. Moodley is also the physician who tells Donna she is HIV-positive. The film also focuses on Zackie Achmat and the TAC.

Various interlocutors describe Mbeki as the 'biggest impediment' to treatment. 'Everyone is utterly perplexed' by his insistence to emphasize extreme poverty only as a cause for AIDS rather than talk about the transmission of HIV-AIDS as a communicable disease: 'If only he had said "I'm Thabo Mbeki and HIV causes AIDS," he would have seized the moral high-ground', says one of Mbeki's critics.

Mbeki's actions are also contrasted with those of Nelson Mandela. Though Mandela had dithered in tackling the pandemic during his tenure at the expense of other priorities (before AIDS peaked in South Africa), he compensated for it after he retired as president by publicly criticizing Mbeki and openly siding with the TAC.

Multinational pharmaceutical companies, including Pfizer, are mentioned in text displayed on the screen but are never interviewed or really revealed as an actual actor on the ground. How is the TAC identified? The TAC is embodied by the figure of Zackie Achmat, its charismatic leader who flouts the law (he per-sonally imports antiretroviral drugs illegally from Thailand), explains what its like to be sick with HIV–AIDS, rejects arguments about the financial costs of treatment, and by footage of him speaking with a megaphone in front of an audience.

The TAC is also identified by marches and signs carried by supporters ('HIV-Positive', 'Love Life' and 'HOPE'). The TAC fights social conditions of poverty and ignorance, and engages with the political environment by highlighting the government's negligence and ambivalence in dealing with the pandemic. The movement and its leader are seen as flouting patent law, but in doing so do not appear as unruly. This is also presented as an exception as the TAC is presented as working *within* the law by taking the government to the Constitutional Court for its decision to await more data in order to accept conventional science on the link between HIV and AIDS. On the whole, the TAC comes across as practical, *flouting the law* when it is the *morally* correct thing to do, but also fighting through the courts. The movement wins its case in court, forcing the government to accept donations and to begin distributing anti-viral drugs.

The film was made for the US public television station, PBS, and shows all the conventions of documentary films accepted for screening there: the linear structure, the closed story (there is a definite beginning and end), resolution and the appearance of talking heads, among others. However, unlike most PBS documentary films, the film is open about its bias. The main message of the film is that until drug companies make further concessions, treatments will remain out of reach of South Africans. It also criticizes the actions of President Mbeki and Health Minister Tshabalala-Msimang. By the film's end the TAC continues the fight while more people are being infected with the virus by the thousands.

Abahlali on film

Abahlali baseMjondolo originated among shack-dwellers in Durban in 2005 when squatters living in the Kennedy Road settlement blocked roads in protest against the sale of a piece of nearby land to a developer, despite the local municipal councillor promising the land to shack-dwellers for housing. Since its inception it has been subjected to police harassment, arrest of its members, attacks and death threats (Abahlali n.d.). It has since grown into a national movement and identifies itself as a 'radical poor people's movement', along with the Cape Town-based Western Cape Anti-Eviction Forum and the Landless People's Movement (Abahlali n.d.). These movements reject electoral politics. In March 2006 Abahlali organized a boycott of the March 2006 elections under the slogan 'No Land, No House, No Vote'. (In contrast, the TAC have consistently supported the ANC during elections.)

Abahlali has been very outspoken about its right to define itself. It often rails again 'Northern donors, academics and NGOs' who they accuse of assuming 'a right to lead the local struggles of the poor in the name of a privileged access to the "global"'. In contrast to the TAC, Abahlali have posted a wide range of short videos, short documentary films and news or raw footage – whether by journalists, media activists or NGOs – on its website. These include the films: *Kennedy*

Road and the Councillor, made shortly after Abahlali was formed in 2005; *Breyani and the Councillor* (also made in 2005); *The Right to Know*, a film by Ben Cashdan[3] about attempts by communities to use new freedom of information laws. The NGO Open Democracy Advice Centre (ODAC) made the film. More recently there have been the films of Jenny Morgan (*A Place in the City* released in November 2008), Elkartasun Bideak's films (mainly in Zulu, the language of the shack-dwellers, with Basque subtitles) and the US-based filmmakers Dara Kell and Christopher Nizza's *Dear Mandela*.

Below I will closely discuss *Kennedy Road and the Councillor*, *Breyani and the Councillor* and *Dear Mandela*. (I will not discuss *The Right to Know* as it is more an infomercial for the work of ODAC than anything else and Bideak's films have a limited reach because of his use of language.)

Kennedy Road and the Councillor is a 16-minute documentary made by the Irish filmmaker, Aoibheann O'Sullivan, about land issues at Kennedy Road Settlement. Much of the film consists of close-up interviews of members of Abahlali as well as their main opposition, local councillor Yacoob Baig (the 'councillor' of the title), over promised improvements to infrastructure and their housing needs. The community also accuses Baig of calling the police when they protest. The police harass a number of Abahlali members and supporters. The film climaxes with a march by residents to Baig's offices. By the film's end, Baig remains in office.

The film definitely sides with the slum-dwellers. The main antagonist is councillor Yacoob Baig. Though the film gives ample time to Councillor Baig, the filmmakers feature his point of view only to contrast it with the day-to-day reality of living in the slum. Baig's claims are contradicted in interviews with residents and activists (Abahlali leader S'bu Zikode, as well as residents Nomhlanhla Princess Mzobe and Thobigile Zulu) as well as by strategically placed text (by the director) that indicts Baig. For example, when Mzobe claims that there are six toilets for the whole settlement and that Baig promised to install more toilets, Baig responds that he had contacted the health department, emphasized the 'urgency' of the problem and expected it to be done 'very, very shortly'. Cut to text: 'The interview with Yacoob Baig took place on 20th April 2005. By June 2005 there are still no new toilets in the area.' The interviews humanize and give a cogent argument to shack-dwellers' demands and show them to be self-sufficient, articulate and with clear objectives. At various times Abahlali leaders are shown ordering their members not to break the law during the march to Baig's offices.

While the film shares some of the qualities of documentaries produced for film festivals or television broadcast, it seems more likely to have been produced for a domestic advocacy audience. For example, the film assumes the viewer is familiar with aspects of post-apartheid politics, local Durban politics or the linkages Abahlali makes between its struggles and that of the anti-apartheid movement.

Breyani and the Councillor, which has a DIY feel to it, was made by media activists 'Giles and Khan' (the latter refers perhaps to trade union and media activist,

Fazel Khan) to document 'the struggle' of the squatter communities on Durban's outskirts for housing. The film takes its title from the local councillors' penchant to bribe residents with Indian food when they protest or complain about sub-standard housing. That may be deliberate.

The film's protagonists are the shack-dwellers and activists of Abahlali. The antagonists are councillors Yacoob Baig and Jayraj Bachu, the focus of shack-dwellers' anger. The film shares some of the characteristics of *Kennedy Road and the Councillor* in that some of the same protagonists (e.g. Nomhlanhla Mzobe) are central characters. The film consists of interviews with squatters, who invite the filmmakers into their houses and show them the conditions. The film also focuses on more controversial aspects of Abahlali's activism, including the tactic to conduct 'mock funerals' for unpopular councillors. The tactic was discouraged after two councillors were murdered in Durban. The film does not acknowledge the darker side of this tactic.

Finally, I want to discuss the short documentary film *Dear Mandela*, which I think points to a new stage in film portrayals of Abahlali. *Dear Mandela* is an eight-minute film directed by Dara Kell and Christopher Nizza. The film, which acts as a teaser for a feature-length documentary (at the time of writing in production), aims to expose South Africa's 'new apartheid', that is forced evictions, shack fires, homelessness and dire poverty for most of the country's majority black population. Members of Abahlali who live in three squatter camps outside Durban are the central focus of the film. These include S'bu Zikode, and Abahlali members Shamita Naidoo, Mnikelo Ndabankulu, Mazwi Nzimande and Zinashe Hohlo.

Kell, who is a South African, and Nizza, an American, started a filmmaking collective, Sleeping Giant Pictures, which aims 'to advance years of anti-poverty organizing via the medium of documentary films'. From the outset the film – which has no narrator – wants to establish its 'South African voice'. Zinashe Hohlo, a 16-year resident and activist, shows the filmmakers around a fire at her shack. Zikode reads from the preamble to the constitution to place Abahlali's struggle within the current legal context, and historical footage (police strip-searching or demanding pass books from black South Africa, protest marchers, and Nelson Mandela's release from prison, among others) is used, not to celebrate the end of apartheid, but to contrast it with the present reality of shack-dwellers (fires, police brutality, house demolitions). This tension is maintained throughout the film in interviews with Abahlali activists who emphasize their present conditions. Abahlali's members and supporters, while taking an active part in how they are perceived, are portrayed as 'everyday people' (washing clothes, cutting grass, etc.) who merely want full citizenship. They consciously make reference to the country's constitution, and place their struggle in a historical context in which they are the heirs of Mandela's protest tradition.

Unlike other films on Abahlali the antagonists aren't clearly identified (i.e. not a specific city official). However, the ANC is clearly at the heart of squatters' grievances. Abahlali members speak of disappointment with the post-apartheid order and how ANC leaders are now imposing economic apartheid and oppressing the shack-dwellers. 'There is no democracy for the poor', says one of the interviewees, while Nzimande, a high school student, talks about a 'a new apartheid between the rich and the poor', and Ntabankulu tells the filmmakers: 'We are really serious about life. This is not life.'

Most significantly, while *Dear Mandela* appears to be *more* grassroots than the films about the TAC (for example, it uses footage shot by Giles and Khan, the filmmakers discussed above), its aesthetic is definitely more professional and breaks with the explicitly DIY aesthetic of Giles and Khan's *Breyani and the Councillor*, for example. As a result, *Dear Mandela* seems to be made at once for a domestic audience as well as for creating international awareness and advocacy around their plight and, crucially, suggests that in contrast to other films about the movement, cinematic portrayals of Abahlali will become closer to those of the TAC.

Conclusion

What do the film representations of these two social movements tell us about popular media and democracy? The TAC's media strategy set out to access the mainstream. It could afford to. The mainstream was receptive to its struggle; not just because local media were generally negative towards the new democratic government (or more specifically the new ruling party and keen to promote any kind of oppositional movement), but because the TAC's demands around AIDS treatment and healthcare could be presented as acceptable in mainstream discourse. Journalists and filmmakers also want to work with TAC, and want to tell its story. In contrast, Abahlali and movements like it (the Anti-Eviction Campaign and the Anti-Privatization Campaign also come to mind) are less successful in accessing mainstream media. Their message is less receptive to the mainstream, particularly their demand that housing is a right. So is their claim that apartheid is far from over, but has merely shifted its basis from race to class: 'They say apartheid is over. Yes, we agree that apartheid is over. But there is a new apartheid system that is operating in South Africa and that apartheid is between the rich and the poor', one of the Abahlali activists tells the filmmakers of *Dear Mandela*. The less formal, more bottom-up and dispersed media strategy therefore makes sense to Abahlali (which does not command the kinds of resources that the TAC has access to). And the democratic potential of the Internet (no gate-keeping regarding exhibition and distribution of films made about Abahlali, for example), points to new democratic potentials for social movements' relationship to film and cinema in transitioning societies like South Africa.

Notes

1 With research assistance from Adam Esrig.
2 Achmat was not the only AIDS activist who made a comparison between the AIDS pandemic in South Africa and the Nazi Holocaust. Edwin Cameron, an openly gay,

HIV-positive judge, accused Mbeki of the same charge in a front-page article published in the weekly newspaper the *Mail & Guardian* (see Cameron 2005).
3 Ben Cashdan also directed *Two Trevors Go to Washington* (2000), a 35-minute film contrasting the different experiences of Trevor Manuel, South Africa's first black finance minister, and Trevor Ngwane, the leader of the Soweto Electricity Crisis Committee, at the meetings of the World Bank and IMF in Washington in 2000.

References

Bosch, T. (2003) 'Radio, Community and Identity in South Africa', unpublished PhD dissertation, Athens, Ohio University.
Cameron, E. (2005) *Witness to AIDS*. New York: I.B. Taurus.
Dugger, C. (2009) 'Breaking with Past, South Africa Issues Broads AIDS Policy', *New York Times*, 2 December, p. A6.
Friedman, S. and Mottiar, S. (2006) 'The TAC and Politics of Morality', in Ballard, R., Habib, A. and Valodia, I. (eds) *Voices of Protest; Social Movements in Post Apartheid South Africa*. Pietermaritzburg: University of KwaZulu-Natal Press.
Johnson, K. and Jacobs, S. (2004) 'Democratization and the Rhetoric of Rights: Contradictions and Debate in Postapartheid South Africa', in Englund, H. and Nyamnjoh, F. (eds) *Rights and the Politics of Recognition in Africa*. London: Zed Books.
Karon, T. (2001) 'South African AIDS Activist, Zackie Achmat', *Time*, 19 April.
Masilela, N. and Balseiro, I. (eds) (2003) *To Change Reels: Film and Film Culture in South Africa*. Detroit: Wayne State University Press.
Nixon, R. (1994) *Homelands, Harlem, and Hollywood: South African Culture and the World Beyond*. New York: Routledge.
Rogosin, L. (2004) *Come Back Africa: Lionel Rogosin – A Man Possessed*. Johannesburg: STE Publishers.
Sparks, A. (2003) *Beyond The Miracle: Inside the New South Africa*. Chicago: University of Chicago Press.
Steps for the Future (n.d.) Online, available at: www.steps.co.za/films_more.php?id=241 (accessed 1 December 2009).
Switzer, L. and Adhikari, M. (eds) (2000) *South Africa's Resistance Press: Alternative Voices in the Last Generation under Apartheid*. Athens, OH: Ohio University Press.
Treatment Action Campaign (n.d.) Online, available at: www.tac.org.za (accessed 15 November 2009).
Van Kessel, I. (2000) *'Beyond Our Wildest Dreams'. The United Democratic Front and the Transformation of South Africa*. Charlottesville: University of Virginia Press.

Part III

Audiences, agency and media in everyday life

Chapter 10

The Amazing Race in Burkina Faso

H. Leslie Steeves[1]

In November 2007 the US reality hit *The Amazing Race* aired two episodes filmed in Burkina Faso, a seldom visited or televised West African country. Contestants raced in pairs to milk camels, teach schoolchildren, catch chickens, learn dance moves, pan for gold, and navigate a congested market. Their remarks indicate a range of reactions: ignorance about Burkina Faso, excitement to visit Africa, disgust with flies and hygiene, discomfort with African poverty, and a renewed appreciation for the material comforts of home. In contrast, the many Africans encountered on the race are entirely silent beyond their few scripted lines.

While Burkina Faso's appearance on the programme counters the historic neglect of Africa in Western media, the silent Burkinabé[2] also mirror a central critique of modernist development paradigms, that is, their top-down approaches, with little voice for local people in decisions and strategies that affect them. Imperialist development aid is supported by media concentration and globalization, resulting in the spread of Western values via popular culture, which helps sustain and extend neoliberal discourses.

Over the past decade US primetime reality programmes such as CBS hits *The Amazing Race* (*TAR*) and *Survivor* have greatly increased the presence of developing countries in Africa and elsewhere in globalized Western media, a trend that has been praised for increasing audience awareness of these countries. Others have critiqued the representations for reinforcing colonial narrative patterns and commodifying cultures (e.g. Delisle 2003; Hubbard and Mathers 2004; Jordan 2006; Wright 2006; Steeves 2008). Few studies, however, have followed these programmes to their destinations to find out how they are experienced and negotiated at the grassroots and how the programmes may benefit and harm host countries. This study therefore explores the impressions and responses of Burkinabé involved with *TAR*, as the programme was being filmed in July 2007.

Briefly, *TAR* is a global pairs race, with pairs related in some way. Pairs compete in contests ('challenges') as they race; the first team to arrive at the end point for each episode or 'leg of the race', wins a prize, which is often a trip courtesy of Travelocity, the programme's main sponsor. The last team to arrive is usually eliminated. The team to arrive first at the final destination wins US$1

million. *TAR* debuted in the United States in September 2001, and the first destination was Zambia. *TAR* has since earned eight Primetime Emmy Awards,
including seven for 'Outstanding Reality-Competition Program'. The programme has been lauded for providing positive representations of seldom-seen
destinations. In fact, up to season 12, when two episodes were filmed in Burkina
Faso, 14 different African countries had been the primary sites for 23 episodes.
Hence, Africa had appeared 15 per cent of the time, much more than on *Survivor*
or on any other primetime network programme (Steeves 2008: 429).[3]

In this study I sought to gain insight into Burkinabés' relative agency in influencing representations; local participants' and observers' understandings and
experiences of the production; and their perspectives on its relative costs and
benefits. I begin by situating the study in Burkina Faso, a land-locked country in
francophone West Africa. Next I review the postcolonial framework for the study
and related research on Africa's representation in media. A review of the methodology and summary of the episodes follow. I then discuss the findings regarding:
agency in decision-making, experiences reported by Burkinabé, and costs and
benefits.

Context of the study

As tourism-related companies such as Travelocity, American Airlines and Royal
Caribbean sponsor *The Amazing Race*, the context of Burkina Faso[4] and the country's attractions for tourism warrant consideration. Of all the countries appearing
in *TAR* thus far, Burkina Faso is the most challenged to meet its people's basic
human needs, according to the UN Development Programme's Human Development Index (2007).[5] Burkina Faso, at number 176, is ranked second to lowest,
just below Mali, Niger and Guinea-Bissau and above Sierra Leone. None of these
other countries have thus far appeared in *TAR*.

With about 90 per cent of its 15 million people engaged in subsistence agriculture, Burkina's economy depends almost entirely on agricultural exports (e.g.
cotton) and international aid. The rural population suffers from drought and trop-
ical diseases, and healthcare resources are scarce (UNDP 2007; CIA 2008).
French is the language of the government and media, yet most Burkinabé speak
an ethnic language as their first language. The Moré-speaking Mossi group constitute over 40 per cent of the population, while the other 60 per cent is comprised of well over 50 minority ethic groups (CIA 2008).

Burkina Faso is hardly a popular tourism destination. Only 300,000 people
visit annually and most for business purposes (Debo Hobo dot Com 2007).
Burkina's share of Africa's tourism revenues is so small that it is not among the 22
African countries listed by the UN World Tourism Organization (2007) in its
annual *Tourism Highlights*.[6] Despite these statistics, plus a weak tourism infrastructure, Burkina has initiated a campaign to increase tourism, holding an international exhibition in the capital Ouagadougou in the autumn of 2007 (Debo Hobo
dot Com 2007). Attractions include the country's arts. Burkina hosts FESPACO,

Africa's largest film festival, and also is known for its novelists, playwrights, music, unique mask and dancing traditions, and its handicraft industry. The government's willingness to cooperate with *TAR* probably aligned with efforts to attract tourists for these and other features, including historic mosques, dramatic landscapes and wildlife.

Postcolonial framework and related studies

Postcolonial studies aim to critically examine and theorize 'the problematics of colonization and decolonization' while offering 'interventionist theoretical perspectives' in order to push for more equitable relations with subaltern groups (Shome and Hegde 2002: 250, 261). Postcolonial questions became increasingly salient as a result of post–Second World War independence movements, immigrant migrations to Western cities, and Western contact via aid (Said 1978). The limitless reach and impact of globalization sparked further postcolonial debates and theory building (Bhabha 1994; Shohat and Stam 1994; Garcia Canclini 1995; Kraidy 2002; Shome and Hegde 2002).

Postcolonial studies address these phenomena in part via 'resistant readings of the invisible operations of power produced through media accounts, representations and practices', with careful attention to historical and local context (Hegde 2005: 62). The Marxian concept of commodification has been especially helpful in postcolonial critiques of hegemonic process in highly commercialized representations (Spivak 1988, 2000; Slater 1999; Shome and Hegde 2002; Kraidy 2005; Jhally 2006; Steeves 2008). Marx and Engels argued that the bourgeoisie exploited personal worth and converted previously non-material relations into exchange value. They predicted that commodification would spread globally and that nothing would be immune (1948: 11–12). Marx later introduced the notion of commodity fetish, an analogy to highlight the power and appeal of commodities to negate values previously central in society, replacing non-material values with material things (1967: 72).

Since then postcolonial scholars and political economists have continued to analyse the global reach of capitalism. Tracing the evolution of advertising, Jhally (2006: 92) observes that the primary theme since the 1960s has been totemism, which merges elements of previous stages (of idolatry, iconology and narcissism) into forms of 'lifestyle advertising', in which products signify group values. Watts and Orbe (2002) use the term spectacular consumption to describe the ways in which advertising may appropriate otherness as a commodity, thereby masking differences between groups represented and media audiences. Steeves (2008) applies this concept to reality television, showing how these programmmes construct cultural authenticity as a market value, also hiding the fear and ambivalence US audiences feel towards foreign cultures, particularly in Africa.

Analyses of tourism similarly show how tourism is commodified as a lifestyle, often motivated by a search for authenticity, in which tourists aim to experience personal transformation via exposure to cultural difference (MacCannell 1992;

Wirosardjoino 1992; O'Barr 1994; Mowforth and Munt 1998; Mustonen 2005). In fact, exposure to difference by venturing outside one's comfort zone often does lead to personal growth. Benefits for host countries frequently emphasized in articles about tourism – including alternative forms, such as ecotourism, cultural tourism and altruistic tourism – may include sustaining cultural pride and providing a crucial source of revenue (Caton and Santos 2007). These and other benefits must be recognized alongside any critique.

Overlapping postcolonial processes that contribute to commodification include erasure, lack of agency and hybridity, all of which help sustain hegemonic Eurocentrism and racism (Spivak 1988; Shohat and Stam 1994; Kraidy 2002, 2005; Shome and Hegde 2002; Steeves 2008). Erasure is evident both in the absence of particular peoples and places from Western media and in their homogenization, i.e. the obscuring of diversity and context into 'static categories of ethnic culture' (Shome and Hegde 2002: 263). Patterns of erasure have been observed in Africa's representation in news and media entertainment (e.g. Hawk 1992; Brookes 1995; Steeves 2008) and in tourism advertising (e.g. Boynton 1997; Butcher 1997; Sobania 2002). Erasure is closely related to agency or voice, as erasures often occur because the colonized lack agency to create their own representations (Spivak 1988; Shone and Hegde 2002). Finally, hybridity is concerned with the nature and outcomes of cultural mixture as a result of colonization and globalization. The concept has many different meanings, including interpretations viewing hybridity as form of resistance by the colonized (e.g. Bhabha 1994). Kraidy (2002, 2005) contests such views, arguing that they neglect hegemony and power. At the same time, however, hybridity is not the same as imperialism: 'a critical hybridity theory considers hybridity as a space where intercultural and international communication practices are continuously negotiated in interactions of differential power' (Kraidy 2002: 317). Hence, agency and hybridity are also related, in that agency significantly shapes the power dynamics of the hybridity process. Many studies of global media and popular culture have observed links between hybridity and power, hegemony, and commodification (e.g. Kraidy 2002, 2005; Parameswaran 2002; Darling-Wolf 2006).

In studying Africa's representation on reality television I proposed the notion 'hybrid encounter' as a means of distinguishing the brief interactions on these programmes from hybridity resulting from extended contact (Steeves 2008). In doing so, I borrowed from studies of colonial fiction describing travellers as 'border creatures', who freely appropriate from native cultures, revealing superior power in the relationship (Dixon 1995: 62–5). Similarly, tourists, including *TAR* contestants, briefly become border creatures in their encounters along the way. Numerous studies of tourism likewise observe inequality and appropriation (e.g. O'Barr 1994; Dann 1996; Edwards 1996; Sobania 2002). Previous studies of reality television reveal consistent themes (e.g. Delisle 2003; Hubbard and Mathers 2004; Jordan 2006; Wright 2006). My study of the hybrid encounter on three US reality programmess found considerable evidence of power asymmetries indicated by: erasure via homogenization; the near complete-absence of Africans' voices alongside abundant contestant voices; and other indications of inequality and commodification in the hybrid encounter, which took several forms: of tourism, imitation and altruism (Steeves 2008).[7] This study extends my previous research via a case study of how Burkinabé, who revealed little agency in the hybrid encounters televised by *TAR* in November 2007, in fact experienced and negotiated these encounters during production.

Method

The primary methodology was via qualitative interviews with numerous Burkinabé at their homes and workplaces in order to understand the local implications of globalized media (e.g. Fontana and Frey 1994: 365–8; Murphy and Kraidy 2003). Certainly my interview encounters are vulnerable to postcolonial critique, perhaps somewhat comparable to my critique of *TAR* encounters: I visited only briefly and obviously had the means to travel and initiate relationships, making exchanges fundamentally unequal. Yet I agree with Kraidy and Murphy (2003: 300–1) and others who argue for the value of contextualizing our studies of hybridities in order to move away from sweeping generalizations – based exclusively on textual analyses – to better understand how power operates locally.

I hired a Burkinabé interpreter fluent in English, French and Moré, the dominant language in the rural areas surrounding Ouagadougou. All but one of *TAR*'s contests took place in predominantly Moré-speaking locations. The interpreter and I jointly watched and discussed the episodes twice. Two American expatriates watched with us, sharing additional questions and reactions. These sessions were helpful both in preparing the interpreter and in contributing some insights in advance. For instance the interpreter recognized locations in Ouagadougou, as well as some Burkinabé participants as actors. Additionally, I interviewed three people affiliated with the Ouagadougou-based company that was hired to co-produce the episodes: a production assistant, the production manager for the episodes and the director of the company (referred to as co-production assistant, co-production manager and co-production director).

Interviews in Burkina Faso were conducted at every production location over a period of one week in late February and early March of 2008 – three rural villages and two adjoining markets in Ouagadougou, as well as at the co-production company. In all contest locations my interpreter and I first met with the appropriate chief or other person of authority (e.g. market head) to seek permission to enter, explain the project, find out about the individual's knowledge and experience of the production, and obtain recommendations for interviews with others. My presence sparked considerable interest at contest sites, resulting in group interviews and discussions with as many as ten or 20 at a time. Respondents were not paid, but I brought kola nuts to chiefs, a sign of respect in the culture, as well as T-shirts, which I gave to chiefs and others who provided assistance, including co-producers. I brought a Polaroid camera and took dozens of photographs to give respondents following interviews. My interviews with the co-producers enabled me to clear up remaining questions and find out about the timeline of their involvement with *TAR*, their knowledge of the programme, and their role in influencing production decisions. I also interviewed a local broadcast journalist, Ouézen Louis Oulon, who provided information on the content of local television and its availability.

Following my return to the United States I conducted two phone interviews: with a producer familiar with *TAR* (referred to as television producer) and with Bertram van Munster, *TAR*'s Executive Producer, Director and Co-Creator. Finally, I carried out an informal focus group session with four Burkinabé students at my university. I invited them to watch the episodes and share their reactions. These later conversations were helpful in validating responses on-site, as well as providing further insight into the production process. See the Appendix for a list of all interviews referenced.

The episodes

A summary of the episodes is necessary before discussing findings. The two episodes studied were filmed on 13–16 July 2007 and aired on 18 and 25 November 2007. Both included comments by host Phil Keoghan describing Burkina Faso as 'a small developing country in West Africa' (18 November) and a 'developing West African nation famous for international festivals celebrating music, art and filmmaking' (25 November).

The 18 November episode begins in Amsterdam, where contestants find out that their next destination is Ouagadougou, which most have neither heard of nor can pronounce. They arrive in Ouagadougou via Paris, where they are directed to take taxis to the train station. There, a clue box tells them to 'travel by train to Bingo'. As the train doesn't leave until the following day, they stay at a nearby hotel, where they dance and drink beer. Upon arriving in Bingo, a rural village west of Ouagadougou, they find a clue box directing them to a 'road block' contest, where a member of each team competes to milk the camels of Tuareg nomads, who viewers are told inhabit the area. After this, teams must lead four camels along a path to their next clue, which directs them to a nearby school where they choose to 'teach it or learn it', i.e. use flash cards to teach English words to schoolchildren or learn Moré words taught by the children. Upon completion, they are directed to follow a marked path to the outskirts of Bingo and to the end of this leg of the race. There, teams are greeted by Phil Keoghan and a Burkinabé woman, and the last team to arrive is eliminated. At this point, torrential rain begins to fall, so everyone is soaked at the finish line in Bingo, which Keoghan says is the 'pit stop'.

The 25 November episode begins at the pit stop, which viewers again are told is in Bingo,[8] and where contestants are directed to follow a path to a nearby village, give a gift to 'Chief Dakisaga' and catch a chicken in his compound – as a gift from the chief. They must then carry the chicken and travel by taxi approximately 100 miles north to Bouda-Pelegtanga, where they choose to 'shake your pan' (pan for gold) or 'shake your booty' (learn traditional dance moves, then perform before three local celebrity judges). Following the completion of either task, contestants must walk to the Pelegtanga market and get their next clue. Along the way they encounter a 'U-turn' option, where any team may require a team behind them to go back and complete the task not chosen previously. (One team, the team eventually eliminated, is in fact U-turned.) Teams are next instructed to travel by taxi to the Tambouy Goat Market on the outskirts of Ouagadougou. The 'road block' context there requires one member of each team to load up a bicycle with an enormous quantity of supplies, including a baby goat, then successfully bring ('juggle') the supplies to a specific vendor in the neighbouring Tambouy market.[9] After completing this task, contestants finally travel by taxi to the pit stop at the Hotel DeVille, where they are greeted by Keoghan and a Burkinabé policeman, and where another team is eliminated. This also marks the close of *TAR* in Burkina Faso.

Agency and representation

According to *TAR* Executive Producer, Director and Co-Creator Bertram van Munster, he personally selects destination countries based on his extensive travel experiences. He selected Burkina Faso, in part because it would be 'very unknown' to most viewers, and because of his familiarity with and affinity for the country based on several previous visits. Plus he knew he could get co-production assistance there. According to the television producer interviewed, factors that are considered in selecting *TAR* destinations include: fit within the travel logistics of the show; potential to include interesting activities and cultural features; safety and security; and balance between familiar versus less familiar, seldom visited destinations. Additionally, van Munster said he seeks a range of climatic conditions: dry and rainy, hot and cold.

According to the co-production director, *TAR*'s initial contact was unexpected, and no one at the company had heard of *TAR* before then.

> One day I got a phone call saying they would like to shoot the program here. At that time I didn't know about the show, but they explained what they wanted and I understood better. It was also just before FESPACO[10] and we were too busy to add one more project. They explained that this could wait until after.

Just as destination countries are decided by *TAR* producers, decisions about contests are likewise made by the *TAR* team, and do not originate from co-producers or others within countries visited. In fact, van Munster personally creates and decides 98 per cent of the programme's contests, often also as a reflection of his travel experiences. For instance, the train segment in the 18 November episode was included because it resonated with an 'old memory' of van Munster's train travel in West Africa, one trip in particular from Ivory Coast to Ouagadougou.

Although van Munster and the CBS *TAR* team had decided on contests for the episodes in advance, the co-production company also had some influence, with a primary concern that the country's culture not be represented in a disrespectful manner:

> From the beginning we were very vigilant about what would be false or give a false impression of Burkina Faso. We tried to correct a lot of things. We need to be very cautious about the image of Burkina Faso. Our films are rooted in our culture. We don't want our cinema to go in a direction that we would have remorse about. We had frank exchanges with the Americans. They said that the programme is entertainment but also aimed to help viewers see the people in their environment. I believed them. They listed the kinds of activities they wanted – a wide range of activities. We coached them so they would have a more precise vision of things.
>
> (co-production director)

As an example, the co-production director recounted his successful argument against filming the Mossi emperor or his palace for the episodes:

> We went to visit the emperor of the Mossi kingdom twice to explain and seek permission. He holds the moral power over much of our country. Very many of our people share this culture. He knows my reputation. He did not want us to take pictures of him. He saw no problem with our goal to get closer to the everyday lives of people if we would do it in a gentle and respectful way. The US team wanted to shoot the emperor's palace, if not the emperor, and use it in background shots. I understood why, that it would be good cinema, but it would not be appropriate. We explained that is not appropriate here and everyone respected our position. It was important that it be done in our own way as gentlemen. We were very eager that it would not give false impressions. We did not want to show anything about the people that would diminish their dignity.

While the above comments show that respectful representations in line with cultural values would be important, it was also evident that *TAR*'s primary status as an entertainment show meant that accuracy would be weighed against entertainment value and expedience. Being previously unfamiliar with *TAR* and having never seen it, in this grey area the co-producers were reliant on the CBS team's explanation of the programme and on CBS editorial decisions. Most American and other fan audiences undoubtedly understand that *TAR* is an entertainment programme and not a serious documentary, but rather a 'post-documentary', in combining traditional documentary elements with staging for 'engagement and pleasure' (Corner 2002: 263–5). Nonetheless its 'reality' status, its many Emmy awards, and its travelogue qualities strongly suggest that locations are represented accurately. Accuracy also is often suggested in comments by the programme host, contestants, and in articles about the programme (e.g. Beck and Smith 2006).

In fact, the accuracy or 'reality' of the representations was mixed. Locations filmed in the two episodes do exist, as do elements of activities replicated in contests. However, the production teams used considerable creative license and embellishment in staging contests. Additionally, while many of the seemingly ordinary people who appeared in the episodes were in fact ordinary Burkinabé, others were actors, producers or politicians, identified via casting call or invited to participate.

Interviews with the co-production crew and villagers in Bingo confirmed one of the most significant deviations from reality: the programme host's claim in the 18 November episode that Tuareg nomads and camels inhabit the area. According to the co-production director (and further confirmed by van Munster), the co-producers' role was primarily to help select locations and make arrangements for the contests that had already been planned. Bingo was selected because *TAR* needed a village with a school by the railway: 'Bingo was the nearest village that met their needs.' Whether or not Tuareg lived there did not matter. According to the co-production assistant, 'There are no Tuareg in Bingo. Bingo is savanna, and Turareg inhabit the desert'. According to a villager in Bingo, 'First the film people came to say they wanted friendship, then they installed things, then the camels came – about 60 camels and 10 Tuareg' (Bingo villager #1). Several villagers in Bingo reported seeing Tuareg and camels come on foot. The co-production director described getting the camels and Tuareg to and from Bingo as particularly complicated:

> That was one of the most challenging things. They all came walking, about 35 from the north, 250 km. away, and the rest from a place – not so far away – that keeps camels for milk. Afterwards we took the ones from the north back by truck.

In another representational inaccuracy, the contestants' quick success in panning for gold suggests that Burkina must possess great wealth in gold. Burkinabé who watched the episodes found this contest particularly amusing, given the country's natural resource limitations. The co-production director said that Bouda-Pelegtanga[11] was selected because it was the nearest site to Ouagadougou with gold. According to a local gold-washer in Bouda: 'Ten persons were hired to dig five holes, so two men dug each hole. They put water in each hole just before the Americans arrived. Gold was put in so they could find it easily.' Finally, sorting out ordinary Burkinabé from actors and others also arguably reveals a type of deviation from accuracy or 'reality', as *TAR* is edited such that Burkinabé participants appear to be ordinary local people who have been invited to participate. Conversations with the co-producers and others confirmed that the schoolchildren and teacher who appeared in the 'teach it or learn it' contest in Bingo were actors obtained via a casting call in Ouagadougou (co-production director;

Bingo School headmaster). Chief Dakisaga was supposed to be played by a local actor named Dakisaga; but as Dakisaga was unexpectedly unavailable, the co-production manager played the chief. In this instance, not only was the chief of Bingo misrepresented, but also the location, as the pit stop was Bazoule, not Bingo, as stated by the host in both episodes. Here it is important to note that the dress of a traditional Mossi chief was deliberately misrepresented so that any Burkinabé viewing the programme would know that a real chief had not appeared in the programme (co-production director).[12] Other actors played the judges at the Pelegtanga dance contest and the greeters at both pit stops.[13] On the other hand, many ordinary Burkinabé also appeared in the episodes. These included taxi drivers at the airport, some gold diggers and washers in Bouda, dance spectators in Pelegtanga, and all of the vendors at the two Tambouy markets, including the eight vendors who held clues for contestants (co-production director).

Perceptions and experience of the 'film'

Burkina Faso's broadcast media are government owned and controlled; over 70 per cent of the national television content is produced in Burkina; the rest comes from France, with some from Latin America and other parts of Africa. In addition, most rural areas of Burkina where 90 per cent of the people live are minimally electrified, if at all; therefore, television access is widespread only in urban areas (Oulon).[14] Hence most Burkinabé had virtually no familiarity with *TAR* or other Western reality entertainment programmes prior to their encounter with the production.

The co-production director's roles included that of 'local facilitator', or explaining in advance to people what was going to happen and having many of them sign release forms:

> I always explained want we wanted to do and the aim of the production – an American programme, for fun, but also to show about the Burkina way of life. So people accepted that before they participated. If people did not accept that, they did not have to participate. The US side understood this. These people may look shy in the programmes, but they knew exactly what it was about and were free to accept or not accept.

While the co-production director undoubtedly did his best under difficult and hurried circumstances, virtually none of the people I spoke with at any of the contest locations, even including the production assistant interviewed, had more than a vague idea of what was going on. According to the co-production assistant, 'We knew it was some type of race, but since it is not in our habit to see such races, we didn't actually know what it was'.

Part of the reason of course was lack of prior exposure. However, additionally, the co-production team was constrained by rules emphasizing secrecy about destinations, contests and outcomes: 'Our own friends didn't know what we were working on' (co-production director). The television producer and van Munster confirmed that everyone close to the production – including thousands each season of *TAR* – must sign a strict confidentiality agreement. However, impoverished local people in developing countries generally would not be asked to sign (television producer). At every production location I sought out people who observed and/or somehow participated in the production, and asked the simple questions: 'What was it about?' 'What did you think of it?' Responses included the following:

We are still wondering (what it was about).

(Bingo villager #1)

It was a film of some type.

(Bingo villager #2)

I didn't know why they brought camels and everything else. No one told us.

(Bingo villager #3)

They promised to come and tell us about it later, but then a heavy rain came so they left in a hurry without ever telling us.

(Bingo villager #4)

I don't know. I saw everything. I saw the white people trying to milk the camels and drink the milk (laughter).

(Bingo villager #5)

Was it a race? We in Burkina don't have time for things like that.

(Bingo villager #6)

I don't know exactly, some type of race with an objective to it. One of the producers explained that they go many places and end here. The rain came while they were filming, so they left quickly.

(Bingo School headmaster)[15]

I was surprised. I wasn't informed about the film until that day. There were many cars and about 200 people. They brought their own food, so I didn't cook that day. The only thing they asked me for was ten chickens.

(chef, Bazoule)

I was not informed until that very day. They didn't take the time to explain. I was told that a production team was making a film involving a dancing group and a gold site. I thought it was a film about dancing and extracting gold. I even asked to meet with them, but they didn't come, so I never learned anything about it. I saw young white men and women dancing with the local dancers, but I didn't know what it was about ... I am very pleased that you have come and explained because the film people didn't care.

(Chief of Pelegtanga)

I was not informed until that day. They got permission from the owner in Ouaga. I still don't know the purpose.

(security guard for the gold site)

I have no idea what it was about.

(Pelegtanga villager #1)

I don't know. We saw white people dancing and holding sticks trying to imitate the local dancers. We all laughed. We had a good time. Is it possible that they will come back?

(Pelegtanga villager #2)

They explained that they want to show the African way of living, so they are making a film to show how the African people live. But everyone was in a big hurry. They said they had another thing to do in the other market.

(Head of Tambouy Goat Market)

A promotion team came two weeks before filming and met our staff. I don't know why they chose our market or much about the film except that it will be shown in the country of the white people. They want to know more about the way of living of the black people. Many aspects of our living they do not know, not even what is a goat.

(Head of neighbouring Tambouy Market)

It was for a film, but I don't know what type. They promised to send it, but I haven't seen it. No one even called to say thank you.

(Tambouy vendor #1)

I don't know anything about the film, except it will be shown in America. I would like to see the film and find out whether or not it was successful.

(Tambouy vendor #2)

I have included these extended comments not to criticize the co-producers, who were working with hundreds of Burkinabé with no prior exposure to US reality television. Even they were unfamiliar with *TAR*, relying on what they were told; plus they were heavily constrained by confidentiality rules, and the pace of production created time and resource constraints. However, the comments do help give voice to the silent Burkinabé who observed and participated in contests, encountering US contestants and producers in the process.

The dominant voices of US contestants show a range of reactions. Particularly significant were confessional remarks aired towards the close of the second episode. Several contestants comment on the profound impact of witnessing such stark poverty, one even breaking down in tears. Typical examples of their reactions include the following:

> Fly from Amsterdam to Ou ... wherever this place is.
>
> (reading the clue, 18 November)

> Fly to Ouaga. We need to find out where the hell it is.
>
> (18 November)

> We just got our tickets and I'm really excited. I never thought I'd ever be going to Africa in my whole life.
>
> (18 November)

> This place is a little scary.
>
> (18 November)

> There is just trash piled up. It's beyond dirty. Nothing is clean. I couldn't live this way.
>
> (18 November)

> It is absolutely an incredible sight – just seeing how people live, that places like this actually exist and how lucky we are to be here.
>
> (18 November)

> This has been an emotional day ... The people here are wonderful. I mean, they grow up and they live, and this is it for them.
>
> (25 November)

> It's OK, the people don't have anything here. Money doesn't make you happy ... We'll make our million another way.
>
> (eliminated team member, 25 November)

In contrast, Burkinabé are almost entirely voiceless, and audiences learn nothing of their culture or views from their perspectives. Only one has unscripted lines, a taxi driver, who is accused by two white female contestants of cheating them in the 18 November episode. His lines are limited to his insistence on a certain price. For a US audience, this image of a black man cheating white women arguably resonates with a racist history, which is further evoked when one of the women adds that Burkina is 'scary' and she fears being kidnapped and 'sold to people for money'.

Burkinabé I spoke with certainly could have provided illuminating information on their culture. They might also have asked questions such as: 'What is this film about?' 'Why are you in a hurry?' 'How do you have time for such a race?' 'Will you come back?' 'Will you send the film so we can see it?' As 'postcolonial intervention pushes for more socially responsible problematizations of communication' that will 'lead eventually to a more just and equitable knowledge base about the third world' (Shome and Hegde 2002: 261), more effort to include Burkinabé voices and answer their questions may have made a difference towards this goal.

Benefits and costs

While *TAR*'s representations of Burkina Faso obviously benefited the CBS network, global sponsors, the US cast, and global consumers, what were the benefits and costs for Burkinabé? Mostly obviously, *TAR* exposed a large prime-time audience to Burkina Faso's existence, perhaps for the first time. Although African catastrophes appear occasionally in news (e.g. Hawk 1992), Burkina Faso's vibrant culture, and its poverty and routine cyles of rain and drought, have seldom been deemed newsworthy. Several African countries have appeared since 2000 in US reality television, but *TAR*'s visit to Burkina Faso was the country's first appearance as a destination in any programme. This is not insignificant, and I note that all four Burkinabé students who watched the episodes reported considerable excitement that Burkina Faso had been featured so prominently on US television.

A previously noted motive for Burkina Faso's cooperation probably was to support tourism via exposure. The Ministry of Culture has launched a campaign to increase tourism, and Burkina does offer some attractions. However, the challenges are great, including a poor infrastructure and language barriers. Nonetheless, Burkinabé did express hopefulness that *TAR* would attract tourists; and the co-production manager said it was his primary motive for participating, even citing my presence as evidence: 'For myself, I wanted to do it because I wanted to help give a good face to Burkina Faso for tourism. Because of *The Amazing Race* you came here. I hope that others also will.' At the same time, type of exposure also matters. For the most part, imitation contests in the episodes resonate with previous critiques of Africa in travel and tourism marketing in their use of homogenizing activities and scenery that do entertain but also symbolize – and fetishize – the continent (e.g. Kratz and Gordon 2002; Sobania 2002; Wright 2006; Steeves 2008). These include the dancing and camel milking contests. The one contest ('teach it or learn it') that suggests altruistic tourism resonates additionally with critiques of modernist development and of Western news, in implying that Africans are victims in need of rescue by the West – by Western English teachers in this instance (Hawk 1992; Fair and Chakravartty 1999; Steeves 2008).[16] Some of the contestants' negative and emotional comments about trash and poverty support a related stereotype, one that Africans are quick to reject. These comments also were least appreciated by the Burkinabé who watched the episodes. An exception, and the favourite of Burkinabé viewers, was the contest requiring the 'juggling' of loaded bicycles through a congested market. As over-loaded bicycles and mopeds are abundant in Ouagadougou, this contest does reveal a common yet somewhat unique quality of Burkina's culture.[17]

In addition to tourism exposure, *TAR* arguably helped Burkina Faso's economy a little by employing hundreds of local people over a period of four months: the production crew, actors, interpreters, drivers, porters, cooks and dozens at each contest site to build shelters and latrines, dig holes, hand out clues and myriad other tasks. According to the co-production director, CBS gave his company the funds and authority to hire Burkinabé, therefore, also giving the company control over fees for various tasks and the responsibility to decide what would be fair, yet not too exorbitant for the context.

At each location I asked what tasks people were hired to do and how much they were paid. In general, payments were sufficient to make the work worth-while, but not too much to create conflict. For instance, the eight vendors selected by the Head of the Tambouy Market to hand clues to contestants were paid 20,000 CFA apiece (about US$40), more than a vendor would typically earn in a month. The head of each adjoining Tambouy market was paid 50,000 CFA (about US$100) to film there. At Bingo, at least 20 villagers were hired to build three toilets and ten straw shelters,[18] earning about 6,000 CFA apiece (US$12), and 50,000 CFA (US$100) was given to the school. At least two others were paid 20,000 CFA apiece (US$40) for the use of their houses during the preparations for filming. At Bouda-Pelegtanga, two Burkinabé hired to demonstrate gold panning were paid 10,000 CFA apiece (about US$20). Ten people hired to dig five holes for gold were each paid 5,000 CFA (US$10). Seven people hired to sweep the area where the dancing took place were each paid 3,000 CFA (US$ 6), and a contribution was made to the local school.

These wages are obviously low by Hollywood standards, particularly for those few Burkinabé who appeared on camera (the vendors holding clues in the Tambouy Market), and also in contrast to what *TAR* undoubtedly must pay for co-production assistance in European, Asian or other more economically developed countries. Political economic critiques of reality television have argued how the genre makes enormous profits while exploiting and commodifying ordi-nary people who have no control over their representations (e.g. Deslisle 2003; Jordan 2006; Wright 2006; Steeves 2008). This occurs because the programmes bypass professional actors and writers (and their unions), because they attract high-paying sponsors eager to associate their products with the programmes' life-style values, and because they are viewed by a global audience, given the many reruns aired around the world. Such critiques become highly relevant in settings such as Burkina Faso where people are unfamiliar with genre, few will ever see the programme, and they desperately need additional income to meet basic needs.

At the same time, most who I spoke with at production sites expressed much more curiosity than concern. Many also enjoyed their brief encounters with the production, finding considerable humour in the contestants' clumsy efforts to carry out supposedly ordinary tasks that were at best creative embellishments of the daily experiences of Burkinabé. Their greatest disappointment was the lack of opportunity for dialogue with the US visitors, as well as the producers' failure to provide information about the 'film'. Almost everyone seemed pleased with the payments received. The only complaint was by the Chief of Pelegtanga, who expected to be given a contribution for the village, but said he did not receive payment. The Chief of Bingo, who was not present during the production, also was not paid. However, he recognized that many villagers were paid for their work and he thought that on balance the village benefited: 'I was not informed, and I was not paid, but if it is for the welfare of the village and if it shows a different image of Burkina, then it doesn't matter.'

Conclusion

US reality television's recent ventures into developing countries such as Burkina Faso on the surface indicate a counter-hegemonic trend within mainstream media, as well as possible resistance to modernist discourses dominated by Western images and values. Yet closer examinations of two *TAR* episodes, alongside interviews with participants in this study, reveal underlying neoliberal values and postcolonial commodification. The programme's many cultural misrepresentations and embellishments, while being presented as 'reality', contribute to the critique, indicating erasure via homogenization. The US contestants' participation in traditional activities also contribute, as their freedom to drop into or out of local culture highlights the privilege of those in the game versus those (the 'subaltern' or 'other') who do not have such options, a difference clearly recognized in comments such as, 'We in Burkina don't have time for things like that' (Bingo villager #6). To the extent that Western audiences hold fearful or ambivalent views of Africa, the imitation contests also indicate spectacular consumption in suggesting equity and thereby obscuring differences between groups – by class, culture, race and nation (Watts and Orbe 2002). Further, Burkinabé, including the co-production team, had no role whatsoever in either creative decisions or in the editing process. Although the episodes were aired in late November 2007, the co-producers had not yet seen them at the time of my interview with them on 3 March 2008.[19]

At the same time, as this study also shows, an assertive co-production team may reduce the extent of postcolonial commodification that might otherwise take place, for instance, by ensuring that culturally sacred people and locations are not disrespected. In fact, some *TAR* contests at other destinations have not shown sufficient cultural respect, as in the staging of a contest at a historic church in Ethiopia in season six (Steeves 2008: 434). According to the television producer, *TAR* tries very hard to *not* be culturally insensitive: 'All decisions are made with respect to the culture. We are the one reality show that is always looking for positive outcomes, not negative.' Van Munster also noted the importance of cultural sensitivity in production decisions. In the Burkina episodes, the co-producers' input was crucial in this regard.

It is also difficult to weigh the value of Burkina Faso's mere appearance on a popular primetime programme. For Burkinabé in the United States, the episodes did reinforce their cultural pride; and the Burkinabé students I spoke with reported many phone calls and emails from friends and family following the broadcast. The programme may have had some educational value for US audiences, perhaps even motivating some to visit Burkina Faso. However, Burkina's primary tourism attractions – the arts – received little more than a mention by the host and were not a focus of contests. The one exception, the dancing contest, does little to distinguish Burkina from other African countries, and hence also contributes to erasure via homogenization.

TAR's production in Burkina Faso did provide income for the local co-production company and for the hundreds of Burkinabé who were hired to appear in the episodes and provide support services. Also, while Burkinabé had little agency in the hybrid encounters, they also expressed little concern. They wished the Americans well and hoped that the film – whatever its purpose – was successful. They felt amused that these visitors had so much time on their hands that they could engage in this strange pastime, but also wondered why everyone was in such a hurry. Slowing down the race just a little, or otherwise allowing more opportunities for exchange and information sharing, might help reduce the extent of commodification in the production and representations, perhaps altering editing decisions, and increasing the episodes' educational value for all participants and audiences – even within a highly commodified, 'postdocumentary' entertainment format (Corner 2002).

Finally, no matter how great the benefits for some Burkinabé and how small the perceived harm, *TAR*'s visit to Burkina Faso produced a primetime tourism commercial not so unlike those critiqued by others for homogenizing and commodifying ethnic culture while giving overwhelming agency and benefits to the visitors. The biggest beneficiaries, however, were the tourism related sponsors who were able to associate their products with the lifestyle values of global adventure travel. Further studies are needed documenting the political economic dimensions of reality programmes filmed in developing countries, as well as cultural consequences and exchanges that occur in many different contexts.

Appendix: interview respondents cited

Head of Tambouy Goat Market, 29 February 2008
Goat vendor, 29 February 2008
Head of Tambouy Market, 29 February 2008
Vendor #1, 29 February 2008
Vendor #2, 29 February 2008
Chief of Bingo, 1 March 2008
Bingo villager #1, 1 March 2008
Bingo villager #2, 1 March 2008
Bingo villager #3, 1 March 2008

Bingo villager #4, 1 March 2008
Bingo villager #5, 1 March 2008
Bingo villager #6, 1 March 2008
Bingo School headmaster, 1 March 2008
Bazoule guide, 1 March 2008
Chef, Bazoule, 1 March 2008
Chief of Pelegtanga, 3 March 2008
Head of security for gold site, 3 March 2008
Gold-washer, 3 March 2008
Pelegtanga villager #1, 3 March 2008
Pelegtanga villager #2, 3 March 2008
Co-production director, 3 March 2008
Co-production manager, 3 March 2008
Co-production assistant, 2 March 2008
Ouézen Louis Oulon, National Radio of Burkina Faso, 4 March 2008
Television producer, phone interview, 2 June 2009
Bertram van Munster, phone interview, 16 November 2009
Focus group interviews with four Burkinabé in the United States, 18 April 2009

Notes

1 A previous version of this chapter was presented to the International Communication Association, May 2009. I am grateful to John Liebhardt and Rose Armour for their assistance with fieldwork and networking in Burkina Faso, and to my interpreter Blandine Tianassé. Thanks to the dozens of Burkinabé both in Burkina and the United States who shared their insights with me; and to producers familiar with *TAR*, particularly Bertram van Munster. I appreciate support provided by the University of Oregon African Studies Programme. Finally, thanks to Herman Wasserman for his encouragement and helpful feedback.

2 The term Burkinabé is both a noun (singular and plural), referencing the people of Burkina Faso, and an adjective, referencing the culture of the country.

3 I note that Africa was not a destination during seasons 13, 14 or 15 (through autumn 2009); therefore, Africa's proportionate presence on *TAR* has gone down since season 12. *TAR* franchises have been sold for productions in Asia, Europe and South America. Plus the original (US) version has been purchased for viewing as reruns in many countries globally.

4 Burkina Faso is often shortened to Burkina in popular discourse.

5 The Human Development Index is derived from data on: life expectancy at birth; adult literacy rate; school enrollment; and GDP per capita.

6 Data show that Egypt, Morocco and South Africa by far dominate Africa's tourism market, though there have been recent increases in visits to poorer sub-Saharan countries, particularly Kenya, Tanzania and Botswana (UN World Tourism Organization 2007).

7 In tourism encounters, contestants perform typical tourism activities, such as going on safari; in imitation encounters, they perform the everyday activities of local people, such as maneuvering animals; and in altruistic encounters, they do helping activities, such as bringing supplies to a hospital.

8 In fact, the pit stop is at least 20 miles away in Bazoule.

9 The neighbouring market differs in that it does not specialize in one product. It is

much larger and more congested than the goat market, with hundreds of vendors selling a broad array of everything from fabric to food to electrical parts.

10 FESPACO took place in late February 2007.

11 Pelegtanga refers to the whole village area, and Bouda is the gold site.

12 My interpreter, the production assistant, the American expatriates who saw the episodes and the Burkinabé in the focus group all knew immediately that Dakisaga was not a real Mossi chief because he was not wearing a traditional red hat. Additionally, they had heard of a Burkinabé actor by that name.

13 According to the co-production manager, the three dance judges were: Blandine Yameogo, an actor; Vincent Koala, of Burkina's National Cultural Centre; and Souleyman Ouedraogo, the Head of Programs for Burkina's National Television. The two greeters were well-known local actors.

14 Cable television, which carries CNN and other US network and French programming is available in Ouagadougou for those who can pay, almost exclusively 'VIP', such as government ministers, others in high positions, and expatriates (Oulon).

15 The Bingo schoolmaster was displaced by actors, but observed the filming. I asked if he knew it was a television programme, and he said he did not.

16 As Steeves (2008) observes, the English words taught include skyscraper, baseball and cowboy, words largely irrelevant to rural Burkinabé.

17 The television producer interviewed said that some *TAR* contests are selected in a manner that will resonate with audiences. In Africa, that would obviously include contests involving dancing or well-known ethnic groups such as Tuareg. However, *TAR* also includes some contests that feature aspects of the culture that are unknown or lesser known to audiences, such as the bicycle juggling contest.

18 The shelters blew away, but the toilets are still there and remain in use.

19 CBS had promised to send copies of the episodes, but had not done so as of 3 March 2008.

References

Beck, M. and Smith, S.J. (2006, 13 February) 'Keoghan Glad "The Amazing Race" Counters Negative World View', *The National Ledger*. Available online: www.nationalledger.com/artman/publish/article_27263446.shtml (retrieved 1 September 2006).

Bhabha, H. (1994) *The Location of Culture*. New York: Routledge.

Boynton, G. (1997) 'The Search for Authenticity: On Destroying the Village in Order to Save it', *The Nation*, 265: 18.

Brookes, H.J. (1995) ' "Suit, Tie and a Touch of Juju"—the Ideological Construction of Africa: A Critical Discourse Analysis of News on Africa in the British Press', *Discourse and Society*, 6(4): 461–94.

Butcher, J. (1997) 'Sustainable Development or Development?', in M.J. Stabler (ed.) *Tourism and Sustainability: Principles and Practice*. New York: CAB International, pp. 27–38.

Caton, K. and Santos, C.A. (2007) 'Heritage Tourism on Route 66: Deconstructing Nostalgia', *Journal of Travel Research*, 45(4): 371–86.

Central Intelligence Agency (CIA) (2008) *The World Factbook: Burkina Faso*. Available online: www.cia.gov/library/publications/the-world-factbook/print/uv.html (retrieved 14 October 2008).

Corner, J. (2002) 'Performing the Real: Documentary Diversions', *Television & New Media*, 3(3): 255–69.

Dann, G. (1996) 'The People of Tourist Brochures', in T. Selwyn (ed.) *The Tourist Image: Myths and Myth Making in Tourism*. New York: John Wiley and Sons, pp. 61–81.

Darling-Wolf, F. (2006) 'The Men and Women of *Non-no*: Gender, Race, and Hybridity in Two Japanese Magazines', *Critical Studies in Media Communication*, 23(3): 181–99.

Debo Hobo dot Com (2007) 'Burkina Faso's Bid for More Tourism'. Available online: www.debohobo.com/2007/10/26/burkina-fasos-bid-for-more-tourism (retrieved 15 October 2008).

Delisle, J.B. (2003) 'Surviving American Cultural Imperialism: Survivor and Traditions of Nineteenth-century Colonial Fiction', *The Journal of American Culture*, 26(1): 42–55.

Dixon, R. (1995) *Writing the Colonial Adventure: Race, Gender and Nation in Anglo-Australian Popular Fiction, 1875–1914*. Cambridge: Cambridge University Press.

Edwards, E. (1996) 'Postcards: Greetings from Another World', in T. Selwyn (ed.) *The Tourist Image: Myths and Myth Making in Tourism*. New York: John Wiley and Sons, pp. 197–221.

Fair, J.E. and Chakravartty, P. (1999) 'Touring Disaster: American Television Coverage of Famine in the Horn of Africa', in K. Nordenstreng and M. Griffin (eds) *International Media Monitoring*. Cresskill: Hampton, pp. 145–61.

Fontana, A. and Frey, J.H. (1994) 'Interviewing: The Art of Science', in N.K. Denzin and Y.S. Lincoln (eds) *Handbook of Qualitative Research*. Thousand Oaks: Sage, pp. 361–76.

Garcia Canclini, N. (1995) *Hybrid Cultures: Strategies for Entering and Leaving Modernity*. Trans. C.L. Chiappari and S.L. Lopez. Minneapolis: University of Minnesota Press.

Hawk, B. (1992) 'Introduction: Metaphors of African Coverage', in B. Hawk (ed.) *Africa's Media Image*. Westport: Praeger, pp. 3–14.

Hegde, R.S. (2005) 'Disciplinary Spaces and Globalization: A Postcolonial Unsettling', *Global Media and Communication*, 1(1): 59–63.

Hubbard, L. and Mathers, K. (2004) 'Surviving American Empire in Africa: The Anthropology of Reality Television', *International Journal of Cultural Studies*, 7(4): 441–59.

Jhally, S. (2006) *The Spectacle of Accumulation: Essays in Culture, Media, and Politics*. New York: Peter Lang.

Jordon, C. (2006) 'Marketing "Reality" to the World: Survivor, Post-Fordism, and Reality Television', in D.S. Escoffery (ed.) *How Real is Reality TV? Essays on Representation and Truth*. Jefferson: McFarland & Co, pp. 78–95.

Kraidy, M.M. (2002) 'Hybridity in Cultural Globalization', *Communication Theory*, 12(3): 316–39.

—— (2005) *Hybridity and the Cultural Logic of Globalization*. Philadelphia: Temple University Press.

Kraidy, M. and Murphy, P. (2003) 'Media Ethnography: Local, Global, or Translocal?', in P.D. Murphy and M. Kraidy (eds) *Global Media Studies: Ethnographic Perspectives*. New York: Routledge, pp. 299–307.

Kratz, C.A. and Gordon, R.J. (2002) 'Persistent Popular Images of Pastoralists', *Visual Anthropology*, 15: 247–65.

MacCannell, D. (1992) *Empty Meeting Grounds*. London: Routledge.

Marx, K. (1967) *Capital: A Critical Analysis of Capitalist Production, Volume I*. Ed. F. Engels. New York: International Publishers.

Marx, K. and Engels, F. (1948) *The Communist Manifesto*. New York: International Publishers.

Mowforth, M. and Munt, I. (1998) *Tourism and Sustainability*. London: Routledge.

Murphy, P. and Kraidy, M. (eds) (2003) *Global Media Studies: Ethographic Perspectives*. New York: Routledge.

Mustonen, P. (2005) 'Volunteer Tourism: Postmodern Pilgrimage?', *Journal of Tourism and Cultural Change*, 3(3): 160–77.

O'Barr, W.M. (1994) *Culture and the Ad: Exploring Otherness in the World of Advertising*. Boulder: Westview Press.

Parameswaran, R. (2002) 'Local Culture in Global Media: Excavating Colonial and Material Discourses in *National Geographic*', *Communication Theory*, 12(3): 287–315.

Said, E.W. (1978) *Orientalism*. New York: Random House.

Shohat, E. and Stam, R. (1994) *Unthinking Eurocentrism: Multiculturalism and the Media*. London: Routledge.

Shome, R. and Hegde, R.S. (2002) 'Postcolonial Approaches to Communication: Charting the Terrain, Engaging the Intersections', *Communication Theory*, 12(3): 249–70.

Slater, D. (1999) *Consumer Culture and Modernity*. Cambridge: Polity Press.

Sobania, N.W. (2002) 'But where are the Cattle? Popular Images of Maasai and Zulu Across the Twentieth Century', *Visual Anthropology*, 15: 313–46.

Spivak, G.C. (1988) 'Can the Subaltern Speak?', in L. Grossberg and C. Nelson (eds) *Marxism and the Interpretation of Culture*. Urbana: University of Illinois Press, pp. 271–313.

—— (2000) *A Critique of Postcolonial Reason*. Boston: Harvard University Press.

Steeves, H.L. (2008) 'Commodifying Africa on U.S. Network Reality Television', *Communication, Culture, and Critique*, 1(4): 416–46.

United Nations Development Programme (2007) *Human Development Report 2007/2008*. New York: Palgrave Macmillan.

United Nations World Tourism Organization (2007) 'Tourism Highlights 2007 Edition'. Available online: www.rotoruanz.com/rotorua/info/stats/global_tourism.php (retrieved 13 October 2008).

Watts, E.K. and Orbe, M.F. (2002) 'The Spectacular Consumption of "True" African American Culture: "Whassup" with the Budweiser Guys?', *Crtical Studies in Media Communication*, 19(1): 1–20.

Wirisardjono, S. (1992) 'Cultural Tourism and Marketing: An Anthropological Perspective', in W. Nuryanti (ed.) *Universal Tourism: Enriching or Degrading Culture?* Yogyakarta, Indonesia: Gadjah Mada University Press, pp. 195–201.

Wright, C.J. (2006) 'Welcome to the Jungle of the Real: Simulation, Commoditization, and *Survivor*', *The Journal of American Culture*, 29(2): 170–82.

Chapter 11

(South) African articulations of the ordinary, or, how popular print commodities (re)organize our lives

Sonja Narunsky-Laden

one cannot talk about black identity without mentioning the role that pop culture has played in reawakening and redirecting black pride in South Africa after 1994. Fashion and music are major players in building societies. South Africa experienced a fashion revolution in which we looked at our black selves and our black history for inspiration and rediscovered the face of Steve Biko, vintage *Drum* covers, and terms such as 'freedom fighter' and 'shebeen queen' ... Ours is a beautiful generation of opposites and oxymorons – rich and poor, hungry and angry, gluttons and philanthropists, artists and subjects, weaves and dreadlocks, multisexuals and clerics, doctors and patients. ... We have nothing to feel bad about, nobody to hate or envy anymore. *Being black has never been so cool and never been so desirable.*

Milisuthando Bongela (2008: 63; my emphases)

Popular culture in (South) Africa: Africanized modalities of modernity

This chapter examines popular print media in (South) Africa from a critical, socio-semiotic perspective which situates the popular in Africa firmly in the realm of the social, and argues that popular media in Africa function seminally as agents of socio-cultural change (Laden 2003). In keeping with this book's approach to the ways popular media often operate unexpectedly in both colonial and postcolonial settings, I argue that even as popular magazines are products of modern capitalism, whatever this may mean, the sense of cultural citizenship they inspire in the African context relates to historical processes of agency in the framework of urbanization and the emergence of civil society. Popular magazines are known to be fuelled principally by advertising revenue, and are unquestionably intended to profit their propagators. However, this does not reduce them to tools of cultural imperialism: in the (South) African context they are mediated by both black and white editors, journalists and advertisers, although this was not always the case. Moreover, despite the political economy dynamics of ownership and editorial policy, it is noteworthy that magazine-reading in (South) Africa and elsewhere is not, nor has it been over the years, a mandatory social practice, but has rather been taken up by vast numbers of readers on a consensual basis.

The cultural work of popular magazines in Africa lies way beyond the financial interests of their propagators, facilitating newly gendered modes of social action, and new modalities of being for contemporary Africans at large, and for South Africans in particular, who would see themselves as modern(izing) citizens, or 'Afromodern' subjects. As part of the broader working apparatus of popular culture, also integral to commercial culture(s) of consumption, popular media in Africa are also presumed to function as key drivers of, and vehicles for the dissemination of, urbanization and modernity. Focusing on the longstanding, successful consumer magazine directed at black (South) African women, *True Love*, by way of exemplification, I describe the *transformative power* and *local reworkings* of popular media and consumer culture as they come to bear on:

1   gendered constructions of women's roles in South African society; and
2   encounters with new and transforming market formations in South Africa.

At least since the nineteenth century, importations and borrowings in Africa have been more or less successfully shaped and constrained through convergence(s) with local popular traditions and media technologies, in the fields of print, film, music, radio, television, performance and drama (on such convergences in African and South African contexts, respectively, see Barber 2006: 3–8; De Kock 1996: 40; Laden 2001a, 2001b; Kruger and Watson Shariff 2001). Popular culture in Africa is hence viewed as constituted primarily through borrowed or imported cultural practices and artefacts, newly imagined, mediated and adapted through a range of media technologies. As borrowed cultural forms, print commodities have long since enabled Africans to access new resources and repertoric options, and motivate social-cultural change (see Even-Zohar 1990, 1997, 1999; Laden 2001a, 2008).

In addressing the highly successful, longstanding glossy women's publication, *True Love* (launched in 1972), I also refer briefly to *Thandi*, which first materialized in the late 1970s as a pull-out women's supplement of *Bona*, and was launched as a separate publication in 1985, as well as *True Love East Africa* (launched 2004), published in Kenya (by East African Magazines Ltd, a joint venture between Nation Media Group and MIH Print Africa), and *True Love West Africa* (launched 2005), written in Lagos, Nigeria, and published in South Africa.

Popular media technologies have inspired, and are intricately intertwined with, new popular cultural forms in Africa (see Barber 2006: 3–8). Mediatized forms of popular culture are becoming ever more prevalent, and the impact of convergences between media technologies and local popular traditions in Africa cannot be dismissed merely as 'cultural imperialism' (see Laden 2001a, 2001b, 2003; Barber 1997, 2006). For 'it is important to recognize the extent to which African cultural innovators have seized upon the possibilities of the media to revitalize their traditions and generate new forms' (Barber 2006: 3), although neither should popular cultural forms be simplistically celebrated as emancipatory without determining the uses Africans actually make of new media technologies.

While I concur with Barber on the centrality of ethnographic research, conceptually, it is important to note that, like many other commercially-oriented cultural practices, popular cultural forms frequently represent aspired to, not necessarily given, states of affairs. It is therefore their evocative power (see McCracken 1990: 104–17), and that of the commodities and beliefs they recommend, that should concern us, for these provide valid ways for people to imagine as plausible alternative realities which may be structurally opposed to their existing reality. Popular cultural forms function both as didactic and aspirational tools, and as means of proclaiming social membership. That is, it is not always what people actually do with media technologies that brings about social change, as much as the way media technologies operate as transmitters of 'elements … out of which scripts can be formed of imagined lives' (Appadurai 1997: 35). As everyday artefacts through which 'the work of the imagination is transformed' (Appadurai 1997: 9), popular media discourses in (South) Africa today provide 'a staging ground' (Appadurai 1997: 7) from which new options for 'strategies of action' (Swidler 1986) may be constructed. They represent sources of data that generate new understandings, images and concrete instructions for recommended social and individual conduct, or, more specifically, they comprise part of the toolkit from which 'actors select differing pieces for constructing lines of action' (Swidler 1986: 273).

Taking up new options in Africa is often imbued with *conviviality* (Nyamnjoh 2002: 111–17), which speaks to a sense of being 'in-fellowship', and addresses 'the interests of communal and cultural solidarities' (Nyamnjoh 2002: 111), so that individual agency and subjectivity are re-negotiated in terms of shared corporate and communal interests, social interconnectedness, interpenetration and interdependence. At the same time, it is precisely the practices and discourses of consumption that should urge us to acknowledge that African popular culture is not simply displaying the culturally homogenizing effects of 'going-West' (see Nyamnjoh 2000: 9–10), but also suggests new local reworkings of a rudimentary 'South African' idiom. Appadurai's view of practices of consumption as a 'force of habituation', as a central means of regulating, among other things, 'the rhythms of accumulation and divestiture that generate particular states of material wealth' (Nyamnjoh 2000: 26), converges with my own view of consumption and popular cultural practices as ways of regulating change, increasing the stabilizing effect of the emerging social order, and standardizing global structures of common difference(s) in the age of globalization (Wilk 1995).

Anderson's concept of the nation as an 'imagined community' (Anderson 1983) serves here as a useful point of entry into what Robert Foster has dubbed commercial, rather than strictly political or ideological, 'technologies of nation making' (Foster 1999: 265–7; Foster 1997: *passim*). In the context of postcolonial Africa and South Africa, reciprocal links obtain between mass-consumption, mass culture and the constitution of national entities (similar studies on the West include Boorstin 1973; Bronner 1989; Ewen and Ewen 1992; Fox and Lears 1983; Marchand 1985). For our purposes here, the 'commercial' technology of nation-making alludes to the ways advertising, and other forms of mass media and culture, such as soap operas, talk shows, magazines, chatrooms and blogs, popular music, film, fashion and popular fiction, all provide, *inter alia*, a variety of material and stylistic sources for 'trying on' new identity options. These cultural practices represent ways for the diverse heterogeneity of Africans and South Africans to forge a sense of themselves as sharing discursive patterns, images and objects (Miller 1995: 277–8; Foster 1999: 154; 2002: 69; LiPuma 2000). In this way (South) Africans will eventually come to believe that collectively they constitute a consumption-oriented, corporate 'national entity', which nonetheless exists, as it were, 'outside themselves'. The literature addressing the manifold and multi-layered links between popular culture, public space(s) and notions of cultural citizenship, inquiring into how imported mass or popular cultural forms have contributed to reorganizing people's lives in Africa and elsewhere, is sizeable; the present chapter is informed largely by Coplan (1985), Fiske (1987, 1990), Barber (1997, 2006), Kupe (1997), Hermes (1998, 2005), Dolby (2001, 2003, 2006), Newell (2002, 2006), Hofmeyr *et al.* (2003) and Simone (2008).

From the *kgoro/khotla* to the women's magazine?

Given the way the traditional chiefdom courtyard, the *kgoro/kgotla*, was dislocated under the impact of colonization, Christianity, migration and urbanization, the social organization of public gatherings among indigenous people necessarily changed in both urban and rural social settings. In pre-colonial times, the *kgoro/kgotla* was the principal and legal forum for public assembly and debate, settling family disputes, negotiation and participation in shared social agendas, including informal learning (i.e. hunting, obedience and manly conduct), storytelling and marriage ceremonies, even as it was also extremely hierarchical. In addition, 'the advantages of seniority, position and patronage' in the *kgoro/kgotla* 'were offset by the authority granted to eloquent disputation in its own right' (Coplan 1994: 38). However, neither the social functions of the *kgotla* nor the rhetorical skills it authorized were accessible to women (see Schapera 1938: 28; Ngcongco 1989; cf. Preston-White 1974: 210; Hofmeyr 1993: 78–102 and *passim*; Coplan 1994: 38). While the *kgoro/khotla*'s inaccessibility to women is striking (see Schapera 1938: 28; Ngcongco 1989: 42–7; cf. Preston-White 1974: 210), given the way African cultural conventions are known to have shaped and constrained the status of women in indigenous African societies (Mikell 1997), this exclusion is not surprising. Although this exclusion may appear to resonate with gendered critiques of Habermas' notion of the public sphere, the complex conventions of how social stratification determines participatory debate within the *kgoro/khotla* renders a straightforward comparison between the African *kgoro/khotla* and the European public sphere highly problematic, if not anachronistic.

On a different level, print technology has facilitated a link, however tenuous, between aural/oral and visual forms of popular culture (see Laden 2001a, 2004). I believe *True Love* maintains linkages between the participatory forum of the *kgotla/kgoro*, issues of gender and consumption, and the very (en)gendering of consumption in South Africa. For although, or perhaps because, women were barred from the traditional public space of the *kgoro/khotla*, it would appear that women's magazines published specifically for black South African women, have come to represent a newly accessible social arena in which women are urged to become actively participant. That is, many of the conventional formats, departments, modes of representation and discursive registers manifested in *True Love* bear continuities with, even as they extend and transform, indigenously (South) African social structures and oral narrative traditions (cf. Brown 1998, 1999; Gunner 1999; Coplan 1985, 1994; Hofmeyr 1993: 78–102; and Cobley 1990: 65–8, 75–91).

Since the emergence of the magazine-form for black South Africans dovetails with the consolidation of the apartheid regime in the late 1940s, I view it, however implicitly, as a dislocated, urbanized version of the *kgoro/kgotla*, through which people were able to generate a sense of social order within a climate of heightened socio-political instability. Correlations are suggested between the social and discursive function(s) of the *kgoro/kgotla* and those ascribed to the magazine-form: both provide a more or less public participatory forum for a collaborative collectivity of people, in which literal exchanges take place, whether orally or in writing. They both represent spaces in which to impart information, voice opinions, articulate disapproval and criticism, express humour, offer help and restitution to injured parties, and discuss current issues, political and non-political alike. Thus, although the physical space of the *kgoro/kgotla* has disappeared, some of its social functions may be seen as having been relocated, transformed and democratized within the textual, printed space of the magazine-form in South African urban environments.

Domesticity and gender in *True Love*

Although in the Anglo-American world the magazine-form has been yoked to the overall 'feminization' of society (see especially Douglas 1988; Huyssen 1986), the producers of magazines for black South Africans, and their readers, had little or no preconceived perception of the magazine-form as intended for and consumed primarily by women; there is scant evidence to suggest the contrary (cf. Daymond and Lenta 1990). In this regard, it is interesting that although 'middle-class' elements, practices and commodities have readily been imported and transformed from the so-called white or Western culture in South Africa, a separate magazine specifically targeting black South African women has only been in circulation since 1984. *Thandi*, the first such magazine publication, initially appeared in the late 1970s as a pull-out women's supplement of *Bona*, and was launched as a separate publication in 1985. *True Love* came into being in 1972 as a male-targeted magazine for migrant mine workers, and became a women's publication in 1984, with the sale of *Drum* and *True Love* by Jim Bailey to Nasionale Pers (Laden 2001b, 2003). From its inception until 1981, *True Love* was compiled by a group of sub-editors working on a collaborative basis, until Barney Cohen was formally appointed editor. Former editors include Barney Cohen (1981–4), Pearl Mashabela, the first black female magazine editor in South Africa (1984–8), and Bessie Tugwana and Dorah Sithole, co-editors (1988–95), who shared the editorial load (Bessie), marketing and home front assignments (*True Love* June 2002: 100–4). Tugwana notes that 'one of the challenges during our time was that many black people had no interest in reading. We made it more pictorial and pitched the magazine at a large market – which was a huge mistake. Sales fluctuated' (*True Love* June 2002: 104). Noteworthy here is Tugwana's perception of increased pictorials and a mass-market orientation at the time as erroneous. Whether this had to do with market conditions at the time, or with *True Love*'s more upmarket image, must remain unresolved for the moment. Perhaps political changes occurring in South Africa during the early 1990s (Mandela's release from prison, the referendum and first democratic elections) encouraged the publishers, Naspers, to invest in *True Love*, in the hope of reaping the fruits of the anticipated expansion of a newly viable black middle-class. *True Love* was revamped again in July 1995, just over a year after South Africa's first democratic elections (April 1994), and Khanyi Dhlomo-Mkhize, daughter of political figure Oscar Dhlomo, was appointed editor. Targeting younger black South African women 'determined to make every aspect of their lives a success' (editorial, Khanyi Dhlomo-Mkhize, *True Love* July 1996), the new, updated version of *True Love* printed on glossy paper with chrome plates, high-tech layout, typeset and design, removed the '& Family' appendix, and was given a new, still current slogan: 'All a Woman Needs'. Late in 2003, Dhlomo-Mkhize stepped down to pursue an MBA in Paris. Busisiwe Mahlaba served as editor from February 2004 until August 2007; in March 2008, Dora Sithole, currently at the editorial helm, was appointed. *True Love East Africa* (launched 2004, edited by Wayuli Muli (www.truelove.co.ke)) and *True Love West Africa* (launched 2002, written in Lagos and produced and printed in South Africa, edited by Bolla Atta (www.true-love-west-africa)), both appear to follow a similar model to the more recent glossy aspirational South African version of *True Love*, claiming to target readers who are 'vivacious, upwardly mobile and contemporary, keeping up with the constantly changing trends of the modern world as they continue to proudly celebrate the diversity and richness of their traditional society' (Bolla Atta, editor, *True Love West Africa* (www.true-love-west-africa)).

The ironies of *True Love*

For our purposes, the case of *True Love* provides a benchmark for assessing some of the ways consumer magazines for black South Africans have effected changes in the socio-cultural dynamics of contemporary South Africa and, by implication, of Africa at large. *True Love*'s steadfastness and growing readership suggest that the magazine has successfully authorized and contributed to the social mobility of male and female black South Africans residing in urban environments. Today, *True Love* is a flourishing woman's monthly, which has endured over several decades. In 2000 *True Love*'s circulation figures stood roughly at 110,000, with readership figures at 1,100,000; this corroborates the pass-on readership suggested to this author by Barney Cohen, editor of *Drum*, in 1992 (personal communication with then Deputy Editor and Features Editor, Glynnis O'Hara, 19 June 2000). In 2004 readership figure estimations stood at 2,200,000 (AMPS 2004); total circulation figures in January–March 2008, according to ABC estimations, reached 94,468, with readership figures of 2,267,000, and current readership figures are estimated at 2,943,000 (AMPS 2009).

A recent (2009) mission statement claims that 'as the premier black women's lifestyle magazine in South Africa, *True Love* is the trusted handbook for upwardly mobile black women in South Africa' (www.thought24.co.za/articles/view/true-love-magazine). Moreover, the *True Love* reader is described as:

> proudly black, dynamic, ambitious, enlightened, mature and sexy. She seeks empowerment through self-development, relationship advice, career guidance and spiritual inspiration. She respects and honours her cultural traditions and aspires to live a successful, fulfilling and dynamic life in a country that continuously presents her with interesting challenges and opportunities. She may be single or married, with or without children. She generates her own income and seeks financial security and independence, in order to fulfil her desires and to enjoy her many choices as a consumer.
>
> (www.thought24.co.za/articles/view/true-love-magazine)

By providing a platform for journalists and readers to articulate and comment on the experiences of urban black women as wives, housewives, homemakers, mothers and working women in a variety of professional and other occupations, over the years *True Love* has secured a growing, predominantly female readership, although it also has a large male readership; a demographic profile from July–December 1999 estimated the gender breakdown for *True Love* at 58.1 per cent female and 41.9 per cent male, but more recent figures are still pending. More significantly, *True Love* has contributed to recasting, through the domestic domain, the repertoire of roles played by women both at home and in society into a new, informal public and/or social sphere where shifting social responsibilities are (re-)negotiated and gradually institutionalized. In so doing, *True Love* confirmed and placed beyond question the urban status of South Africa's black middle-class, enhancing the roles and social standing of black women within it.

Although both traditional and modern variations of the family are typically held to limit women's roles as homemakers, mothers and wives to the domestic domain, similarities between Western and African societies cannot be taken for granted. This is partly due to the complex interaction between traditional, rural institutions and practices, and urban, 'capitalist' ones, manifested, among other things, in the different ways male and female migrancy in South(ern) Africa came to bear on processes of urbanization and the repatterning of domestic economies in the townships and other urban environments. For example, the shift from subsistence-oriented modes of livelihood in rural homesteads to more market-oriented options in urban environments, and the ways these were taken up by women in the cities, cannot be viewed straightforwardly as having been oppressive and denigrating to women. Women themselves were often motivated to move to the cities, and accrued benefits from urbanization, despite their many hardships (see Bozzoli 1991). Indeed, the reshaping of gender and familial roles within the framework of accelerated urbanization in South Africa was central in motivating a new range of 'popular' cultural options for black women in South Africa. Hence, the publication of both *Thandi* and *True Love* must be understood as both conditional on, and facilitated by, the changing political, socio-cultural and material circumstances of South Africa's black population in various stages of transition from rural to urban environments.

While domestic work is typically cast as epitomizing experiences of exploitation for all women, in the South African conjuncture this is far from straightforward. Social historian Belinda Bozzoli (1991) has shown that the experiences of black women as domestic workers in white suburban homes were frequently perceived by the women themselves strategically, as a constructive way of pursuing and legitimizing their own needs and interests (sending money back to their parents' rural households and investing in their own future ones), and as a means of gaining new prestige and respectability. Bozzoli implies that their sense of humiliation and exploitation at working in other women's homes was frequently marginalized relative to the benefits that accrued to them. It seems to be the case that the urban household was indeed presented in *True Love* as a site of social and cultural respectability.

True Love articulates many of the routine, trite, yet often representative uses black South African women make of material goods, social patterns and practices, experiences and beliefs in organizing their individual and collective identities and everyday lives. These goods and lifestyle practices contribute to changes in traditional versus modern, urban patterns and social positions concerning, for instance, rights for women, marital and sexual relationships, notions of sexuality, rites of courtship and sexual attraction, the 'nuclear' versus the traditional, extended family, kinship relations, witchcraft and sorcery, access to contemporary modes of household economy and household utility services (running water, sanitation and electricity), new work options, careers and occupations, media options (print and broadcast), patterns of reproduction and contraception, gendered roles both within and outside the household unit, the kitchen (as a concrete social space in its own right), changing systems of provision and patterns of consumption (foods such as maize, potatoes, corn, sugar and eggs alongside rice, tea, coffee, ketchup, breakfast cereals, canned foods such as pilchards and sardines, canned fruit, cakes and biscuits, and pizzas), procedures of food preparation, eating and drinking as social activities and as 'entertainment', changing physiognomies and uses of the body, body images and gestures (often epitomized by current and former beauty queens), clothes and fashion, bodily attributes and deportment, and standards of beauty. One example features a smiling portrait of former Miss South Africa (1995), Basetsana Makgalemele, promoting a hair relaxant (*True Love* May 2000: 4). Hair relaxants are frequently (if controversially) used by black women to straighten ('relax') their typically curly or frizzy hair. In this advert, the photographed model's elegantly coiffed hair is relaxed and shining, foregrounding aspects of respectable middle-class femininity through the model's celebrity status, acclaimed good-looks, euphemistic reference to the advertised product as 'a hair relaxer', and repeated use of the word 'relax' to induce a leisurely sense of slowing down and unwinding.

Another example stresses similarities between stereotypical beauty concerns among black and white teenagers. Featuring two teenage girls, one black and one white, the case in point is an advert for a product called Clean & Clear, a Shine Control Mattifier (*True Love* July 2000: 17). Both girls photographed are in their mid-teens, attractive, lightly made-up, and both have long hair. Although the black model's hair is braided in loose dreadlocks while the white model's is loose and flowing, similarities between them are foregrounded more than are differences. The product is one that may be used by people of all skin types and colours, and the ad appears to be directed at all potential consumers/readers. The copy treats both girls equally stereotypically, as middle-class teenagers, 'outstanding' individuals who 'shine' and are 'self-absorbed', even as they wish to remain 'shine-less', i.e. perspiration-free, respectably under control, and 'squeaky clean'. All topicalities are negotiated through both verbal and visual strategies in a variety of magazine departments and discourses (editorials, feature articles, readers' letters, advice columns and other regular columns) and in a wide range of advertisements.

Over the years *True Love* has facilitated the introduction of a range of new representational options for black South African women (behavioural, discursive and visual), new forms of sociality and neighbourliness (in work situations, in both city and suburban environments, and in areas of residence such as informal settlements, townships and, more recently, in previously 'white' suburbs), and new understandings of what might constitute feasible, appropriate and desirable domestic figurations (household arrangements binding members by marriage, kinship or familial relations, or any other domestic arrangements whereby individuals choose or agree to share a single dwelling).

True Love regularly recommends new behavioural models for women and other family members in domestic and public spheres, work and/or leisure-oriented, and in neighbourhood streets. *True Love* has motivated changing ideas for the individual and collective production of selfhood, notions of femininity, respectability and correct social etiquette, defining desired social affinities and determining critical and discriminatory standards, authorizing moral codes for 'meaningful' modes of existence and shared solidarity, 'new understandings of subjectivity, personal relationships and sex roles, ideas of domesticity, leisure, and reproduction, aspirations for new modes of employment, political and recreational pursuits, and, no less importantly, changing standards and styles, both individual and collective, of beauty, fashion, material culture, and comfort and design.

A less prominent, yet equally regularized feature of *True Love* is the inclusion of investigative articles on topical socio-political issues such as 'Women who love women: why do they?' (*True Love* September 1990), 'Domestic workers: who protects their rights?' (*True Love* October 1991) 'Murder for money: the link between insurance policies and murder' (*True Love* October 1993), 'Are women soldiers less feminine?' (*True Love* February 1994), 'Why black women MPs want to leave parliament' (*True Love* December 1998: 66–8), 'Financial abuse: men who manipulate with money' (*True Love* October 2003), 'Rape behind bars' (August 2002) and 'A war of words: silencing the free press in Zimbabwe' (*True Love* April 1993). This type of magazine reporting is not always dismissed from women's magazines, nor is it a distinguishing feature; it is typically included in upmarket international magazines such as *Elle* and *Marie Claire*, and I believe this is the motivation underlying their inclusion in more recent editions of *True Love*, from 1995 on.

Interestingly, *True Love*'s past, like its name, is steeped in irony and is quite paradoxical: it was conceived as a soft-porn publication targeted at a male readership of migrant labourers, many of whom worked in the mines (former editor Barney Cohen, *True Love* June 2002: 102). In 1972, following *Drum*'s declining sales due to steady competition from *Bona*, *Drum* editor Jim Bailey decided to issue a 'sister' publication which he named *True Love*. Modelled largely on the photo-comic magazine introduced into South Africa via *Zonk* (1962), *True Love* focused mainly on sex scandal stories, and its name was initially an attempt to cover-up for a publication that bore no likeness whatsoever to a women's magazine. Presumably aware of a similar attempt by an editor of *Ebony* USA who used the 'cheesecake' 'girlie magazine' option as a means of boosting *Ebony*'s sales (see Wolesley 1971), Bailey clearly hoped a magazine based on this model would be successful enough to offset losses incurred by *Drum*. *True Love* indeed

> became the migrant workers' bible, who were fascinated by the sex stories, while those who couldn't read were only too happy to follow the picture-stories. By then the magazine was over 100 pages and we sold enormously in mines and hostels.
>
> (former editor Barney Cohen, *True Love* June 2002: 102)

This version worked well for several years, but eventually Bailey was forced to succumb to censorship and forgo the sex scandals, and *True Love* lost tens of thousands of readers, and Bailey finally sold *Drum* and *True Love* to the Afrikaans publishing house Nasionale Pers in Cape Town (personal interview with Barney Cohen, executive editor of *Drum* and *True Love* 1992). During the 1970s Bailey also published another women's title, *Trust*, which was marketed in Nigeria, and presented itself as *Drum*'s younger sister. Nasionale Pers' proprietors sought 'to tap the growth market of black print-media readers' (Chapman 1985: 217) and decided to recast *True Love* as a women's magazine; until then, magazines for black readers in South Africa had targeted a predominantly male readership (e.g. *Zonk*, *Drum*, *Bona* and *Pace*) although they all also addressed women, as indeed did other magazine publications, including *Tribute* and *Ebony South Africa*. Needless to say, though, by 1984 there was already a thriving market for magazines targeting white South African women. The new women's magazine format of *True Love* published by Nasionale soon prompted the Argus group, Nasionale's main rival, to launch a second magazine for black South African women, and in 1985 *Thandi*, sister publication to *Bona*, was born. The new women's format of *True Love* was given an expanded title, *True Love & Family*, and a slogan: 'For the Woman Who Loves Life', coupling the Western romantic notion of 'true love' with an idealized notion of the household unit identified in Western modernity as 'the family'. Ironically enough, this version of *True Love* seems to have been impervious, 'blind' or indifferent to conventional magazine depictions, both discursive and visual, of 'romantic love'. This is not to say that it did not refer to love, sex and marriage – quite the contrary, these and many related issues systematically concerned the editors and readers of *True Love* over the years. However, these were typically construed as shared social and socializing concerns and experiences, rather than as romantic paradigms of personal intimacy between two individuals, which is, more often than not, the primary focus in most Western women's magazines (see, for instance, Zeldin 1994; Illouz 1997). This suggests that, in the past, prevailing Western understandings of privacy, passion and sexual intimacy, the self-evident correlations typically drawn between love (and marriage) and personal happiness, and between romantic love, consumer culture and leisure practices, may not knowingly correspond with African concepts of personhood and ways of being, wherein a person's sense of individuality is often largely determined by prevailing collectivist norms of sociability that do not endorse portraying the self, or 'being alone', in positive terms (see Morris 1994; Jacobson 1973). However, this has changed, as attested in recent issues of *True Love* which include sections on relationships: 'My love, are you out there?' and sex: 'Lessons in sex: liberating sex teachings' (*True Love* July 2009: 108 and 104, respectively), and 'The scrub detector: is your boyfriend a loafer?' and 'Single and loving the sex! Sister, do it for yourself!' (*True Love* November 2009: 118 and 112, respectively).

In conclusion, this chapter has addressed some of the nuanced ways in which the everyday lives of women in South Africa, and by implication in Africa at large, are refined, enhanced and shared through a popular print media commodity, the women's magazine *True Love*. I hope I have shed new light on *True Love*'s seminal function as a forum which over time has enabled black South African women to revalue their everyday lived experiences and attitudes, contributing to their sense of social wellbeing and enabling their active participation in procedures of socio-cultural change, democratization and cultural citizenship

References

AMPS (2004) *All Media and Products Survey, January to June 2004*, SAARF (South African Research Foundation). Online, available at: www.archive.saarf.co.za (last accessed 21 February 2010).

——. (2009) *All Media and Products Survey, January to June 2009*, SAARF (South African Research Foundation). Online, available at: www.saarf.co.za (last accessed 21 February 2010).

Anderson, B. (1983) *Imagined Communities: Reflections on the Origins and Spread of Nationalism*, Oxford: Oxford University Press.

Appadurai, A. (1997) 'Consumption, duration, and history,' in *Streams of Cultural Capital*, edited by Palumbo-Liu and Gumbrecht, Stanford: Stanford University Press, pp. 23–46.

Barber, K. (ed.) (1997) *Readings in African Popular Culture*, Bloomington: Indiana University Press.

——. (ed.) (2006) *Africa's Hidden Histories: Everyday Literacy and Making the Self*, Bloomington and Indianapolis: Indiana University Press.

Bongela, M. (2008) *True Love Babe* March 2008: 63.

Boorstin, D. (1973) *The Americans: The Democratic Experience*, Millers Falls: Vintage.

Bozzoli, B., with M. Nkotsoe (1991) *Women of Phokeng: Consciousness, Life Strategy and Migrancy in South Africa, 1900–1983*, Johannesburg: Ravan Press.

Bronner, S. (ed.) (1989) *Consuming Visions: Accumulation and Display of Goods in America, 1880–1920*, New York: W.W. Norton.

Brown, D. (1998) *Voicing the Text*, Cape Town: Oxford University Press.

——. (ed.) (1999) *Oral Literature and Performance in Southern Africa*, Oxford: James Currey, David Philip.

Chapman, M. (1985) *The Drum Decade: Stories from the 1950s*, Pietermaritzburg: University of Natal Press.

Cobley, A. (1990) *Class and Consciousness: The Petty Bourgeoisie in South Africa 1924–1950*, New York and London: Greenwood Press.

Coplan, D. (1985) *In Township Tonight: South Africa's Black City Music and Theatre*, Johannesburg: Ravan Press.

——. (1994) *In the Time of Cannibals: The Word Music of South Africa's Basotho Migrants*, Johannesburg: Witwatersrand University Press.

Daymond, M. and Lenta, M. (1990) 'Workshop on black women's writing and reading: Boitumelo Mofokeng, Thandi Moses, Sanna Naidoo, Leboang Sikwe, Veni Soobrayan and Nomhle Tokwe', *Current Writing* 2(1): 71–90.

De Kock, L. (1996) *Civilizing Barbarians: Missionary Narrative and the African Textual Response in Nineteenth-Century South Africa*, Johannesburg: Witwatersrand University Press and Lovedale Press.

Dolby, N. (2001) *Constructing Race: Youth, Identity, and Popular Culture in South Africa*, Albany: State University of New York Press.

——. (2003) 'Popular culture and democratic practice', *Harvard Educational Review* 73(3): 258–84.

——. (2006) 'Popular culture and public space in Africa: the possibilities of cultural citizenship', *African Studies Review* 49(3): 31–47.

Douglas, A. (1988) *The Feminization of American Culture*, New York: Anchorday.

Even-Zohar, I. (1990) 'Polysystem studies', special issue of *Poetics Today* 11(1).

——. (1997) 'Culture repertoire and the wealth of collective entities: parameters for contrastive culture analysis'. Available online: www.tau.ac.il/~itamarez (retrieved 8 January 2010).

——. (1999) 'The making of repertoire, survival and success under heterogeneity', paper presented to the 5th IASS Congress, Dresden. Available online: www.tau.ac. il/~itamarez (retrieved 8 January 2010).

Ewen, S. and Ewen, E. (1992) *Channels Of Desire: Mass Images and the Shaping of American Consciousness*, Minneapolis: University of Minnesota Press.

Fiske, J. (1987) *Television Culture*, London: Methuen.

——. (1990) 'Women and quiz shows: consumerism, patriarchy and resisting pleasures', in Brown, M. (ed.) *Television and Women's Culture: The Politics of the Popular*, London: Sage, pp. 134–43.

Foster, R. (ed.) (1997) *Nation Making: Emergent Identities in Postcolonial Melanesia*, Ann Arbor: University of Michigan Press.

——. (1999) 'The commercial construction of "new nations"', *Journal of Material Culture* 4(3): 263–82.

——. (2002) *Materializing the Nation: Commodities, Consumption and Media in Papua New Guinea*, Bloomington and Indianapolis: Indiana University Press.

Fox, R. and Jackson Lears, T. (eds) (1983) *The Culture of Consumption*, New York: Pantheon Books.

Gunner, L. (1999) 'Remaking the warrior? The role of orality in the liberation struggle and in post-apartheid South Africa', in Brown, D. (ed.) *Oral Literature and Performance in Southern Africa*, Oxford: James Currey, David Philip, pp. 50–60.

Hermes, J. (1998) 'Popular culture and cultural citizenship', in Brants, K., Hermes, J. and Van Zoonen, L. (eds) *The Media in Question: Popular Cultures and Popular Interests*, London: Sage, pp. 157–67.

——. (2005) *Re-reading Popular Culture*, London and New York: Blackwell.

Hofmeyr, I. (1993) *'We Spend Our Years as a Tale That is Told': Oral Historical Narrative in a South African Chiefdom*, London: James Currey.

Hofmeyr, I., Nyairo, J. and Ogude, J. (2003) '"Who can Bwogo me?" Popular culture in Kenya', *Social Identities* 9(3): 373–82.

Huyssen, A. (1986) 'Mass culture as woman: modernism's other', in *After the Great Divide: Modernism, Mass Culture, Postmodernism*, Bloomington: Indiana University Press, pp. 44–62.

Illouz, E. (1997) *Consuming the Romantic Utopia: Love and the Cultural Contradictions of Capitalism*, Los Angeles: University of California Press.

Jacobson, D. (1973) *Itinerant Township: Friendship and Social Order in Urban Uganda*, California: Cummings Publishing Company.

Kruger, L. and Watson Shariff, P. (2001) '"Shoo–this book makes me to think!" Education, entertainment, and "life-skills" comics in South Africa', *Poetics Today* 22(2): 475–513.

Kupe, T. (1997) 'Voices of the voiceless: popular magazines in a changing Zimbabwe, 1990–1996', unpublished PhD thesis, University of Oslo.

Laden, S. (2001a) '"Making the paper speak well", or, the pace of change in consumer magazines for black South Africans', special issue of *Poetics Today* on 'South Africa in the Global Imaginary', guest edited by Leon De Kock, co-edited by Louise Bethlehem and Sonja Laden.

——. (2001b) 'Magazine matters: toward a cultural economy of South Africa's (print) media', in Tomaselli, K. and Dunn, H. (eds) *Media, Democracy and Renewal in Southern Africa*, Denver: International Academic Publishers, pp. 181–208.

——. (2003) 'Who's afraid of the black bourgeoisie? Consumer magazines for black South Africans as an apparatus of social change', *Journal of Consumer Culture* 3(2): 191–216.

——. (2004) '"Making the paper speak well", or, the pace of change in consumer magazines for black South Africans', in de Kock, L., Bethlehem, L. and Laden, S. (eds) *South Africa in the Global Imaginary*, Pretoria: University of South Africa Press, pp. 248–77.

LiPuma, E. (2000) *Encompassing Others: The Magic of Modernity in Melanesia*, Ann Arbor: University of Michigan Press.

McCracken, G. (1990) *Culture and Consumption: New Approaches to the Symbolic Character of Consumer Goods and Activities*, Bloomington and Indianapolis: Indiana University Press.

Marchand, R. (1985) *Advertising the American Dream: Making Way for Modernity 1920–1940*, London and Berkeley: University of California Press.

Mikell, Gwendolyn (ed.) (1997) *African Feminism: The Politics of Survival in Sub-Saharan Africa*, Philadelphia: University of Pennsylvania Press.

Morris, B. (1994) *Anthropology of the Self: The Individual in Cultural Perspective*, London and Colorado: Pluto Press.

Narunsky-Laden, S. (2008) 'Identity in post-apartheid South Africa: "learning to belong" through the (commercial) media', in Hadland, A., Louw, E., Sesanti, S. and Wasserman, H. (eds) *Media Power, Politics and Identity in South African Media*, Cape Town: HSRC Press, pp. 124–48.

Newell, S. (ed.) (2002) *Readings in Popular African Fiction*, Bloomington: Indiana University Press.

——. (2006) 'Entering the territory of elites: literary activity in Ghana', in Barber, K. (ed.) *Africa's Hidden Histories: Everyday Literacy and Making the Self*, Bloomington: Indiana University Press, pp. 211–34.

Ngcongco, L. (1989) 'Tswana political traditions: how democratic?', in Holm, J. and Molutsi, P. (eds) *Democracy in Botswana*, Gaborone: Macmillan, pp. 42–7.

Nyamnjoh, F. (2000) '"For many are called but few are chosen": globalization and popular disenchantment in Africa', *African Sociological Review* 4(2): 1–45.

——. (2002) 'A child is one person's only in the womb', in Werbner, R. (ed.) *Postcolonial Subjectivities in Africa*, London and New York: Zed Books, pp. 111–38.

Preston-Whyte, E. (1974) 'Kinship and marriage', in Hammond-Tooke, W.D. (ed.) *The Bantu-speaking Peoples of Southern Africa*, London: Routledge, pp. 177–210.

Schapera, I. (1938) *A Handbook of Tswana Law and Custom*, London: Frank Cass.

Simone, A. (2008) 'Some reflections on making popular culture in urban Africa', *African Studies Review* 51(3): 75–89.

Swidler, A. (1986) 'Culture in action: symbols and strategies', *American Sociological Review* 51: 273–86.

Wilk, Richard (1995) 'Learning to be local in Belize: global systems of common difference', *Worlds Apart: Modernity through the Prism of the Local*, ed. Daniel Miller, London and New York: Routledge, pp. 110–133.

Wolesley, Roland E. (1971) *The Black Press, U.S.A*, Iowa: Iowa State University Press.

Zeldin, T. (1994) *An Intimate History of Humanity*, New York: HarperCollins.

Chapter 12

Popular TV programmes and audiences in Kinshasa

Marie-Soleil Frère

The Congolese media have undergone significant changes in the last 15 years, especially the media based in Kinshasa: a 2008 survey (Frère and IMMAR 2009) showed that the Congolese capital counted no less than 125 registered publications, 41 radio stations and 51 TV stations. TV's popularity is particularly noticeable: recent audience surveys[1] indicate that TV has surpassed radio to become the most consumed medium in the Congolese capital and is especially popular with a female audience. The aim of this chapter is to underline how, beyond the regular newscasts of the main TV stations in Kinshasa, TV has become the vehicle for alternative forms of local information and other types of representation of citizens. Indeed, new kinds of popular programmes are now bypassing both regular TV newscasts in French or those in one of the four national languages. These broadcasts have proven to be highly popular, probably because the public, which is usually ignored in traditional TV broadcasts, can recognize itself in these new shows. Following a description of the main features of TV audiences in Kinshasa, a number of media initiatives will be presented which, though undeniably popular with the public, have been strongly criticized by professional journalists, academics and media regulatory or self-regulatory bodies.[2]

TV: the prime medium in Kinshasa

With some 81 TV channels nationwide, the Democratic Republic of the Congo (DRC) presents a particularly wide range of broadcasting outlets. Whereas 88 per cent of the 381 radio stations are based outside the capital, TV stations are concentrated in Kinshasa, where 51 out of 93 (55 per cent) of all TV stations are located.

The DRC has one public TV broadcaster, the Radio Télévision nationale du Congo (RTNC), which includes two channels based in Kinshasa (RTNC1 and RTNC2) and regional services in each province.[3] The RTNC is meant to be available nationwide via satellite, but it is often unable to pay its provider and its broadcasts are thus often interrupted. The RTNC has repeatedly been accused of being a 'state' rather than a 'public' broadcaster: not only does the presidential party (the PPRD) receive extensive and almost exclusive coverage, but the

Minister of Communications and the Media, who is the authority responsible for the RTNC, is a close ally of the presidential majority.

Most numerous in the country are the private commercial stations, which total 52 stations (including two which are broadcast nationwide via satellite). They are followed by 24 religious stations, mostly located in Kinshasa, and which are linked to 'Awakening Churches'. Many of these stations are used to promote the ministry of pastors or prophets and to attract new members to their churches. TV stations belonging to more traditional Protestant, Catholic or Kimbanguist churches are rare.[4] On the contrary, their many radio stations, which are mostly located in the provinces, play a crucial role in broadcasting local information and promoting development.

Though community broadcasters dominate the radio sector, there are only four community TV stations nationwide.[5] The televisual landscape also includes two international TV stations which are freely available in Kinshasa (the French-speaking consortium TV5 Monde, and the European channel Euronews). More stations are available to the very few in possession of a proper satellite dish.

Several factors have contributed to the rapid increase in the number of TV stations in Kinshasa. New digital technologies have undoubtedly facilitated the establishment of new audiovisual broadcasters, but the lack of a clear legal and regulatory framework has also facilitated the allocation of broadcasting frequencies. The first private stations were created in the early 1990s. Antenne A (1991), Canal Kin 1 (1993), Canal Kin 2 (1995), Radio Télévision Kin Malebo (1995) and Raga TV (1996) were among the first private TV stations in Africa. In 1996, a press law formally ratified the liberalization of the Congolese media sector, but the text centred mostly on the written press, not establishing an appropriate legal framework for broadcasting. Congolese TV stations thus still operate without a mission statement, which would define their scheduling rights and obligations.

The proliferation of stations in Kinshasa has led to tensions with neighbouring Congo-Brazzaville. Indeed, DRC stations have pirated frequencies allocated to the Republic of Congo by the International Union of Telecommunications, since Kinshasa and Brazzaville are just separated by the Congo River.[6]

Moreover, recent political developments have encouraged greater television pluralism. In particular the 2006 parliamentary and presidential elections resulted in a large number of TV stations being set up to support the political careers of candidates who believed that in order to count as a Congolese decision-maker, one has to have one's own TV station. During the 2006 elections, six stations in Kinshasa were linked more or less directly to one of the 33 presidential candidates: CCTV (Canal Congo Télévision) and CKTV (Canal Kin Télévision) belonged to Jean-Pierre Bemba; Digital Congo to Joseph Kabila's sister; Afrika TV to Azarias Ruberwa; Global TV to Nzuzi wa Mbombo; Radio Lisanga Télévision to Roger Lumbala. Seven other stations belonged to parliamentary candidates aiming for a seat at the National Assembly or the Senate: RTG@ (Radio Télévision du Groupe L'Avenir) belongs to Pius Muabilu Mbayu; Tropicana TV and Numerica TV to Jean-Pierre Kibambi Shintwa; Molière TV to

Léon Nembalemba; Télé 7 to Modeste Mutinga; Horizon 33 to Jean-Charles Okoto; RTKM to Aubin Ngongo Luwowo. Mirador TV is owned by Michel Ladi Luya, a Transition deputy.

Other private commercial stations (such as Antenne A or Raga TV), whose shareholders are businessmen not directly involved in politics, are therefore operating in a complex environment, where their attempts to remain neutral are often jeopardized by the fear of their owners of putting off the major political players.[7]

TV audiences in Kinshasa

Audience surveys (IMMAR 2006, 2007, 2008) show that in recent years TV has become the most popular medium in Kinshasa.

Access to TV now equals access to radio, and is far ahead of access to mobile phones and the Internet. Given that a huge majority of Kinshasans do not have access to satellite dishes, they mostly view local programmes.

In other towns, TV has achieved limited penetration, because of the high cost of TV production and reception equipment, and because televisions require electricity, which is often lacking or unstable.[8]

While the written press and the Internet can be called elite media, used mostly by men with a secondary school level of education, TV is the only medium for which the audience is completely balanced between men and women, but also between the different age categories and education levels.

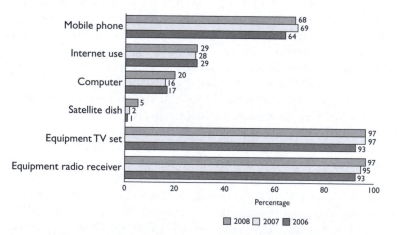

Figure 12.1 Equipment in Kinshasa, 2006–8.

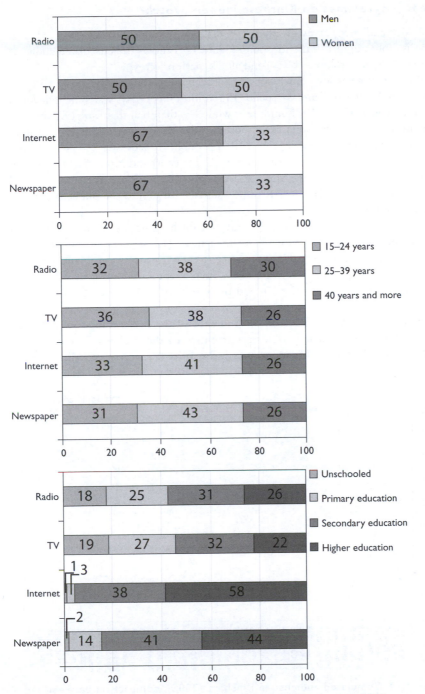

Figure 12.2 Audience profile for the news media in Kinshasa in 2008.

What programmes do Kinshasa viewers watch?

The 2008 audience survey clearly shows that TV is viewed at nighttime, whereas radio is more popular in the morning. Figure 12.3 shows the cumulated audience curves of all radio stations (black) and all TV stations (grey).

Viewing time is also much longer for television. The study shows that, on average, women in Kinshasa spend 196 minutes per day watching television (men, by contrast, spend 158 minutes), while less than half that time (97 minutes) is spent listening to the radio. The most popular station is Mirador TV, with 45 per cent viewing figures, far ahead of the public broadcaster RTNC (22 per cent)[9] and the private stations Antenne A (22 per cent) and Numerica TV (16 per cent). As for viewing time, Mirador TV is also the station that is most viewed (about 100 minutes a day), whereas the audience tunes into the public station for less than an hour a day.

RTNC is still watched every day, but not for long periods of time. The only programme drawing viewers is the evening news (13 per cent of the audience). The ongoing popularity of the national 8 p.m. newscast is easy to explain: people need access to important official decisions, such as appointments for civil servants, transfers within the administration and the results of national recruitment exams for public services.

Figure 12.5, which focuses on the audience of the four most popular stations in Kinshasa, helps to identify which programmes are the audience's favourites.

Nigerian TV serials (broadcast under the title *Love Story* on Mirador TV)

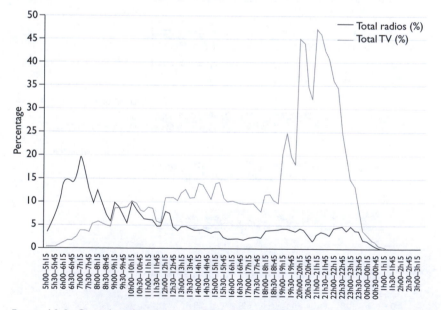

Figure 12.3 Cumulated audience in Kinshasa (2008), comparison between radio and TV over a week.

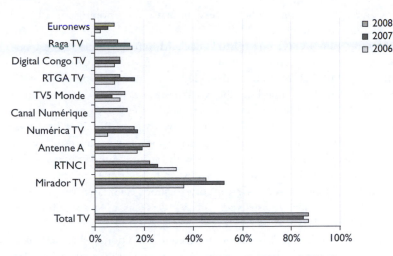

Figure 12.4 Cumulated audience for TV in Kinshasa, 2006–8.

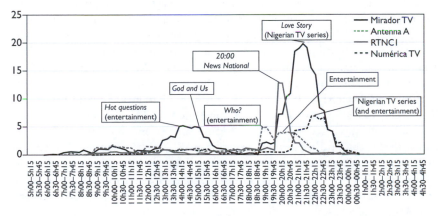

Figure 12.5 Cumulated TV audience for the top four TV stations (Monday to Friday) – Kinshasa (2008).

clearly dominate an audience which has been fragmented since the multiplication of TV channels.[10] It is clear that the audience peaks at the moment when those programmes are on air. These video productions, very roughly dubbed in French or Lingala, focus on violence, sex, witchcraft and money. 'Today, people are drawn to anything which will enable them to hope for a bit more happiness and well-being', notes Donat M'Baya, the president of Journaliste en Danger (JED), an NGO which supports press freedom in the DRC. 'These themes allow the audience to dream, in a country where everyone has ceased hoping for a better situation' (personal communication 2009).

Reports by the CEMPC (Centre d'Etude et de Monitoring de la Presse Congolaise, i.e. the monitoring center of the regulatory HAM – High Authority for the Media) and OMEC (Observatoire des Médias Congolais, professional self-regulation body) regularly underline the weakness of local TV programmes (OMEC 2008). Most stations do not have enough resources to produce their own quality programmes, even though the press law requires that they broadcast a quota of 50 per cent locally produced content (1996 press law, art. 66).[11] Many broadcasters are forced to fill in their schedules with musical entertainment, video clips, sketches, televised theatre, studio debates or programmes received from foreign countries or donors, with little capacity to shoot their own programmes outside.[12] Schedules are rarely respected, and viewers are used to improvised agenda and recurrent delays.

What is on offer thus largely depends on production conditions, which are characterized by limited operating budgets (televisions are operating with a monthly budget from USD 10,000 to 125,000) and a shortage of material, human and technical resources. With limited vehicles, filming equipment or staff, the journalists mainly work in the newsroom and each programme has to be supported by an advertiser or sponsor. Therefore, educational programmes are the first to go. 'Commercial sponsors are not interested in this type of programme', says Jo Tala Ngaï, the director of Antenne A, and Vice-President of ANEAP, the association of private broadcasters. 'They prefer to support sports or entertainment' (personal communication 2008). A small number of political debates are very popular: *Table Ronde* ('Round Table') on Congoweb TV, *Entretien* ('Discussion') on Digital Congo, *Droit à la parole* ('Have Your Say') on Antenne A, *Profondeurs* ('Depths') on Numérica, *Polele* ('Openly') on CCTV, and *Tosolola yango* ('Let's Talk About It') on RLTV. But most of these are not sufficiently grounded in fieldwork – instead the microphone is repeatedly handed to the same participants that have been nicknamed 'débatteurs' ('debating guys'), going from a station to another to express their views.

Congolese TV stations also rely on programmes pirated from other stations in complete violation of broadcasting rights.[13] According to Lwemba lu Masanga, the HAM's legal advisor:

> We don't know exactly if they have the rights to broadcast these imported productions. The legal and regulatory framework is certainly lacking, but if we adopt new rules and regulations, people will claim that we are violating the freedom of the press.
>
> (personal communication 2008)

Retrieving the signal of foreign TV stations is especially prevalent in the case of sports events, whose broadcasting rights are beyond the reach of African stations. According to Jo Tala Ngaï, the rights for the last African Cup of Nations amounted to USD 2 million:

It's impossible for us to meet such huge fees. Last time, the government managed to lower the rights to USD 250,000. Otherwise, the Congolese would have been deprived of soccer. During the last European Cup, the rights for some of the games were granted for free to African stations, which could not afford to buy any.

(personal communication 2008)

Another major characteristic of the TV stations in Kinshasa is their tendency to overwhelmingly use French: the official language takes up more than three-quarters of airplay.[14] As Fulgence Muganga has shown (2007: 34), 'the local vernacular Lingala is marginalized in TV broadcasts, only featuring in entertainment programmes like TV drama and music'.

The success of 'popular' programmes

The data about audiences in Kinshasa displays a number of interesting trends,[15] including the wide success of 'local/community news'. Two of these news broadcasts have generated a tremendous following among the audience as well as much debate among the media authorities. The first of these is a television station named Molière TV; the second is a programme called *Journal en lingala facile* ('The News in Easy Lingala').

The popularity of these programmes is due to the fact that they are seen as really reflecting the daily lives and concerns of Kinshasans. But they all also have in common that they have been suspended or called to order by the media regulatory body because of excesses in form and content.

Molière TV: the popularity, and excesses, of a 'local' television station

Until it was shut down in 2008, Molière TV was a striking illustration of a television station that was both populist (connected with the ideas and opinions of ordinary people) and popular (enjoyed by many people), grounding its success in the fact that it showed everyday life on the streets of Kinshasa, though often at the expense of professional journalistic ethics. Established in 2005 by Léon Nembalemba, Molière TV wanted both to reflect the everyday life of Kinshasans and to be a platform for them to freely express their concerns. The station became greatly popular by broadcasting raw images shot by the TV station's owner on the streets of the capital, without the consent of the protagonists, and then broadcast without being edited.

'When something happens in the city, people call Molière TV and the director will immediately head out into the field', explains Godefroid Bwiti, director of the press agency InterCongo Média:

It's a real 'local' television which invites people on the street to talk about their lives on air, even if sometimes it's nonsense. In a situation where the public station RTNC never hands over the microphone to the man in the street, it's to be expected that Kinshasans will recognize themselves in such a channel and watch it.

(personal communication 2008)

Though this type of 'reality television' has sometimes tended towards sensationalism – paying attention to 'man bites dog' news items, showing dead or mutilated bodies, displaying the faces of rape or murder victims – it has also convinced Kinshasan viewers that presenting their daily problems publicly on television could help solve them. In one neighbourhood, for instance, a boy whose hand had been crushed by a machine was treated for free by a professional surgeon after Molière TV had broadcast shocking images of his bloodied hand. In another broadcast, a woman who had been expelled by her landlord with her baby was able to find a new shelter after Molière TV showed them living on the streets (Léon Nembalemba, personal communication 2009). 'The phone number of the station is permanently displayed on the TV screen', Nembalemba explains. 'Thanks to our motorcycles, as soon as we receive a call, we can arrive straight on the spot'.

Another of the station's famous shows allowed people to come and denounce live on air any act of gross misconduct affecting them. The show soon turned into a platform of uncontrolled exposés invading people's privacy. Some cases which were still pending in court were delivered a televised guilty verdict, in total violation of the presumption of innocence. By contrast, 'some court cases which were bogged down in the incompetent jurisdiction suddenly found an outcome after the case had been debated on screen' (M'Baya, personal communication 2009).

A 2007 survey of civil society leaders showed that Molière TV was viewed the most reliable Congolese media in the field of advocacy, 'thanks to its sensational reports on political current events as much as on scandals affecting the social fabric' (Experts 2007).

Molière TV's success also reflected how wary Kinshasan viewers had become of other TV stations which mostly focus on politics, covering official presidential activities (as regards the RTNC and other televisions close to the presidential majority) or formal ceremonies involving ministers or local authorities, events which were given paid coverage to ensure their visibility.

'Unfortunately, popularity doesn't guarantee quality', notes Bosamba Malanga, an advisor to the service responsible for compiling the cases submitted to the regulatory body HAM (personal communication 2008). Molière TV became famous for receiving one of the biggest numbers of warnings or sanctions by the regulation authority, the HAM: it was reproached for broadcasting unedited sequences, elements that could violate privacy rights or an individual's reputation, the dissemination of rumours and unverified information. The HAM summoned the director Nembalemba many times in order to draw his attention to the many excesses in the content of these live programmes.

In May 2008, Molière TV was given a one-month suspension, following the broadcast of rumours involving the highly emotive 'disappearance of the sexes' urban legend. In Kinshasa, as has happened before in Benin, for instance (Duplat 2002: 3–4), a rumour circulated in the city that some men had experienced the disappearance or shrinking of their genitals after having shook hands with a foreigner supposedly from the Ibo community in Benin and accused of being a sorcerer in Kinshasa (Mandel 2008). Molière TV interviewed these 'victims' extensively, showing their diminished sexual organs on screen. The High Authority for the Media criticized the station's 'blatant lack of professionalism in the treatment of information' and 'the broadcasting of images and sounds which constituted acts of gross indecency' and condemned it for contributing to 'a campaign to incite hatred and murder' towards the alleged sex-thieves. Once the one-month suspension had ended, Molière TV's director discovered that their allocated signal was occupied by TVS1, a new station set up by Adolphe Muzito, the then Minister of the Budget (and who would become Prime Minister following Antoine Gizenga's resignation on 25 September 2008). After lengthy judicial procedures, Léon Nembalemba managed to recover his station's signal and started broadcasting again on 24 September 2008. Two days later, police officers raided the station's headquarters and took away all their material. The station, which was also one of few stations to give voice to the political opposition, has thus lost its own voice through procedural irregularity. For the people of Kinshasa, this meant the closure of one of the only TV stations that reflected the daily life of the city's inhabitants.[16]

The News in Easy Lingala

In March 2006, Kinshasan viewers discovered a new programme broadcast on the channel Horizon 33: *Le journal en indoubil* ('The News in Indoubil'). Indoubil is Kinshasa slang, a pidgin language made up of Lingala, French and elements from other local vernaculars. Zacharie Bababaswe, the programme's founder, justified its creation on the following grounds:

> There are 9 million people in Kinshasa with no access to information on democracy and development. The education system has not been functioning properly since the 1980s. The people no longer understand French. The language that people use and understand in the city is Indoubil, the language of the ghetto. If we want to reach them, that's the language we have to use.
> (personal communication 2009)

A BBC World Service Trust report calls it the language of 'marginalized people', a language 'associated with criminals' (AMDI 2006: 7). The show was an immediate and undeniable success, but it soon fell foul of the regulatory authority. On the one hand, it was reproached for using this 'vulgar' language instead of the official language (French) or one of the country's four vernacular languages (Lingala, Swahili, Kikongo and Tshiluba). On the other hand, the show's recurrent violations of professional conduct (mainly the respect for privacy) was also strongly criticized. On 5 May 2006, barely two months after its creation, the show was suspended by the HAM. Those two months, however, were enough for Bababaswe to see the tremendous interest of Kinshasans in his project, and so two years later, on 3 March 2008, he launched a new programme entitled *Le journal télévisé en lingala facile* ('The News in Easy Lingala').

This new programme borrowed its title from *Le journal en français facile* ('The News in Easy French'), a Radio France International newscast intended for listeners with limited knowledge of French. Launched on the second public station (RTNC2), it followed in the footsteps of the earlier initiative. Independently produced by Zacharie Bababaswe and sold to various stations, *The News in Easy Lingala* distinguishes itself from newscasts on public and private stations. As regards form, the same pidgin is still in use and the tone is the familiar one used in the city. As regards content, news items are intended to be close to the Kinshasa population. Everyday societal information is thus dominant: road accidents, erosion, pollution, criminality, difficulties in getting around, bad weather, water and electricity shortages, etc. According to Bababaswe:

> We respond at once when people call us. That's how we were able to denounce the lack of drinking water or electricity in some neighbourhoods. As soon as *The News in Easy Lingala* brings up a subject, the SNEL and REGIDESO[17] are prompt to react.
>
> (personal communication 2009)

The programme's slogan ('an initiative in support of access to information by all and for all') reflects the desire not only to cover local news, but also to let the people have their say, people who do not usually have access to information media. Whereas other TV stations' newscasts have provoked great suspicion from the audience towards politically oriented and biased medias, *The News in Easy Lingala* traditionally ends with one or other of the following expressions: 'bondimela nga' ('believe me, it's true') or 'kokamwa' ('it's astounding'). The very nature of what constitutes news is being challenged: media personalities are no longer public figures which newscasts serve to promote. With *The News in Easy Lingala*,

> the people are what matters, people who sometimes come from remote places and who are not there to talk politics, but to talk about daily hardships, the lack of water, electricity, transport, etc. *The News in Easy Lingala* has become a means for the people of Kinshasa to express their concerns to the public authorities. The information is no longer coming from the top to the bottom, but reaches the top from the bottom.
>
> (M'Baya, personal communication 2009)

This approach, which is intended to contrast with that of Molière TV by being more professional, with a journalistic treatment and editing process of the information material, has been a great success. Besides RTNC, five stations currently broadcast the daily 45-minute newscast (TVS1, Ratelki, Couleurs TV, CBS TV, CMB Digi), sometimes several times, meaning that it can be shown up to 21 times a day. The show's popularity has also led to undeniable financial success. According to Zacharie Bababaswe:

> Production costs are around USD 2,000 per month, but we earn a lot more. First of all, we have sponsors: the Rawbank has bought all advertising slots before and after the programme. And then there are the TV stations which buy the programme. And there are also people who pay to be on the programme.
>
> (personal communication 2009)

That is one of the consequences of its popularity: politicians and private companies are now keen to appear on *The News in Easy Lingala* and are willing to pay to do so. The newscast is thus gradually becoming a succession of short promotional clips for the Head of State, his wife (for whom Bababaswe claims to be a communications counsellor), or other public authorities. Not wanting to be left behind, mobile telephone companies regularly ensure that their promotional stunts are given sufficient coverage.

The newscast is also criticized because its founder, Zacharie Bababaswe, repeatedly uses it to harangue various personalities (including the resigning Speaker of the Assembly, Vital Kamhere). Bababaswe has been called 'the king's fool' (Rogeau 2009), a media buffoon or an opportunistic *griot*, but this has not spoilt his success. The HAM has repeatedly called to order the founder of the programme, whom it believes regularly violates professional ethics.

The popularity of *The News in Easy Lingala*, like that of Molière TV, reveals the frustration felt by the inhabitants of Kinshasa, faced with a plethora of TV stations in whose programmes they do not feel represented. Whereas audiovisual media should attempt to reflect the daily concerns of citizens and to represent the various components of the Congolese population, the latter is almost absent from the information media, which focus on political and institutional 'news from above'.

Preachers, pastors and messiahs to save the Kinshasans

Molière TV and *The News in Easy Lingala* are not alone in making use of original TV programmes, which are often problematic from a legal and ethical perspective, but very popular with audiences longing to see their concerns taken into account. Besides time slots purchased by denominational churches on general news channels, numerous denominational stations in Kinshasa belong to pastors and preachers who use them not only to evangelize, but also to intervene in the civilian life of their congregations.[18] If religious songs and sermons 'have become the true means to save the Congolese people in a time of crisis' (Muganga 2007: 41), their success is mostly grounded on the fact that they address directly the country's social and political situation, trying to give some hope to the faithful.

The televised sermons of these pastors, as well as the call-in shows they present, answering questions from their congregations, are often politicized and have regularly necessitated the intervention of the HAM. In 2004, the HAM had to suspend *Tribune populaire*, a programme broadcast on Nzondo TV, owned by pastor Denis Lessie, which had broadcast live a 'prophetic message', predicting serious trouble if the general elections were not held on the fixed date. Viewers, described as 'no less excited' than their charismatic pastor, had then called in to back the words of their pastor (Lwemba 2008: 56).

Likewise, in April 2005, the HAM announced the suspension of RTMV (Radio Télévision Message de Vie) for having allegedly broadcast messages inciting rebellion and violence. The station's director, 'Archbishop' Fernando Kutino, launched a campaign led by his Eglise Armée de la Victoire (Church of the Army of the Victory) under the slogan 'S.O.S. Sauvons le Congo' ('Let's Save the Congo'), which was widely broadcast on his station. During the election campaign, he backed Jean-Pierre Bemba and endorsed some of his campaign slogans, notably in his programme *Mwana Congo*, accused of encouraging xenophobia, until the HAM suspended the programme.

Général Sony Kafuta, the pastor behind RTAE (Radio Télévision Armée de l'Eternel) put his faith, and his media, into Joseph Kabila's election campaign, for which he was called to order in August 2006 by the HAM for 'inciting violence'.

Besides being overly politicized, these religious channels have also been criticized for exploiting the despair and credulity of viewers, some pastors freely promising visas to travel abroad, miracles of all kinds, weddings, and even promising to heal AIDS victims if they lay their hands on the TV set. They thus attract large numbers of people to their churches who are in search of hope and who are willing to pay (sometimes no less than a tenth of their meagre income) in the belief that this will ensure them better days (Mbiye 2007: 79). Television is a key part of their strategy, leading some to talk of 'electronic churches' or of an 'electronic religion': the pastors become TV celebrities, just like show-business celebrities (Kamate 2007: 89–96). The success these stations and their founders enjoy probably also reveals that they are meeting the viewers' expectations, which are not being fulfilled by traditional media (Pype 2009).

Popular music in the service of politics

Lastly, when TV stations are not showing political debates, imported series or religious sermons, it is popular music that holds centre stage. Yet popular Congolese music is not so much an individual or collective artistic enterprise aimed at ensuring an audience, a name or financial revenues. It generally has a political objective, which is 'either to support political players, or to condemn politics' (Bagalwa 2004: 212). And it is undeniable that it can mobilize the troops: for decades, musicians have acted as role models not only for youths, but for the whole of the population of Kinshasa.[19] Yet, according to a sociologist from the University of Kinshasa, Léon Tsambu Bulu (2004: 193), from the beginning of the Transition in 1990, popular Kinshasan music 'has become increasingly violent, like the power struggles which have monopolized the country's attention', and the same holds for artists and the audience.

Thus, some believe that in 1998, at the start of the second war, the call by President Laurent Désiré Kabila to the Kinshasa population to rise up against the Rwandans and the Ugandans (former allies turned aggressors) population 'is in part due to the backing of musicians'. Indeed, Laurent Désiré Kabila, seeking to legitimize his position with the Kongophones in the west of the country, is alleged to have recruited the group of the singer Werrason, to support his political movement AFDL. The mass media would have an important impact on the audience, and television in particular, which, through its numerous musical programmes, contributes to the widespread broadcasting of these commissioned productions. Why so? Because, according to Bagalwa (2004: 213),

> the political message spread by musical actors would be followed by the masses ... since it emerges from social actors with no political ambition, since politics and its venal and versatile professionals have little value in the popular imagination (people talk of 'politichiens') [i.e. 'politiciens'/'politicians' and 'chiens'/'dogs'].

In 1998, more than 20 Congolese pop stars gathered to sing 'Tokufa mpo na Congo', encouraging the Congolese people to give their lives for their country which had been invaded by foreigners.

Moreover, a number of Congolese pop stars are deeply involved in politics, and use their music to sing the praises of personalities who pay them to do so. The music critic of the private daily Le Potentiel observes that 'Congolese society no longer trusts its musicians. ... When Congolese singers such as Koffi Olomide and Werrason praise politicians in their songs, all they can think about is their profit' (Nzau 2006b: 13). In September 2005, the president of the National Censorship Commission for Songs and Shows published a decree banning Congolese musical groups from singing during the elections. 'We have recently observed in your songs, whether in public or destined for the public, that you mention the names of civilian and military figures. This practice is dishonouring our music' (quoted in Nzau 2006b).

That practice is called 'libanga'[20] and consists of citing dozens of names in a single song, each person mentioned paying the singer or rewarding him with luxury gifts. 'Libanga' fits in a tradition of laudatory songs that became very popular under Mobutu. Franco Luambo Makiadi, for instance, in part built his career on his odes to the Mobutu regime, which punctuated the evolution of the Zairean Republic with songs entitled, for instance, 'Contentieux belgo-congolais' or 'Candidat na biso Mobutu'. From 1998 onwards, the names of important political figures started featuring more prominently in songs, and today it is a widespread phenomenon. Pushing this practice to its extreme, several key figures of Congolese music (Werrason, J.B. Mpiana, Koffi Olomidé, Papa Wemba, etc.) clearly stated their support for Joseph Kabila during the elections, and put their music at his service.

During the election campaign, the HAM was forced to ban certain songs,[21] which were being broadcast continuously on radio stations close to certain candidates, and to set up a service in charge of analysing the contents of the advertisements, songs, video clips and jingles. Just as pastors and their congregations were courted by politicians, so too popular singers were put to the task. Beyond the propaganda-like character of certain refrains, one should not overlook the artists' ability to express social criticism. In the DRC, radio stations were suspended for having played popular songs that were critical of the public authorities. Thus, the act of playing the song 'Binashindakana' ('The Situation is Becoming Impossible' in Swahili) or Kélix Wazekwa's 'Que demande le peuple' ('What are the People Asking for') were considered rebellious acts by the public authorities.

Conclusion

Based on one of the first audience surveys of TV stations in Kinshasa and grounded in a reflection on some of the most popular programmes, this chapter has attempted to put forward some of the main features of TV consumption in popular environments. Television is currently the prime medium in the Congolese capital, both as regards penetration and daily viewing times. Yet it has largely been ignored by international organizations and researchers, who primarily pay attention to radio stations, which have traditionally enjoyed greater popularity in Africa. Today, however, television is unavoidable if one wishes to reach the people of Kinshasa, women and youths in particular.

On the TV screens, new programmes have emerged which have proven to be hugely popular among the lower classes, in the face of a public broadcaster which is finding it hard to reform itself and to leave behind a monolithic pro-governmental discourse inherited from the one-party period; in the face also of commercial stations which are often overly politicized and whose news programmes serve exclusively to promote one or other individual. Call-in shows, local news, religious sermons and popular music are among those programmes which are tremendously successful with the wider public, and are thus courted by advertisers, even if they are looked down upon by Kinshasa's intellectual elite. The Kinshasan public's interest for these programmes no doubt reveals their disaffection towards 'politichiens' ('politicians'/'dogs') and elitist news programmes. They have in common the fact that they are pretending to take into account the daily concerns of the Kinshasa inhabitants, to give them a voice and to 'speak the truth' in a public space which is widely occupied by politicians establishing their own media or paying journalists to relay their views.

As we have seen, these new programmes have raised a number of issues for the stakeholders of the media sector, including the regulation authority: verbal abuse, unbridled sensationalism and biased reporting have made their way into these broadcasts, whether they cover 'local' news, entertainment or are of a religious nature. Given their big audience, and these programmes' claims to provide an alternative to the mainstream 'top to bottom' type of communication, they have also drawn the attention of the politicians wanting to benefit from their wide popularity. The same 'politichiens' that those programmes wanted to challenge are now courting the producers of these newscasts in order to reach their audience, generating a political drift in the content. The reaction of the professional journalists' organization and regulatory authority has so far been either to disparage these newscasts as been 'non-professional', or to take sanctions in order to suspend them.

Is that the proper attitude towards the phenomena? Would it not first be better to look into, and perhaps learn from, the reasons for their success and the gap they are filling in the expectations of the Kinshasan audience? All these shows aim to reflect an image of life in Kinshasa which is closer to daily reality; they all want to relay the real concerns of the marginalized urban population, while sometimes uncovering the lies and manipulations of politicians. They all also wish to express themselves in a language that is more easily understood by people when the overwhelming majority is excluded from political issues mostly debated in French. It goes without saying that the populist excesses and abuses of these media and shows have to be condemned. But it is also necessary to reflect on the best way to take into consideration these needs and expectations, while also ensuring that the answer will take into account the media's obligations in matters of responsibility and ethical respect in the treatment of information.

These programmes are not only gathering a large audience because they are sensationalist. They undoubtedly relate to the political opinions of the viewers. On 27 July 2006, 48 hours before the first run of the presidential election, Jean–Pierre Bemba's militants walked out of a campaign meeting at the stadium and ransacked at least three buildings in the neighbourhood: the HAM, Pastor Sony Kafuta's church and the Zamba Playa Studio belonging to the singer Werrason. All three were accused of a biased involvement in the campaign and of supporting Bemba's major challenger, Kabila. The incident is worth mentioning because it shows that religion, music and the media regulators are all viewed as actors in the political landscape.

The popular TV programmes can reach an audience that is obviously out of the scope of traditional newscasts, and therefore it could be useful to try to think of ways to help these broadcasters and producers to become more professional and more aware of ethics. This is a huge undertaking that, as well as the public authorities, will also involve TV station owners and presenters, musicians, directors, advertisers, and perhaps even the preachers, too. But this undertaking will be crucial to the future of Congolese citizens that are still in the phase of building a new civic consciousness after years of dictatorship and war.

Notes

1 Audience surveys are conducted in Kinshasa by three companies: BERCI, Experts Sprl. and Le Point. Major advertisers generally have their own internal survey systems, as well as International broadcasters (RFI and BBC, mainly). The figures in this chapter are from surveys conducted over 2006, 2007 and 2008 by the French company IMMAR on a sample of about 1,000 individuals above 15 in Kinshasa.

2 The author wishes to thank Donat M'Baya Tshimanga and Pierre N'Sana for their suggestions in finalizing this chapter, as well as Patrick Lennon for his help in the translation.

3 The RTNC is currently trying out a third channel, RTNC3. This so-called 'institutional' channel broadcasts parliamentary debates live but aims to establish a complete daily schedule.

4 In Kinshasa, the Catholic Télé Elikya was only created in 2009, joining Télévision Sango Malamu (Protestant) and the Kimbanguist Television RATELKI, each of them being an extension of the radio station first created under the same name. Outside Kinshasa, the most important religious stations are Télévision Amani (an initiative of the Archdiocese of Kisangani), Télévision Fraternité (an initiative of the diocese of Mbuji Mayi) and RATELKI, which is found in most towns of the Lower Congo.

5 These include, for instance, Radio Télévision pour le Développement Intégral (RTDI) in Kisangani; Radio Télévision Graben in North Kivu (Béni and Goma) and Radio Télé Boma (RTB) in the Lower Congo. The huge costs of audiovisual productions make it difficult for local communities or civil society organizations to support such a media.

6 Many media specialists believe that the Brazzaville government takes this as a very good excuse not to have to allocate more broadcasting frequencies to local applicants and thus to maintain complete control of the broadcasting sector.

7 On the role played by television in the competition between political actors during the election, see Frère (2007 and 2009).

8 In another study conducted by the Experts Sprl. (2007) for the NGO Search for Common Ground, figures indicate that almost 31 per cent of the people polled said they listened to the radio because it was the only medium they could have access to. The most recent figures published by the ITU date back to 2006 and mention a general equipment rate of 37.9 per cent for radio and 0.5 per cent (3.8 per cent of the household) for television.

9 The RTNC's audience has gradually been eroded over the past ten years. Until 1996, the national TV broadcaster was ahead of private stations (TKM, Raga, Antenne A and Canal Kin) by more than 20 per cent. After the second public channel was created in 1996, TKM and Antenne A took the lead. See Kasongo Mwema (2001: 487–8).

10 The other programmes featured in the figure are: a political debate which is open to the political opposition that has no seat in Parliament (Questions brûlantes/'Burning Hot Issues'); a religious programme (Dieu et nous/'God and Us'); a short spot introducing a masked prominent person (Qui?/'Who?'); and televised theatre (Divertissements/'Entert aiment').

11 According to Fulgence Muganga (2007), locally produced programmes make up 76 per cent of the broadcasting time of Antenne A, 63 per cent of Canal Kin, 54 per cent of Raga TV, 61 per cent of RTKM, 79 per cent of Horizon 33 and 96.5 per cent of RTG@.

12 Some UN agencies offer programmes to local TV channels, as do NGOs specializing in audiovisual productions. For instance, the Lokolé Centre, established by the American NGO Search for Common Ground, is producing radio and television shows that promote peace and citizenship. It includes a reality TV show entitled *Tosalel'ango* ('Let's Do It'), based on a group of young people under 30 who have been challenged to bring positive changes to their local community. The show is aired on Digital Congo.

13 See the HAM observation (n°Ham/AP/007/2004) of 8 December 2004 on the fraudulent broadcasting of programmes, shows and other filmic materials belonging to foreign broadcasters.

14 Seventy-five per cent of the air time of Antenne A, 69 per cent of Raga TV, 62 per cent of RTKM and Horizon 33, and 49 per cent of Tropicana TV and RTG@.

15 In this chapter we will not consider the case of fictional programmes such as Nigerian TV serials or TV dramas even though they enjoy a very large audience their main purpose is not to inform the Kinshasa audience. They therefore not seen as the place where 'truths' could be expressed about what is going on in the city.

16 This time it was shut down on strictly political grounds, since the regulatory authority did not condemn any content-related abuse. Molière TV started broadcasting again on another frequency in November 2009, more than a year after it had been shut down. According to the station's manager, it had once again attracted a large audience within a few weeks.

17 The SNEL (Société nationale d'Electricité) and the REGIDESO (Régie de Distribition d'Eau) are the state companies providing electricity and water in the city of Kinshasa.

18 Thus, for example, 'Radio Télé Message de Vie' (RTMV) de l'Archbishop Fernando Kutino, 'Radio Télé Armée de l'Eternel' du Général Sony Kafuta Rockman, 'Amen TV' de l'Apôtre Léopold Mutombo, 'Radio Télé Puissance' (RTP) de l'Evangéliste Jean Oscar Kiziamina, 'Radio Télé Voix de l'Aigle' du Révérend Baruti, 'Télé Sentinelle' de l'Apôtre E. Mbiye, 'Radio Télé du Dieu Vivant' de l'Apôtre Sikatenda Iyadi, 'Canal CVV' de Mama Olangi, 'Hope TV du Pasteur Kankienza', etc. See Mbiye (2007: 75).

19 Music plays an important part in the social lives of people (weddings, baptisms, etc.). In recent years, however, youths have seen music as representing material and social success, in stark contrast to the weakened living conditions of civil servants and employees, whose careers are no longer seen as enviable models.

20 In Lingala, *Kobwaka libanga* means 'to cast the first stone'. The singer J.B. Mpiana holds the record with almost 200 names mentioned in a song entitled 'Lauréats', recorded in 2000. See Monsa (2006).

21 On 15 October 2006, at the start of the campaign for the election second round, the HAM decided to ban two songs: 'Bawuta', which was favourable to Jean-Pierre Bemba; and Joseph Kabila's campaign ad, performed by Madilu and Lacoste Muke Tonga.

Bibliography

AMDI (African Media Development Initiative) (2006) *Democratic Republic of Congo. Research Findings and Conclusions*, London: BBC World Service Trust.

Bagalwa-Mapatano, J. (2004) 'La chanson politique face à la violence politique au Congo-Zaïre post-Mobutu', in R.M. Beck and F. Wittmann (eds), *African Media Cultures. Transdisciplinary Perspectives*, Köln: Rüdiger Köppe Verlag, pp. 193–214.

Duplat, D. (2002) *Liberté de la presse, responsabilité des medias, l'Afrique sur la voie de l'autorégulation*, Paris: GRET.

Experts Sprl. (2006) 'Survey on Media in Kinshasa', 24th edition, July.

Experts Sprl. (2007) 'Rapport Etude qualitative de base', commissioned from Search for Common Ground, Kinshasa.

Frère, M.S. (2007) 'Médias et élections en RDC', in S. Marysse, F. Reyntjens and S. Vandeginste (eds), *L'Afrique des Grands Lacs, Annuaire 2006–2007*, Paris: L'Harmattan, pp. 165–200.

Frère, M.S. and IMMAR (2009) *Le paysage médiatique congolais. Etat des lieux, enjeux et defis*, Kinshasa: FCI.

IMMAR (2006, 2007, 2008) *Etude d'audience des medias de Kinshasa*, unpublished reports.

Kamate Mbyiro, R. (2007) 'Médias et propagande religieuse à Kinshasa', *Revue africaine de Communication sociale* 2(1): 83–99.

Kasongo Mwema, Y.A. (2001) *La Télévision, ses enjeux et ses publics au Zaïre depuis 1990*, PhD thesis, University of Bordeaux III.

Lwemba lu Masenga (2008) *Régulation et sanctions des médias en République démocratique du Congo*, Master Thesis, Unesco Chair in Peace and Human Rights, University of Kinshasa, March.

Mandel, J.J. (2008) 'Les rétrécisseurs de sexe. Chronique d'une rumeur sorcière' *Cahiers d'Etudes africaines*, no. 189–190/1–2, pp. 185–208.

Mbiye Lumbala, H. (2007) 'Message religieux télévisuel. Chances ou menaces pour l'unité familiale', *Revue africaine de Communication sociale* 2(1): 73–82.

Monsa Iyaka Duku, F. (2006) 'Elections en Rdc: la place du musicien congolais', *Le Potentiel* 3710 (24 April).

Muganga Kawanda, F. (2007) 'La programmation télévisuelle kinoise. Problèmes et defis pour les familles congolaises', *Revue africaine de Communication sociale* 2(1): 29–42.

Nzau ne Diop, J. (2006a) 'La place de la chanson dans la 3ème République', *Le Potentiel* 3892 (2 December).

Nzau ne Diop, J. (2006b) 'La chanson congolaise n'aborde pas la politique et les élections', *Le Potentiel* 3794 (5 August).

OMEC (2008) 'Report on the audiovisual sector of Kinshasa', May–June.

Pype, K. (2009) 'We need to open up the country: development and the Christian key scenario in the social space of Kinshasa's teleserials', *Journal of African Media Studies* 1(1): 101–16.

Rogeau, O. (2009) 'Le fou du roi', *Le Vif L'Express*, May.

Tsamba Bulu, L. (2004) 'Musique et violence à Kinshasa', in T. Trefon (ed.), *Ordre et désordre à Kinshasa. Réponses populaires à la faillite de l'Etat*, Paris: L'Harmattan/Musée Royal de l'Afrique Centrale, pp. 193–212.

Chapter 13

New technologies as tools of empowerment

African youth and public sphere participation

Levi Obijiofor

Introduction

The use of new communication technologies for participatory communication in the public sphere is seen largely as an important pathway to the development of deliberative democracy in developing and developed countries. This is not surprising. History suggests that whenever new technologies are introduced, there is widespread optimism about how the technologies will affect the methods of communication in human societies. As Kandell (1998: 110) notes:

> (E)ach significant technological development fundamentally changes the way the world works. Just as the invention of the electric light enabled a multitude of nocturnal activities to occur and the VCR created an entire industry of video retailers, the development of the Internet and the World Wide Web have spawned a revolution in communication, commerce and interpersonal behavior.

To what extent do these assumptions apply to university students in the African context, where access to new media technologies is not as prevalent as in developed countries? Do new technologies such as the Internet, electronic mail (email), mobile phones and interactive multimedia systems have parallel effects on users in developing and developing countries? This chapter examines the extent to which university students use new technologies as forms of popular media for participatory communication in the public sphere and to complement the traditional news media.

Celebration of the new media is based partly on the perceived negative influence of traditional mass media on audience members. Communication researchers Lerner and Schramm (1976) and Tehranian (1989) documented the dysfunctional role of the mass media in developing countries. This was against the prevailing beliefs in the decades of the 1960s and 1970s during which the mass media were projected as facilitators of socio-economic development in developing countries. According to Lerner and Schramm (1976: 341–2):

Throughout the less-developed regions, people have been led to want more than they can get. This can be attributed in part to the spread of the mass media, which inevitably show and tell people about the good things of life that are available elsewhere ... As people in the poor countries were being shown and told about 'goodies' available in developed countries, they were also being taught about their own inferiority – at least in terms of wealth and well-being. Recognition of the disparities between the rich and poor countries produced among some a sense of hopelessness, among others a sense of aggressiveness. Both apathy and aggression usually are counterproductive to genuine development efforts.

Similarly, Tehranian (1989: 183) cited former President Sukarno of Indonesia who lamented the destructive influence of Hollywood and the mass media on Indonesia because the media induced Indonesians to demand goods and services which the country could hardly afford.

This chapter focuses primarily on university students' use of new media because, in many societies, students are perceived as future leaders. In the African context, university students are classified as elite because they hail from elite backgrounds and also because university education is seen as a gateway to securing high-profile jobs and higher social status in society. Therefore, what students do with new technologies now may provide us with insights into how they will use the technologies to empower themselves. Habermas (1989) had argued that in the Europe of the seventeenth and eighteenth centuries, the public sphere privileged the elite, especially men. The question must be asked: will new media confer a similar privilege on African university students in the twenty-first century?

A number of researchers have documented the relationship between students and new technologies. For example, Kubey et al. (2001: 366) note the increasing use of the Internet by university students while Jones et al. (2009) report that students are 'heavy users of the Internet' (2009: web document). According to Jones et al. (2009), 'New online technologies such as Napster were invented on college campuses, and the initial development of the Internet took place in an academic setting'.

In Africa, research suggests that students constitute the main consumers of new technologies (Omotayo 2006; Mwesige 2004; Sairosse and Mutula 2004; Odero 2003; Robins 2002). Research also shows that young people constitute the main users of the Internet (Aoki and Downes 2003; Adomi et al. 2003; Alao and Folorunsho 2008; Furuholt et al. 2008; Furuholt and Kristiansen 2007). However, the extent to which university students in Africa use new technologies as popular media to empower themselves and to participate in the public sphere (e.g. online forums) remains largely unknown. While there is evidence that university students in Nigeria and Ghana use the Internet (e.g. Awoleye et al. 2008; Omotayo 2006; Kwansah-Aidoo and Obijiofor 2006; Jagboro 2003), little is known about the extent to which these students use new technologies for participatory communication in the public sphere. This is the key issue explored in this chapter.

New technologies and participatory communication

Research has underscored the relationship between new technologies and greater citizen participation in the democratic process in both Western and non-Western cultures. Essentially, it is argued that new technologies serve as an engine that galvanizes public interest and participation in modern democracies. Why is popular participation a precondition for democratic civic engagement and socio-economic development? The answer lies in the role of new technologies in society, such as the use of new technologies for promotion of a healthy democracy (e.g. freedom of expression and respect for human rights), and as facilitators of strategic links between political leaders and citizens. At the heart of all these is the question of access. For new technologies to empower citizens to participate in the political process, civil society must have unimpeded access to the technologies. In the African situation, there is a huge gap between those who have access to new technologies and those who don't. In Nigeria in particular, university students' access to Internet services remains restricted because of a combination of factors such as the high cost of Internet services, scarcity of public Internet sites, regular disruptions to electricity supply, and official apathy by the federal government towards science and technology development.

For example, owing to the paucity of telecommunications facilities in the public sector in Nigeria, including official apathy towards the uptake of new technologies, Nigeria's National Universities Commission's (NUC) Internet project for universities has remained largely an unfulfilled dream (Omotayo 2006). According to Ani *et al.* (2007: 355):

> (I)n Nigeria, there is a disparity in the level of accessibility to ICT between the private and public sectors of the economy. In most public institutions, such as universities, polytechnics, primary and post-primary schools, and government ministries, access to ICT, if not completely lacking, is inadequate.

This is the grim situation that confronts university students in Nigeria.

The dismal situation in Nigeria and other African countries differs starkly from the widespread access to and use of Internet and computer technologies in the United States and Western Europe. For example, university and college students in the United States are not only exposed in their early years to computer technology but they are also provided with access to the Internet. Kandell (1998: 16) notes that in the United States, 'Computer use by college students is strongly encouraged, implicitly if not explicitly, and in some courses is required'. A study of college students at 40 US-based tertiary education institutions showed that 'College students continue to be early adopters of new Internet tools and applications in comparison to the general U.S. Internet-using population' (Jones *et al.* 2009). As the authors note, 'students overall have exhibited clear preferences towards using the Internet as a medium for social interaction and, in most cases, used it with great frequency in their everyday lives' (Jones *et al.* 2009).

Beyond the disparity in students' access to technologies, the relationship between new media and the democratic process has been underscored in the literature. Bonaga (cited in Tambini 1999) has noted how new media are transforming democracy and socio-economic development on a global scale:

> all over the world a new dimension is evolving with unbridled momentum and making a major impact on democracy and development, stretching the horizons of citizens: this is the world of new communication and information technologies, destined to revolutionise democracy and the economy.
>
> (Bonaga 1994, cited in Tambini 1999: 310–11)

Tambini (1999: 306) also observes that 'a very broad notion of democracy and participation is necessary to come to terms with the implications of new media for democracy'. If citizens must participate in the democratic process, they need information. Information is vital to how citizens participate in the political process (e.g. voting) and how they make judgments about the performance of their political leaders. Information is also necessary to enable citizens to make decisions about their own welfare. But information must be free and readily accessible to everyone. New media technologies are regarded as popular means of communication because they are free from control by political authorities and market forces. The popular appeal of new media is based on their characteristics: they are interactive; and they allow citizens the freedom to select the kind of information that appeals to them when they want it. In the new media environment, citizens switch roles as information producers and consumers. This implies that new media have diminished the gate-keeping role of journalists in traditional media. However, even as new media promote freedom of choice, ease of access and greater citizen participation in the public sphere, they have their drawbacks. As Tambini (1999: 319) points out:

> The very characteristics that are seen as positive in encouraging participation (cheapness, anonymity) are seen as a problem when they foster less appealing forms of online political organization.... The legal status of inflammatory or libellous material posted in the semi-public worlds of discussion groups remains contested, and the links between the virtual identity of users and the real identity unclear.

Tambini (1999: 319) further makes the point that 'The degree to which new forms of democratic participation can be developed using the new media will depend upon how new media are regulated and who has access, and also on the design choices made'. He argues that the future of civil networking will depend on three key factors: access; motivation; and 'collective interest' (i.e. notions of local communities and political participation).

Cybercafés providing space for expression of popular culture

While there is a vast range of literature on how people use new technologies such as the Internet and email at home and in the workplace (e.g. Haythornthwaite 2001; Howard *et al.* 2001), other studies have explored how cybercafés serve as a public sphere (Dahlberg 2007; Brants 2005; Dahlgren 2005; Papacharissi 2002), including how and why people patronize the cybercafés, as well as the needs they seek to gratify by surfing the Web (Kaye and Johnson 2004; Kaye 2007). In Africa, researchers have also analysed: patterns of Internet use by Ghanaian university students (Kwansah–Aidoo and Obijiofor 2006); ICT use by Congolese refugees at tertiary educational institutions in Cape Town (Wasserman and Kabeya-Mwepu 2005); Internet cafés in Tanzania (Chachage 2001); Internet use in Gaborone city, Botswana (Sairosse and Mutula 2004); the cybercafé industry in Africa (Mutula 2003); and information technology diffusion in Botswana (Jain and Mutula 2001).

In analysing the use of Internet services, researchers have also examined the major access points for Internet use and found that cybercafés are particularly popular among students because of the diverse range of services and the convenience they provide. For example, Sairosse and Mutula (2004: 61) report that in Botswana,

> Cybercafés are becoming preferred Internet access points because most of them open for long hours, charge reasonably, provide assistance to users, have diverse services and are generally convenient and flexible places for searching the Internet. Students studying in various universities through distance education, for example, find using cybercafés to access course syllabuses and material convenient.

Cybercafés also provide important social services which promote greater interaction among Internet users, including strengthening of community belonging and identity. Sairosse and Mutula (2004: 65) note that 'cybercafés provide Internet access points for users to socialise, provide meeting places for different people, are centres of communication through e-mail, and pursuit of education through e-learning'. What these suggest is that, apart from providing access to a deliberative public sphere, cybercafés also offer a space for expression of various forms of popular culture.

The overarching aim of this chapter is to explore how university students in Nigeria and Ghana use new media technologies as forms of popular media to participate in the public sphere. The chapter also examines whether new media serve as tools of political and economic empowerment such as participation in online forums and social networking sites. The chapter also explores the primary reasons why students use new technologies. In order to advance the discussion, the chapter draws on the theoretical frameworks of uses and gratifications, as well as Jürgen Habermas' (1989) theory of the public sphere.

Theoretical frameworks

The uses and gratifications theory, as well as Habermas' theory of the public sphere, are central to the discussion in this chapter. The uses and gratifications theory is important because many of the studies that examined how people use new technologies (especially Internet-based studies) have been explained within the framework of uses and gratifications (e.g. Kaye 2007; Kaye and Johnson 2004; Charney and Greenberg 2001; Papacharissi and Rubin 2000). The uses and gratifications framework examines media audiences rather than the media message (Littlejohn 1992: 364). It views audience members as active consumers of media contents, who make conscious decisions about what type of media and media content to expose themselves to. According to Kaye (2007: 129): 'Uses and gratifications studies investigate how the audience uses the media rather than how the media use the audience.' According to Bucy et al. (2007: 149), the key assumptions of uses and gratifications theory are:

> (a) that the audience for news and other genres of media content is active and goal directed. (b) that media are an important source of need gratification whose fulfillment lies with audience choices, and (c) that media compete with other sources of need satisfaction.

Littlejohn (1992: 365) states that the gratification an individual seeks from the media relates to 'one's beliefs about what a medium can provide and one's evaluation of the medium's content'.

Public sphere in the digital age

The emergence of new media technologies has raised optimism about the resurgence of the Habermasian public sphere in the digital era. The enthusiasm is based on the popularity of new media and the fact that they enjoy relative autonomy from state and commercial control and influence. Hurwitz (1999: 656) notes, for example, that, 'The Internet has become a new tool and venue for political groups of all stripes. Advocacy and interest groups use it to organize their supporters for online lobbying of local, national, and foreign officials'.

The African context: how university students use new technologies

One of the key questions examined in this chapter is the extent to which university students in Nigeria and Ghana use new technologies such as the Internet, mobile phones and email to participate in the public sphere. What kind of activities do the students engage in with the aid of new media technologies?

The discussion presented here draws on three studies – one study conducted in Nigeria by the author (Obijiofor 2009), one study conducted in Ghana by this author and a colleague (Kwansah-Aidoo and Obijiofor 2006) and a study conducted in a Nigerian university (Omenugha 2009). The three studies are related and recent. Above all, they are relevant to the issues explored in this chapter. Obijiofor (2009) surveyed students at the University of Lagos. A total of 240 questionnaires were administered to students at the Akoka main campus of the university. Of this number, 142 valid questionnaires (59.58 per cent) were returned and analysed. Omenugha's (2009) study utilized mixed-method approaches which involved focus group interviews with 18 students, assessment of 110 students' examination scripts, and personal observations of the Nnamdi Azikiwe University students' use of information and communication technologies in the classroom environment. In the Ghanaian study, Kwansah-Aidoo and Obijiofor (2006) selected four major Internet service providers at the premises of the University of Ghana, Accra. The four Internet cafés were given a total of 200 questionnaires (i.e. 50 questionnaires per Internet café) to administer to their student patrons. Questionnaires were administered only to those students who agreed to answer questions. A total of 180 of the 200 questionnaires were returned, resulting in a return rate of 90 per cent.

Studies conducted at the University of Lagos (Obijiofor 2009) and the University of Ghana (Kwansah-Aidoo and Obijiofor 2006) showed a low frequency of Internet use by the students. Less than one-third of the students at the University of Lagos (31.7 per cent) and the University of Ghana (24.9 per cent) used the Internet on a regular basis (i.e. three to six times per week). The results suggest that, although the students enjoyed Internet access, they used the Internet less frequently per week. This implies that mere access to the Internet does not suggest that students will use the technology more frequently or in any particular way. Also, access to the Internet is not an indicator of why students use the Internet. As Kwansah-Aidoo and Obijiofor (2006: 362) argued, mere exposure to new technologies is not a good indicator of whether people will use the technologies or how the technologies will be used. High cost of accessing Internet services and lack of basic Internet skills have been cited as reasons for low frequency of Internet use among university students in Africa (Omotayo 2006; Awoleye et al. 2008; Ugah and Okafor 2008; Mwesige 2004).

Primary reasons for Internet use

A high percentage of the students surveyed at the University of Lagos (70.4 per cent) and the University of Ghana (68.3 per cent) identified email communication as their primary reason for accessing the Internet. Secondary reasons include: to search for special information; to read news; to relax; and to buy goods and services. Previous research has found similar reasons why university students in Africa use the Internet (Alao and Folorunsho 2008; Awoleye et al. 2008; Ugah and Okafor 2008; Sairosse and Mutula 2004; Jagboro 2003; Robins 2002; Chachage 2001).

Use of Internet applications and resources

To determine the extent to which University of Lagos students utilized the various applications and resources on the Internet, they were requested to indicate how often they used online search engines to find material of interest to them (Obijiofor 2009). It was assumed that ability to use search engines would demonstrate the students' Internet skills, including the extent to which they utilized the many important applications and services available on the Internet. Kaye and Johnson (2004: 198) note that 'Web users actively search out information when they click on links or employ search engines, suggesting Web use is goal directed and that users are aware of the needs they are attempting to satisfy'.

Of the 142 students surveyed at the University of Lagos, only 18.3 per cent used Internet search engines 'every time', while 43.7 per cent used the search engines 'sometimes'. Also, 22.5 per cent used the search engines 'not very often' and 9.2 per cent said they 'never' used the Internet search engines. Nearly 3 per cent said they couldn't remember how often they used the Internet search engines. Although a different question was used in Ghana to test students' Internet skill levels, the results bear some similarity with the findings from the University of Lagos. For example, at the University of Ghana only 28.3 per cent of the 180 students said they had basic Internet skills while 48.9 per cent said they were moderately skilled, and 22.8 per cent considered themselves as highly skilled (Kwansah-Aidoo and Obijiofor 2006: 362).

Theoretical implications

When students at the University of Lagos (Nigeria) and the University of Ghana identify email communication as their primary reason for accessing the Internet, they seem to suggest that participatory communication in the public sphere is not a priority. This does not mean that the students do not consider the Internet as a form of popular media. Arguably, the Internet constitutes a form of popular media among these students but its popularity seems to be restricted to email communication. Additionally, using the Internet largely for email communication suggests that students use the technology basically to satisfy their communication needs in the private sphere rather than for participatory communication in the public sphere. There are possible reasons why the voices of these students are noticeably absent from the public sphere. The reasons include: poverty; lack of basic Internet skills; technical, infrastructural and structural problems that hinder wider access to the Internet; lack of knowledge of gratifications derivable from participation in social networking sites; lack of awareness of the significance of participation in online forums, etc.

By failing to use the Internet search engines more regularly, University of Lagos students in particular made very limited use of the various applications and resources on the Internet, perhaps owing to their lack of basic skills for surfing the Internet. If uses and gratifications theory argues that Internet (or media) use is goal directed, certainly there are limits. Overall, the predominant use of the

Internet for email communication by those students surveyed in Nigeria and Ghana implies that the students have very limited goals for using the Internet. This is not restricted to students only. Oyelaran-Oyeyinka and Adeya (2004) found in their study of Internet use by Kenyan and Nigerian university teachers that only a small number of the respondents nominated electronic commerce as their main reason for using the Internet, implying that university academics in Kenya and Nigeria made limited use of the applications offered by the Internet.

Different students, different uses of new technologies

The way undergraduate students at the University of Lagos and the University of Ghana consume new technologies differs from the way Nnamdi Azikiwe University students in Nigeria use new technologies. In her study, Omenugha (2009) outlines how the use of new technologies has significantly affected academic performance and social behaviour of students at the Nnamdi Azikiwe University. She observed that while mobile phones and 'all night browsing of the Internet' may have empowered the students in various ways, the technologies have also impacted the students in negative ways (Omenugha 2009: 11). Specifically, while mobile phones and the Internet constitute the most prevalent technologies used by the students, the students also reported a major shift towards the use of 'Facebook, which is gradually eroding the use of emails' (Omenugha 2009: 11). The students also perceived web surfing as 'becoming outmoded as their mobile phones were often imbued with software for surfing the net' (Omenugha 2009: 11). The diverse uses which students make of the mobile phone imply that, across cultures, mobile phones are used as a form of popular media among youths.

Although the studies at the universities of Lagos and Ghana did not address the use of mobile phones, the results presented by Omenugha (2009) provide interesting insights into comparative uses of new technologies by university students in different settings. While previous studies by Obijiofor (2009) and Kwansah-Aidoo and Obijiofor (2006) showed a majority of the students at the University of Ghana and University of Lagos accessed the Internet essentially for email communication, students at the Nnamdi Azikiwe University (Omenugha 2009) did not find email communication an important incentive for accessing the Internet. Rather, the Internet attracted the students because it empowered them through participation in Facebook where they could 'meet' and communicate with important people and their peers.

Despite the popularity of new technologies among students, Omenugha (2009: 12) cautioned about the negative consequences of excessive dependence on or use of new technologies:

> 'addiction' to Facebooking had actually done some damage to the youths – someone lost his job because he was caught by the boss Facebooking during office hours; another nearly lost his life because he lost concentration as he was sending a text message while walking along the streets and nearly got hit

by a vehicle. The mobile phone has assumed a symbol of power and status for the students that many go for the very expensive and sophisticated ones that have the 3G features that would make the phone perform multiple tasks such as browsing, facebooking, emails, etc. Students who do not have such phones feel inferior and are reluctant to bring their phones out in public. The result is that some could even steal, lie or engage in fraudulent practices to be able to get the phone of their dream.

Omenugha also reported that the students did not feel it was 'fashionable' any longer for them to access the Internet for purposes of viewing pornography. As she noted,

> the use of the Internet for pornography has drastically reduced amongst their peers as they see people who do that as "childish". More so, computer games and phone games, including play stations are available ... and many have turned to them rather than pornography.
>
> (Omenugha 2009: 12)

Conclusions

These studies suggest that popular uses of new media by university students (e.g. Facebook) tend to divert attention from the more 'serious' use of new media for public deliberation and civic engagement in other cultures. Tanner (2001: 383), for example, reports how Chileans used Internet online forums 'to create spaces for public debate on political and social topics', such as the debate that ensued following the arrest and detention in London of former Chilean leader Augusto Pinochet in October 1998.

As shown in the preceding analysis, students at the universities of Lagos and Ghana tend to use new technologies such as the Internet and email mostly to fulfil their needs for private communication, for access to special information, for access to news, for relaxation and other entertainment purposes, as well as for online shopping. However, students at the Nnamdi Azikiwe University engage in more convergent use of new technologies (e.g. mobile phones, the Internet and social networking sites such as Facebook) that empowered them because it allowed them to 'meet' and interact with different people, to make new friends, to relax, and to 'keep busy'. Incidentally, Boyd and Ellison (2007) identified social networking sites such as Facebook, MySpace and Twitter as popular forms of media whose uses cut across generational differences.

> What makes social network sites unique is not that they allow individuals to meet strangers, but rather that they enable users to articulate and make visible their social networks. This can result in connections between individuals that would not otherwise be made, but that is often not the goal.
>
> (Boyd and Ellison 2007: 211)

See also Boyd (2008) and Hargittai (2007).

One conclusion to be drawn from these studies on the diverse uses of new media is that the use of new technologies among university students in Nigeria and Ghana is not homogenous. Different students use new technologies in different contexts. However, it could be argued that the popularity of new media among students did not extend to the more 'crucial' use of the technologies for self-empowerment in the public sphere and to promote deliberative democracy.

Failure to use new media for participatory communication in the public sphere could be attributed to general economic and infrastructural problems that are common in developing countries. These include poor network services provided by telecommunications providers, poverty, illiteracy and the high cost of accessing the Internet. Studies conducted in Nigeria identified other problems such as 'slow response time, network fluctuation at cyber café' (Ani et al. 2007: 362); 'slowness of the server, inadequate knowledge of how to navigate on the Internet, financial problems and insufficient cyber cafés' (Omotayo 2006: 219); irregular supply of electricity and high cost of access and use of the Internet (Ugah and Okafor 2008); low connectivity (Jagboro 2003); as well as 'financial constraint ... inefficient Internet links and servers ... no personal access to the Internet, not being computer literate, cyber congestion, lack of reliable storage facilities, long distance and pop-up of pornographic sites (spyware)' (Awoleye et al. 2008: 88–9). In Tanzania, Chachage (2001: 230) found problems such as 'slow responses or server not working, junk mail and failure of previous users to sign out', all of which inhibit Internet users.

Future research should explore specific factors that inhibit university students' engagement with new media for participatory communication in the public sphere.

References

Adomi, E.E., Okiy, R.B. and Ruteyan, J.O. (2003) 'A survey of cyber cafés in Delta State, Nigeria', The Electronic Library, 21(5), 487–95.

Alao, I.A. and Folorunsho, A.L. (2008) 'The use of cyber cafés in Ilorin, Nigeria', The Electronic Library, 26(2), 238–48.

Ani, O.E., Uchendu, C. and Atseye, E.U. (2007) 'Bridging the digital divide in Nigeria: a study of Internet use in Calabar metropolis, Nigeria', Library Management, 28(6/7), 355–65.

Aoki, K. and Downes, E.J. (2003) 'An analysis of young people's use of and attitudes toward cell phones', Telematics and Informatics, 20(4), 349–64.

Awoleye, O.M., Siyanbola, W.O. and Oladipo, O.F. (2008) 'Adoption assessment of Internet usage amongst undergraduates in Nigerian universities: a case study approach', Journal of Technology Management & Innovation, 3(1), 84–9.

Boyd, D. (2008) 'Can social network sites enable political action?', International Journal of Media and Cultural Politics, 4(2), 241–4.

Boyd, D.M. and Ellison, N.B. (2007) 'Social network sites: definition, history, and scholarship', Journal of Computer-Mediated Communication, 13(1), 210–30.

Brants, K. (2005) 'Guest editor's introduction: the Internet and the public sphere', Political Communication, 22(2), 143–6.

Bucy, E.P., Gantz, W. and Wang, Z. (2007) 'Media technology and the 24-hour news cycle', in C.A. Lin and D.J. Atkin (eds) *Communication technology and social change: theory and implications*, Mahwah: Lawrence Erlbaum Associates, pp. 143–63.

Chachage, B.L. (2001) 'Internet cafés in Tanzania: a study of the knowledge and skills of end-users', *Information Development*, 17(4), 226–32.

Charney, T. and Greenberg, B.S. (2001) 'Uses and gratifications of the Internet', in C.A. Lin and D.J. Atkin (eds) *Communication technology and society: audience adoption and uses*, Cresskill: Hampton Press, pp. 379–407.

Dahlberg, L. (2007) 'The Internet, deliberative democracy, and power: radicalizing the public sphere', *The International Journal of Media and Cultural Politics*, 3(1), 47–64.

Dahlgren, P. (2005) 'The Internet, public spheres, and political communication: dispersion and deliberation', *Political Communication*, 22(2), 147–62.

Furuholt, B. and Kristiansen, S. (2007) 'Internet cafes in Asia and Africa – venues for education and learning'. Online, available at: http://ci-journal.net/index.php/ciej/article/viewFile/314/352 (accessed 5 July 2009).

Furuholt, B., Kristiansen, S. and Wahid, F. (2008) 'Gaming or gaining? Comparing the use of Internet cafés in Indonesia and Tanzania', *The International Information & Library Review*, 40, 129–39.

Habermas, J. (1989) *The structural transformation of the public sphere: an enquiry into a category of bourgeois society*, Cambridge, MA: MIT Press.

Hargittai, E. (2007) 'Whose space? Differences among users and non-users of social network sites', *Journal of Computer-Mediated Communication*, 13(1), 276–97.

Haythornthwaite, C. (2001) 'Introduction: the Internet in everyday life', *American Behavioral Scientist*, 45(3), 363–82.

Howard, P.E.N., Rainie, L. and Jones, S. (2001) 'Days and nights on the Internet: the impact of a diffusing technology', *American Behavioral Scientist*, 45(3), 383–404.

Hurwitz, R. (1999) 'Who needs politics? Who needs people? The ironies of democracy in cyberspace', *Contemporary Sociology*, 28(6), 655–61.

Jagboro, K.O. (2003) 'A study of Internet usage in Nigerian universities: a case study of Obafemi Awolowo University, Ile-Ife, Nigeria', *First Monday (Peer-reviewed Journal on the Internet)*, 8(2–3). Online, available at: http://firstmonday.org/htbin/cgiwrap/bin/ojs/index.php/fm/article/view/1033/954 (accessed 6 July 2009).

Jain, P. and Mutula, S.M. (2001) 'Diffusing information technology in Botswana: a framework for Vision 2016', *Information Development*, 17(4), 234–40.

Jones, S., Johnson-Yale, C., Millermaier, S. and Perez, F.S. (2009) 'Everyday life, online: U.S. college students' use of the Internet', *First Monday (Peer-Reviewed Journal on the Internet)*, 14(10). Online, available at: www.uic.edu/htbin/cgiwrap/bin/ojs/index.php/fm/article/view/2649/2301 (accessed 13 October 2009).

Kandell, J.J. (1998) 'Internet addiction on campus: the vulnerability of college students', *CyberPsychology & Behavior*, 1(1), 11–17.

Kaye, B.K. (2007) 'Blog use motivations: an exploratory study', in M. Tremayne (ed.) *Blogging, citizenship, and the future of media*, New York: Routledge, pp. 127–48.

Kaye, B.K. and Johnson, T.J. (2004) 'A web for all reasons: uses and gratifications of Internet components for political information', *Telematics and Informatics*, 21(3), 197–223.

Kubey, R.W., Lavin, M.J. and Barrows, J.R. (2001) 'Internet use and collegiate academic performance decrements: early findings', *Journal of Communication*, 51(2), 366–82.

Kwansah-Aidoo, K. and Obijiofor, L. (2006) 'Patterns of Internet use among university students in Ghana', in O.F. Ayadi (ed.) *African development: what role for business? Proceedings of* the *International Academy of African Business and Development Conference*, Vol. 7, Accra, Ghana (23–27 May 2006): Ghana Institute of Management and Public Administration, pp. 359–65.

Lerner, D. and Schramm, W. (1976) 'Looking Forward', in W. Schramm and D. Lerner (eds) *Communication and change: the last ten years – and the next*, Honolulu: The University Press of Hawaii.

Littlejohn, S.W. (1992) *Theories of human communication*, 4th edn, Belmont: Wadsworth.

Mutula, S.M. (2003) 'Cyber café industry in Africa', *Journal of Information Science*, 29(6), 489–97.

Mwesige, P.G. (2004) 'Cyber elites: a survey of Internet café users in Uganda', *Telematics and Informatics*, 21, 83–101.

Obijiofor, L. 'Perceptions and use of Internet and email technologies by Nigerian university undergraduate students', paper presented at the African Council for Communication Education (ACCE) conference, University of Ghana, Accra, August 2009.

Odero, J. (2003) 'Using the Internet café at Technikon Pretoria in South Africa: views from students', paper presented at the Norwegian Network on ICT and Development Annual Workshop, Bergen, Norway, 14–15 November. Cited in Wahid, F., Furuholt, B. and Kristiansen, S. (2006) 'Internet for development? Patterns of use among Internet café customers in Indonesia', *Information Development*, 22(4), 278–91.

Omenugha, K.A. (2009) 'Nigerian students' use of information and communication technology – a blessing or a curse?', paper presented at the African Council for Communication Education (ACCE) conference, University of Ghana, Accra, August 2009.

Omotayo, B.O. (2006) 'A survey of Internet access and usage among undergraduates in an African university', *The International Information & Library Review*, 38, 215–24.

Oyelaran-Oyeyinka, B. and Adeya, C.N. (2004) 'Internet access in Africa: empirical evidence from Kenya and Nigeria', *Telematics and Informatics*, 21, 67–81.

Papacharissi, Z. (2002) 'The virtual sphere: the Internet as a public sphere', *New Media & Society*, 4(1), 9–27.

Papacharissi, Z. and Rubin, A.M. (2000) 'Predictors of Internet usage', *Journal of Broadcasting & Electronic Media*, 44, 175–96.

Robins, M.B. (2002) 'Are African women online just ICT consumers?', *Gazette*, 64(3), 235–49.

Sairosse, T.M. and Mutula, S.M. (2004) 'Use of cyber cafés: study of Gaborone City, Botswana', *Program: Electronic Library and Information Systems*, 38(1), 60–6.

Tambini, D. (1999) 'New media and democracy: the civic networking movement', *New Media & Society*, 1(3), 305–29.

Tanner, E. (2001) 'Chilean conversations: Internet forum participants debate Augusto Pinochet's detention', *Journal of Communication*, 51(2), 383–403.

Tehranian, M. (1989) 'Communication, democracy, peace, and development: some theoretical considerations for the future', in D.S. Sanders and J.K. Matsuoka (eds) *Peace and development: an interdisciplinary perspective*, Hawaii: School of Social Work, University of Hawaii.

Ugah, A.D. and Okafor, V. (2008) 'Faculty use of a cybercafé for Internet access', *Library Philosophy and Practice* (a peer-reviewed electronic journal). Online, available at: www.webpages.uidaho.edu/~mbolin/lpp.htm (accessed 6 July 2009).

Wasserman, H. and Kabeya-Mwepu, P. (2005) 'Creating connections: exploring the intermediary use of ICTs by Congolese refugees at tertiary educational institutions in Cape Town', *Southern African Journal of Information and Communication*, 6, 94–103.

Part IV

Identity and community between the local and the global

Chapter 14

Transnational flows and local identities in Muslim northern Nigerian films

From *Dead Poets Society* through *Mohabbatein* to *So...*

Abdalla Uba Adamu

Introduction

In analysing Muslim Hausa film viewing and preferences for Hindi cinema, Brian Larkin (1977) coins the term 'parallel modernities' to refer to the co-existence in space and time of multiple economic, religious and cultural flows that are often subsumed within the term 'modernity'. Larkin argues that his formulation resonates with the term 'alternative modernities' used by Arjun Appadurai (1991) but with a key difference. Appadurai links the emergence of alternative modernities with the increased deterritorialization of the globe and the movement of people, capital and political movements across cultural and national boundaries. I want to contribute to the debate by suggesting 'concurrent modernities' to explain the use of Hindi film motifs in northern Nigerian Muslim Hausa video films. In this, I argue that none of these conceptions of modernities – parallel and alternative – as applicable to the cinematic development of young urban Muslim Hausa filmmakers took into consideration the violent intrusion of small media technologies that helped to create *media identities* – rather than *social* identities divorced from the religious, political and economic transnational flows both Larkin and Appadurai alluded to. These small technologies, in fact, enable transnational communities to use filmic templates 'in their own image', exploring *similar* contexts as those being copied.

I explore this concurrent modernity by examining how a Hollywood film, *Dead Poets Society* (1989, dir. Peter Weir) was reworked in two different countries; first as *Mohabbatein* (2000, dir. Aditya Chopra) in India, and then as a Muslim Hausa, northern Nigerian video film *So...* (2001, dir. Hafizu Bello). Both Indian and Nigerian titles of the remake mean the same thing: love. In my analysis I want to look at the appropriation styles used and how the Muslim Hausa filmmaker attempted to domesticate Indian social reality as Hausa social identity.

Peter Levine argues that 'we often think of democracy as a political system in which the people are ultimately in control of their government's budget, important laws, and relations with foreign nations' (2007: 34). However, it is at least as important for a people to control its own identity and self-image. In order to be self-governing, a community or a nation must be able to illustrate and memorialize its values and present its identity to outsiders and future generations of its own people through works of art and literature, rituals and traditions, forms of entertainment, public spaces and prominent buildings. Small media technologies have provided Nigerian filmmakers with an opportunity to create what I see as 'industries of representation' in which each region of the country demonstrates its democratic right to represent its society in its own way. For instance, the southern Nigerian film industry, Nollywood (Onishi 2002), is characterized by the notion of statehood in which plotlines of corruption, crime and governance are interspersed with African ritual beliefs. The northern Nigerian video film industry, Kanywood, is on the other hand characterized by romantic themes of relationships between boys and girls (and occasionally, married couples) in which conflicts are identified and resolved. This focus on the private sphere in Kanywood films, reflecting itself a deeper social focus on gender relationships, is reflected in Hindi films that the most successful Hausa filmmakers directly copy. It is for this reason that I provided 'concurrent modernity' as an alternative to Larkin's 'parallel modernity' because both Hindi and Muslim Hausa societies share an antecedent concurrent common interface of the role of Islam and traditional conservative values in mediating social relationships.

Nigerian media policies became liberalized only in 1992 during one of the episodic periods of military dictatorship (Onwumechili 2007). The liberalization came about because of 'international lenders' pressure and the government's inability to control access to international satellite signals' (Onwumechili 2007: 128).

Eventually, the government issued the National Broadcasting Commission (NBC) Decree No. 38 in 1992 to liberalize the broadcast market. This liberalization led to high expectations about the use of media in at least a liberal, if not democratic, Nigerian society. These expectations included diversity of the media, availability of new media technologies, enhanced customer service and others. This accelerated the development of the Hausa video film industry which started with a video film titled *Turmin Danya* in 1990. When in 1999 Nigeria became democratic again, the Hausa video film had developed into a viable industry. The Hausa youth who developed the industry used it as a marker of identity – for their video films were more focused on the self, in contrast with the southern Nigerian video film industry that focuses more on the nation.

Democracy therefore provides an element of control. Thus the argument for the continuing role of national identity in cementing a sense of common citizenship is that 'it provides the political cohesion necessary for a democratic community' (Schwarzmantel 2003: 86). Within this context, popular culture therefore becomes a forum for the negotiation of race, gender, nation and other identities, and for struggles for power within a society (Dolby 2006).

In this chapter I specifically look at the transcultural intertextuality of the three films, not only within the notions of identity, but also within the larger context of media liberalization in Nigeria brought about by democratic opportunities for choices of what to adapt or appropriate. In this transcultural intertextuality, the same message goes through different cultural climates and negotiates its acceptance. There are two processes involved in this: vertical intertextuality, which looks at textual migrations of the message from the West to the East to Africa; and horizontal intertextuality, which looks at the migration of text from the East to Africa. As Brian Larkin (2003: 172) notes,

> Indian film offers Hausa viewers a way of being modern that does not necessarily mean being Western ... For Nigerian Hausa, Indian film offers a space that is alter to the West against which a cultural politics (but not necessarily a political one) can be waged. The popularity of Indian film with Hausa audiences is so great that, in the north of Nigeria at least where Hausa are based, they are used by both Hausa and their others as means of defining identity and locating the temporal and political nature of that identity.

It is these commonalities in identity that makes Hindi films ready templates for remakes and appropriation by Hausa filmmakers, even if the Hindi film itself is based on another film from another culture. It is this commonality that I refer to as 'concurrent modernity'. Having been first rendered into a more traditional setting of Indian audiences, Hollywood films therefore become more palatable to conservative Hausa via Hindi cinema. This reveals a unique channel of transnational flow of media identities little explored in media and cultural studies. For while studies of the itineraries of Bollywood cinema tended to focus on consumption (e.g. Banaji 2006; Sangita Gopal and Sujata Moorti 2008), there is little by way of actual cinematic transfers, especially between Hindi films and communities that do not have any form of Indian presence, as in northern Nigeria. In this way, therefore, Hausa filmmakers with their adherence to Hindi films as templates of either direct reproduction or artistic inspiration provide the significant locus for understanding how deep transnational media flows to other communities in Africa. This should reveal how their influences goes beyond intertextuality and international border crossings to emerge as authentic local texts capable of telling a local story – even if started transnationally.

Textual migrations and transnational entertainment

In his discussion of the remake, Thomas Leitch identifies 'four possible stances a remake can adopt, each with its own characteristic means of resolving its contradictory intertextual claims' (1990: 142). These are the 'readaptation', the 'update', the 'homage' and the 'true remake'. These stances actually refer to intertextual relationship between the remake and the source text – rather than the general approach (model) that motivates the *need* for the remake. Thus Leitch's 'stances' gives us another perspective on the specific strategies adopted when a decision to remake is taken.

In analysing transnational media flows in popular culture, it becomes inevitable to discuss the issues of adaptation and appropriation. While adaptation is clearly intermedial – shifting from source text to another, usually more visual medium, appropriation is seen as 'a more decisive journey away from the informing source into a wholly new cultural product and domain' (Sanders 2006: 26). Thus appropriation is often intramedial – circulating within the same media. In remaking *Mohabbatein* as *So...*, the Hausa filmmaker clearly adopts appropriation as a strategy, evidenced in his attempt to move away from the original source material and create a whole new focus. It becomes intramedial because the core messages of the two films did not shift media – they both shared the same small-technology video media, rather than if shifts were made from celluloid to video film.

These perceptions of the narrative as an intertextual form would seem to fit in with visual theoretical precepts of the remake as 'a special pattern which represents and explains at a different time and through varying perceptions, previous narratives and experiences' (Horton and McDougal 1998: 2). Yet a series of subtleties are introduced when actually dissecting the juxtaposed texts and narratives between the source and the remake, especially when crossing cultural borders. This is illustrated by the way popular commercial Hindi cinema appropriates films from Hollywood. As pointed out by Paul Cooke (2007: 4):

> it could be argued that Hollywood is so powerful economically because it is the best at providing the world with the most appealing film aesthetics and narrative structures as well as the most attractive message, setting the norm for mainstream film-making, against which all other cinemas must be judged.

The link between Hollywood and Indian cinema was well established right from the inception of the cinema industry in India. As observed by Kaushik Bhaumik (2007: 201):

> The dialogue between Hollywood and Bombay cinema is a long-standing one that can be dated back to the earliest years of film history. Imported films were seen in Bombay from 1896 onwards creating a film culture that was to define the shape of Bombay cinema in crucial ways.

As a result of this, charges of being mere clones of Hollywood films have followed films, especially from the popular Bombay cinema. It is not mere blind copying, however, for as Tejaswini Ganti (2002) pointed out, Hollywood films that are considered adaptable to the Indian context are those with more universal appeal, rather than the more esoteric, and often intellectually demanding, regional cinema of directors such as Satyajit Ray. Consequently

> Films that have been adapted in the recent past – *Sabrina, Kramer vs. Kramer, Mrs. Doubtfire, The Hard Way, Sleeping with the Enemy, French Kiss*, and *An Affair to Remember* – are all centered on relationships – romantic, marital, parental, filial, or friendship – allowing Hindi filmmakers to add new twists to narratives that are predominantly about romantic love, kinship, or the myriad levels of duty.
>
> (Ganti 2002: 287)

The Americanization of global cinema, of course, sees the reproduction of the same Hollywood films across cultures, or what Andrew Horton (1998: 173) calls 'the cross-cultural makeover'. In Horton's original conception, he looks at how minority cultures appropriate Hollywood because such strategies can prove 'instructive for both narrative film studies and cultural studies' (Horton 1998: 173). In his particular example, he analysed how Bosnian-born Yugoslav director Emir Kusturica remade Francis Ford Coppola's *Godfather* and *Godfather II* as *Time of the Gypsies*.

Other cinemas, such as Turkish cinema, borrow from Indian cinema. For instance, according to Ahmet Gurata (2009: 2), in Turkey

> Indian films were modified and adapted into the local context by the local distributors, exhibitors or censorship bodies. These modifications took the form of various programming and translation methods from trimming to dubbing. Furthermore, certain scenes were removed or in some cases performances or acts featuring local stars were inserted into the original prints.

This is similar to the Hausa cinema in northern Nigeria which draws its main inspiration from Hindi cinema, such that over 130 Hindi films were appropriated in one form or the other as Hausa video films (see Adamu 2009).

Thus what is of further significance is the way media is used to construct identities and share these constructs with communities sharing these identities. Obviously, then, the usage of identity-construct kits from different communities may communicate different conceptions of the communities and consequently lead to misrepresentation of identities. This is the scenario that creates issues of the role of entertainment in such communities. I will illustrate this by analysing the three films and later discussing their intertextual and cultural linkages that focus on identities of their individual societies.

I will first present a brief plot summary of each, and then later discuss how the core elements of *Dead Poets Society* are reworked by each filmmaker to domesticate the elements to the recipient audiences by looking at the fidelity of the narrative structures of the remakes.

Source text 1: *Dead Poets Society* (United States)

Dead Poets Society is about the discovery of identity and reaffirmation of identity. It focuses on the discovery of an inner core of personal beliefs and uses these beliefs as a central engine to social engagement and reaffirmation – the alternative to denial of these inner personal beliefs is, often, tragic. It seeks to show the dangers of conformity.

The plot revolves around seven boys who attend a prestigious preparatory school, the Welton Academy, in Vermont, the United States, which is run on four principles: *tradition*, *honour*, *discipline* and *excellence*, as explained by the dour principal, Gale Nolan.

The school recruites a much more cheerful and adventurous English teacher, John Keating, whose extremely unorthodox (to the school) teaching methods included ripping out whole pages from a poetry book, and encouraging the students to stand on their classroom desks as new ways of looking at the world. While not openly encouraging rebellion against constituted authority, the new teacher nevertheless encourages the students to engage on a process of self-discovery – including egging them to revive an old school club, the Dead Poets Society. His whole teaching methods revolve around showing the students the 'dangers of conformity'.

Their contact with the new teacher and his unorthodox approach to life and personal freedom enables each of the seven boys to embark on a personal journey of discovery – which leads to the conclusion that authority acts only as a guide, but the true identity of a person is inside – thus confirming Keating's teaching about the dangers of conformity.

One of the boys, Charlie Dalton, takes his new personal freedom too far and publishes a profane and unauthorized article in the school's newsletter. In this article, Charlie states that he wants to have girls allowed at Welton. Another student, Neil Perry, opposes his father by appearing in a stage play, an obsession his father thinks will only derail the boy from pursuing a more rewarding career in medicine, which the boy does not want. On being told that he must quit the play, Neil commits suicide by shooting himself – committing the ultimate defiance of authority. An investigation is conducted by the college, and John Keating is blamed as being the causative factor that leads to Neil's death. Subsequently, John Keating is dismissed as a teacher from the school – although he leaves thanking the students for standing up – literally in the last scene – to their own identity in the end.

Target-source text (T-ST) I: *Mohabbatein*

As far as I could tell, the director of *Mohabbatein*, Adrit Chopra, did not seem to have made any explicit recorded statement about the cinematic relationships between his film and *Dead Poets Society*. Nevertheless, numerous websites alluded to the seemingly obvious fact that *Mohabbatein* is a direct intertextual reading of *Dead Poets Society*. Further, María Seijo-Richart (2008) has covered the issue of the relationship between the two films in a more structured manner.

In *Mohabbatein* the plot revolves around three boys admitted to the Gurukul, a preparatory college in India run by Narayan Shankar, a strict disciplinarian, who runs the college on the basis of three principles: *tradition, honour* and *discipline*. He has been running the Gurukul on these principles for 25 years, and sees no reason to change.

The regime at the Gurukul includes banning any romantic liaisons between the students and any females outside the college – a difficult task, as right next door to the Gurukul is a girl's hostel. One of the three students recites the story he heard of a former student of the Gurukul who fell in love with a girl and had his love denied – leading to the girl committing suicide. The student was expelled from the Gurukul. It happened that the girl was Principal Narayan's daughter.

Soon a music teacher, Raj Aryan Malhotra, applies to teach music at the Gurukul. He is given the job reluctantly on the condition that he finds students who like music enough to be taught. He comes across as footloose and fancy-free. He sets out to prove the power of love (*mohabbatein*) over the fear of the principal that permeates the school. His idea of teaching music is to liven things up a bit. Thus he is as unconventional as could be, in an institution that prides itself on its conventions.

It is clear he is different because his main thematic message is for his wards to follow their hearts and fall in love. Further, his main mission is to bring about change to fill the school with love and sunshine. His strategy includes arranging a party for the students, which allowed almost all the girls from the nearby hostel to join in a frenzy of singing and dancing typical of commercial Hindi cinema. The principal catches them in the act and in a disciplinary administrative session demands to know if they were made to defy the school authorities by 'someone'. They replied that they did everything on their volition because they were 'following their hearts' – literally, 'seizing the day', as John Keating would put it. The teacher, however, goes to the principal, goes down on his knees and pleads for the students not to be dismissed because they were made to do what they did by the teacher. He pleads, however, because he does not want another student to be expelled from the Gurukul for simply following their heart's desires – as he was; and reveals himself to Narayan as the student who was expelled for falling in love with the principal's daughter, who killed herself.

The principal agrees to forgive the students on the condition that the teacher confess at the school assembly that whatever he has been teaching – love – is wrong; and then he must leave the Gurukul 'and never come back'. He tells the teacher, 'in the battle of love and fear, fear will always win'. The teacher retorts that is not fear (i.e. Narayan) that has won, but fear that has lost – for the teacher has returned to the Gurukul to break the hard barrier that Narayan surrounds his heart with and in time be accepted as a son. Now Narayan has lost both a daughter and a son.

At the morning assembly Narayan addresses the students and, in a surprise move, renounces his hard stance on life and accepts that 'life is about giving and receiving love, nothing else, nothing else'. Consequently, 'the old generation will have to change their old traditions, so that a new generation can create a new tradition'. With this, he requests the new teacher to take over from him as principal of the Gurukul, to provide a better, happier, future for the students, one filled with love.

Target-target text (TT): *So...* (northern Nigeria)

So..., like *Dead Poets Society* and *Mohabbatein*, but most particularly the latter – which it remakes in many shot-by-shot scenes, is about identity – this time, social identity. In Hausa societies the individual's pedigree ('usuli') is one of the markers of identity and acceptance in any social grouping. A person with no traceable pedigree is considered unworthy of either being married or having his daughter married – unless of course it is to the social layer of those without pedigree.

So... is based in an orphanage, not a college. The settings of Welton Academy in *Dead Poets Society*, as well as the Gurukul in *Mohabbatein* – both stern, sober and extremely establishment – provide a perfect setting for a conservative schooling environment in the Hausa remake.

Early in the film, the principal of the orphanage, Kabiru Nakwango, orients the residents to the four fundamental principles of the orphanage. These are: *ladabi* (good manners), *biyayya* (obedience), *addini* (Islam) and *kyawawan dabi'u da al'adu* (good cultural deportment). He has run the orphanage for 30 years – suffering only a tragic personal loss – on these principles, is deeply set in his ways, and does not accept any form of change.

Soon a new teacher, Mansur Abdulkarim, joins the faculty to teach choreography. The new teacher believes that the orphanage lacks love, and sets out to change this. He tells the boys the story of a former resident of the orphanage who fell in love with the principal's daughter. She was banned from seeing him and he was expelled from the orphanage. Distraught, the principal's daughter killed herself.

Naturally the boys are wildly enthusiastic about the subject of choreography in such a sober establishment, and therefore welcome the idea of radical change. To embellish the choreography lessons, the new teacher involves the girls from a nearby orphanage for girls. The principal is against this move as he believes that such co-educational configuration is likely to lead to undesirable consequences, particularly among young teens. Despite this, the new teacher goes ahead and organizes more choreography competitions (along the same song and dance patterns in *Mohabbatein*).

When the students break the school rules for the first time, the principal chides them. When they do it the second time, he asks them to write a letter of apology in which they should indicate that they were forced into breaking the orphanage's rules. The students insist that they did everything on their own volition. He then asks them to leave the school within 24 hours. On learning this, Mansur Abdulkarim goes to the principal's house, bends on his knees and begs him to forgive the students, as it was he, not they, who was responsible for their behaviour, also revealing himself as the former resident who had fallen in love with the principal's daughter. The principal agrees to reinstate the boys but only if Mansur will appear in the assembly the following morning and renounce all he has been teaching them as illusion.

In the morning assembly of the orphanage, the principal reiterates that Mansur is deceiving them about love. He then asks Mansur to explain what he means by love. After a long explanation of the virtues of love, and his acceptance that Kabiru will never change, Mansur produces a letter of resignation from the orphanage as a teacher. The students protest loudly. This suddenly makes the principal accept that since they protested so vigorously, his time is over, he belongs to an older generation. He then asks Mansur, the choreography teacher, to take over the leadership of the school and to fill it with love.

Intermedial transitions of identities across borders

A single commonality that binds all the three films is desire for change from the status quo. Yet this declared desire for change is constructed through narrative styles typical of the audiences for each film. While the change desired in the *Dead Poets Society* is in tandem with American liberal social philosophy, the conservatism of Welton Academy's authorities is institutional, not personal. Nolan is merely acting out a script written over 100 years ago. John Keating's influence on the students deals with them as individual units, rather than as institutional appendages. This is consistent with notions of personal freedom – an entrenched American social philosophy (see, for instance, Smith 1983).

In *Mohabbatein* the impetus is not to change a group, but an individual, and his stern ways that led to tragic personal consequences. Yet it was the tragedy that drove him further into his isolated cold world of conformity to his own beliefs. This personal tragedy was domesticated from the institutional tragedy of *Dead Poets Society* where Neil Perry commits suicide. Yet in both cases, the tragedy served as a catalyst to bringing about change – though not necessarily in the direction anticipated.

So... would seem to have greater impact on the desire for change, and with it a reconstructed identity. This is indicated in the way the filmmakers chose an orphanage, rather than a prestigious school, as the setting for their secondary remake of *Dead Poets Society*. Elitist preparatory schools such as the Welton Academy or the Gurukul do not exist in northern Nigeria. The producers therefore shifted away from elitism to non-identity, and there is no place where the residents lack identity as much as in an orphanage. In northern Nigeria children in orphanages are mainly abandoned, lost children or those whose mothers (rarely fathers) do not have any means of sustaining them. Being taken into an orphanage is considered 'amana' (trust) by the Islamic public authorities (Kirk-Greene 1974: 5).

Consequently, the social regime in such establishments tended to be extremely orthodox to Islamic teachings – to ensure that the orphanage becomes truly *in loco parentis*. It is against this background that we come to understand Principal Nakwango's adherence to the orphanage's principles.

Even the choice of the curriculum at the heart of the contention between the new teacher and the principal reveals another shift in identity focus. The new teacher is recruited to teach them choreography, not music or poetry. It is significant that the producers of *So*... did not choose music (as done in *Mohabbatein*), because it is not a taught subject in the curricula of Muslim Hausa public educational establishments of northern Nigeria, due in part to the low status of musicians (Podstavsky 2004) – unlike in India where music is part of religious life. Further, according to Smith (1959: 249), the Hausa system of social status has

> three or four 'classes'. Sometimes the higher officials and chiefs are regarded as constituting upper 'class' by themselves, sometimes they are grouped with the Mallams and wealthier merchants into a larger upper class. The lowest

'class' generally distinguished includes the musicians, butchers, house-servants and menial clients, potters, and the poorer farmers who mostly live in rural hamlets. The great majority of the farmers, traders and other craftsmen would, therefore, belong to the Hausa 'middle-class'.

However relevant their roles are, Hausa entertainers are among the lowest groups in the status scale. Their condition is reflective of their generic dependence on the largesse of others, and their arts are, in essence, instruments of mendicancy, their walk of life. The Hausa word *roko*, begging, denotes this condition.

Even the choreography the producers chose is associated with low status in a conservative society. Dancing is, however, a popular urban pastime, particularly in the era of transnational musical genres such as electro/techno, disco and hip-hop. In my interviews with the director of *So...* Hafizu Bello, he explains his awareness of the lack of career focus of choreography for Muslim Hausa orphans; but in fact choreography was introduced to brighten the dark and sober atmosphere of the orphanage and make life more fun and lively (personal communication, 1 June 2009). Being in an orphanage is depressing enough, without the severity of the principal's philosophy of life that seems to be anti-fun.

In its construction of individual identity, *So...* bases its plot on the social acceptance of a person without identity – for orphanage children in northern Nigeria are considered precisely that; no established pedigree ('asali, asalan'). Consequently, for marriage purposes, a suitor is not sure of the good training and behaviour of children from such care homes. It is therefore necessary for *So...* to establish the principle tenets of *in loco parentis* as the entrenchment of parental responsibility – in the absence of biological parents.

At the same time, *So...* reveals contradictions in the acceptance of constructed identity. Although the principal insists on his principles being implemented in the school, he also seems to have little faith in the impact of those principles on his students. This is reflected in the way he refuses to allow his own daughter (with a good pedigree) to marry one of the orphans, Mansur Abdulkarim (later to return as a choreography teacher in the school), a refusal that leads to her committing suicide. It would have been obvious from his strict disciplinarian disposition which he imparts not only to his students, but also his family, that marrying his daughter to one of his students – as Islamic teachers in northern Nigerian often do – would have been a perfect test of the results of his principles. However, since the suitor is an orphan, and thus has no pedigree, the principal refused to allow such a liaison. In a way, *So...* critiques the Hausa society that insists on the pedigree of an individual, despite having all the proper traits of a 'perfect gentleman'.

In departing from the ideological veneer of *Dead Poets Society*, and accepting the more flexible adaptations of popular culture as in *Mohabbatein*, *So...* uses the Muslim Hausa Islamic social universe and cultural realities to entrench an established tradition of the Muslim Hausa in researching the pedigree of suitors before marriage commitment. At the same time, it applauds the institutional basis for identity construction, which enables residents from orphanages to acquire an Islamic upbringing.

Conclusion

In analysing appropriation and dialogue in Japanese cinema, Rachel Hutchinson (2007: 172) points out that:

> There are many ways to read the relationship between a film and its remake: in terms of fidelity, imitation, plagiarism, appropriation, or other enactments of power. For the most part, such models rely on a binary system to analyse the relationship between two films in isolation from their surroundings.

This binary system includes appropriator versus appropriated, subject versus object. However, it is clear that not all the elements of the relationship identified by Hutchinson could apply wholly to understanding the intertextual relationship between the three films discussed in this chapter. Thus, in my conclusion, I focus mainly on fidelity discourse as a means of understanding why Hausa filmmakers chose to appropriate *Mohabbatein*, rather than its source text, *Dead Poets Society*.

In choosing Hutchinson's fidelity discourse, I accept her distinction between the fidelity discourse and the remake theory, where she sees the latter as an attempt to explain what is going on when one director remakes the film of another. My use of the fidelity discourse is not so much on its structuralist core, but as a tool for extracting shared commonalities in identity formation between three divergent cinemas and audiences – from the United States, India and Nigeria.

The reason for this choice is practical enough: in my interviews with the director of *So . . .*, Hafizu Bello, he stated his unawareness of *Dead Poets Society*, and insists that his template for *So . . .* was *Mohabbatein*. This is not surprising because mainstream Hollywood films are not shown in Nigeria – except via pirated copies available on DVDs containing as many as 20 full features and sold for about a dollar or less from wheelbarrows. Thus in the case of the Hausa remake of *Mohabbatein*, there is no attempt on the part of Hafizu Bello as a director to, as it were, enter Aditya Chopra's mind as the director of *Mohabbatein* to understand his technique in the remake. Hafizu Bello's technique was rooted in the social reality of Hausa societies and their treatment of individuals without identified parental pedigree. In his remake, he uses the majority of ideas from *Mohabbatein*, but rejects quite a few that he felt were not applicable to his audience (e.g. the concept of elitist preparatory school, confrontations between the daughter who committed suicide and her father), while at the same time incorporating what I call supra-realistic icons to the Hausa society – such as teaching young orphans choreography in a society that does not accept dancing as a religiously acceptable occupation.

The second reason for using the fidelity framework is the closer 'emotional grammar' between the messaging and social contexts of *Mohabbatein* and *So . . .* than between *So . . .* and *Dead Poets Society*. For in the latter the principal's stern visage is readily identifiable as institutional – something in fact which parents would approve of as entrenching responsibility. In the remakes in *Mohabbatein* and *So...*, however, the principals cut an authority figure that is in line with the didactic nature of the environment that expects total submission to authority – complete with the white beard of an elder. Conformity to traditional authority therefore becomes expected fare of conservative behaviour as, for instance, exemplified by the refusal to allow inter-gender mixing in the two settings. In *Mohabbatein* the reason for this was because it might introduce an element of diversion to the male students. In *So...* it is because teen co-educational institutions are on a collision course with Islamic tenets – 'addini' (religion and, in this case, Islam), being one of the four pillars of the orphanage.

Thus in using fidelity discourse as an analytical framework, I compare *So...* with *Mohabbatein* by beginning with the former and looking back to the latter in order to analyse what was included or omitted in the remake. For as Sanders (2006: 17) pointed out, 'the interleaving of different texts and textual traditions, which is manifest in the intertextual impulse', has also been linked to the postcolonial notion of 'hybridity' by, for instance, writers such as Homi Bhabha, whose account of hybridity suggests how things and ideas are 'repeated, relocated and translated in the name of tradition' (1995: 207).

Yet this hybridity must essentially respect differences because, as Homi Bhabba suggests, synthesis or homogenization of multiculturalism 'proves stifling' (Sanders 2006: 17). Consequently the choices between hybrid intertextuality and homogenization of multiculturalism based on the notion of sharing common interfaces between translocating and receptive media climates will have to be made at the altar of cultural negotiation.

References

Adamu, A.U. (2009) 'Media Parenting and the Construction of Media Identities in Northern Nigerian Muslim Hausa Video Film', in Kimani Njogu and John Middleton (eds) *Media and Identity in Africa*, pp. 171–86. Edinburgh: Edinburgh University Press.

Appadurai, A. (1991) 'Global Ethnoscapes: Notes and Queries for a Transnational Anthropology', in Richard Fox (ed.) *Recapturing Anthropology: Working in the Present*, pp. 191–210. Santa Fe: SAR Press.

Banaji, S. (2006) *Reading 'Bollywood': The Young Audience and Hindi Films*, London: Palgrave Macmillan.

Bhabha, H.K. (1995) 'Cultural Diversity and Cultural Differences', in B. Ashcroft, Gareth Griffiths and Helen Tiffin (eds) *The Post-Colonial Studies Reader*, pp. 206–12. London and New York: Routledge.

Bhaumik, K. (2007) '"Lost in Translation: A Few Vagaries of the Alphabet Game Played Between Bombay Cinema and Hollywood"', in Paul Cooke (ed.) *World Cinema's 'Dialogues' with Hollywood*, pp. 201–17. New York: Palgrave Macmillan.

Cooke, P. (2007) 'Introduction: World Cinema's "Dialogues" with Hollywood', in Paul Cooke (ed.) *World Cinema's 'Dialogues' with Hollywood*, pp. 1–16. New York: Palgrave Macmillan.

Dolby, N. (2006) 'Popular Culture and Public Space in Africa: The Possibilities of Cultural Citizenship', *African Studies Review* 49(3): 31–47.

Ganti, T. (2002) '"And Yet My Heart Is Still Indian": The Bombay Film Industry and the (H)Indianization of Hollywood', in F.D. Ginsburg, Lila Abu-Lughod and Brian Larkin (eds) *Media Worlds: Anthropology on New Terrain*, pp. 281–300G. Berkeley: University of California Press.

Gopal, S. and S. Moorti (eds) (2008) *Global Bollywood: Travels of Hindi Song and Dance*, Minneapolis: University of Minnesota Press.

Gurata, A. (2009) 'Remaking Indian Films', paper presented at international workshop on Indian Cinema Circuits: Diasporas, Peripheries and Beyond, held on 25 and 26 June, at The Old Cinema, Regent Campus, University of Westminster, London.

Horton, A. (1998) 'Cinematic Makeovers and Cultural Border Crossings: Kusturica's *Time of the Gypsies* and Coppola's *Godfather* and *Godfather II*', in A. Horton and Stuart Y. McDougal (eds) *Retakes on Remakes*, pp. 172–90. Berkeley: University of California Press.

Hutchinson, R. (2007) 'A Fistful of *Yojimbo*: Appropriation and Dialogue in Japanese Cinema', in P. Cooke (ed.) *World Cinema's 'Dialogues' with Hollywood*, pp. 172–87. New York: Palgrave Macmillan.

Kirk-Greene, A.H.M. (1974) *Mutumin Kirki: The Concept of the Good Man in Hausa*. The Third Annual Hans Wolff Memorial Lecture, 11 April 1973, Bloomington: African Studies Program, Indiana University.

Larkin, B. (1997) 'Indian Films and Nigerian Lovers: Media and Creation of Parallel Modernities', *Africa* 67(3): 406–39.

Larkin, B. (2003) 'Itineraries of Indian Cinema: African Videos, Bollywood, and Global Media', in E. Shohat and Robert Stam (eds) *Multiculturalism, Postcoloniality, and Transnational Media*, pp. 170–92. New Brunswick: Rutgers University Press.

Leitch, T.M. (1990) 'Twice-Told Tales: The Rhetoric of the Remake', *Literature/Film Quarterly* 18(3): 138–49.

Levine, Peter (2007) *The Future of Democracy: Developing the Next Generation of American Citizens*, Lebanon: UPNE.

Onishi, N. (2002) 'Step Aside, L.A. and Bombay, for Nollywood', *New York Times*, 16 September, online edition.

Onwumechili, C. (2007) 'Nigeria: Equivocating while Opening the Broadcast Liberalization Gates', in I.A. Blankson and Patric D. Murphy (eds) *Negotiating Democracy: Media Transformations in Emerging Democracies*, pp. 123–42. New York: SUNY Press.

Podstavsky, S. (2004) 'Hausa Entertainers and their Social Status: A Reconsideration of Sociohistorical Evidence', *Ethnomusicology* 48(3): 348–77.

Sanders, J. (2006) *Adaptation and Appropriation*, Oxford: Routledge.

Schwarzmantel, J. (2003) *Citizenship and Identity: Towards a New Republic*, London: Routledge.

Seijo-Richart, M. (2008) 'A Bollywood Remake: Mohabbatein (2000, dir. Aditya Chopra) and Dead Poets' Society (1989, dir. Peter Weir)'. Paper presented at the conference on Cultural Borrowings: A Study Day on Appropriation, Reworking and Transformation, University of Nottingham, 19 March 2008.

Smith, J. (1983) *The Spirit of American Philosophy*, New York: SUNY Press.

Smith, M.G. (1959) 'The Hausa System of Social Status', *Africa*, 29: 239–52.

Chapter 15

Local stories, global discussions
Websites, politics and identity in African contexts

Inge Brinkman, Siri Lamoureaux, Daniela Merolla
and Mirjam de Bruijn

Introduction

In this chapter we will compare websites related to various regions in Africa emphasizing ethnic or regional identity as politically important. Four cases – websites relating to the Moroccan Berber context, websites that stress 'Kongo' and 'Nuba' identity respectively, and websites produced by people from English-speaking West Cameroon – will be presented separately followed by a comparative interpretation. In all four cases, interrelations between marginality and mobility have directly informed the patterns of identity construction and political engagement in the local and (inter)national contexts and hence need to be described before discussing the virtual realm. The discussion of marginality and mobility will be followed by an outline of the various ways in which identity is represented on the websites related to that case.

Our discussion will speak to the central themes of this book – popular media, development and democracy – in a number of ways. In our comparative approach we have paid specific attention to websites as connected and embedded instances of social relations and media histories. Another related issue has been the notion of the 'popular', leading in turn to a discussion of the social hierarchies involved in the production of and activities related to websites. This includes the influence of 'access', but also 'voice' and control. Instead of focusing on 'democracy' per se, we took the concept of 'the political' in its broadest sense and viewed identity construction as a political process.

Case 1: 'Kongo' websites

Introduction

The word 'Kongo' resonates widely: the old Kongo kingdom is one of the more well-known aspects of African history, and early Christianity, literacy and the Portugalization of its elite have inspired a relatively large body of literature.[1] While the Kongo region once formed a political and economic centre, now it is regarded as marginalized. Colonialism divided the area: the old heartland of the kingdom belonged to Angola, another part formed the Bas-Congo province (now Kongo Central) in Belgian Congo. In Congo-Brazzaville and Gabon there remain Kikongo speakers. It became an area of exclusion, limited in terms of political authority, state services in the realm of communication, transport, health, education, etc.

Because of this, many people from the region moved to Léopoldville (Kinshasa). As war broke out in Angola in the 1960s and continued to plague the region until 2002, migration intensified: mainly to Congo Kinshasa, but also to Angola's capital Luanda and the more well-to-do moved intercontinentally. In all contexts, migrants had a difficult position.

Throughout, there were people who felt that the division of the Kongo-speaking region upon colonialism had been unjust and the importance of Kongo nationalism grew after the Second World War (Brinkman 2003; MacGaffey 1995: 54). Clearly the case discussed here points to the multiplicity of identities: national, ethnic and other forms may be equally important for people.

A recent context for Kongo identity is online media, e.g. websites. In this case study the focus will be on two such websites, namely: www.nekongo.org ('Nekongo') and www.luvila.com/Oyeto.html ('Luvila'). The aim is to look into the ways 'Kongo' identity is represented in cyberspace. Although a number of other 'Kongo' sites exist, these two websites were selected because they are currently the only sites that are relatively active.

The Nekongo website is in French and started in 2001 under the name Lusikamu. It is described as a 'virtual foyer of Kongo people anywhere'. The home page consists of recent news items on the DRC, Congo-Brazzaville, Angola and Gabon and is regularly updated. Under the headings, issues of the information bulletin *Observateur Kongo en ligne* ('Kongo Observer on-line') can be found, with archives since 2002. Although described as a monthly, it only appeared around every three months and no issue has been released since mid-2008. The issues contain articles on Kongo history and culture, interviews, links to Kongo music, etc. Political issues relating to Bas-Congo and Northern Angola are given much attention.

In contrast to the Nekongo website, Luvila has a strong Kikongo language component. It starts in Kikongo, followed by translations in Portuguese, English and French. On the site a call is made to people to 'tell about our tradition'. The site is US-based and was created by Angolan residents abroad, organized in the 'Bakongo Research Institute' in Montgomery, United States. Links with Northern Angola exist in several ways, for example a book from a Mbanza Kongo resident is published online. The website also contains video clips and audio material with interviews.

Viewing an Internet community in isolation based on one website is hardly fruitful. In many cases multifarious relations exist between the 'virtual' and the 'offline' world. On the Belgian-based site www.congonline.com/COnekongo.htm, for example, announcements are made about upcoming events. From the exchanges it is clear that some participants know each other personally.

Consulting the two selected websites does not directly reveal offline connections, but references are made to the 'offline' context. Thus on Nekongo it is announced that one of its participants has opened a cybercafé in Matadi. Apart from this, there exist a number of links within the context of the World Wide Web. A clear example is the reference made in November 2001 by a certain Mavambu on the forum 'village Kongo – vata dia Kongo' to the Nekongo website (http://forum.lixium.fr/cgi-bin/liste.eur?mavambu). In another instance of cross-referencing, the musical artist Muinguilo of Kongo background uses the Luvila guestbook to invite people to visit his website at www.muinguilo.com. Such cross-referencing reveals the intertextual nature of websites.

Intertextual links also exist between various media. Both sites post references to written publications, including newspapers, relating to Kongo language, history and culture. YouTube clips of television programmes are included as well as pictures that first appeared in print. Similar remediation of items from older media have been mentioned elsewhere (Merolla 2009; also Spitulnik 2002: 187; Issa-Salwe 2006: 157). The 'Kongo' websites thus extend to the offline world, as well as to various other media and the virtual world itself.

The most striking aspect of the Kongo websites is the relevance attributed to 'tradition' and 'history'. Luvila starts with: 'Please tell us something about our tradition. We need to learn more about our tradition. As we all know the world is moving and we need to make sure that our tradition does not die.' On Nekongo, tradition and history feature less prominently and the focus is on current events, but also here there are references to tradition: e.g. pictograms of a Kongo coat of arms, and references to historical figures of the region, such as Kimpa Vita, Simon Kimbangu and Kasa-Vubu. Interestingly, Kongo history is often related to the Bible and aspects of Christian religion. For example on 19 April 2009, an article was posted on the Nekongo site entitled: 'La Bible: un texte Kongo?', in which the Kongo language is classified as 'Chaldéo-Hébraïque' and the Kongo people interpreted as the 'lost tribes of Israel'.

Especially on Nekongo, historical aspects are often explicitly related to present political issues: boundary disputes, toponyms, modern religious movements, etc. A striking example of this is a reference to Holden Roberto, long-time leader of the Angolan nationalist movement FNLA. His picture on one of the pages is captioned with 'Holden Roberto mort il y a quelques mois avait rêvé à sa façon à la grande nation Kongo' ('Holden Roberto – deceased a few months ago – dreamt of the great Kongo nation in his own way'). Also in the *Observateur Kongo en ligne* of August 2008 a federal Congo state is advocated with the argument that the present borders constitute a colonial legacy. Such overt references to federalism obviously concern a politically sensitive issue. On Luvila, the home page states that the website functions 'Within a united Angola, from Cabinda to Cunene. ONE PEOPLE and ONE NATION (Say No To Racism)'. The issue of national unity and the form of the nation-state is hence treated very differently on the two websites.

The issue of 'politics' on websites is not easy to investigate. As Debra Spitulnik indicates, new small media may challenge the notion of politics as an 'open domain', flouting the borders between private and public spheres. Because websites and fora can be characterized more as 'diffused dialogues' than direct interactions with the state, their political content or influence is difficult to measure (Spitulnik 2002: 179, 181). In some instances political engagement is very clear and direct, the Nekongo site also contains several memoranda: in October 2009 one was posted to ask the Presidents of Angola and DRC to limit the expulsions of Congolese from Angola and the expulsions of Angolans from the DRC, as 'migrations have always been a human phenomenon'. Likewise in 2008 a 'memorandum of the Kongo community in the diaspora' asked the Congolese authorities to stop the violent repression related to the religious movement Bundu dia Kongo in Kongo-Central. Also the polls on the Nekongo site often have clear political overtones: 'Is Ne Moanda Nsemi [leader of the religious movement Bundu dia Kongo] right in creating a political party?' and 'What should be done about the two villages in Bas-Congo annexed by Angola?'.

The 'political', however, is also found in indirect and unexpected ways. The mere fact that people manifest themselves as 'Kongo' is a response to the history of state formation in colonial and postcolonial times. In Angola as well as in the DRC Kongo identity is in principle regarded as a threat to the central state (Brinkman 2003; MacGaffey 1995). Representing identity as such constitutes a political act.

Case 2: 'Nuba' websites

Out of the mountains and into the diaspora

The diverse inhabitants of the Nuba Mountains in central Sudan have, since British colonialism, attracted the interest of outsiders due to their 'bewildering complexity' (Nadel 1947) of features. The superordinate label 'Nuba' was not used by the people themselves. 'It is only very recently ... that some sense of a common 'Nuba-ness' has developed' (Stevenson 1984). But this Nuba-ness is better defined as their common predicament in relation to the dominant 'Arab' culture than based on internal similarities. Due to discriminatory policies, the independent Government of Sudan (GOS) privileged local Arab traders, allowing them access to Nuba land and bringing many Nuba migrants out of the mountains to work in mechanized farming or to Khartoum, paradoxically facilitating both an increased awareness of a regional identity alongside integration into the national picture through Arabization and Islamization (Baumann 1987; Manger 2001, 2004).

The 1960s and 1970s saw the increased representation of the Nuba elite in national politics (Salih 1995). Komolo, a clandestine Nuba youth movement with a racial orientation took hold at the University of Khartoum (Manger 2001). When members of Komolo returned to the Nuba Mountains and sought political representation, they found sympathy and a voice, not with the GOS, but within the political programme of the Sudan People's Liberation Army/Movement (SPLA/M), a rebel movement which has fought against the GOS since the early 1980s. The

Komolo movement and the SPLA/M meant to represent all Nuba people and sought the reinforcement of a united Nuba identity based on a common past.

In 1992, the GOS authorized a jihad (holy war) against the Nuba people (De Waal and Abdel Salam 2004), condemned as an 'ethnic genocide' by the SPLA/M and the international humanitarian community because of widespread killings, torture, rape or the separation of people from their families to be relocated in so-called 'peace villages'. Hundreds of thousands migrated. Most left for Khartoum, other urban centres, or refugee centres in Cairo or Nairobi, where they remain today. Many obtained political asylum or refugee status in Europe or North America. They joined a small community of highly educated migrants who already settled in the diaspora in the 1970s (Sharkey 2004).

SPLA/M leaders, aware of the benefits of propaganda for the war, made contact with filmmakers, photographers and a range of NGOs and, supported by international media, forged a discourse referring to the 'genocide of the Nuba People'. The ongoing economic marginalization of Nuba people and later the war against its people has provoked a strong sense of Nuba coherence, a new identity born out of politics, victimization and war. The combined efforts of local elites with the resources available to educated diaspora are responsible for the new Nuba identity.

Introduction to websites

A part of the identity project mentioned above, several websites appeared to reflect the 'Nuba cause'. Several 'offline' relations link Nuba Survival www. nubasurvival.com and Nuba Times www.nubatimes.com. Their producers and contributors were chairmen of the Nuba Mountains Solidarity Abroad (NMSA).

Dutch visual artist and photographer Nanne op 't Ende's website, the Nuba Mountains Homepage (www.occasionalwitness.com), is also an outcome of a collaboration with the NMSA Chairman in the Netherlands, Salih Kaki, an active SPLA/M member. Two websites were founded by the Nuba diaspora in the United States to represent their local organizations, www.nmiausa.com and www.morointernational.com.

These websites illustrate plainly that the virtual realm cannot be separated from real life events, but that people are connected in a variety of 'technosocial' ways, that relationships and hierarchies are transported intermedially from one context to another.

Content

All of the websites here draw on the identity category introduced above. NMIAUSA clearly subscribe to an exotic notion of Nuba-ness on their website:

> The Nuba Mountains are the black hole of the planet Earth, and yet one of the rare examples of primordial human sensibility and the symbiotic

relationship between Man and Nature, a people that has managed to survive the twilight of the ancient gods.[2]

All of the websites have subsections entitled, 'Nuba culture', 'Nuba songs', 'poetry', 'rituals' or some version thereof. Nuba Survival sports titles such as 'The forgotten war...', 'Nuba of Sudan: treasures of Africa' or 'Wrestling in the Nuba Mountains: past and present'. Moro International dedicates a section to Moro language, and one subsection to 'Traditional naming', listing several Moro male and female names (Kaka, Kuku etc.), clearly motivated by a concern over identity loss due to Arabization or even Americanization, since this group is based in the United States. This concern is endorsed by images, e.g. pictures of traditional Nuba dancing, stick-fighting or wrestling and many landscape images, the mountains, agricultural activities, the iconic Nuba village, with small circular dwellings. Nuba Times posts images of political figures, SPLA Commander Yousif Kuwa Makki and Fr. Gaboush. As Manger (2001: 56) points out, 'the hegemonic view in the contemporary discourse of the Nuba is one based on the Nuba of the Central Mountains, of the areas liberated by SPLA' such that the images are not only dominated by representations of 'traditional' life, but also by representations of one part of the Mountains. For the more Arabized areas, these images may not be representative. Nuba Survival posts images by Leni Riefenstahl, Hitler's infamous filmmaker, who spent close to a decade in the Nuba Mountains in the 1970s. She was blamed for dehumanizing the Nuba in her photography, yet this identity has been absorbed by these websites. On her death in 2004, condolences were posted on Nuba Survival to 'remember Leni for her good work ... the last historical records of what was once a Nuba way of life'.

The identity project serves several aims: to bring attention to the Nuba Mountains, call for external support, demonstrate cultural purity and unity for political purposes and provide an agenda for development and modernization. Nuba Survival's text 'A Call for Relief' appeared in its first newsletter issue (1995), the same year as Julie Flint's film, *Sudan's Secret War*, and illustrated the early purpose of these media: a documentation effort and an appeal to international sympathy. Over time it took a more development-oriented approach, adopting the logo of a maize plant. Sections are dedicated to water, agriculture and education, and most websites call for economic investment in the Nuba region.

A third political aim is the need for cultural and political unity stated in several of the websites' constitutions: 'to establish brotherhood', 'the unification of the Nuba is our first concern' etc., and is largely a reaction to the outcomes of the Navaisha Agreement in 2005, when the GOS and SPLM/A agreed on a power-sharing deal (55 per cent and 45 per cent, respectively) for the Nuba region. The two signatories were blamed for bypassing Nuba leadership, and thus the Agreemnent is a source of disappointment for Nuba expatriates. In recent years, several conferences have been held to address this; the invitations, and outcomes of such conferences are a central part of all the websites' content. It is thus apparent that Nuba unity abroad is not coming out of increased network activity in the virtual realm; rather these websites reflect ongoing real life events.

None of the websites are very interactive. Although Nuba Times, in journalistic format and in Arabic, is a more open sphere of interaction, its contributors are few and it is not considered very up-to-date. However, all make direct political assertions. Nuba Survival posts downloadable copies of letters written to government officials, mediators and the military. Moro International and NMIAUSA make clear statements about their political and financial support of the SPLM's agenda in the Nuba region. In contrast, Nuba Survival displays a different political outlook, by being critical of the actions of the SPLA/M. Its postings and articles reflect the position that the Nuba leaders need an independent government, and autonomy to make local decisions within a united secular Northern Sudanese state. Thus, we see two distinct nationalist agendas, one which takes consolation in Southern Sudanese support, and the desire for possible secession, the other, putting secession as a last option, hoping for Nuba self-determination and a voice in government.

Another website, Sudanese Online (www.sudaneseonline.com) is the primary source for all Sudanese in the diaspora, including the Nuba. It is a much richer source for up-to-date news and its forum is highly active. This is telling, and an actual reflection of the reality of things: people seek a voice within the national arena online as they do offline.

Case 3: Cameroonian anglophone websites

Introduction

The political and cultural identity in anglophone Cameroon historically interacted with processes of physical and social mobility. Mobile telephony and the Internet have contributed to the lowering of communicative barriers across broad geographical swaths, with resultant transformations in identity construction and representation. A survey of websites originating from communities in the diaspora from and in anglophone Cameroon evokes three broad formats – those representing cultural and development associations, news organizations and personal weblogs in addition to closed listservs. In this particular case we seek to analyse the interactive nature of journalistic websites as a platform for debates on political identity and cultural and development websites as windows into the cultural heritage of Cameroonian diaspora communities.

Cameroonian anglophone identity

The current Republic of Cameroon is the product of a bifurcated colonial history, which brought together the minority former British Cameroons into a union with the former French Cameroon majority in 1961. Thus, anglophone Cameroon identity is born out of demographic and political structuring within which political authority since independence has been controlled by majority francophone elements. This marginalization is manifested in the lopsided distribution of infrastructural and service provision assets to the disfavour of minority anglophone regions of the country: absence of road infrastructure, paucity in public health investment, inadequate representation in government and attempted co-optation of the anglophone educational system (see Nyamnjoh and Konings 2003; Nyamnjoh and Jua 2002). Many anglophones view themselves as marginalized within the overall Cameroonian setting.

Transnational communities

Experiences of marginality have given rise to a high degree of mobility from the area. The first wave of migrants from Cameroon to the United States arrived in the early 1960s as part of educational exchange programmes. However, the political upheavals and economic crises of the early 1990s, coupled with the establishment of the Diversity Visa lottery programme by the US government, ushered in a new wave of Cameroonian migrants for educational, economic and political reasons. This mobility has led to a highly dynamic anglophone Cameroonian transnational community; one that maintains active relations with Cameroon in many ways. Actual visits to and from Cameroon are infrequent, but people seek other means to stay in contact, one being the establishment of cultural and development organizations such as the Bakossi and the Bafut Manjong Associations based in Maryland, United States, where a large anglophone diasporic community has settled. Our analysis of websites related to these associations shows that representations of Cameroon probably are informed more by diasporic images of 'home' than by lived reality in present-day Cameroon. In the words of one of the informants in Maryland:

> We stay here for years without going back home. And in our minds are frozen the images of home as we left it. Despite what we are told is happening out there, we feel that time back home is frozen while here we move along.

Such statements make us reflect about how 'political and cultural identities' are imagined and represented, in this case by a diasporic elite in communication with an elite resident in West Cameroon.

Cameroon anglophone news

Local and global representations of the elite have contributed to both the articulation and representation of disparate political dimensions of anglophone identity and shows the interaction between online and offline contexts. In Maryland, where fieldwork was carried out, 'politics' at 'home' is an important theme in discussions among members of the Cameroonian community. This political platform is reinforced by the stream of information about Cameroon that people read daily on the Internet. *The Post* newspaper, issued from Buea in the Southwest region of Cameroon has a bi-weekly hard copy and an identical online edition (www.thepostwebedition.com). It posts local news stories from Cameroon as well as abroad, but with local interpretations. Contrary to the hard copy, the website version is interactive, offering its visitors the possibility to comment on published news stories. It provides a platform for ongoing debates between local and diasporic elites, linking the website to a published newspaper and so forming an online–offline construction.

Since it made its debut in July 2004, *The Post Online* has, in both content and structure, presented news stories following editorial guidelines that clearly represent the dominant anglophone Cameroon political identity. The riots that gripped urban centres in Cameroon in February 2008, and the reporting of them in *The Post Online*, provide a prime example for an understanding of the articulation of Cameroon anglophone political identity. Articles published in *The Post Online* elicited passionate debate amongst anglophone Cameroonians, both at home and in the diaspora.

Cameroon anglophone culture

Meanwhile, at the sub-regional level, communities have appropriated the Internet to portray cultural manifestations of marginality in an attempt to curate their cultural heritage and ostensibly contribute to 'development' initiatives at home. This is demonstrated by static web representations of homeward-looking diaspora in websites of the following associations: Bakossi Cultural and Development Association (www.bacda.org) and Bafut Manjong Cultural Association (http://bafutmanjongculturalassociation.org/index.html).

The websites of the Bakossi and Bafut Manjong cultural associations, in their form and representation, are static, frozen in time and primarily informative. There is no space for interaction and the categories on which one can click are closed. Neither are updated any longer, although the Bakossi website was updated until 2009 and also shows moving images. Interestingly, here we see a totally different representation of Cameroonian identity compared to the discussion above. Politics is quasi-absent in these websites. Both websites show pictures of cultural festivals: masks, dances and people in colourful costumes, and the famous broidery. These are presented as exemplary of the ethnic and linguistic groups involved. Also intriguing are pictures taken of development activities in Cameroon that the Bafut Manjong Association funded with money from the diaspora. Contributions to healthcare are the most important forms of help. The image of a rich or wealthy diaspora community supporting their compatriots back home represents the inequality between home and diaspora.

The cultural websites are mainly inward-looking representations which feed off the hierarchical positioning of diaspora and home communities, thereby creating new forms of economic marginality – with the economically endowed

diasporic elements seeking to contribute to development projects in the economically underprivileged home. These constructions play into broader manifestations
and dominant representations of Cameroon anglophone political identity. In this
The Post website offers a somewhat more dynamic picture, although here also the
main participants belong to the elite, both local and diasporic. Closed listservs,
where relatively young people from different places around the globe and within
Cameroon discuss Cameroonian politics might show a different picture.

Case 4: Berber websites

Berber/Amazigh[3] websites managed in North Africa as well as in diasporic locations (mostly in France, Belgium and the Netherlands) well express the 'glocal'
combination of transnationalism and local identification enhanced by new media
connections worldwide (Robertson 1995). Historical elements need consideration to understand the flourishing of Berber/Amazigh diasporic websites and, in
particular, their choice for 'culturalism' and restrained positioning in political
discourse.

The 'Berber question' in short

The postcolonial linguistic policy in Northwestern Africa has centred on Arabization, the re-adoption of Arabic in the public sphere. Notwithstanding the
huge percentages of Berber speakers (around 20 per cent in Algeria and 40 per
cent in Morocco), Tamazight/Berber[4] enjoys little recognition. Those request-
ing official status for Berber were accused of 'localism', of 'French acculturation' and a threat to national unity as represented by the Arabic language (cf.
Chaker 1989; Gallissot 2000; Merolla 2001: 70–101; Roberts 1983: 218–35 and
1993: 79–92). The censorship and sometimes open repression of the Berber
language gave rise to mass protests in the Berber-speaking region of Kabylia
(Algeria), while in Morocco cultural activism increased over time. At the end
of the twentieth century, both Algerian and Moroccan governments became
receptive to a more flexible language policy. Despite the foundation of Berber
institutes and increasing usage of Berber at school, many felt that changes were
slow and dissatisfaction is growing among Berber activists at home and in the
diaspora.

The Berber diaspora, mainly based on labour migration, increased in the last
quarter of the twentieth century. Apart from the considerable Algerian immigration to Europe, migration flow from Berber-speaking areas of Morocco started in
1945 and was directed towards the former colonial powers France and Spain and
towards French-speaking Belgium. After the 1980s, new migration flows towards
the Netherlands and Italy started, reaching a total of about 335,000 persons of
Moroccan origin in the Netherlands (official statistics CBS 2008) and about
365,000 in Italy (official statistics CENSIS 2008). Berber immigration is estimated
at 70 per cent of the total Moroccan community in the Netherlands.

Berber websites

The growth of Berber websites is not an isolated phenomenon but should be seen in the framework of the cultural effervescence of Berber songs, theatre and popular films since the mid-1980s. The Internet in fact aids the diffusion and creation of Berber artistic production due to its characteristic remediation – refashioning – of other media (Merolla 2002, 2005).

The cultural factor has been crucial in Berber activism and mass protests. Since the colonial period, Berber intellectuals and writers promoted the re-appreciation of Berber languages and oral genres thanks to Berber transcriptions and French translations of poetry and storytelling. An extensive corpus of novels, poetry, song texts, theatre and films, in Berber as well as in French and Dutch, have emerged. Such artistic productions – and in particular songs with political and migration themes – have played a central role in the activation and diffusion of Berber identity that is deeply rooted in the specific linguistic area (Kabyle, Rif, Tuareg, etc.) but it is supra-national as well (Berber/Amazigh), because of the common language (at least at the linguistic level) and the common condition of marginalization in the postcolonial nation-states. The Internet has offered a new medium and showcase for cultural activism.

Here two Berber sites managed from the Netherlands are presented as examples of the glocal character of diasporic Berber websites and their relationship to culture and politics. The first site is Tawiza, one of the first Berber sites in Dutch. The second is the English/Arabic Agraw, presently very popular among young Berbers in the Netherlands and in Morocco.

Tawiza.nl

Tawiza.nl provides information on the Tamazight (Berber) language, history, literature, arts and identity. The Tawiza cultural association also aims to help Berber youths find their way in the diasporic context of the Netherlands. The site's main language is Dutch, though the Tarifit (Riffian Berber) language is also present. Tawiza supports Berber linguistic and cultural rights in Morocco. Though regularly updated, and with forum pages that have been heavily visited in the past, the site currently seems static.[5]

Identity markers appear on the Tawiza homepage: its name ('Tawiza' means solidarity and cooperation) and the use of the Berber Tifinagh alphabet on the banner. The logo, with the words 'tawiza', 'stichting' ('foundation' in Dutch) and again 'tawiza' written in neo-Tifinagh, visually encapsulates the linguistic and cultural conundrum of Berber diasporic groups. At the same time, it is a statement of cultural autonomy as the Arabic script dominant on the Moroccan linguistic market is absent.

The Tawiza homepage is devoted to public discussions and news, while an index contains hyperlinks to 'Literature', 'Language', 'Cuisine', 'Music', 'History', etc. An account of a festival in Rabat (Morocco), quoted from the blog of a

Dutch anthropology student, is the only one that openly tackles political questions. The blog reports policemen rudely dispersing Berber youth rejoicing in the Moroccan-Riffian-Dutch band Imetlaâ ('immigrants') displaying an Amazigh flag. Summarizing current interpretations by activists and researchers alike, the blogger clarifies the contradiction (songs accepted – flag opposed) by explaining that the open political expression of ethnic identity, as in the case of the flag, is harshly suppressed in Morocco, while cultural expressions of being Berber – and, if possible, touristy folklorized forms of it – are accepted.

Although political statements are not openly made, its social and cultural discourse is committed to the preservation of the Berber language in the diaspora and in Morocco, the recognition of Berber in the public sphere (at school, in written form, as a religious language, etc.) and by the local Dutch people. The use of Tarifit and Dutch well summarizes this dual belonging, the desire to distinguish oneself in a larger, diasporic and multinational, perspective.

Agraw.com

The website Agraw ('assembly') uses English on the home page and main index. One-third of Agraw users are Moroccan, the remainder more or less equally distributed among Belgium, Algeria and the Netherlands. The choice of English is a solution to the challenges posed by the audience's multilingualism and by the global showcasing of the website.[6] At the same time, the use of Arabic and Rif Berber on sub-pages and in the forum reveals a pragmatic attitude that counters the ideological 'anti-Arabic' position of a number of Kabyle Berber websites, and allows those who can use different language and to choose the language in which they can best express themselves. Moreover, choosing English as main language is linked to a 'humanistic' positioning on the World Wide Web as indicated in the mission statement ('Agraw.com does encourage dialogue in the society, promotes tolerance, secular education, non-violence, the emancipation of women and overall humanistic universal values').

The name 'Agraw' meaning 'assembly' emblematically refers to the traditional forms of the village's (or better: village men's) shared political decision-making and to the creation of a renewed collective form of 'getting together'. The subtitle 'Portal Dedicated to Amazigh Culture' synthesizes the mission statement while the images of a woman in traditional clothes playing the bandir (tambourine) and of the Amazigh flag visually encapsulate the 'culturalist' approach to politics.

Political discourses and commitment are given room in the forum. In the interview titled 'Salem Chaker and Autonomy', the interviewee[7] defines the situation of the Kabyle Berbers – forerunners in Berber culturalism and activism – as an 'impasse' because their movement sticks to cultural promotion without being able to organize a political and juridical project requiring political autonomy. Although read by a relatively high number of visitors, this interview (in French) provoked no reactions. The theme of political goals and the possible (military/pacific) means to reach them is however present in message boards of topics discussed in Arabic. Messages on the political position of Berbers on Islam and the Palestinian/Israeli conflict are equally visited and get many reactions. As a whole, Agraw offers more space to 'politics' than Tawiza, but the culturalist approach remains 'mainstream'.

Interpretative remarks

Several analytical themes have emerged from the four case studies presented here: multifarious links that reach beyond the websites, the social hierarchies involved, the role of 'tradition' in identity formation and the width of the concept 'politics'.

In much of the literature, the 'virtual world' is discussed as if it were completely separate from 'real' life. This approach has already been qualified by some authors (Bernal 2006; Issa-Salwe 2006; Marneweck 2006), and also the cases presented here reveal that there are links between the 'offline' and the 'online' world. Hence these websites should be interpreted in relation to wider contextual circles and historical dimensions. In the Sudanese case, for example, the main producers and contributors are part of an elite in-group of expatriates, many or perhaps all of whom knew each other from their common experience in the war. In this case, political activities and intra-elite power struggles are conducted both online and offline.

Another element of linkages are the 'intertextual' links within the Internet context: on fora people may refer to websites and vice versa, links to clips on YouTube are provided etc. The latter can also be regarded as an instance of 'intermediality' or 'remediation', in which items that appeared in other forms are recycled. These may be items from printed journals, articles from journals, and even entire books. Especially in the Berber case, we saw an emphasis of integrating oral genres, like songs and stories (see also Lafkioui and Merolla 2008). Far from the Internet being a sterile, separate realm – a virtual world detached from other spheres – there are many connections, lines of interaction and mutual links.

In some contributions on the Internet, 'voice' and 'equality' are stressed. As Victoria Bernal (2006; also Mitra 2001; Anyefru 2008) states: 'the internet can be seen as decentralized, participatory, unregulated, and egalitarian in operation compared to mass media such as newspapers, radio, or television'. Through the Internet people from anywhere can contribute without others even knowing their whereabouts, social background, etc. If, however, we interpret websites as embedded and interacting with offline connections, it would follow that real life hierarchies are also discernable on the World Wide Web. In all four cases, the analysed websites argue for a careful consideration of the often stated claim that the Internet offers a voice to the marginalized, that it allows for democratization through popular participation, that it offers a natural space for the diaspora to create and perpetuate a virtual nation. Our findings would subscribe to Spitulnik (2002) who holds that future research may be carried out into the importance of factors – 'out of country residence, computer access, and privileged background' – as constitutive in the use of website as a medium.

In all four cases, it is obvious that website production and participation is predominantly an elite and male affair, in some cases interpreting 'their' position as marginal so as to garner support for a political cause. Social hierarchies from 'real world' relations interact with website constructions in all four cases. Especially in the Sudanese and DRC/Angola cases, even having the skills to use the Internet and regular access to it puts its users into an elite category. Furthermore, most of them are set up on servers in the United States or Europe and their use is highly restricted inside the country: they mainly remain a diasporic affair. In the Cameroonian and Moroccan cases, local participation is greater, as is the number of websites, but also here there exist limits in terms of accessibility. In the realm of production, the websites remain an affair exclusive to the elite. The majority of the users are members of the more well-to-do with relatively high social status. This obviously calls for a reconsideration of the notion of 'the popular'.

Far from being a platform representing various political tendencies, these websites often reveal a particular point of view within elite politics. On news sites, there is room for debate and difference of opinion, but on the whole the websites are showcase formats, in which unity and purity form the leitmotiv in the representation of identity. The Nuba case, for example, illustrates this clearly: despite the fact that many are divided according to whether they want to join with the North, whether they would like to secede with the South or whether they want regional autonomy, the websites keep up an appearance of unity and hardly represent the diversity of opinions among the Nuba peoples. Art, music, language and discourse on these websites all endorse the Nuba identity project and use it as part of a political agenda and a development programme.

In this culturalist project, history and 'tradition' form a crucial ingredient of identity formation. As Barber (1997: 1) has said, 'For the nationalist African elites, celebrating the "traditional" was an affirmation of self-worth, an assertion that African civilizations had long had their own artistic glories.' But where is the locus of modernity for the Nuba people who do not appear on these websites? One YouTube video of Nuba 'traditional' dancing shows women fully clothed in *towbs*, the national dress representative of Northern Arab-Muslim Sudanese style. This shows that a 'traditional' locally based alternative model for development may never take hold.

Similar tensions can be discerned in the Berber case. Images and discourses on the websites Tawiza and Agraw converge in presenting an endangered Berber cultural identity in need of the active engagement of Berber speakers worldwide. 'Traditional' images are used, but the visual construction of Berber-ness is very much focused on the present due to photos and videos of pop music bands and festivals. The transnational character of these websites – whether linguistically rooted in the Dutch diasporic location for Tawiza or with the English global attire for Agraw – is strongly related to the presentation, diffusion and construction of an artistic, positively qualified, characterization of 'being Berbers'. This is a common, almost unanimous, discourse that crystallizes identity elements emerged in the (past and present) reactions to long-term historical modifications. Political discourse, in such a framework, is not yet free from the weight of the political censorship in the Maghreb, and direct references to political issues are avoided or packed in cultural discourse.

In this case, then, politics is mainly conducted through culture and direct references to political events are lacking. Yet, in the 'Berber' as well as in the 'Kongo' case, merely referring to ethnic identity categories constitutes a political act and may be interpreted as a threat to statist policies. The Cameroon websites show a diversified picture in themselves: some websites ostensibly focus on culture and development, while others contain passionate debates about politically sensitive issues. Also here, however, intra-elite debates as well as positioning vis-à-vis the state play a role in all websites and the 'cultural' cannot be interpreted as isolated from 'the political'. In the Nuba case, direct links can be discerned between levels of politicization and the history of identity formation. As was indicated, Nuba coherence is strongly related to politics, victimization and warfare. In other words, Nuba identity cannot but be politically charged. Comparatively speaking, the Nuba websites are all overtly political, and have clearly emerged as a consequence of conflict and war.

This discussion of the similarities and differences of the role of the 'political' in websites focusing on particular forms of identity reveals that a generalized image of the Internet as contributing to equality and democratization per se cannot be sustained. This new form of media in all four cases is strongly related to elite intra-politics. In this the websites may differ strongly from other new ICTs, especially small media such as email exchange and the mobile phone. A generalized image of the 'impact of new ICT' is also in this sense uncalled for, and would underpin our arguing for a differentiated, qualified approach that views people and technologies as mutually interacting, often in unexpected ways.

Notes

1 'Kongo' is used to designate an ethnic group, Kikongo refers to the language, while 'Congo' refers to a river, a region, and the countries Congo-Kinshasa and Congo-Brazzaville. For further reading: Jan Vansina, *Kingdoms of the Savanna* (1966); Ann Hilton, *The Kingdom of Kongo* (1985); John K. Thornton, *The Kongolese Saint Anthony: Dona Beatriz Kimpa Vita and the Antonian Movement, 1684–1706* (1998).

2 www.nmiausa.com/nuba.htm.

3 The language is still commonly called 'Berber', but increasingly referred to with the local word *Tamazight* (Amazigh/Imazighen for singular/plural).

4 Tamazight/Berber is the second language of North Africa after Arabic and is spoken in several variants by approximately 15 million people in Morocco, Algeria, Tunisia, Libya, Mali and Niger.

5 A possible explanation is the advent of newer Berber-Dutch websites and the great popularity of the Dutch language site Maroc.nl.

6 French is the colonial language par excellence in North Africa. Many Moroccan youth are literate in Arabic first and only second in French. Kabyle Berbers from Algeria, France and Belgium do not master Arabic. Similarly, the youth from the Netherlands master Berber at home and Dutch and English at school, but are not literate in Arabic.

Using Rif Berber and Dutch as main languages would limit the access of Berbers from other Berber areas/diasporas and of the international audience.

7 Salem Chaker was Professor of Berber Linguistics at the Inalco, Paris (National Institute of Oriental Languages and Civilizations) and now at the IRCAM at Aix-en-Provence.

References

Anyefru, E. (2008) 'Cyber-nationalism: the Imagined Anglophone Cameroon Community in Cyberspace', *African Identities* 6(3): 253–74.

Barber, K. (1997) 'Preliminary Notes on Audience in Africa', *Africa International* 67(3): 347–62.

Baumann, G. (1987) *National Integration and Local Integrity. The Miri of the Nuba Mountains in the Sudan*, Oxford: Clarendon.

Bernal, V. (2006) 'Diaspora, Cyberspace and Political Imagination: the Eritrean Diaspora Online', *Global Networks* 6(2): 161–79.

Brinkman, I. (2003) 'War and Identity in Angola. Two Case-Studies', *Lusotopie*: 195–221.

Chaker, S. (1989) *Berbères aujourd'hui*, Paris: L'Harmattan.

De Waal, A. and Abdel Salam, A.H. (2004) 'Islamism, State Power and Jihad in Sudan', in De Waal, A. (ed.) *Islamism and Its Enemies in the Horn of Africa*, Bloomington: Indiana University Press.

Gallissot, R. (2000) *La Maghreb de traverse*, Paris: Éditions Bouchene.

Hilton, A. (1985) *The Kingdom of Kongo*, Oxford: Oxford University Press.

Issa-Salwe, A.M. (2006) 'The Internet and the Somali Diaspora: the Web as a New Means of Expression', *Bildhaan* 6: 54–67.

Lafkioui, M. and Merolla, D. (eds) (2008) *Oralité et nouvelles dimensions de l'oralité: intersections théoriques et comparaisons des matériaux dans les études africaines*, Paris: Inalco.

MacGaffey, W. (1995) 'Kongo Identity, 1483–1993', in Mudimbe, V.Y. (ed.), *Nations, Identities, Cultures*, special issue of the *South Atlantic Quarterly* 94(4): 45–58.

Manger, L. (2001) 'The Nuba Mountains: Battlegrounds of Identities, Cultural Traditions and Territories', in Kastfeldt, N. (ed.), *Sudanese Society in the Context of Civil War*, Copenhagen: University of Copenhagen Press.

Manger, L. (2004) 'The Nature of the State and the Problem of a National Identity in the Sudan', in Pausewang, S. and Sørbø, G.M. (eds), *Prospects for Peace, Security and Human Rights in Africa's Horn*, Bergen: Fagbokforlaget, pp. 62–85.

Marneweck, M. (2006) 'Internet Chatrooms: Real or Virtual Identities?', in Alexander, P., Dawson, M.C. and Ichharam, M. (eds), *Globalisation and New Identities: a View from the Middle*, Johannesburg: Jacana Media, pp. 237–59.

Merolla, D. (2001) 'Questioning Gender, Nationalism and Ethnicity in the Maghreb', *Gender, Race & Class* 8(3): 70–101.

Merolla, D. (2002) 'Landscapes of Group Identities: Berber Diaspora and the Flourishing of Theatre, Videos, and Amazigh-Net', *The Journal of North African Studies* 4(7): 122–31.

Merolla, D. (2005) 'Migrant Websites, WebArt and Digital Imagination', in Ponzanesi, S. and Merolla, D. (eds), *Migrant Cartographies, New Cultural and Literary Spaces in Post-Colonial Europe*, New York: Lexington Books, pp. 217–28.

Merolla, D. (2009) 'Dutch Moroccan Websites: Religion, Secularism, and Music', unpublished paper, AHRC-ESRC workshop: 'Performance, Media and the Public Sphere'. University of Leeds.

Mitra, A. (2001) 'Marginal Voices in Cyberspace', *New Media and Society* 3(29): 29–48.

Nadel, S.F. (1947) *The Nuba: An Anthropological Study of the Hill Tribes in Kordofan*, Oxford: Oxford University Press.

Nyamnjoh, F.B. and Jua, N.B. (2002) 'Scholarship Production in Cameroon: Interrogating a Recession', *African Studies Review* 45(2): 49–71.

Nyamnjoh, F.B. and Konings, P. (2003) *Negotiating an Anglophone Identity: A Study of the Politics of Recognition and Representation in Cameroon*, Leiden and Boston: Brill.

Roberts, H. (1983) 'The Kabyle Question in Contemporary Algeria', *Government and Opposition* 18(2): 218–35.

Roberts, H. (1993) 'Historical and Unhistorical Approaches to the Problem of Identity in Algeria', *Bulletin of Francophone Africa* 4: 79–92.

Robertson, R. (1995) 'Glocalization: Time-Space and Homogeneity-Heterogeneity', in Lash, M.S., Featherstone, M. and Robertson, R. (eds), *Global Modernities*, London: Sage, pp. 25–44.

Salih, M.A.M. (1989) 'Africanism and Islamism in the Nuba Mountains', in Hurreiz, S.H. and Abdel Salam, E.A. (eds), *Ethnicity, Conflict and National Integration in the Sudan*, Khartoum: Institute of African and Asian Studies.

Salih, M.A.M. (1995) 'Resistance and Response: Ethnocide and Genocide in the Nuba Mountains, Sudan', *Geo Journal* 36(1): 71–8.

Sharkey, H.J. (2004) 'Globalization, Migration, and Identity: Sudan, 1800–2000', in Schaebler, B. and Stenberg, L. (eds), *Globalization and the Muslim World: Culture, Religion, and Modernity*, Syracuse: Syracuse University Press, pp. 113–37.

Spitulnik, D. (2002) 'Alternative Small Media and Communicative Spaces', in Hyden, G., Leslie, M. and Ogundimu, F.F. (eds), *Media and Democracy in Africa*, New Brunswick: Transaction, pp. 177–205.

Stevenson, R. (1984) *The Nuba People of Kordofan Province: An Ethnographic Survey. Vol. Monograph 7*, University of Khartoum: Graduate College Publications.

Thornton, J.K. (1998) *The Kongolese Saint Anthony: Dona Beatriz Kimpa Vita and the Antonian Movement, 1684–1706*, Cambridge: Cambridge University Press.

Vansina, J. (1966) *Kingdoms of the Savanna*, Madison: University of Wisconsin Press.

Overview of websites

'Kongo' case:
www.luvila.com/Oyeto.html
www.nekongo.org
'Nuba' case:
www.morointernational.com
www.nmiausa.com
www.nubasurvival.com
www.nubatimes.com
www.occasionalwitness.com
'Berber' case:
www.agraw.com
www.tawiza.nl
Anglophone Cameroon case:
http://bafutmanjongculturalassociation.org/index.html
www.bacda.org
www.thepostwebedition.com

Chapter 16

Survival of 'radio culture' in a converged networked new media environment

Okoth Fred Mudhai

Introduction

Radio remains significant in socio-cultural and political landscapes in Africa. One would expect radio to naturally be a casualty of the proliferation of newer information and communication technologies – even if ICTs are still more expensive at present, they make local and cross-border communication much simpler and easier. Yet the loosening of the state's grip on the broadcast sector in African countries post-1990, through the licensing of several private FM stations – though mostly in cities – has rekindled 'radio culture'. This culture has been boosted by social networking applications via the Internet and mobile phones that enable erstwhile rare audience feedback and participation. It is argued in this chapter that although radio's survival as a major cultural phenomenon may appear to be under threat from new media technologies such as the mobile phone, convergence makes it possible for it to remain a significant arena of information dissemination and exchange, particularly in rural and deprived urban areas underserved by modern cabled ICT infrastructures. These converged media platforms may be seen as forms of popular media that contribute to a higher level of democratic participation and enable alternative discourses of media development to take shape outside the more established mass media channels.

Significance of radio in a converged mediascape

There are an estimated 10 million radio sets in South Africa, with listeners many times that number, broadcasting a range of programming from ultra-hip urban music to community news and information in the deep rural areas. You can listen to radio on the airwaves, via satellite and on the internet, with most of the major stations – and even some community ones – offering live audio streaming from their websites.

(Alexander n.d.)

The statement above captures how far radio in Africa has come, adapting to the new media environment as the need arises – and playing a pivotal role in Africa's public life over the years.

Although some scholars have underscored the significance in Africa of other media such as television (Wresch 1998), the historical and contemporary significance of radio on the continent is generally accepted (Domatob 1988: 168; Meischer 1999: 14, 19; Alhassan 2004: 25, 63–4).

Portability, cost-effectiveness, versatility and orality make it 'the people's medium' (Van der Veur 2002: 81), 'the one to watch' (Girard 2003a). A recent detailed look at 40 African countries projected that although television ownership will grow by an average of 17 per cent, radio remains dominant – especially in rural areas – with a rapid increase in channels (Bizcommunity 2008; ITU 2008). Reliable data are hardly available, but from previous – sometimes disparate – figures (Fardon and Furniss 2000: 1; Jensen 2002; UNESCO 1963: 13) it is estimable that radio sets in Africa have grown from 1.4 million in the 1950s to 5.3 million around the 1960s; from 170 million in 1997 to around 205 million in 2002; reaching 270 million in 2009. Like any technology, radio diffusion has been uneven within African countries and between the continent and the rest of the world, but the penetration rate – initially as low as one receiver per 1,000 inhabitants in 1950 (UNESCO 1963: 13) – has improved over the years, especially post-independence (Mytton 1986: 304; Bourgault 1995: 75).[1] However, the place of radio as a favourite medium is no longer guaranteed.

The story of exponential diffusion in Africa has changed from radio to newer ICTs. The number of Internet users in Africa increased from three million in 2000 to 32 million in 2008 while that of mobile phone users grew from 11 million in 2000 to 246 million in 2008, with growth in both services on the continent from 2003 to 2008 being twice that of the world – although penetration rates remain low by current benchmarks (ITU 2009: 1).[2] Little wonder Francis Kasoma told this author in Lusaka in the early 2000s that the mobile phone is 'the new mass medium of Africa' (see also de Buijin et al. 2009) – although the place of radio is still safe owing to technological convergence.

Although Nyamnjoh (2005: 211) points out that the 'sweeping affirmation' that radio (and television) 'are indeed popular ... is more imagined than real', he seems to underscore the significance of radio through the allusion to this medium in reference to informal media in the African context, in particular rumour or unconfirmed information circulated by word-of-mouth. A number of Kenyan communities call this 'radio without battery'. It is 'pavement or sidewalk radio' in Cameroon and most of francophone Africa (radio trottoir) and lusophone Africa (rádio boca boca), not to mention other Cameroonian terms – 'radio one-battery', 'radio kongosa', 'radio 33', 'radio Kaake no-battery' and 'FM Malabo' (Nyamnjoh 2005: 209–10. See also Fardon and Furniss 2000: 2; Hyden and Leslie 2002: 24–5). Indeed the ubiquity of such informal media and that of radio, with some of the content crossing both media, forms a vital element of convergence – even if not technologically sophisticated. Of course the cross-feeding of such content between radio and other media has been done cautiously in sensitive political and cultural contexts.

Part of radio's appeal is its historical-nostalgic value, especially as 'the barometers and the agents of change' (Fardon and Furniss 2000). Yet in most African countries, colonial and postcolonial governments maintained their stranglehold on state radio, enjoying around 90 per cent national coverage, to serve elitist and propaganda interests as Althusserian ideological state apparatuses, until the rulers gave in reluctantly amidst reform agitations mainly from the 1990s (see also Bourgault 1995; Meischer 1999: 14; Van der Veur 2002; Alhassan 2004: 129 and 136; Nyamnjoh 2005: 125; Olorunisola 2005). 'Broadcasting ... now come in all shapes and forms, with various ownership and funding models, supervisory mechanisms, missions and programme offerings' (AfriMAP/NMP 2007: 2). A recent comprehensive survey of 12 countries covering 2007–2009 identified six categories mainly by ownership and control – state, public, commercial, political-interest, community and other special-interest – and recognizes Internet broadcasting 'with possible overlaps, hybrids and yet other forms' (AfriMAP/NMP 2007: 2). The reluctant state slackening of control (Alhassan 2004: 128; Nyamnjoh 2005: 125; Ansu-Kyeremeh 2007: 104) brought much needed variety and pluralism in the realms of radio – with subtle and obvious implications for democratic practice and theory on the continent.

The recently licensed mainly commercial FM stations are not perfect, or a panacea for the socio-political and cultural shortcomings of the state-controlled model. Writing on Ghana, Alhassan (2004: 129) notes that 'if the early postcolonial broadcasting was characterized by elite to elite communication the current media scene suggests that it is now an intra-urban affair with marginal participation from non-city dwellers'. The highly commercial stations feature a large musical and advertising menu (Meischer 1999: 14, 18). Their 'different' infotainment rather than news-information approach is nevertheless an injection of variety that has a role in present-day Africa. Presenters and disc jockeys at these stations may at times lack professionalism, but Mytton (1986: 303) points out that there is a place for such media workers beyond emphasis on 'education achievement' as 'the point is surely to ensure that talented creative people receive adequate training'. Although the community model is participatory, it has not been spared the criticism of being too donor dependent (Meischer 1999: 14–15, 18). So no model is perfect, but all – the state one included – have a role to play in facilitating mediated democratic participation in African societies.

The model that has attracted most scholarly and activist attention is the political-interest or 'independent' one – characterized by extra-judicial attacks (Ogblondah 2002: 66) forcing many to operate clandestinely.[3] It is worth noting that a number of the radio categories identified by AfriMap/NMP (2007: 2) are not necessarily mutually exclusive – so private commercial radio as well as community and religious broadcasters, such as Angola's Radio Ecclesia, can face state censure due to their perceived political stance.

The focus of this chapter is not on the cases of radio forming part of direct agitation for political change, in the process being more vulnerable to censorship, and of radio being used for overt public interest information-education programming defined and covered by others (AfriMAP/NMP 2007: 3ff.), but on the increasingly popular contemporary entertainment content – most common in private commercial radio, although other categories also try to incorporate such material in a bid to retain and win audiences in an increasingly competitive environment. In fact, some authors trace the commercialization of broadcasting (even within the state model), with investors focusing on cities 'where consumers with money could be located', to the 1960s and 1970s when state control was much tighter (Bourgault 1995: 80). The approach to the examination of infotainment here is not to lament about understandably detrimental aspects and trends already covered by other scholars, such as imperialism or 'foreignization' (Ansu-Kyeremeh 2007) and dumbing-down. There is no denying that 'privatization could well lead to increased domination of Africa's airwaves by foreign services and to greater opportunities for elite profiteering from scarce financial resources available around capital cities' (Bourgault 1995: 68). Indeed, some of the owners of private stations have very close links to ruling elites – with preferential treatment when it comes to licensing and other control measures. However, some of the unintended consequences of pluralism and competition have been attempts to meet audience desires – which have included popular culture content with messages of political resistance that are often subtle, yet accessible to the discerning.

Popular culture, radio and democratic theory

The term 'mass', linked to culture, may no longer be fashionable but it is 'used to identify those everyday things that we all share through mass media and industrial technology ... that which is mass-produced, and is successful, is "popular" culture' (Roberts 1987: 276). Integral to popular culture – as distinguished from 'elite culture' – are 'pervasive' and 'invisible' icons, which 'reflect and communicate our values, hopes and dreams' and 'are given uncritical devotion' – with popularity entrenched 'principally by intense circulation, publicity and mass advertising' (Roberts 1987: 277). Radio plays a significant role in purveying these icons and related artefacts.

In examining 'radio's role within popular culture', Hendy (2000: 194) identifies three main areas:

> The first is in the area of democratic life ... radio ... as a medium of information and discussion. The second is in the more diffuse area of identity – how radio might nurture, or destroy, people's sense of 'belonging'.... The third area has a more specific focus ... radio ... shape trends in popular music.

Although the focus in this chapter is on the third aspect – associating radio culture with consumption, this is inextricably linked to the first and second. In the early years of radio, 'collective acts of reception became a feature of everyday life' (Loviglio 2005: xiv). New media may have reduced or eliminated this in the developed world, but in Africa it is not unusual to listen to loud radio music on public transport and in shops, especially in small rural towns. From some homes, the 'intimate space of reception' of radio (Loviglio 2005: xiv) exists alongside a public one – 'a complex web of social performances' (Loviglio 2005: xvi), not unimaginable in a mobile-phone environment once units are appropriately enabled. 'Radio's promiscuous mixing of the interpersonal and mass communication' in the context of identity and difference – evoking 'intense pleasure and anxiety' (Loviglio 2005: xviii) – remains durable and popular, including in Africa.

Despite the ingredients of contradictions such as 'repression and ... *face-powder democracy*' that are apparent in attempts to embrace liberal democracy in Africa, 'there is no doubt about the liberalizing, mobilizing and empowering *potential*' of the conventional and new media in the continent (Nyamnjoh 2005: 23). Popular culture is one of the ways in which 'democracy comes in bits and pieces' (Ogundimu 2002: 235) – sometimes through subtle rather than direct struggle or agitation. A number of theories have been used to examine popular culture in general and in the African context in particular. One is the social learning theory of modelling or imitation espoused by scholars such as Melvin DeFleur and Everette Dennis (Roberts 1987: 278). A related concept is the 'cultural norms theory ... [which] ... indicates that the media tend to establish the standards or norms which define acceptable behaviour in society' (Roberts 1987: 278). An unrelated but common approach is that of imperialism or (neo-/post-)colonialism or 'cultural synchronisation' (Domatob 1989: 162). While the concerns in this last approach are valid, there is also a need to take hybridization into account.

Dominant foreign content is not an all-pervasive ill, affecting all media areas all over the continent. Mytton (1986: 304) notes that in Nigeria 'flourishing record labels mean that ... most music on the radio in that country' is local. Mytton raises a different problem – ethnicity. 'Nigerians don't much like Nigerian music unless it is from their own area. With some exceptions, you don't hear much Hausa music in the clubs and bars of Lagos. The same cultural exclusivity is seen everywhere' (1986: 304). Although one may argue that the ethnic-linked ownership and target audiences of some of the recently licensed FM stations may exacerbate such ethnic exclusivity, popular artists who have borrowed from the West and from other African cultures have wider appeal, resulting in radio airplay beyond ethnic lines. In Kenya, popular hybridized songs – in terms of language and style – such as 'Unbwogable' ('Unscarable' or 'Unfrightenable') and modified previously ethnic-based artefacts or even genres have enjoyed popularity all over the country, especially if they have subtle political undertones around election time, though it is worth noting that in the 2008 post-election violence radio was both catalyst (by accentuating the ethnic stereotypes especially in speech programming) and alleviator (by giving airplay to 'Music for Peace' songs and joining other media in the 'Save Our Beloved Country' peace programming). Hybridization is crucial, especially given that one of the consequences of unshackling airwaves has been an increase in often localized 'ethnic' radio – such as Kenya's Kass FM (www.kassfm.co.ke). A recent report points to 'an explosion in the number of radio stations, particularly ... in local languages. ... the "vernaculars" ... have been a high growth area over the last five years' (Bizcommunity 2008; ITU

2008). Ethnic-based or regional radio is not a new phenomenon, with some of the previous, often state-backed, ones being segregative in the case of Namibia (Meischer 1999: 15) or hate-based in the well-known case of Radio Milles Collines in Rwanda. A more useful perspective – rather than that of provincialism – is the role of these ethnic-based radio stations in the expansion of the public sphere in a manner that is more in tune with ordinary local populations and beyond. These stations may be seen as holding an emancipatory appeal in relation to open, free and fair discourse.

Although his study was based on pre-radio seventeenth- to nineteenth-century Western Europe, radio epitomized Habermasian concerns in blurring public-private spheres. His theory has been linked to 'the ritual power of radio to conjure a new social space – public and private – national and local' (Loviglio 2005: xiv). The Habermasian idealistic yet pessimistic early public sphere theory has been criticized for its emphasis on elitism, state-centrism, singularity, rationality and universalism. To postmodernist Mark Poster, 'when Habermas defends with the label of reason what he admires in Western culture, he universalizes the particular, grounds the conditional, absolutizes the finite' (Crack 2008: 29). Scholars like J.B. Thompson point out that in the new public sphere, ICTs – increasingly converging with radio – increase the 'vulnerability and visibility' of political leaders 'before audiences' – limiting their control on content reception and interpretation (Crack 2008: 36). In the recent 'revisions of the public sphere theory, the mass media are not considered the source of a sham public but rather the site for a reconceptualization of the meanings and the uses of publicity' (Loviglio 2005: xx). This new conceptualization is that of a pluralist, differentiated, inclusive and extra-territorial public sphere (Crack 2008: 47–68). In a converged digital environment, radio still finds a place in the 'complex mosaic of differently sized, overlapping and interconnected public spheres' (Keane 2000: 76).

Nugdalla (1986: 102) points out that broadcasting – especially radio – can contribute to 'cultural renewal' through 'the arts: music, songs and drama' which broadcasting has made 'popular' and given 'a touch of respectability'. He elaborates: 'It is in the sphere of artistic production that broadcasting becomes more of a cultural than an ideological or propaganda institution' (Nugdalla 1986: 102). Of course there is the paradox that the political ideology and propaganda 'manifest and repulsive in talks, speeches, and preaching' via radio is replaced by what may be considered imperialist ones 'latent and subtle in the works of art' (Nugdalla 1986: 102), but the question is whether change is more likely to be achieved through some toleration of what McPhail (1981) terms electronic colonialism or by embracing ideologies of self-centred African political elites. Although popular culture is mostly associated with commercial broadcasters, the works of scholars such as Fairchild (2001) show community radio can also play a role in this area. There is a place for a radical political approach by clandestine and legitimate radio, but commercial and community radio broadcasts can also play a role in democracy by strategically focusing on popular culture – in spite of what Kellner

$(2003),^4$ echoing Guy Debord, would term the triumph of the spectacle under technocapitalism in a high consumption society with commodity pleasures.

Radio's popular culture content under convergence

Content, regardless of media, is king – technologies only offer varying conveniences. There is no doubt that some popular culture content, especially in private commercial FM stations in African cities, exhibits 'Western' features that Ansu-Kyeremeh (2007: 108) identifies as 'use of foreign languages; imitation and mimicry of foreign programs with their broadcast formats; and ... less diversified programming' but at the same time, as the author indeed acknowledges, resistance rather than victimhood has been expressed in the audience preferences. In fact a great deal of creativity and blending in modern radio programming injects local style, languages or dialects, idioms, anecdotes, jokes, rumours and music. Hendy (2000: 194) notes that although radio 'is very much the global purveyor of both American music and American formatting conventions', there is really no longer – and perhaps never has been – pure cultures, with radio as an enabler of hybridization. Fardon and Furniss (2000: 1) note that 'the growth of African broadcast culture on radio has been spectacular ... Via radio, African cultures are broadcast, both widely and narrowly, and is influenced by the broadcasts of other cultures'. In other words, popular culture content is not necessarily always 'culture-corroding' (Ansu-Kyeremeh 2007: 101).

What constitutes popular culture content? Abdulkadir (2000: 129–30) lists music request programmes, drama and comedy and variety shows but this is not all.

> Local popular cultural genres, such as proverbs, catchphrases, jokes and funny stories abound, while whatever people are talking about on the streets regarding fashion, personalities and events – in short all of current popular discourse – form the stuff of chart shows and other discussion programmes.
>
> (Abdulkadir 2000: 130)

'Much of the most popular content tends to be music on the radio' (ITU 2008). This is more so the case in the recently licensed FM stations across Africa, as confirmed by a recent survey.

> The most striking trend in terms of audiences is the rise in radio listenership. There is a huge appetite for FM music radio ... Africans, both sub-Saharan and North African, surround themselves with music in cars, public transportation, shops and homes. Wherever deregulation has taken place, multiple FM channels have emerged.
>
> (Analyst Hugh Hope-Stone – Bizcommunity 2008; ITU 2008)

To Hendy (2000: 214), 'radio's intimate connection [is] with *music* ... Music, rather than talk, is the main component of most of the world's radio stations and networks'. Citing M. Pickering and R. Shuker who, while recognizing the *enriched–swamped* paradox with a view that 'quotas on radio' could 'help rebalance the forces of localism and internationalization' appreciate 'radio's role in the *dynamic* aspect of popular music culture', Hendy (2000: 224–5) notes that radio is 'capable of providing "the conditions of interaction" in the ongoing creation of "hybridized" symbolic forms and practices'. Such conditions could lead to segmented 'taste publics' (Hendy 2000: 227) and what S.J. Douglas has called barrier-erecting 'mutually exclusive auditory niches' (Hendy 2000: 229). These niches may be ethnic, generational, extra-territorial or virtual, but with intersections among them – so the barriers may not necessarily be exclusive in a networked society. 'In its pervasiveness and variety, radio thoroughly disrupts any neat association between the local and global as geographical referents' (Fardon and Furniss 2000: 2), given the presence of local broadcasters online and the retransmissions via local FM stations of output from international broadcasters. Whether among mass or niche audiences, music remains the most popular content – and a carrier of socio-cultural and political nuances-messages.

Like other content, the ruling elite have used music – especially the traditional type – on state radio to serve them.[5] In the early stages of private radio in Africa, music was mainly American with most news being re-broadcast. Peter van der Akker (in Van der Veur 2002: 101) captures the recipe for success thus: take 'a huge dose of Western pop music, lard it with talk radio and commercials and your popularity is guaranteed'. In Kenya, music was virtually the only content that the initial private radio disseminated (Van der Veur 2002: 90). This was partly because, as journalist Charles Onyango-Obbo notes, owners mostly supportive of the ruling elite 'know a respectable news program is likely to annoy someone in government' (Van der Veur 2002: 100). In recent years, some of the music contents have increasingly become political, thanks to 'socially conscious musicians' (Karimi 2009). That 'their message – in a mixture of English and native languages – is popular with locals', underscoring hybridization, means private radio ignore them at their own commercial peril.

> Kenyan musician Eric Wainana became a household name after he released the Swahili song 'Nchi ya Kitu Kidogo' ('Land of Petty Bribery'). The song, which became an unofficial anthem, left government officials uncomfortable. State-run broadcasters did not play it for years.
>
> (Karimi 2009)

The 'independent radio' that appeals to the 'young urban audience' may prefer the 'immensely popular rappers' for commercial reasons (Ruigrok n.d.), but the musicians are increasingly injecting political messages in their popular songs. Yet this is not always a safe escape route away from news. A 2009 report on fragile Somalia by the International Press Institute indicated that radical Islamist militants

Al-Shabab that controlled the southern town of Baidoa shut down private Radio Warsan, and took the station's director and news editor into custody, for airing 'un-Islamic' content, 'especially songs and music' (Hunt 2009). In Zimbabwe, 2005 presidential candidate Jonathan Moyo's election campaign 'smashing hit', 'Phambili Le Tsholotsho' ('Go Tsholotsho!') could be heard on mobile phone soundtracks and bars but it was banned from national radio using the very rules he put in place as Information Minister under Mugabe (Ruigrok n.d.; also see Chapter 6 in this volume).

Popular music is not just a feature of private commercial radio; it is embraced by some state and community broadcasters – only these are often more selective in attempts to avoid upsetting the status quo. For example, South Africa's (Western Cape) community Bush Radio music shows included *Everyday People*, on local music and artists, mid-weekly *Soul Makossa*, on music from around Africa, and Friday's *Head Warmers*, on American hip-hop music and the related culture (Olorunnisola 2005). Radio Zibonele in the South African township Khayelitsha is popular for its trendy music in shows such as *Party Time* and *International Top 20 Countdown* (Olorunnisola 2005). It is not just the music that is popular, but all that goes with it during a number of shows. These include commentary by hosts and contributions from audience members. Before privatization, a popular radio commentary was a monologue on the Kenya Broadcasting Corporation (KBC), Leonard Mambo Mbotela's *Jee Huu ni Ungwana?* (Is this really gentility/decency?), criticizing the daily habits of ordinary people – safely eschewing the foibles of the powerful. In recent programming, especially on private radio, talk or chat shows have become more interesting and critical of the powerful and music shows are increasingly interspersed with comment. The style is often informal, satirical and jocular – sometimes with rumours and innuendos. With the ethical problems raised by such formats, one is reminded of Habermas' reference to 'talk shows as the epitome of the "sham public" that had replaced the authentic one' – 'in a strange echo of Walter Lippman's "phantom public"' (Loviglio 2005: xx). In Africa, such shows have opened up spaces of expression, right from before privatization. Although Nugdalla (1986: 96, 97) found in a 1980s Sudan study that talks and discussions were 'generally monotonous', they 'contributed ... to the promotion and consolidation of the new human values and practices' – which included acceptance of women's contributions. Nugdalla (1986: 97) recalls that 'religious fanatics and rigid traditionalists' found the spectre of a woman singing or acting on radio 'an unforgivable sin' and even males who did so 'were spoken of as "vagabonds"' but with time singers became 'popular and singing acceptable'. Recent attempts to stretch the boundaries in controversial chat shows by state broadcasters such as Namibia's national radio 'on occasion leads to the termination of a broadcast' (Meischer 1999: 16).

Recently licensed private stations have found it more exciting to push boundaries in chat and discussion. Kenyan Kiss FM presenters Caroline Mutoko and Walter Mong'are's indecent language against cabinet minister Martha Karua in a memorable 2004 edition of *Big Breakfast* was beyond the bounds of decency, but it was in keeping with the satirical style that the presenters had adopted and which made their show popular (Barth 2004).[6] This was perhaps their way of building genre-awareness, with the legal risks that came with the experiment. This was within what Boler (2008: 393) sees as 'the function of political satire … saying what is otherwise unsaid within a given political climate', given that the controversial minister Karua had declined to respond to Kiss FM's crucial questions of public interest relating to her significant water ministry.

> Satire speaking truth to power is a central place of optimism in political discourse … It is not a coincidence that political satire is popular during times of political repression and censorship. People respond to satire because it pokes holes in the entire edifice of lies that have been built.
>
> (Boler 2008: 22)

Boler argues, with S. Turpin, that the appeal of 'ironic approach to truth' – at multiple levels in form and content – challenges and critiques complicity in what Guy Debord terms a 'spectacular society' (Boler 2008: 387).

Under freer airwaves, audience participation, for instance through phone-ins, signalled 'that private-enterprise radio may be experimenting with forms of political expression that contradict prevailing orthodoxy' (Van der Veur 2002: 101). An example is Ugandan Capital Radio's *Capital Gang* discussion show, which includes live phone-ins, and which has sometimes been in trouble with the government – although it has featured President Museveni on occasions. As part of demonstration of resistance to 'foreign' content in Ghana, Ansu-Kyeremeh (2007: 107) points out that 'discursive, and especially interactive, listener phone-in programs on radio that usually focus on local issues are very popular'. Due to the discomfort of authorities with audience input – and the live nature of some of these – such shows have been met with bans, for instance in Togo (RSF 2009), or threats of various forms. Audience input and chat usually offer opportunities for radio to converge with informal media, which is characterized by innuendos and rumour, a risky territory that has led Kenya to propose 'legislation on broadcasting seeking to criminalise unconfirmed reporting' (Maina 2009).

A more significant form of convergence in recent times involves dissemination of radio content via modern ICT platforms in an adaptation to the digital future (McCauley 2002; Attias and Deflander 2003; Girard 2003b; Ilboudo and Castello 2003; Jallov 2003). Radio has not been left out in the increasing intersection between mass media, social media and personal media. Radio has joined creative appropriation of new media platforms such as the Internet and mobile phones that, along the lines of arguments by Spitulnik, offer 'real alternatives, if well harnessed to serve popular social causes' (Nyamnjoh 2005: 205). Values associated with African realities, and that have made such convergence easier, are listed by Nyamnjoh (2005: 4, 15–17, 20, 205), citing others such as Gecau and Olorunnisola, including: sociality, negotiation, interconnectedness, interdependence, coexistence, creativity and conviviality. These qualities have been catalysed by 'communicative hurdles and hierarchies ... [and] ... histories of deprivation, debasement and cosmopolitanism' (Nyamnjoh 2005: 4). Radio's appropriation of new ICT media, despite such risks as exploitation (through commodification, commercialization and conglomeration), inequality (through the digital divide) and Orwellian surveillance, show that 'globalization does not necessarily or even frequently imply homogenization or Americanization' (Appandurai, cited in Nyamnjoh 2005: 7). One of the best examples of radio convergence, in political realms, is that of London-based Zimbabwean exile radio, SW Radio Africa (www.swradioafrica.com) which uses short message service and podcasts (Bunz 2009).

The Internet has been the most dominant platform of convergence for the radio. Indeed, 'radio is now proving itself versatile enough to go hand in hand with the Web' (Gardner in Girard 2003a: blurb). Although pointing out that 'many ... argue that the Internet is the ultimate Western tool for the acculturation of the South', Ansu-Kyeremeh (2007: 107) acknowledges that 'the Internet may somehow relate the global/international to the community'. In Ghana, Alhassan (2004: 196) notes that 'several FM stations stream their audio content on their web pages and also provide alphanumeric content. ... the "digirati" [the new elites of digital literacy in Ghana] prefer to get their news via the Internet'. Radio broadcasters in most other African countries have similar online presence – some offering live streaming.[7] A number of websites for African radio stations, especially South African and Kenyan ones, have improved over the past few years – with a number of features that allow audience participation and choices. One level of interactivity and convergence is that subjects covered on radio find their way onto the websites of national daily newspapers. For instance, a dispute between Kenya's Kiss FM and the water minister often featured on the comment pages of the online editions of the *Daily Nation* and *Sunday Nation* newspapers (Barth 2004).

An emerging phenomenon, especially for Africans in the diaspora, is that of popular music broadcasts based mainly or entirely online – with sites hosted in Europe and the United States. These include: African Internet Radio or A.I.R. (www.africaninternetradio.com); Radio Africa Online (RAO), formerly Soukous Radio (http://soukous.org or www.live365.com); Tanzania's Bongo Radio (www.bongoradio.com); Addis Live (www.addislive.com/ethiopian-music.html). RAO has an icon for various qualities of connection, including one for slow dial-up internet; it is also possible to listen via mobile phone (http://soukous.org/mobile.htm) – which means it would be usable by Africa-based audiences. Music played on these websites includes popular genres such as Soukous, Coupe Decal, Ragga, Kwaito, Hip Hop and Genge. That these websites use AutoDJ make some of them rather robotic and consumerist. However, some of the songs are linked to the themes relevant to Africa. For instance, when I listened one weekend in November 2009, one of the songs played on Germany-hosted A.I.R. was 'Soldat Tirera' (Concert Radio Blagon 2006) by Cameroonian Idy Oulo, on multiparty democracy, good governance and human rights. On RAO, which has comments and discussion sections, one of the discussions was about 'Protest Music', partly referencing recent media stories on political significance of music – such as Femi

Kuti's music.[8] In his contribution to the discussion thread, 'Protest Music – a Genre on its Own?' on RAO, Kenyan listener Wuod Kwatch writes:

> I am left thinking/wondering that certain strains of African music are really suited for agitation and protest. Afrobeat, Reggae (historically), S African music (not sure what to call it, I mainly listen to SA Jazz) and now this new thing in Kenya – 'Genge' … It seems to me that some musicians will forever get stuck doing their 'shtick' about vocalizing or channeling their anger toward the political order of the day in their music. And they do this day in and day out. It's their right all right to do whatever. This is where Franco and the likes of DO Misiani, Remi Ongala, Mbaraka Mwinshehe excelled. They knew how to strike a balance, singing about the mundane from clothing and tailors, to adverts for cars, to women (backstabbing ones) and philandering men.[9]

He concludes with a critical reflection on the efficacy of Kenya's current crop of so-called politically and socially conscious musicians, especially for hardly using clever metaphors as their predecessors did.

While the Internet is currently the main convergence platform for radio broadcasting, the mobile phone has the potential to be the really true mass platform in Africa – given the right applications at the right price. With the help of the UK's Guardian Media Group, SW Radio Africa is looking for a better solution to broadcast to Zimbabwe cost-effectively – with the mobile phone being an option (Bunz 2009). At the City University of New York Graduate School of Journalism, one of Professor Jeff Jarvis' students, Adeola Oladele, won a $3,000 prize in 2008 for her proposal to audio-broadcast via mobile phone.[10] However, it is not an easy option as one has to go through phone companies.

> After contacting phone companies, I'm finding out that it would be more expensive for me to broadcast through phone companies. The original plan was to have people call in to listen to the News or have me call them with the News and shows. Now I'm thinking it might be better for me to start a community radio station and people can tune in on their cell phones free of charge … People are already listening to radio on their cell phones back home. So, it will still be broadcasting via cell-phones, except that I would also have a station instead of going through phone companies.
>
> (Oladele 2009)

Conclusion

Along the lines of the original concerns of Habermas about the refeudalization of the public sphere, there are arguments that the consequences of recent liberalization of the airwaves in Africa include the tabloidization or dumbing-down of radio through over-emphasis on infotainment, especially urban popular youth music and related genres, at the expense of serious news and information useful to rural dwellers who are most reliant on the medium. 'According to the report *Making*

Waves by censure guardian Index on Censorship, the information now heard on the radio in many African countries is even more shallow [*sic*] than it was under strict government censure' (Ruigrok n.d.).

Before and soon after independence in most African countries, radio broadcasting was an ideological tool for the ruling elite – the colonial regimes followed by the mostly authoritarian postcolonial governments. One way of escape from this stranglehold, part of politico-economic reform bargains into liberalization and privatization, has been the initially gradual (1980s) and later rapid (1990s) move from dominantly political propagandist-ideological programming to the increased incorporation of cultural content not directly threatening to the status quo – but subtly significant for change politics, especially in the less restrictive new media environment. The paradoxical processes of globalization, media ownership convergence or conglomeration and content homogenization on the one hand, and glocalization-hybridization, proliferation of alternative small-scale entrepreneurial initiatives and fragmentation of content-audiences on the other hand reduce the force of arguments about radio, or any other electronic media, as cultural-media imperialism or electronic (post-/neo-)colonialism instrument.

While this chapter has shown that popular culture is mostly associated with commercial radio in Africa, a number of state and community broadcasters attempt to engage with the public cultures in order to remain relevant. Popular culture content such as music can sometimes – not always – be used to communicate political, in addition to social, messages, often in less direct ways. To win over the younger generation in particular, radio broadcasters are embracing convergence through the use of new network media as an alternative platform.

Notes

1 Radio receivers per 1,000 grew from 32 in 1965 to 69 in 1975 and 164 in 1984 (L.J. Martin, cited in Bourgault 1995: 75). National surveys in the late 1980s found that 42 per cent of rural households in Kenya and 62 per cent in Nigeria had a radio set (Mytton 1986: 304).
2 In 2008, penetrations were: Internet users – 4.2 per 100 inhabitants (compared to 15 for developing countries and 23 for the world); mobile-phone subscriptions – 32.6 per 100 (49 and 59). See ITU (2009: 1–2).
3 A useful database for clandestine radio, including in Africa, is at: www.clandestineradio.com.
4 Note that Kellner does not specifically single out radio as a platform for today's 'infotainment society' – along the lines of Debord's idea of the spectacle society.
5 For brief overviews, see B. Posthumus in 'Radio and Music Industry', www.powerofculture.nl/uk/specials/radio/muziekindustrie.html and M. Oord, 'Radio and Traditional Music, www.powerofculture.nl/uk/specials/radio/traditie.html (accessed 9 November 2009).
6 Case details at Kenya Law, 'Martha Karua v. Radio Africa and Two Others', available at: www.kenyalaw.org/CaseSearch/view_preview.php?link=42963595429445554955793&words= (accessed 11 June 2010). Also see BBC report of 3 May 2004, 'Kenya's Private Radios Face Curbs', available at http://news.bbc.co.uk/1/hi/world/africa/3680377.stm (accessed 11 June 2010).

7 More details available on the directory at Radio Station World (http://radiostation-world.com/africa.asp) and another extensive list is available at the University of Stanford African Radio Online site, Radio Stations – Radio in Africa (www-sul.stanford.edu/depts/ssrg/africa/radio.html). For North Africa, check Radio Culture Tunisia (www.listenarabic.com/Radio+Culture+Tunisia+radio174.php).
8 CNN online, 'Femi Kuti: Blending Afrobeat and Politics', 11 November 2009, www.cnn.com/2009/WORLD/africa/10/26/african.voices.femi.kuti/index.html and CNN TV, 'African Voices', 31 November 2009; Karimi (2009).
9 Online, available at: http://soukous.org/discussion.htm (accessed 6 November 2009).
10 'Three '08 Students Win Entrepreneurial Journalism Contest, CUNY Graduate School of Journalism', www.journalism.cuny.edu/2008/12/23/three-08-grads-win-entrepreneurial-journalism-prizes (accessed 12 November 2009).

References

Abdulkadir, M. (2000) 'Popular Culture in Advertising: Nigerian Hausa Radio', in R. Fardon and G. Furniss (eds) *African Broadcast Cultures: Radio in Transition*, Oxford: James Currey, pp. 128–43.

AfriMAP/NMP (2007) 'Public Broadcasting in Africa: a Survey', African Governance Monitoring and Advocacy Project and Open Society Initiatives Network Media Programme. Available at: www.misa.org/downloads/afmd/AfriMAPOpenSociety.pdf (accessed 9 November 2009).

Alexander, M. (n.d.) 'South Africa Radio Stations, SAinfo'. Available at: www.southafrica.info/about/media/radio.htm (accessed 8 November 2009).

Alhassan, A. (2004) 'Development Communication Policy and Economic Fundamentalism in Ghana'. Dissertation, University of Tampere, Finland. Available at: http://acta.uta.fi/pdf/951–44–6023–5.pdf (accessed 13 November 2009).

Ansu-Kyeremeh, K. (2007) 'Implications of Globalization for Community Broadcasting in Ghana', in L.K. Fuller (ed.) *Community Media: International Perspectives*, New York: Palgrave Macmillan, pp. 101–10.

Attias, S. and Deflander, J. (2003) 'The Information Highways are Still Unpaved: the Internet and West African Community Radio', in B. Girard (ed.) *The One to Watch: Radio, New ICTs and Interactivity*, Rome: FAO, pp. 39–48.

Barth, K. (2004) 'Kiss FM Breached Ethics, but Karua Courted Trouble', Media Maverick column, *Sunday Standard* (Nairobi), 4 November 2004. Also available at: www.kodibarth.com/downloads_standard/Commentaries%20%20Kiss%20FM%20breached%20ethics,%20but%20Karua%20courted%20tro.htm.

Bizcommunity (2008) 'Rapid Increase in Radio and TV Channels in Africa, Says New Report', 29 February 2008. Available at: http://africa.bizcommunity.com/Article/412/59/22458.html (accessed 11 November 2009).

Boler, M. (2008) *Digital Media and Democracy: Tactics in Hard Times*, London: MIT Press.

Bourgault, L.M. (1995) *Mass Media in Sub-Saharan Africa*, Bloomington: Indiana University Press.

Bunz, M. (2009) 'How Your Internet Knowledge Can Help African Radio'. Blog, *Guardian* (UK), 4 November 2009. Available at: www.guardian.co.uk/media/pda/2009/nov/04/digital-media-radio-zimbabwe-african-radio (accessed 11 November 2009).

Crack, A.M. (2008) *Global Communication and Transnational Public Spheres*, New York: Palgrave Macmillan.

de Bruijin, M., Nyamnjoh, F.B. and Brinkmann, I. (eds) (2009) *Mobile Phones: The New Talking Drums of Everyday Africa*, Leiden: African Studies Centre.

Domatob, J.K. (1988) 'Sub-Saharan Africa's Media and Neocolonialism', *African Media Review* 3(1): 149–74.

Domatob, J.K. (1989) 'Black Africa's Cultural Synchronisation through Pop Music', *Neohelicon* 16(2): 303–15.

Fairchild, C. (2001) *Community Radio and Public Culture: Being an Examination of Media Access and Equity in the Nations of North America*, Cresskill: Hampton Press.

Fardon, R. and Furniss, G. (eds) (2000) *African Broadcast Cultures: Radio in Transition*, Oxford: James Currey.

Girard, B. (ed.) (2003a), *The One to Watch: Radio, New ICTs and Interactivity*, Rome: FAO. Also available at: http://comunica.org/1–2–watch/ (accessed 11 November 2009).

Girard, B. (ed.) (2003b) 'Radio and the Internet: Mixing Media to Bridge the Divide', in B. Girard (ed.) *The One to Watch: Radio, New ICTs and Interactivity*, Rome: FAO, pp. 2–13.

Hendy, D. (2000) *Radio in the Global Age*, Cambridge: Polity Press.

Hunt, N. (2009) 'Baidoa Radio Station Shut; Director and News Editor Held by Al-Shabab Militants: Journalist Safety Remains a Serious Concern in War-torn Somalia', International Press Institute report, 1 October 2009. Available at: www.freemedia.at/regions/africa/singleview/baidoa-radio-station-shut-director-and-news-editor-held-by-al-shabab-militants/cd87ac3fea (accessed 16 November 2009).

Hyden, G. and Leslie, M. (2002) 'Communication and Democratization in Africa', in G. Hyden, M. Leslie and F.F. Ogundimu (eds) *Media and Democracy in Africa*, Uppsala: Nordiska Afrikainstitutet, pp. 1–28.

Ilboudo, J. and Castello, R. (2003) 'Linking Rural Radio to New ICTs in Africa: Bridging the Rural Digital Divide', in B. Girard (ed.) *The One to Watch: Radio, New ICTs and Interactivity*, Rome: FAO, pp. 27–38.

ITU (2008) 'Rapid Increase in the Number of Radio and Television Channels in Africa', International Telecommunication Union report on 'African Broadcast and Film Markets Survey' by Balancing Act and InterMedia, 10 March 2008. Available at: www.itu.int/ITU-D/ict/newslog/Rapid+Increase+In+The+Number+Of+Radio+And+TV+Channels+In+Africa.aspx (accessed 11 November 2009).

ITU (2009) 'Information Society Statistical Profiles 2009 – Africa', International Telecommunication Union. Available at: www.itu.int/dms_pub/itu-d/opb/ind/D-IND-RPM.AF-2009-PDF-E.pdf (accessed 3 December 2009).

Jallov, B. (2003) 'Creating and Sustaining ICT Projects in Mozambique', in B. Girard (ed.) *The One to Watch: Radio, New ICTs and Interactivity*, Rome: FAO, pp. 73–80.

Jensen, M. (2002) 'Information and Communication Technologies – A Status Report', ITU. Available at: www.itu.int/osg/spu/wsis-themes/UNMDG/jensen-icts-africa.doc (accessed 13 November 2009).

Karimi, F. (2009) 'African Musicians Going Political', CNN Online, 2 November 2009. Available at: www.cnn.com/2009/WORLD/africa/10/31/kenya.music.influence/index.html (accessed 27 November 2009).

Keane, J. (2000) 'Structural Transformation of the Public Sphere', in L.K. Hacker and J. van Dijk (eds) *Digital Democracy: Issues of Theory and Practice*, London: Sage, pp. 71–89.

Kellner, D. (2003) *Media Spectacle*, London: Routledge.

Loviglio, J. (2005) *Radio's Intimate Public: Network Broadcasting and Mass Mediated Democracy*, Minneapolis: University of Minnesota Press.

McCauley, M.P. (2002) 'Radio's Digital Future: Preserving the Public Interest in the Age of New Media', in M. Hilmes and J. Loviglio (eds) *Radio Reader: Essays in the Cultural History of Radio*, New York: Routledge, pp. 505–530.

McPhail, T. (1981) *Electronic Colonialism: the Future of International Broadcasting and Communication*, London: Sage.

Maina, H. (2009) 'It's Archaic for State to Withhold Information', *The Standard*, 21 November 2009. Available at: www.standardmedia.co.ke/commentaries/InsidePage.php?id=1144028729&cid=15& (accessed 21 November 2009).

Miescher, G. (1999) 'The Political Significance of the Press and Public Radio (NBC) in Postcolonial Namibia', Basler Afrika Bibliographien (Switzerland), Working Paper No. 2.

Mytton, G. (1986) 'Review of *Mass Communication, Culture and Society in West Africa*', *African Affairs* 85: 303–5. Available at: http://afraf.oxfordjournals.org/cgi/reprint/85/339/303 (accessed 13 November 2009).

Nugdalla, S. (1986) 'Broadcasting and Cultural Change', in G. Wedell (ed.) *Making Broadcasting Useful: the African Experience – the Development of Radio and Television in Africa in the 1980s*, Manchester: Manchester University Press (for) the European Institute for the Media, pp. 91–104.

Nyamnjoh, F.B. (2005) *Africa's Media: Democracy and the Politics of Belonging*, London: Zed Books.

Ogblondah, C.W. (2002) 'Media Laws in Political Transition', in H. Hyden, M. Leslie and F. Ogundimu (eds), *Media and Democracy in Africa*, New Brunswick: Transaction, pp. 55–80.

Ogundimu, F.L. (2002) 'Media and Democracy in Twenty-First Century Africa', in H. Hyden, M. Leslie and F. Ogundimu (eds), *Media and Democracy in Africa*, New Brunswick: Transaction, pp. 207–38.

Oladele, A. (2009) 'Cell Phone Radio – Nigeria', email, 9 November 2009.

Olorunisola, A.A. (2005) 'Community Radio as Participatory Communication in Post-Apartheid South Africa'. Available at: www.personal.psu.edu/faculty/a/x/axo8/Joburg/manuscript.htm (accessed 12 November 2009).

Roberts, T.E. (1987) 'Mass Communication, Advertising and Popular Culture: Propagators and Procedures of Consumer Behaviour and Ideology', in J. Domatob, A. Jika and I. Nwosu (eds), *Mass Media and the African Society* (African Media Monograph Series No. 4), Nairobi: African Council for Communication Education, pp. 269–80.

RSF (2009) 'Broadcast Media Forbidden to Let Public Express Views on Air', Reporters without Borders, 21 April 2009. Available at: www.rsf.org/Broadcast-media-forbidden-to-let.html (accessed 13 November 2009).

Ruigrok, I. (n.d.) '(In)dependent Radio'. Available at: www.powerofculture.nl/uk/specials/radio/onafhankelijkheid.html (accessed 9 November 2009).

UNESCO (1963) 'Statistical Reports and Studies', United Nations Educational, Scientific and Cultural Organization. Available at: http://unesdoc.unesco.org/images/0003/000337/033739eo.pdf (accessed 19 November 2009).

Van der Veur, P.R. (2002) 'Broadcasting and Political Reform', in H. Hyden, M. Leslie and F. Ogundimu (eds), *Media and Democracy in Africa*, New Brunswick: Transaction, pp. 81–105.

Wresch, W. (1998) 'Information Access in Africa: Problems with Every Channel', *The Information Society* 14: 295–300. Available at: www.indiana.edu/~tisj/readers/fulltext/14–4%20wresch.pdf (accessed 13 November 2009).

Chapter 17

Policing popular media in Africa

Monica B. Chibita

The media play a key role not just in mediating political discourse based on rational-critical debate, but also in arbitrating cultural recognition and diversity (Örnebring and Jönsson 2004: 285). In many African countries the mainstream media are dominated by official discourse and do not tolerate open criticism of the power elite (Barber 1997: 3; Nyairo and Ogude 2005; Mano 2007). The popular media in Africa therefore have an even more specific democratic contribution to make because for many these may be the only means of expressing themselves on a wide range of matters of concern to them along the political-economic-cultural continuum. Because of their style and their apparent focus on 'soft' and sometimes 'off limits' themes, however, the popular media have been criticized for focusing on trivialities and denying audiences 'wholesome' information to enhance their political efficacy. As such they have not been the focus of regulation debates on the African continent, except to the extent that they are perceived as endangering 'public morality' and 'African cultural values'. However, the democratic contribution of the popular media in Africa has been recognized by scholars such as Nyairo and Ogude (2005), Mano (2007), Wasserman (2008) and Olatunji (2009). The common thread running through these works is that the popular media enable diversity in a way the mainstream media in Africa cannot.

Discussions of diversity tend to go along with other important issues such as democracy, freedom of expression and regulation. The principle of diversity is key in linking the popular media to democracy. The media freedom advocacy organization, Article 19, captures the essence of media diversity: 'a variety of different types of voices being given access to the media and a variety of different types of information and viewpoints being heard' (Article 19 2006: 19). This definition would seem to signal less government control over the media.

The media in most African countries have since the early 1980s made steps towards liberalizing and privatizing their media sectors. In the context of the globalization and commercialization of the media worldwide, though, local media content as it relates to diversity has become a major issue especially as the media in Africa have had to respond to both challenges and opportunities arising out of these world trends (Sreberny-Mohammadi 1991: 123; Strelitz 1999: 53; Kariithi

2003: 171, 174–6). The idea of 'policing' popular media, in the context of 'freeing' the media, not surprisingly, therefore, is highly contested. Article 19 summarizes the anxiety associated with media regulation in general thus: 'The word "regulation" is worrying to some people. There is an assumption that outside intervention of any sort will be an interference that reduces freedom of expression and consumer choice' (Article 19 2006: 14). Based on this assumption commercial media owners in Africa have challenged the regulation of the broadcast media other than by the broadcast industry itself or the market.

However, as Article 19 (2006: 14) observes, 'regulation is about more than just allocating frequencies. What regulation should also do is to increase access to the media and make sure that a greater variety of voices are heard' (cf. Siune 1998: 24–5). Although much of popular media content in Africa is available in the indigenous languages, the globalization, rapid expansion and commercialization of the media industry have raised concerns about the need to shield local (African) media industries from being flooded out by Western cultural products which are often cheaper, backed by superior technological and distribution capacity and in a 'global' language like English (see Kariithi 2003). The local media have also tended to appropriate the 'global' languages such as English or French in some form or another to expand their catchment area.

Much of Africa is characterized by shaky democratic structures, linguistic heterogeneity and economic inequalities. There are also related issues such as poverty and conflict that make diversity harder to achieve. While the latest developments in the media would seem to increase access and variety for some Africans, there are sections of the African population whose access to these opportunities cannot be taken for granted or left to the market to regulate. These issues make it imperative to continue discussing how best to secure a kind of diversity in the popular media in Africa that leans towards citizenship rather than just consumerism.

This chapter, therefore, discusses popular media in an African context influenced by global trends, and the significance of popular media for diversity and democracy. The chapter examines key arguments relating to the regulation of popular media and makes a case for 'policing' popular media in Africa. The arguments of the chapter are situated within a critical political economy framework and backed by illustrations from Kenya, Nigeria and Uganda. The chapter aims to situate popular media in Africa in wider global developments and make a case for regulating popular media in the public interest.

Popular media in Africa

Popular culture and popular media are separate by an invisible line. Abah (2009) characterizes popular media as alternative to the mainstream. The popular media for Abah are media that represent the culture from, or of, 'the people'. Like Barber (1997: 4–5), Abah (2009: 731) sees popular culture – the stock in trade of popular media – as a continuous attempt to 'define, contest and expand the boundaries of class, hierarchy and access' (cf. Kaarsholm and James 2000: 194).

Popular culture in Africa according to Abah should denote 'what is popular' and connote popular concerns as well as that which enables people to define their existence or plight (Abah 2009: 733). Barber (1997: 4–5) further contends that even if class boundaries are harder to define in the African context than, for instance, in Europe, popular culture always conjures up a sense of 'them' and 'us' where 'them' represents those perceived to be rich, powerful or in some other way privileged and 'us', the rest of the 'ordinary' people.

Popular media and everyday life in Africa

Popular media in Africa offer information and cover themes from everyday life, carry critiques of the lifestyles of celebrities, the wealthy and the politically powerful as well as of 'ordinary' people, and project local culture onto the marketplace (Abah 2009: 733). According to Van Zoonen (2000: 13) popular media broaden the parameters of debate by bringing into public discourse themes and formats that would otherwise be considered unworthy of the 'public sphere'.

Uganda's leading stand-up comedian 'Pablo', for instance, is known for making fun of Uganda's President Museveni's foibles on stage as well as on radio and television where journalists in the mainstream media would fear to tread lest they be charged with bringing the character of the president into disrepute. Similarly, two local television comedies, *Barbed Wire* and *Side Mirror* also ridicule celebrities or powerful politicians through music, jokes, parody or satire. Both shows are immensely popular in the capital city, partly because, in spite of their English names, they are in Luganda, the language spoken by the largest number of Ugandans. The shows are in Luganda, and use English only to poke fun at those who would claim to be highly educated. Some themes the shows have covered include corruption, nepotism as well as the tense relationship between the central government and the powerful Buganda Kingdom that the government appears to perceive as a political threat.

In 2008, mobile text messages played a key role in mobilizing ordinary Ugandans against a government proposal to give away a large tract of land in Mabira Forest. The mobilization called upon Ugandans to boycott sugar produced by the investor who was supposed to benefit from the land give-away and to march in large number through Kampala city. The march was a massive success and managed to avert the government's decision.

Organizations like Right to Play and The Kampala Kids League have used football matches to raise awareness of the devastating effects of the protracted Lord's Resistance Army insurgency in Northern Uganda, also employing radio and television. In addition, popular musicians like Jose Chameleone, Bebe Cool and Bobi Wine often hold concerts to raise awareness and resources to assist orphans or people living with HIV/AIDS and receive extensive coverage in the media. These examples illustrate the potency of the popular media in addressing issues of concern to ordinary people that may not be aired freely in the more mainstream media.

On the whole, the popular media in Africa tend to be more accessible and sometimes even more portable than the mainstream media (see Abah 2009). In addition, they often have more flexibility to offer content in the indigenous languages and draw from familiar idiom, which offers the only chance for many to participate in public discourse via the media and to witness or to represent their realities. To illustrate this, the video industry in Nigeria has capitalized on Nigerian idiomatic expression drawn from the Ibo, Hausa or Yoruba culture or from pidgin which is a hybrid language that the ordinary Nigerian (regardless of class) tends to be comfortable with (see Abah 2009: 733).

In Uganda a popular music and drama group, The Ebonies, produce cheap videos with simple and highly popular plots in a mixture of Luganda and English. Modelled on the Nigerian 'Nollywood' films, the themes of these videos range from passion to crime to witchcraft, with which viewers from various social positions could identify.

Popular media and citizenship

Understandings of the contribution of the media to the proper working of 'the public sphere' as conceived by Habermas (1989[1962]) have underpinned many debates on the media's democratizing role. Many critics have rejected Habermas' apparent limitation of issues for discussion to specifically those of political concern, arguing that it leaves out popular culture, which constitutes a key aspect of the modern public sphere and is significant for important issues such as identity formation (see Fraser 1993; Goldsmith Media Group 2000; Berger 2002; Wasserman 2008). Critics have also challenged the accuracy of linking the public sphere necessarily with common concerns (see Berger 2002: 30 and Thompson 1995: 253). Habermas' idealistic presentation of the public sphere has also been criticized for ignoring the exclusion of significant categories such as women and workers and a blindness to alternative public spheres created by them; underrating the agency of audiences; prioritizing dialogue and consensus to the disregard of 'dissensus' and failing to take account of the different, pluralistic environment in which contemporary public communication occurs (Thompson 1995: 254–258, cf. Fraser 1993: 521–2; Berger 2002: 31; Willems 2008: 6–14).

Scholars like Berger (2002), Willems (2008: 6–14) and Wasserman (2008) thus contend that the media's democratizing role in an African context calls for a re-envisioning of Habermas' original understanding of the public sphere. Such re-envisioning would have to accommodate political activity that is mediated in forms other than rational–critical dialogue about matters of common concern.

Though the present-day popular media in Africa may not be regarded as the most obvious site for 'rational critical debate' à la Habermas, and may not always 'stand against the state', they are important not only for artistic expression but also for political contestation. Because of their flexibility and tendency to cover not only 'hard' information but entertainment as well, popular media have a special role to play in allowing alternative voices to be heard as well as holding rulers and powerful members of society accountable. They are also valuable in creating, sustaining or challenging cultural values and trends. Finally, popular media in Africa enable public discourse in the languages of the people which may be the indigenous languages, or appropriations of the colonial languages (including pidgin), thus drawing into the public domain voices and representations that would otherwise have been left out.

Since the early 1980s, the majority of African countries have liberalized their economies and, with these, their media sectors. In Uganda in the last decade, for instance, the country has gone from one state radio and television station to an additional 158 radio stations and 32 television stations, the majority privately owned. The telephone sector now has four large private service providers – Orange, MTN, UTL and Zain (www.ucc.co.ug). The Internet, though still an urban phenomenon, is spreading out into the rural areas, with over 17 Internet service providers. In 2009 broadband became an option in Uganda and Kenya. The Uganda government has moved to merge the broadcast and telecommunications regulators, in response to global convergence trends (Tanzania and South Africa also have experienced similar growth and have converged regulators).

At least two media giants (Vision Group and the Nation Media Group), are discernible on the Ugandan media scene: the Vision Group, where government holds majority shares, owns Radio West, Vision FM, Bukedde FM, Bukedde Television, the *New Vision* and *Sunday Vision* newspapers. The English language newspapers have local language counterparts: *Bukedde* (Central region), *Etop* (Eastern region) *Orumuri* (Western region) and *Rupiny* (Northern region). The Nation Media group, where the Aga Khan Foundation is the majority shareholder owns the *The Daily Monitor*, *The Sunday Monitor*, KFM radio and Nation Television (NTV). The Nation Group is equally powerful in Kenya and owns media interests in Nigeria, South Africa and Tanzania.

With all this, it is easy to get fixated at the level of how wonderful all this choice is for the 'consumer', forgetting about the other important identity, that of the citizen. Croteau and Hoynes (2001: 2008) argue that for a polity to function effectively and for citizens to enjoy full rights, access to information and diversity of debate are key. Popular media such as cinema/film, video, the Internet as well as radio and television contribute to the broadening of the arena where self-expression and contestation take place. This is particularly significant in the African context, where many governments are still reluctant to preside over the transformation of state media into public media, and keep a hold on the broadcast media even when they are privately owned.

In Africa, the popular media (such as the Nigerian, South African and Kenyan film industry or the burgeoning music industry across the continent) offer content in languages that may have no space in the mainstream, and yet strike a chord with large sections of audiences. The Yabis music genre in Nigeria, which was popularized by Felá Aníkúlápó-Kútì during the repressive years of military rule (climaxing in the 1970s) has been used to critique the political elite, and also employs pidgin. The music group Gidi-Gidi Maji-Maji used a popular rap song

('Unbwogable') to campaign for the National Rainbow Coalition against the hegemony of the KANU Party, which had ruled Kenya since independence (see Nyairo and Ogude 2005).

Clearly, therefore, the popular media in Africa can contribute to cultural and political diversity and contribute to the democratization process. However, the commercialization of the media, partly occasioned by their globalization, may curtail the media's capacity to play this role optimally.

Commercialization of the media

The changes in the media industry that accompany globalization have not necessarily enhanced the popular media's capacity to offer diversity of information, representation and expression equitably in Africa. Access has become more expensive and exclusive and the diversity of content has been compromised (Murdock 2000: 147–8; cf. Siune 1998; Goldsmith Media Group 2000; Croteau and Hoynes 2001; Nyamnjoh 2008: 32–4). Capitalist common sense seems to suggest that the more homogenous this content is, the more marketable. Peculiarities in theme, language or cultural appeal are therefore kept to a minimum (McChesney 2000: 100–9).

The implications of all this for the media in Africa have been mixed. In many African countries these developments are a welcome relief from monolithic state-owned and controlled broadcasters and limited communication avenues. Many people now have access to FM radio stations that broadcast in the colonial languages (English, French, Portuguese) as well as in the indigenous African languages. The community media sector has grown and has the potential to serve populations that were previously excluded from the media by a range of socio-economic factors. Many more people have access to telephone communication thanks to the advent of the mobile phone. However, as Nyamnjoh (2008: 33–4) has noted, while there has been growth in the pluralism of channels, there has not necessarily been the same amount of growth in diversity. Linguistic minorities, the poor and women continue to be excluded either at the level of ownership, or due to lack of the material and symbolic resources to participate fully in the new media bonanza (cf. Scannell 2000: 120–5). Most notably, the largely commercialized media ignore audiences that are not considered commercially viable. Nyamnjoh argues that Western production companies are reluctant to invest too heavily in the portrayal of African cultures and realities because they consider them 'socially inferior and economically uncompetitive' and when they do invest in them, the products are often stereotypical (2008: 30).

With the commercialization of the media, access to a significant percentage of what the popular media have to offer via video, cinema, tabloids and magazines is dependent on the capacity to pay for it. In Africa the 'public' media in most countries are not a substitute as they tend to be government mouthpieces and/or as commercialized as their commercial counterparts (see Fourie 2003: 10–152). It is partly for this reason that critical political economy observes that the new, commercialized media concentrate more on addressing audiences as consumers than as citizens (Goldsmith Media Group 2000: 54; Croteau and Hoynes 2001: 207). Consumers pursue private interests, services or experiences. They purchase what they want to have. Besides, consumers are by nature unequal, distinguished by their purchasing power (Croteau and Hoynes 2001: 207).

Citizens on the other hand (ideally) are connected to communities and civil life in which they play an active part. In a democratic society citizens are regarded as equal regardless of their consumer capabilities. This, according to Croteau and Hoynes (2001: 207) is what distinguishes democratic societies from markets. In a sense, therefore, if all we had to be concerned about were audience members' identities as consumers, we would not be debating the value of 'policing' popular media since their offerings would, in any case, be available to all who have access to them and who can afford to pay for their 'products'. However, if we view the media – even the popular media – as sites for open contestation of ideas, identities and representations, the bar must be set higher. This observation by the Goldsmith Media Group (2000: 54) helps bring this point home:

> The media, as forms of communication at a distance, raise issues of participation which are not reducible to questions of consumer choice. It is not normally an issue, let alone an issue of public importance, whether you had the opportunity to participate in the production of the clothes you wear. It is an issue, and one of fundamental public importance, what opportunities you had to participate in the representation to others of your living conditions, your opinions, your forms of cultural expression. The latter are fundamentally issues not merely of choice, but of control; they are issues of freedom, which must be addressed at the social level.

There is a growing tendency in the current globalized and commmercialized media environment for media regulation to focus on securing consumer interests only, neglecting citizen needs, thus remaining blind to the way media impact public lives. Critical political economy argues that as a result of this citizens feel that they have no obligation to contribute to identifying solutions to common problems as long as they can solve personal problems by purchasing goods or services. The potential result of this is political apathy. They also are no longer interested in participating in the development of a common identity.

Thus in different contexts Fraser (1993), Gitlin (1998) and Willems (2008) have challenged Habermas' idealized public sphere. Even though their focus is not regulation, the general trajectory of their critique points to the fact that rather than remain fixated on the development of a unitary public sphere, regulation debates should instead focus on smaller sites of democratization which Gitlin calls 'public sphericules' – often made possible by popular rather than mainstream media (Gitlin 1998: 173). Regulation should consider how to make these 'sphericules' more open, diverse and accessible (Fraser 1993: 522–4, cf. Dahlgren 2002; Goldsmith Media Group 2000; Willems 2008). Such sites in an African context would include not just radio and television, but also video, the Internet and mobile telephones.

'Policing' popular media in Africa

In the globalized media economy, access to what the popular media have to offer, and opportunities to receive and give information, reflect and contest cultures and viewpoints through the popular media are unequally distributed. In the African context such exclusion might ostensibly be based on socio-economic status, but this is often linked to other sources of inequality stemming from, for instance, ethnic origin or gender. If we agree that the market is not the best suited to rationalize access to cultural products in a commercialized media environment, then it becomes necessary to discuss how this space could be policed to ensure a degree of equity in access to popular culture.

In this regard, Nyamnjoh (2008: 33) posits,

> The profit motive dictates that various media content are conceived, produced, and disseminated with the primary objective of maintaining economic, political and cultural privileges and advantage, while thwarting any attempt at the social shaping or domestication of media technologies and content that could abolish or overturn such privileges.

Wilkinson (2007: 19), specifically talking about the imminent danger to linguistic diversity in the European Union, also discusses what he calls 'the forces of economic homogenization' which reduce linguistic diversity in the interests of economic expediency. While the liberalized media in Africa have increased the number of languages on air, many of these languages receive token representation unless they can compete with English or French in terms of commercial viability. The experience of the former British and French colonies has been that the primary target categories of the commercial media, i.e. the young and the wealthy, speak a colonial language in addition to, or instead of, their indigenous language. This makes it easier to supply linguistically homogenized content to avoid dealing with the linguistic heterogeneity of the continent. Because such content is often cheaper than locally produced content and often of superior technological quality, the local production industry is the loser.

In a discussion of policing the popular media in Africa, one must be careful not to essentialize 'African media' and 'African content' to justify censoring them. Cultural symbols are 'social constructions subject to constant redefinition' (Morris 2002: 280). This understanding should tone down tendencies to force popular media into a mould, possibly killing them in the process. Having said this, it is important to recognize the importance of local content industries not only in strengthening national identities and enhancing democratic debate, but also in providing employment for local populations and raising revenue. Because of this, the local content industry in Africa warrants a degree of 'policing'.

There have been strong arguments that the state should continue to regulate, especially the broadcast media, to protect 'the public interest'. However, notions like 'national consensus' and 'public interest' are often open to manipulation by political and cultural elite. In Africa, especially immediately following independence, many governments used the urgent need for national development to suppress oppositional views. Once again this goes contrary to the idea of a free and diverse media needing to accommodate not only consensus but also *dissensus*.

Scholars within the framework of cultural studies (see for instance Grossberg 1995: 73; Kellner and Durham 2001: 4; Barker 2002: 13, cf. Ferguson and Golding 1997) have challenged the critique of critical political economy for downplaying the agency of audiences and therefore the possibility of oppositional readings. Critical political economy however maintains that there is only so much one can change working at the level of individual consumption. Lasting solutions need to be targeted at the structural level (Ferguson and Golding 1997: 76–7) and at this level notions of the public interest must be part of the discussion. However, neither the state nor the market is the best or the only agent for the regulation of the media. Citizens can and should play a role in 'policing' their own popular media.

The popular media are typically not as amenable to 'policing' as their mainstream counterparts. Because they are not necessarily modelled on 'rational critical debate', and tend to adopt a light-hearted, entertainment-oriented approach, governments are wont to dismiss them because they do not perceive them as a threat. This perception masks the political potency of these media given their 'popularity' as well as the fact that people who would ordinarily not make their voices heard in the mainstream media see this as a space where they not only could participate in the creation of content, but also use the content as a basis for vibrant debate conducted at a 'wavelength' and often in a language they are comfortable with. Because of the informality of their formats, popular media are able to do this while at the same time addressing a broader range of cultural, economic, political and social issues than the mainstream media (which are often directly or indirectly under the influence of government and/or business interests) would accommodate. Because of characteristics such as these, it is no longer possible to dismiss popular media as just entertainment sites with no significance for citizenship and therefore not in need of any form of regulation. Perhaps what we need to do instead is to distinguish clearly what kind of citizenship (and by what means) these media could engender, and how this can be harnessed to maximize a diversity of voices and representations in the popular media in Africa.

In Africa, the influx of global 'popular content' delivered through radio, television, cinema, video, etc., exists side-by-side with major socio-economic inequalities. Poverty can hinder access to the provisions of the media. Not only do the poor find it harder to own media outlets, they also have a difficult time getting their content onto the air (Herman and McChesney 1997: 190–1; Goldsmith Media Group 2000: 26–7, 39–44; McQuail 2000: 156–7, cf. Nyamnjoh 2008). With more subscription television channels and a demand for accessories to make use of 'available' channels, the issue of exclusion gets more acute. This in turn affects how fully the majority of Africans can participate as citizens in a polity or simply represent their realities or see them reflected in the media. Another reason for policing popular media therefore would be to minimize the consequences of such inequalities.

'Policing' popular media could also be justified on the basis of protecting the interests of vulnerable groups such as minors. Typically, regulation has sought to minimize the presumed negative effects of specific (usually obscene or violent) content by stipulating periods during which such programming cannot be aired (the watershed period) (see Article 19 2006: 72–3). Content of concern would include violence, obscenity, the use of or promotion of harmful drugs and offensive language. The definition of concepts such as 'obscenity' and others, such as 'national cultural values', though, is still contentious. Government agents often hide behind such vague terms to lock out content they consider politically undesirable. Also unresolved is how to 'protect' vulnerable groups without in the process locking out other categories of people. The attempt by a group of women's organizations in 1995 to stage Eve Ensler's play *The Vagina Monologues* in Uganda to highlight escalating violence against women generated vibrant debate with arguments on either extreme of the freedom of expression continuum. The debate revolved around whether it was more important to protect 'national cultural values' surrounding what can be said and shown to and about women in public, or to expose rampant gender-based violence by any means available, even at the risk of ruffling a few cultural 'feathers' (see Makubuya 2005; Jjuuko 2005 for a full discussion of this controversy).

Popular media also raise concerns relating to the content and volume of advertising. Again specific concerns here include advertising directed at children, advertising alcohol, tobacco and other harmful drugs, the veracity of advertisers' claims as well as the proportion of time given to advertising compared to other programming (Article 19 2006: 68–9).

Another area for policing in the context of popular media in Africa is hate speech or speech that incites violence. There may be problems with defining precisely what kind of speech incites violence as well as to what extent states can apply pre-publication censorship to any form of speech without impinging on freedom of expression. However, the consequences of unregulated speech have an ugly precedent in Rwanda that many African countries would want to avoid. For this reason alone, a case could be made for 'policing' speech in popular media.

Protection of reputations is also a relevant area for 'policing'. This is in consideration of how much damage the popular media with their reach can do to an individual. However, it is also in recognition of the fact that public officials hold their positions in the public trust and therefore must be held accountable. Where the official accountability mechanisms are not functioning well, sometimes the popular media move in to provide an alternative accountability mechanism through cartoons, music, drama, etc. Regulation in this area must ensure fairness and as much as possible rely on clearly laid down complaints procedures to allow all parties a fair hearing.

As in other contexts (see Croteau and Hoynes 2001: 211) content (including local production concerns) and access appear to be the two broad areas of regulatory concern in Africa. In Nigeria, South Africa and Uganda there has been some regulation in these areas already. However, given the new developments in the media globally and the opportunities they offer, and yet given the political and economic constraints discussed in this chapter, any policing would do well to proceed with caution, to involve audiences in identifying their needs and challenges in the new media environment and to insulate the media from undue manipulation by government or commercial interests at the expense of cultural and political diversity. Key areas to focus on would include ownership and distribution of media, linguistic diversity, affordability of services and content, particularly with regards to boosting local production as well as the identification and protection of vulnerable groups. It is important to weigh the benefits of self-regulation rather than, or alongside, government regulation in the African context in all these areas as this can guarantee protection from undue influence and manipulation.

Conclusion

Despite the advent of digitalization and satellite broadcasting, media regulation is not redundant, because there is more to regulation than allocating frequencies. The media in Africa are part of global changes in the media sector but they are also part of a unique context characterized by major social and economic inequalities and a weak production sector. Securing diversity in the media is more important now with the momentum moving in the direction of globalization and concentration. The popular media offer great potential for diversity but require a degree of 'policing' if this potential is to be optimized. There is a great likelihood, however, that governments and business interests might hide behind claims of protecting 'national cultural values', freedom of expression or consumer choice to close out oppositional voices or secure business interests. As such, neither of these might be the best political, economic or cultural arbiter. Any 'policing' of the popular media, therefore, needs to be done in the context of protecting fundamental rights like freedom of expression and access to information. Increasingly, regulation by citizens and media professionals/practitioners is preferable to state regulation.

References

Abah, L.A. (2009) 'Popular culture and social change in Africa: the case of the Nigerian video industry', *Media, Culture and Society* 31: 731–48.
Article 19 (2006) *Broadcasting pluralism and diversity: training manual for African regulators*, London: Article 19.

Barber, K. (ed.) (1997) *Readings in African popular culture*, Bloomington: Indiana University Press.

Barker, C. (2002) *Making sense of cultural studies: central problems and critical debates*, London: Sage.

Berger, G. (2002) 'Theorizing the media-democracy relationship in Southern Africa', *Gazette* 64: 21–45.

Croteau, D. and Hoynes W. (2001) *The business of media: corporate media and the public interest*, 2nd edn, London: Pine Forge Press.

Dahlgren, P. (2002) 'The public sphere as historical narrative', in D. McQuail (ed.), *McQuail's reader in mass communication theory*, London: Sage, pp. 194–200.

Ferguson, M. and Golding, P. (eds) (1997) *Cultural studies in question*, London: Sage.

Fourie, P.J. (2003) 'The future of public service broadcasting in South Africa: the need to return to basic principles', *Communicatio* 29(1&2): 148–81.

Fraser, N. (1993) 'Rethinking the public sphere: a contribution to the critique of actually existing democracy', in S. During (ed.), *The cultural studies reader*, 2nd edn, London: Routledge, pp. 518–36.

Gitlin, T. (1998) 'Public sphere or public sphericules?', in T. Liebes and J. Curran (eds), *Media, ritual and identity*, London: Routledge, pp. 175–202.

Goldsmith Media Group (2000) 'Media organisations in society: central issues', in J. Curran (ed.), *Media organisations in society*, London: Arnold, pp. 19–65.

Grossberg, L. (1995) 'Cultural studies vs. political economy: is anyone else bored with this debate?', *Critical Studies in Mass Communication* 12(1 and 2): 72–81.

Habermas, J. (1989) *The structural transformation of the public sphere: an inquiry into a category of bourgeois society*, Cambridge, MA: MIT Press.

Herman, E.S. and McChesney, R.W. (1997) *The global media: the new missionaries of global capitalism*, London: Cassell.

Jjuuko, F.W. (2005) 'To ban or not to ban? A critique of the Media Council ruling', *East African Journal of Peace and Human Rights* 11(1): 172–81.

Kaarsholm, P. and James, D. (2000) 'Popular culture and democracy in some Southern contexts: an introduction', *Journal of Southern African Studies*, Special Issue: *Popular Culture and Democracy*, 26: 189–208.

Kariithi, N. (2003) 'Issues in local content of broadcast media', in *Broadcasting policy and practice in Africa*, London: Article 19, pp. 162–80.

Kellner, D.M. and Durham, M.G. (2001) 'Adventures in media and cultural studies: introducing the keyworks', in D.M. Kellner and G.M. Durham (eds), *Media and cultural studies: keyworks*, Oxford: Blackwell, pp. 1–29.

McChesney, R.W. (2000) *Rich media, poor democracy: communication politics in dubious times*, New York: The New Press.

McQuail, D. (2000) *McQuail's mass communication theory*, London: Sage.

Makubuya A.N. (2005) 'The "Vagina Monologues" saga and free expression in Uganda: exploring the limits', *African Journal of Peace and Human Rights* 11(1): 165–81.

Mano, W. (2007) 'Popular music as journalism in Zimbabwe', *Journalism Studies* 8(1): 61–78.

Morris, N. (2002) 'The myth of unadulterated culture meets the threat of imported media', *Media, Culture and Society* 24: 278–89.

Murdock, G. (2000) 'Concentration and ownership in the era of privatization', in P. Marris and S. Thornham (eds), *Media studies: a reader*, 2nd edn, New York: New York University Press, pp. 143–55.

Nyairo, J. and Ogude, J. (2005) 'Popular music, popular politics: *unbwogable* and the idiom of freedom in Kenyan popular music', *Africa Affairs* 104: 225–49.

Nyamnjoh, F.B. (2008) 'Children, media and globalization' in N. Pecora, E. Osei-Hwere and U. Carlsson (eds), *African Media, African Children*, Göteborg: University of Göteborg, NORDICOM, pp. 29–47.

Olatunji, M.O. (2009) 'Yabis music: an instrument of social change in Nigeria', *Journal of African Media Studies* 1(2): 309–28.

Örnebring, H. and Jönsson, A.M. (2004) 'Tabloid journalism and the public sphere: a historical perspective on tabloid journalism', *Journalism Studies* 5(3): 283–95.

Scannell, P. (2000) 'Public service broadcasting: the history of a concept', in P. Marris and S. Thornham (eds) (2nd edn), *Media studies: a reader*, New York: New York University Press, pp. 120–34.

Siune, K. (1998) 'Is broadcasting policy becoming redundant?', in K. Brants, J. Hermes and L. Van Zoonen (eds), *The media in question: popular cultures and public interests*, London: Sage, pp. 18–37.

Sreberny-Mohammadi, A. (1991) 'The global and the local in international communications', in J. Curran and M. Gurevitch (eds), *Mass media and society*, London: Edward Arnold, pp. 118–38.

Strelitz, L. (1999) 'Globalisation: good and bad', *Rhodes Journalism Review* 18: 53–4.

Thompson, J.B. (1995) 'The theory of the public sphere', in O. Boyd-Barrett and C. Newbold (eds), *Approaches to media: a reader*, New York: Arnold, pp. 252–9.

Van Zoonen, L. (2000) 'Popular culture as political communication: an introduction', *Javnost-The Public*, 7(2): 5–18.

Wasserman, H. (2008) 'Attack of the killer newspapers! The "tabloid revolution" and the future of newspapers in South Africa', *Journalism Studies* 9(5): 786–97.

Wilkinson, K.T. (2004) 'Language, economics and policy: challenges to public service broadcasting in North America and the European Union'. Paper submitted to the culture, and commerce: tensions and dimensions working group of the RIPE at the 2004 international conference: mission, market and management: public service broadcasting and the cultural commons, Copenhagen and Aarhus, Denmark, 3–5 June 2004.

Willems, W. (2008) 'Interrogating public sphere and popular culture as theoretical concepts: on their value in African studies'. Paper presented at the CODESRIA 12th General Assembly, Dakar, Senegal.

Index